Go East, Young Man

Front Entrance to Saltair Pavilion, Great Salt Lake, Utah.

Go East, Young Man

Imagining the American West as the Orient

Richard V. Francaviglia

UTAH STATE UNIVERSITY PRESS
LOGAN, UTAH
2011

Copyright © 2011 Utah State University Press
All rights reserved
Utah State University Press
Logan, Utah 84322-3078
www.USUPress.org

Publication of this book was supported by a grant from the
Charles Redd Center for Western Studies at Brigham Young University.

Manufactured in China

ISBN: 978-0-87421-809-1 (cloth)
ISBN: 978-0-87421-811-4 (e-book)

Library of Congress Cataloging-in-Publication Data

Francaviglia, Richard V.
  Go east, young man : imagining the American West as the Orient / Richard V. Francaviglia.
     p. cm.
  Includes bibliographical references and index.
  ISBN 978-0-87421-809-1 (cloth : alk. paper) — ISBN 978-0-87421-810-7 (pbk. : alk. paper) —
ISBN 978-0-87421-811-4 (e-book)
1. West (U.S.)—Civilization. 2. Orientalism—West (U.S.)—History. 3. United States—
Civilization—Asian influences. 4. Asia—Foreign public opinion, American. 5. United States—
Territorial expansion. 6. East and West. I. Title.
  F591.F76 2011
  978—dc23

The landscape of the West has to be seen to be believed. And, perhaps conversely, it has to be believed in order to be seen.

N. SCOTT MOMADAY, "THE AMERICAN WEST AND THE BURDEN OF BELIEF" (1996)

Contents

Preface   *ix*

Introduction: The Malleable Landscape   *1*

I The Frontier West as the Orient (ca. 1810–1920)

1. The American Zahara: Into and Beyond the Great Western Plains   *25*

2. In Praise of Pyramids: Orientalizing the Western Interior   *64*

3. Chosen People, Chosen Land: Utah as the Holy Land   *87*

4. Finding New Eden: The American Southwest   *126*

5. The Far East in the Far West: Chinese and Japanese California   *155*

6. Syria on the Pacific: California as the Near/Middle East   *176*

7. To Ancient East by Ocean United: The Pacific Northwest as Asia   *202*

II The Modern West as the Orient (ca. 1920–2010)

8. Lands of Enchantment: The Modern West as the Near/Middle East   *223*

9. Another Place, Another Time: The Modern West as the Far East   *257*

10. Full Circle: Imagining the Orient as the American West   288

Notes   *308*

Bibliography   *329*

Index   *344*

Preface

THE AMERICAN WEST MAY SEEM LIKE FAMILIAR TERRITORY, but it is really a land of paradoxes, one of which is the subject of this book. Beyond the stereotypes of cowboys and Indians, modern cities and ghost towns, lies another set of images of a West that is not Western at all but has its origins in Asia and the Middle East. The paradoxical idea that the West can be East—that is, have a connection to what was once widely called "the Orient"—is evident in the region's historical literature and modern-day popular culture. In other words, Eastern or Oriental motifs also brand this otherwise characteristically western American locale.

This Orientalization of the West was apparent to me as a kid growing up in California in the 1950s, where a place named Mecca and its date palms simmered under the intense sun near the Salton Sea. It became even more apparent to me when I moved to Oregon in my early twenties and noticed artists and writers equating the Pacific Northwest's landscape with that of China and Japan. In graduate school at the University of Oregon, I studied the Mormons' role in shaping the landscapes of the Intermountain West. In that desert region, too, the West was Orientalized, as members of this most American of religions had been cast as peoples of the Middle East, most frequently Muslims. Over the years, I collected information on this important but neglected theme of West as East (and westerners as easterners) in American history.

About ten years ago, the theme of the Orient in the American West reemerged as I taught American and transatlantic history at the University of Texas at Arlington (UTA). Asked to teach a graduate seminar, I selected the theme "Orientalism in Transatlantic Perspective." When I presented a lecture on "Orientalism and the Mormon West" in class early in the semester, one of my students asked when I'd be writing a book on that subject. I told her I was actually writing an extensive article that was nearly ready for publication. When she seemed surprised and suggested "Why not write it as a book?" I realized she was correct. The article was becoming too long already, and I had found myself holding back on writing the longer story anyway. However, because the Mormons were only one part of the story, it soon became apparent that the larger story itself—how the entire American West was Orientalized—needed to be told. So, pulling together the many references I'd been collecting about the East in the West, and some that those students had discovered, that paper ultimately became the book you are now about to read.

As part of my research into this subject, I traveled to the real Orient to compare landscapes there with their American counterparts. The Holy Land was one of my first stops. In Israel, Rehav (Buni) and Milka Rubin were my hosts as I compared landscapes of the Middle East with those of the interior American West. I traveled elsewhere in search of prototypes used in Orientalizing the American West, but their hospitality was unmatched. Closer to home, in Utah, friend and associate Phil Notarianni, director of the Utah State Historical Society in Salt Lake City, introduced me to the very helpful archivists there, including Doug Misner and Tony Castro. The staff at the University of Washington Special Collections was also of great assistance. I also received assistance from Southern Methodist University's DeGolyer Library. The US Library of Congress also provided a number of relevant sources, as did the Archives of the Church of Jesus Christ of Latter-day Saints in Salt Lake City, where Michael Landon and Ron Barney were especially helpful. I also gleaned a number of sources from books and articles I'd read over the years; many of these were also found in university libraries and other archives. In Arizona, Joe and Billie Foster provided photos of Hi Jolly's monument, and Roy Purcell of Green Valley opened his studio to me. In California, Peter Blodgett and Dixie Dillon at the Huntington Library proved to be of great assistance, sharing their knowledge of sources with me when I visited San Marino. The staff at the Coachella Valley Historical Society in Indio— especially Connie Cowan—graciously provided examples of advertisements promoting California dates. In Weaverville, Jack Frost at the Joss House State Historical Park provided a behind-the-scenes tour. In Locke, Clarence Chu provided photographs of the town and its celebrations.

Fellow academicians at other universities also helped. When two cultural geographers at the University of Nevada at Reno—Gary Hausladen and Paul Starrs—learned that I was working on this book, they became quite enthusiastic. In a matter of minutes, they began to rattle off numerous exciting references, from Joan Didion's California-based memoir to Los Angeles–based film noir that had Oriental overtones and undercurrents. Similarly, historian David Weber of Southern Methodist University in Dallas introduced me to the intriguing novel *West of Babylon* when he learned of my interest in the subject of the American West as the Orient. At Arizona State University, geographer Dan Arreola and his wife, Susan, graciously provided postcard images from their extensive personal collection. Very close to home, the staff at Willamette University's Hatfield Library here in Salem, Oregon, went out of their way to assist me as I searched for resource materials.

Although many of the sources used in this book were located in archives scattered across the country, others were in my personal collection. Over the years, I've collected many postcards of the American West that revealed aspects of Orientalism— chromolithographs of geographic features in the West with Egyptian or Middle Eastern names; early (as well as fairly recent) color cards with a person, building, or scene in San Francisco or Los Angeles masquerading as the Orient. Some of these I share with readers in this book not because they are factual depictions of places and people but rather because they are just the opposite. They are, in effect, testimonies to a popular tendency to reconfigure the American West (and the American westerner) into venerable Oriental counterparts.

Among the other archives I consulted were those at the Special Collections of the University of Texas at Arlington, where I taught for seventeen years before retiring in 2008. At UTA, Special Collections staff members Kit Goodwin, Cathy Spitzenberger, and Ben Huseman were especially helpful. In addition to my colleagues in the History Department, I also acknowledge the strong support of Ken Roemer (professor of English), Chris Conway (professor of Spanish/modern languages), and Karl Petruso (professor of anthropology and dean of the Honors College). I owe special thanks to my former secretary, Ann Jennings. Ann is the type of lifelong learner who made both my job and hers enjoyable—the kind of secretary who not only typed up the material I provided but also enjoyed looking up unfamiliar terms and people in order to learn more about them. I should also note that several of the students in that graduate seminar are mentioned in the endnotes, as their insights were quite helpful; so too was former student Jeff Stone, who brought several interesting maps to my attention as he completed his doctoral dissertation at UTA. This is yet another example of a professor learning from his or her current and former students, but I also learned a great deal from critics who reviewed the manuscript, including historian David Wrobel of the University of Nevada at Las Vegas, who kindly shared sources pertaining to nineteenth-century travel literature in the American West. David also suggested the two-part design of this book, with an American West Orientalized in the past covered in part one, and the modern West being covered in part two. Above all, though, I owe a debt of gratitude to editor John Alley of Utah State University Press. John suggested many ways in which my original manuscript could be improved while never losing faith in either the subject of American Orientalism or this manuscript.

Introduction
The Malleable Landscape

*All of us conjure up images of lands that we have heard about, intend to visit, or would like
to live in, and retain impressions of those places that we have seen.*

Robin W. Doughty, *At Home in Texas: Early Views of the Land* (1987)

In October of 2004, Israeli geographer Rehav "Buni" Rubin and I were
intently discussing the landscape of the Holy Land as we drove north from
the Dead Sea in the Jordan Valley. Rubin, who has extensive knowledge of the
Middle East, pointed out various irrigation projects and talked about the settlements we passed as if they were personal friends he had watched growing and
changing over the last several decades. Given my extensive travel experience
and fieldwork in the American West, my perspective was naturally quite different from Rubin's. Although I took in every one of his words about the landscape and savored every view of this "new" place, I was amazed by how a lot of
what I observed here in Israel reminded me of a place much closer to home—
namely, the Imperial Valley in Southern California's low desert. Gazing at the
Dead Sea, which receded in the side-view mirror of Rubin's white VW station
wagon, I pondered just how much that body of water resembled the Salton
Sea. Like the Dead Sea, this salt-rimmed inland lake in California lies below
sea level and looks like a slab of blue stone set into a beige-colored plain bordered by bone-dry, heavily eroded hills. Looking left and right as Rubin drove
northward on that clear early October day, I was surprised by how familiar
this otherwise exotic place felt. As date palms and citrus groves flashed by, I
could visualize those same plants that had transformed California's Coachella
Valley into a garden spot—and gave such a similar Middle Eastern "feel" to
the landscape of that part of the Golden State.

My thoughts here were not mere fantasies. There are indeed real geologic,
climatic, and biotic similarities between these two landscapes, which are further connected by agricultural enterprise and human imagination.[1] However,
there are many differences, too. I was conscious of these differences, but what
surprised me most was how readily and repeatedly that Southern California

landscape—more than nine thousand miles to the west— inserted itself into my consciousness here in Israel. Even more surprising is how much time separates these landscapes in the popular mind. Although the Imperial Valley sometimes uses Middle Eastern or Near Eastern metaphors to promote its "exotic" qualities—date palms, oases, a salty sea, and even place names like Mecca—those features date from only the early twentieth century. By contrast, the aura of the Holy Land is far more ancient. Its translated place names—we call them the Dead Sea, Jordan River, Sea of Galilee—are legends associated with at least three thousand years of literature, faith, and folklore. Yet I thought both places could almost pass for one another at times as Buni Rubin and I rolled through the fabled Jordan River valley.

My realization about the similarities between the landscapes of Israel and California reminded me of an incident that took place in Arizona about twenty years earlier. At that time, I was managing environmental programs in southeastern Arizona but often worked with staff from the Arizona Department of Health Services (ADHS) in Phoenix. On one trip into the hilly country just west of Tombstone, I was accompanied by ADHS planner Sam Hadeed, a Lebanese American who had lived in Arizona for about ten years. As we topped the rise of a limestone-ribbed, scrub-covered hill, Sam exclaimed, "This countryside looks so similar to the hills of Lebanon that it feels just like home!" Here, thousands of miles from Lebanon, Sam saw in that landscape stretching off into Arizona's San Pedro Valley a vision of a similar-appearing ancestral landscape. I've thought a lot about Sam's statement, for he was a scientist rather than a romanticist. Yet he could see such clear parallels between a landscape in the American West and one in the Middle East that it prompted him to make that statement about "home" out of the blue.

Much more recently, I informed an associate named Abdul Kelani that I was headed to Phoenix for a meeting. Abdul, who had moved to the United States from Syria about twenty years ago, responded that he loved Phoenix because it "seems so much like Damascus." By this, he meant the look of the landscape of stark hills rising out of the desert floor, and also the quality of the atmosphere—low humidity and often clear skies. Abdul also added that the profusion of date palm trees in Arizona's capital city helped him associate Phoenix with Damascus.

This tendency to imagine or recall a much more familiar place in an exotic place reminds me of an evocative passage in Andrea Barrett's "Servants of the Map." In that short story, a British cartographer mapping the rugged interior of Asia writes: "As I fill in the blank spaces with the bends and curves of a river valley, the dips and rises of a range, the drawing begins to resemble a map of home."[2] When similar feelings come to me, they always prompt me to ask two questions: Am I so beguiled by the familiar that I neglect to really experience the new? Or, conversely, by seeing the familiar in the exotic, am I insightful and sensitive to those factors that link, rather than separate, places located far from each other? I still have no answer to this two-sided question, but I do know that I am not alone when I feel that similarity. What surprises me is how rarely, with few exceptions, scholars have ever studied this phenomenon. Those exceptions include cultural or human geographers like Robin Doughty, David Seamon, and Edward Relph. As Doughty put it in describing how newcomers encountered Texas in the 1800s: "In entering a new environment and in coming to terms with its features, settlers transpose images of the land with which they are familiar and construct new ones by employing terms that they and others understand. They are . . ." he noted, "anxious to inform relatives and friends about what is the same and about what is different."[3]

Obviously, Sam Hadeed, Abdul Kelani, and I are by no means the first people to see similarities between our native lands and places elsewhere. The tendency to make such comparisons is probably as old as humankind. People migrate but they carry, as part of their cultural baggage, memories of other places they have experienced. And yet there is something modern about this tendency, which became an integral part of modern exploration and discovery. Upon experiencing the Caribbean islands in the 1490s, for example, Christopher Columbus declared that what he saw here was "like Andalusia in springtime." This was no doubt a heartfelt sentiment but one perhaps also calculated to stimulate and validate Spain's interest in colonizing the place.[4] These comparisons intensified with time. The comparison of places that are far distant from each other became especially common during the age of tourism and transoceanic migration, which began about 1800. By that time, several centuries of landscape painting had taught people to see places somewhat differently than people had seen them in earlier periods. Through increasingly elaborate descriptions and images, people became aware of details, textures, and compositions. In other words, they now developed skills in "graphicacy," much as Western culture developed skills in literacy after the printing press brought the written word to the masses. As a result, many people became part of the modern, visually oriented world, and nothing would ever be quite the same.

During the nineteenth century, as Americans became sophisticated international travelers, they often compared places at home with the exotic places that they experienced while traveling abroad. Consider, for example, how Mark Twain's writing influenced American attitudes about exotic places. Although his best-selling book titled *The Innocents Abroad*[5] (1869) was written with caustic wit, the typical American traveler found much to admire in the Old World as he or she read Twain's book. Moreover, technology now brought those places closer to the United States. Traveling to Europe, the Near East, and even Asia became increasingly easier as the steamship and railroad greatly reduced travel time on sea and land. In his insightful book *Irreverent Pilgrims*, Franklin Walker noted that Twain's perceptions of the Orient changed with the trials and tribulations of travel: Twain initially observed that for all the misery and poverty that he encountered, "'These people are naturally good-hearted and intelligent, and with education and liberty, would be a happy and contented race'"—if it were not for Turkish oppression. However, "as he traveled south plagued by fatigue, fever, and daily discomfort, the dream of a picturesque land of Arabian Nights or Biblical patriarch dissolved under the glaring Syrian sun into an awareness of a people more miserable than any he had ever seen—even than the Goshoot Indians of Nevada." Twain was, in fact, nearly done in by "the God-forsaken barrenness and desolation of Syria," which he described even more harshly than the barrenness and desolation of Nevada. Moreover, with each mile traversed in Syria, Twain became more and more critical of the Arab men he encountered, describing them in prose that was "either marked by invective or humorously pejorative."[6] This reminds me that one's state of mind, and even health, can determine how one sees and recounts the Orient. When all is right with the world and one's health superb, the Orient can be a glistening, magical place. But when a traveler is nearly doubled over with intestinal cramps, the Orient's people and landscapes can suffer in his or her prose, poetry, and memories.

As Americans traveled with eyes wide open, they inevitably drew comparisons between what they saw abroad and what they remembered in their own country. By century's end, it became second nature to compare and equate coastal California with the Mediterranean, Colorado's Rocky Mountains with the Alps, and Utah's Wasatch Front with the Holy Land. More specifically, as historian Earl Pomeroy noted, Americans often compared California to Italy, the Riviera, or Palestine, and the Rocky Mountains to the Swiss or French Alps.[7] To see how this happened, we need to consult the rich exploration and travel literature consisting of reports, journals, diaries, maps, and advertisements. There, in both words and images, is the world for us to compare and covet. True, these travelers represented a somewhat elite segment of the American public, but many people were avid readers. Many of these travel books became best sellers.

In his preface to the original (1874) edition of *Picturesque America*, William Cullen Bryant observed that even though "our country abounds with scenery new to the artist's pencil," much of it was neglected. By contrast, Bryant noted, "In the Old World every spot . . . has been visited by the artist; studied and sketched again and again." Vexed by this, Bryant challenged artists to visit and portray our nation, where "thousands of charming nooks are waiting to yield their beauty to the pencil of the first comer." Sexual connotations of this metaphor aside, Bryant made an interesting point. Now that the transcontinental railroad reached the Pacific, one could travel to the "Rocky Mountains rivaling Switzerland in its scenery of rock piled on rock, up to the region of the clouds. But . . ." Bryant added, "Switzerland has no such groves on its mountainsides, nor has even Libanus [Lebanon], with its ancient cedars, as those which raise the astonishment of the visitor to that Western region—trees of such prodigious height and enormous dimensions that, to attain their present bulk, we might imagine them to have sprouted from the seed at the time of the Trojan War." Bryant cautioned Americans who compared the American West with similar landscapes in the Old World. There is, as he put it, "an essential difference" the traveler should recognize between America and Eurasia. "So, when he journeys among the steeps, and gorges, fountains of Lebanon and Anti-Lebanon, he will perceive that he is neither among the Alps nor the Pyrenees." As Bryant put it, discerning people (like himself) realize that "the precipices wear outlines of their own, the soil has its peculiar vegetation, the clouds and the sky have their distinct physiognomy." This was certainly sound advice, but it tended to fall on deaf ears at that time. Why? Because the West was not yet the West we know today, but was in the process of becoming that region in the popular mind. Before that happened, people judged the West in terms of what about it was similar to what they had seen elsewhere. Orientalism was a part of this process of testing western North America against other more distant places.

In fact, how we view the landscape of home depends on what we've experienced elsewhere. As cultural historian Neil Harris observed, "Travel was a broad and catholic teacher," and it ultimately led to an increased American cosmopolitanism. In turn, however, that cosmopolitanism was increasingly viewed as heretical. It became "a threat to patriotism," for, as Harris put it, "belief in a peculiar national virtue stretched thin when it encountered the tempting philosophy of cultural pluralism." Equally challenging, perhaps, was the sense of unease that Americans felt when they pondered the Old World's ancient ruins, where "past grandeur and present degradation were so graphically contrasted." This contrast "served to remind the onlooker of the power and brilliance that had once held sway there" and suggested that a similar fate might await the new and promising United States. This concern, according to

Harris, was exacerbated by the growing social discontent in America's increasingly crowded cities. To counter this, the masses needed a worthy diversion. Harris interprets Americans' seemingly insatiable interest in broadening education in great works of art and architecture in the nineteenth century as "tools to maintain a minimum level of public security and contentment, opiates which would quiet and eventually tame the savage beasts who prowled in American cities."[8]

Although Harris specifically addressed America's wholesale fascination with Europe as a cultural center, the Orient, too, was another part of the world that was emulated enthusiastically. In fact, to virtually all Americans, no part of the world was portrayed as more mysterious and more interesting than the Orient. The most surprising thing about the Orient, perhaps, is how many people made reference to that faraway region whether or not they had ever actually visited it. But if the term "Orient" was frequently spoken or penned, just what, and where, was this mysterious place?

Geographically speaking, the Orient is difficult to define, for it literally means any place east of the West. More specifically, though, it meant places where Oriental peoples lived. In European thought, the Orient meant Asia—which was located to the east of Europe, about where the Oder and Don Rivers flow. Europe had long been fascinated by this Orient, but by about 1760, the word *Orientalism* became part of the English language. Asia itself is a Western construct, and that huge part of the Eurasian landmass reaches well into the area of the eastern edge of the Mediterranean Sea.

Given North America's colonization by Europeans over the last half millennium, it is no surprise that a fascination with the East spread westward across the Atlantic. Although this book focuses on North America, it will refer to Europe more or less throughout, as the cultures are so closely allied. Typically, Europeans and Americans in the past spoke of two Orients—the Far East and the Near East. Today, we are more likely to call the Far East by another, but only slightly less West-centric term, *East Asia*. However, I shall use the former term *Far East* when relevant, that is, when discussing Western views of that part of the East in the context of nineteenth-century descriptions of it. Of course, we use the term *Middle East* today for what people in the nineteenth century called the Near East. Both of these Easts—Near and Far—are different enough from the West to be as easily understood intuitively as they are difficult to define geographically.

For their part, geographers, diplomats, and merchants long considered terminology such as the *Far East* too vague and simplistic. To make more sense out of the Orient, they divided it into many subregions—for example, East

Asia, Southeast Asia, and Indonesia. We still refer to the Middle East today but recognize that it has many important subregions, such as Asia Minor, the Holy Land, and the Arabian Peninsula. These subregions of a much larger Orient may seem to be based on real physical geography but are actually cultural constructs. Then, too, historians and social critics may define the East as areas where fundamentally different religions and cultures—for example, Islam or Buddhism—dominate. As will become apparent, I employ a fairly liberal definition of the Orient, one that accounts for the early spread of Islam across northern Africa to Gibraltar on the west; this, paradoxically, means that some of the Orient lies south of Europe. In my definition, then, the Orient sprawls nearly seven thousand miles (11,265 km) longitudinally, from Morocco to Malaysia.

The Orient, of course, is as much a state of mind as an actual place. Therefore, literary critics and writers offer noteworthy definitions that are based less on actual geography than on personal, and sometimes very emotional, beliefs. For example, in attempting to define the Orient, Argentine poet and essayist Jorge Luis Borges stated that there "is something we feel as the Orient . . . but . . . I don't know how I can define it." Despite this disclaimer, however, Borges went on to define the Orient as well as anyone ever has:

> It is above all a world of extremes in which people are very happy or very unhappy, very rich or very poor. A world of Kings who do not explain what they do. Of Kings who are, we might say, as irresponsible as Gods.[9]

There is no separating such a place from the imagination of the individual reader. Timothy Weiss summed up Borges's understanding of the Orient as "having the shape of a story; in this story-within-stories, one eventually finds, he surmises, one's own tale and destiny."[10] This story-inspired definition of the Orient is astute. It not only incorporates a touch of Arabian mystery but may also help explain the nearly insatiable Western interest in the East from ancient times, and certainly the Christian Middle Ages, to the present. Perceptions of this East are not only driven by popular narratives but are also likely to be highly personalized. This East may be far away geographically, but it is psychologically part of us—and we are part of it.

Something else about Borges's description is noteworthy. A despotic ruler playing God is conceivable in this place we have identified as the exotic "other" because we believe that it is a place that has objectively different rules than those by which Western society normally plays.[11] Such an Orient is conceivable, and readily conceived, by westerners as a place that serves as a counterpoint to ours. *We* are the West(erners), *they* are the Orient(als).

It is here that not only the Orient but also *Orientalism* needs to be addressed and defined. The first definition of Orientalism in most dictionaries is "any trait, style, custom, expression, etc. peculiar to Oriental peoples." The second involves "knowledge or use of Oriental languages, history, etc." The third definition involves "imitation or assimilation of that which is Oriental, especially in religious or philosophical thought, or in art."[12] It is this third definition that interests me most in this book because it is central to understanding how and why Americans imitate(d) the Orient and how this played out so commonly and so effectively in the American West.

Orientalism would not exist if there were no underlying interest or fascination with the Orient. I am suggesting not only that Orientalism is part of Western culture's need to identify the exotic "other" but also that it is an integral part of Western culture's own cultural construction. We imitate(d) or assimilate(d) the Orient because doing so helps our culture construct a more complete identity. In other words, the Orientalization of American culture— or in this case, the American West—brings fuller meaning to the people and places we encounter on American soil.

As I use the term here, Orientalism is a mind-set that readily imagines or perceives an East when it encounters non-Eastern peoples and places. It involves the West's fascination with a part of the world identified as the East. In a literal and literary sense, Orientalism is a large and contested body of knowledge about the Orient. According to Edward Said in his pathbreaking 1978 book *Orientalism*, "The Orient was almost a European invention, and had been since antiquity a place of romance, exotic beings, haunting memories and landscapes, [and] remarkable experiences." Said's premise is that Orientalism represents the creation and study of an Orient by westerners (Europeans) for a particular reason, namely, the appropriation and domination of that East. In Said's view, Orientalism is both disingenuous and exploitative. It may offer faint praise, but the Western view of the Orient is ultimately intended to foster inferiority through imperialism. In Said's view, then, Orientalism is a form of containment, defining as the "other" those who are to be subdued.

Said's hypothesis is widely, though not universally, accepted. According to art historian John MacKenzie, Orientalism also involves genuinely positive depictions of, even an admiration for, the peoples and places of the East. We can see this in flattering artistic representations of the East by westerners. As MacKenzie put it, Said's interpretation of Orientalism imagines early Orientalists' "negative stereotyping, slights and insults on the basis of late twentieth-century perceptions." MacKenzie, in other words, sees a great deal of presentism in Said's interpretation. He notes that viewing the past with today's sentiments and sensitivities can misinform us about how people in earlier periods really felt about the Orient and its peoples. Thus, even though MacKenzie sympathizes with some of Said's overtly political concerns about affairs in the recent Middle East, he claims that Said's thesis ultimately "poisons the deep wells of sympathy and respect which artists of all sorts felt for the East in the nineteenth century, which they expressed in distinctively nineteenth-century ways, not necessarily amenable to the critical values of the twentieth century."[13]

Travel accounts are also more complex than they first appear. As Harry Liebersohn noted in *Aristocratic Encounters: European Travelers and North American Indians* (1998), "it is difficult to adopt a method of analyzing travel encounters that is supple enough to follow the movement of travelers and their writings across the many borders" of inquiry about the subject. Liebersohn further notes that "Said's Orientalism has emphasized the moment of pure project[ion] of Western power onto non-Western societies." But "this kind of radical critique . . ." about "an inherent colonialism of Western culture has given way to a blurrier map of cultural encounters." Liebersohn concludes that "romantic travelers have a story of their own to tell, related to yet removed from the world of their predecessors."[14] More recently, historian David Wrobel called for a post-Saidian interpretation of travel narratives in the American West.[15] Orientalism, in this post-Saidian view, emerges as something more refreshingly expansive, providing room for broader interpretation(s) of how the West (in this case, the United States) perceives the East.

A careful reading of the historical literature suggests that people in the United States generally, and the American West in particular, regarded the Orient with affection as well as fear; which is to say that the Orient was regarded with considerable ambivalence. Moreover, because Orientalism is not confined to one portion of the West but is broadly shared by a wide range of people, we do well to expand the definition of sources that can help illustrate and explain it. When studying Orientalism, MacKenzie urges us to consider popular culture as well as elite art and literature. This is good advice. Although Edward Said's *Orientalism* employed elite literary sources almost exclusively,[16] Orientalism itself reaches deeply into all areas of popular culture.[17] It includes sources as diverse as popular novels, architecture, art, advertising, film, and music.[18]

Rather than viewing Orientalism as universally negative, therefore, it might be more profitable to recognize that it may be negative, positive, or both. It has been so ever since the first Greeks looked eastward, the first European Christian pilgrims set out toward the Holy Land, the first Crusaders marched toward Jerusalem, the explorer Marco Polo trekked to China, and the nationalistic Napoleon marched into Egypt. Many people who would never actually visit the Orient also formed opinions about that part of the world and its cultures. In other words, Orientalists are simply people who envision and engage the Orient (and its peoples) for a wide variety of reasons. Rather than brand their interests and motives as good or bad, I simply acknowledge that their Orientalism has yielded considerable information about that part (or those parts) of the world—information that has often been imported into our culture from diverse sources. Orientalism, then, is a vehicle by which knowledge about places and peoples is transferred and applied, however imperfectly, to the non-Orient (i.e., Europe and the Americas). Just as Orientalism may be the result of varied intentions, it may also be well-informed or ill-informed.

Even though the Orientalism imported into the American West originated in Europe, it had its own permutations on American soil. In Europe and France in particular, Orientalism was closely linked to organized military imperial expansion, though aesthetics played a large role, too. In the United States, Orientalism began to flower in a new nation that had just begun to ponder westward expansion as the collective impulse of individuals. The Orientalism they took westward with them was not only complex but (like its European counterpart) also changeable through time. Like its European progenitor, American Orientalism has a dual identity; it may involve either traditional religious and spiritual associations or physical and material excesses (of flesh, wealth, hubris). The former are some of the loftiest aspects of Western civilization, while the latter are considered decadent, and the stuff against which moral crusaders have railed for centuries.[19]

In Orientalism, the East has meaning as both geographical position and metaphor. The Orient as East is associated with the rising of the sun in the east—hence the concept of Jerusalem at the top of early maps. Its position there symbolizes that city's importance, and that positioning persists in our using the word "orientation" to signify up (or top) on a map—even though that position is now conventionally north. The East is metaphorical for another reason: before the sun rises in the east, that region is bathed in darkness. Just as we might seek the sun by traveling west (as it seems to do) and hence find constant renewal, by looking eastward we greet a new day, but in so doing, find far more than the rising sun—we also inevitably encounter the darkness that is banished by the light. The metaphor translates into a basic tenet of Christianity: the sun rises in the east, while the Son (of God) symbolically rises on Easter.

This, coupled with the fact that traveling eastward brought Europeans face to face with new (or, rather, rediscovered) environments such as the desert—with its binary challenges as either tempting wilderness or nurturer of God's spirit through light[20]—led them to perceive the East as a place where one's spiritual mettle could be tested. That kind of desert spiritual test also occurred in the American West when settlers such as the Mormons encountered conditions of increasing aridity with every mile they traveled westward. This new region in the American West, then, was akin to that experienced by Europeans who traveled eastward during the Crusades. Finding something familiar in this new West was no accident or coincidence. Many of our Euro-American values about such desert landscapes were inherited from biblical and other stories that originated in the East.

Nineteenth-century American Orientalism reveals a deep searching for spirituality. In *No Place of Grace* (1981), T. J. Jackson Lears observed that Orientalism was not simply "a trivial exercise in exoticism" nor, for that matter, was it even "a response to the spiritual turmoil of the late nineteenth century." Oriental mysticism, by which Lears particularly meant eastern Asian Buddhism, became popular in the late nineteenth century. Lears attributed this to a strong growing antimodernism: the East suggested mystery while the West at that time, circa 1880–1920, demanded increasing rationality. Oriental mysticism could, as Lears noted using explicitly Freudian terminology, help one recover the "primal irrationality" that had been lost in the West. Among others, Lears used three case studies of elite Bostonians—eccentric surgeon William Sturgis Bigelow, scientist Percival Lowell, and poet George Cabot Lodge—to demonstrate how thoroughly Orientalism consumed, and sometimes exhausted, its practitioners. All three of the Bostonians revealed, like American society itself, the titanic struggles between authority and responsibility in late Victorian society. Lears focused especially on the fascination with Far Eastern—notably Japanese—Orientalism but reminded us that "popular Orientalism was unsystematic and diverse" and that "its adherents were often ignorant of the traditions they claimed to embrace."[21] That ignorance, of course, does not make the Orient any less potent as an influence; in fact, it may have enhanced it.

American Orientalism is as old as the nation itself; in fact it is far older. By restlessly moving westward, settlers were paradoxically moving closer to the Orient by way of the Pacific Ocean. This American movement into the West as a "passage to India" theme was discussed by Henry Nash Smith in his classic book *Virgin Land*.[22] The Asia toward which Americans were destined was itself always vague and ever shifting. Smith quoted Thomas Jefferson—whom he calls "the intellectual father of the American advance to the Pacific"—as a promoter of trade with the East Indies. Smith titled the first "book" of *Virgin Land* "Passage to India" and cited Henry David Thoreau's *Walden* (1854), which speculated that the way to the American West "does not pause at the Mississippi or the Pacific, nor conduct toward a worn-out China or Japan, but leads on direct a tangent to this sphere, summer and winter, day and night, sun down, moon down, and at last earth down, too."[23] By this, Thoreau meant that the East Indies was America's ultimate destiny.

There is, of course, something very Columbian in the belief that by traveling westward, one would find the riches—gems, spices, and the like—of the Indies. This was obvious very early in the European exploration of the Americas. Consider the Spanish conquistador Cortés, who moved into Mexico City in 1519 and soon set his sights on the Pacific Ocean, or South Sea as it was called. Cortés observed that "everybody who has any knowledge and experience of navigation in the Indies is certain that the discovery of the South Sea would lead to discovery of many islands rich in gold, pearls, precious stones, spices and other unknown and wonderful things."[24] By Jefferson's and Thoreau's time, however, the Indies was no longer the Antillean (or West) Indies, but rather the real thing—Southeast Asia and even the Indian subcontinent; in other words, the East Indies that Columbus had sought, but failed to find. More to the point, whereas China and Japan were recognized empires in their own right, the Indies seemed far less coherent, and less claimed by authority. With increased intercourse and increased political ambition worldwide, however, even Japan, Korea, and China would become fair game for American commerce and adventurism. In that way, the entire Orient, as it came to be called, offered seemingly unlimited possibilities to the American imagination.

According to cultural historian Oleg Grabar, at least four "impulses"—one might also call them factors—were operative in popular American Orientalism. The first was a Protestant search for the spaces and sites associated with biblical revelations, as suggested in part by the proliferation of biblical toponyms in many parts of the country. The second impulse involved a fascination with aspects of culture associated with European aristocracy—the very peoples who had obtained Islamic and other Eastern art and artifacts since the Middle Ages. The third was Americans' tendency to incorporate symbols, designs, and other aspects of Eastern culture into public art, architecture, and popular culture. This Orient that Americans copied or mimicked was, according to Grabar, "curiously poised between desire and repulsion, beauty and ugliness, [but] it is an Orient that answers deep psychological and social needs." So far, these three factors are for the most part positive. However, the last impulse was a "critical rather than sympathetic" attitude toward the Orient, or, as Grabar concluded, "The Orient only matters as providing illustrations for some significant moments in the long history that led to the American promised Land, and its very misery is a demonstration of the latter's success."[25] Grabar here quotes Mark Twain, whose scathing comments about places he had visited in the Holy Land formed the essence of *The Innocents Abroad* (1869). Although Grabar does raise many valid points, he fails to note that Twain was not exactly the best choice to illustrate Americans' supposedly critical attitudes about the East. Twain was not only an ailing individual at times, but also the greatest satirist of his era. In his writings and on stage, Twain criticized virtually everything—including his own country and the entire human race. Depending on his mood and mercurial pen, Twain could be as anti-American as he was anti-Oriental.

Orientalism was a powerful force in shaping the way newcomers encountered, and made sense of, the peoples and places they found in the North American West. As a revisionist historical geography of the American West, this book will focus on places and how they are perceived, especially why one place and its peoples can so readily remind us of other places and peoples. Its main focus is on landscapes that capture aspects of their prototypes elsewhere. These landscapes can be thought of as "surrogates" in that they serve as substitutes for the real landscapes they mimic. Similarly, peoples encountered in one place can remind us of peoples seen elsewhere. A major premise of this book is that people and place are in inseparable in this process of creating new cultural identities. As identities shift from place to place and from culture to culture, they are shaped and reshaped through a kind of mimesis through time.

The landscape, as one of the grand artifacts that a culture constructs, is seemingly permanent, but it, like the imagination that encounters it, is actually highly malleable. The landscape is also physically manipulable. To paraphrase Winston Churchill, we shape landscapes and they in turn shape us. When we name a community in North America "Mecca" or "Lebanon," we subliminally imprint it with associations and memories, some very distant or ancient. Like adoptive parents, people experiencing a new landscape may give the new place an older, preconceived identity—much like a parent names a child after a relative and by so doing imposes a series of traditions and expectations. To parents, this is natural enough, but it imposes a preconceived identity on the child. The surrogate, in other words, is granted some of the character given the original through a process that seems harmless enough—perhaps even flattering—and is disarmingly simple.

Studied more closely, however, the adoption of a surrogate landscape is a complex act. The surrogate landscape is on the one hand counterfeit; yet on the other it is a tribute to the original. The fact that such a landscape is copied at all suggests the power of the original in the popular mind. Consider the Holy Land as a case in point. Although the real Holy Land is incomparable, it is also surprisingly susceptible to duplication. Witness its iconization on Christmas cards, wherein wise men are placed against an immediately recognizable background of desert, palm trees, and indigo skies. In the Desert Christ Park near Yucca Valley, California, the rock-ribbed landscape of the New World becomes the Old World as statues of Jesus in various stages of his life are placed in this hilly, boulder-strewn area. Through such conflation, the Mojave Desert landscape of the park becomes, in a word, biblical. Because a place will be copied only if people associate it with something significant—often an event or events—it is therefore replicable elsewhere through surrogacy only if two factors—geographic conditions and human imagination—are present.

Such comparisons may seem timeless or perhaps ageless, but the process by which original places become treasured, even sacred, may occur in a surprisingly short time.[26] Consider, for example, the Navajo (Diné) Indian reverence for the four mountains that anchor their homeland in the "Four Corners" area of the American Southwest. This landscape is an indelible part of Navajo identity today and would seem to have been so for thousands of years. The archaeological and historical record shows, however, that the Navajo people arrived here from the northern Great Plains as late as about 1200 or 1300 AD. Seven or eight hundred years may seem like a rather short time, but traditional Navajo spiritual and cultural identity is now so dependent on that new place in the Southwest that it seems eternal. If we keep in mind that even Western culture as we know it has been evolving, and that most of our national identities (such as Italian, German, or American) are only two or three centuries old, the speed at which identities take shape should not be surprising.

In fact, the process can operate much more quickly, as the Mormon settlement of Utah confirms. Only about 150 years have passed since the Mormons arrived in the Salt Lake Valley in July of 1847, yet it is now their homeland. Moreover, it is worth noting that the Mormons almost instantly transformed the landscape into the center of their religion by equating its landscape with lands mentioned in the Bible. When this place making by the Mormons began, western North America had been in a state of flux geopolitically for more than a century. In the early nineteenth century, the North American West belonged to Spain (then Mexico) and Britain. Russia was a minor player and about to exit the stage, but it did leave an easy-to-romanticize heritage behind. Lewis and Clark's Corps of Discovery expedition helped establish an American foothold in the Far West in 1805. Between then and 1848, the American West was explored and then claimed by the United States at an increasingly rapid pace. A fascination with the Orient was popular in the United States at this time, but most Americans lived along the Eastern Seaboard and were now actively settling the Midwest. This means that the Orientalization of the American West was underway well before settlers, and even explorers, from the United States arrived there in the early to mid-nineteenth century. Still, the American West held special promise. To get a hint of Euro-Americans' mindset, we need only recall that one of Lewis and Clark's goals was to determine whether the Indians there were members of the Lost Tribes of Israel.

From about 1820 into the 1880s, the opening of the Anglo-American West was documented for audiences in American cities along the Eastern Seaboard and in the Midwest. Europeans too were keenly interested in the North American frontier. The West drew European writers who penned reports and stories for their readers back home. The American West, then, was not only explored and settled by real pioneers but also opened in a very dramatic and literary fashion—the drama being a literal acting out of a story for an eager audience. In this story, the landscape was a major player, as so much of the continuity of westward discovery was based on vivid descriptions of Eastern, or Oriental, places—their topography, vegetation, hydrology, and their native residents.[27]

America's deep interest in the Orient helped to transform regions being explored and settled in North America into "exotic" locales. This means that the imagined (if not imaginary) East actually had a role in shaping a formative American region. Ironically, western America was captured by the Orient, rather than vice versa. This, of course, was more of a voluntary surrender to the East in the Western imagination, but that type of self-deception was not necessarily pathological. Rather, it reveals the East as inspirational during the age of romanticism, when it was more or less expected that a writer or traveler would become emotionally engaged with a particular subject. The landscape itself was one such subject, or rather object, that was regarded subjectively.[28]

As will soon become apparent, the Orientalization of the American landscape worked hand in hand with the Orientalization of people in frontier America. This process began early. Consider, for example, how the eastern portion of the early American nation was Orientalized. In describing the Indian wars occurring in the frontier areas of the Southeast in 1775, Indian trader James Adair noted that "a sufficient number of discreet orderly traders"

was needed to bring stability to a dangerous and chaotic situation. "Formerly
. . ." Adair noted, "each trader had a license for two towns, or villages; but
according to the present unwise plan, two and even three Arab-like pedlars
sculk about in one of those villages." These traders, of course, were not really
Arabs, but they acted the way Adair assumed Arabs operated—in a very enterprising fashion but without a European sense of honor, and with little or no
discipline.[29] At the time, this was an effective way to reaffirm how good British
merchants should operate; which is to say honorably, within the law, and with
a sense of the civic good. This upright behavior would in turn ensure that
Indians were treated fairly and that they wouldn't rebel against the Crown.

On the early westward-moving frontier, even Anglo or Anglo-American
subjects were sometimes Orientalized—oftentimes voluntarily. In describing
how he moved about the Southeast in the 1830s, a soldier noted that his
conduct during the Seminole wars left him doubtful. To help the reader better
understand how "a dark, uncertain blank . . . filled my soul with disappointment and dismay," he placed himself in yet another more literary travel scenario, observing that "I felt like the adventurer merchant in the Arabian Tales,
who, in the midst of his exalted enthusiasm, kicked and overset his basket of
crockery, and found himself reduced to nothing; it seemed to me as though, in
Scripture phrase, I had strained at a gnat and swallowed a camel."[30] This literary trope confirms that the unstable frontier encouraged romantic allusions
and illusions. At this time and in this frontier setting, Orientalism flourished.

But even more familiar places could be Orientalized early on. The fact that
nineteenth-century travelers envisioned themselves having real Oriental experiences on the East Coast reveals just how primed they were for exotic adventure. How else would one explain an author describing the area near Cape Cod
in 1838 as follows: "The sand and barreness increase; and in not a few places it
would need only a party of Bedouin Arabs to cross the traveller's path, to make
him feel that he was in the depths of *an Arabian or Lybian* desert."[31] Similarly,
even a rather well-known part of New York State was described exotically in
1845: "Long Island has still many unexpected beauties to reward the attentive
tourist," including its less-populated eastern portion, where after "falling back
upon the isolated farmhouse, and the whistling ploughboy, anon losing itself
in sterile Arabian sands, and frightful cavernous solitudes, it would seem as
if some regions of the noble and beautiful Isle contrasted strangely with each
other, as the first rude huts of twin brothers on Palatine Hill, differed from the
city of the Caesars."[32] In writing the latter passage, Lydia Howard Sigourney
emphasized Long Island's diversity of landscapes using the literary allusions of
the day, which were often Oriental and focused on the Near East.

An essential step in Orientalizing the American frontier, then, involved Orientalizing both places and peoples. It is no surprise, therefore, that the area's indigenous inhabitants were also given Oriental identities. This too took place in steps, both chronologically and geographically. In his dramatically written book, *A History of the Indian Wars* (1812), New Englander Daniel Clarke Sanders stated that "the savage of America" does things in a leisurely way, although "his soul is as active as his body is passive." Sanders then added, however, that "there must always be industry somewhere; and among the savages this falls to the lot of the *women*," who "hoe the corn, and secure the harvest" while also doing the cooking and providing "the comforts of the fireside." This seemed familiar to Sanders. Comparing the Indians' lifestyle to the Arabs, he noted that when these women "have provided a repast, they are not used to eat, agreeably to the custom of Arabian wives, till their husbands have done."[33] By looking to the East, Sanders found a way to understand seemingly exotic human behavior among the Indians on the American frontier.

Studying the writings of the period confirms that the Orientalizing of the American Indians as well as the landscape began on the East Coast and moved westward with the rapidly expanding frontier. This was closely linked to the way that northern Europeans settled North America. By 1820, in describing Detroit, Michigan, which was "called by courtesy a city," J. C. Gilleland observed that the French had a presence here. Because the French were consummate Orientalists, that French connection doubled the likelihood that an Orientalist analogy would find its way into a description. Gilleland cited Volney, who "observes that the ladies in general resemble the Arabian Bedwins, particularly in their shark shaped (low cornered) mouths, and tiger teeth." This may have made these women seem dangerous, but that was not Volney's intent. "Most of them . . ." he added, "have lively, expressive, agreeable countenances."[34]

These exotic descriptions were written about the relatively tame eastern United States, but only marked a starting point. The farther west that the United States expanded on the North American continent, the more exotic the landscapes and peoples seemed to become. In attempting to make sense out of what they saw, pioneers often envisioned other lands they had heard and read about. Consider, for example, how Americans who had never actually seen a desert might react when they encountered one far west of the Mississippi River. They had no firsthand experience, nor had their parents and grandparents. For generations, their experience had been gained in the humid eastern United States and, before that, western Europe. For most of these people, however, the desert was associated with one thing in particular—religion.

That religion was their own Judeo-Christian heritage, whose early history had unfolded in the desert, which was called "the wilderness" in many biblical passages. Moreover, that wilderness consisted of barren mountains from which various prophets had received inspiration from God. The interior American West, with its desert mountain wildernesses aplenty, was positioned to become a surrogate for the landscapes of the Holy Land.

In the nineteenth century, the Far East was also viewed as a place where spirituality, broadly defined, was regarded more highly than in America. This spirituality transcended Christianity, plumbing other Eastern religions like Hinduism and Buddhism. New England was the home of several highly influential writers, including Henry David Thoreau (1817–1862), who sought alternative spiritualities. Among these seekers of alternatives was Ralph Waldo Emerson (1803–1882), who longed for the "unity of Asia" and "the infinitude of the Asiatic soul," which he contrasted with the more superficial West. Although Emerson is "regarded as the first Orientalist, and indeed the Orientalist *par excellence*, of American literature,"[35] many other writers were also engaged philosophically with the East from the 1830s to the 1860s.

At the same time that serious thinkers like Emerson pondered the Orient philosophically, the lavish ornamentation of the East also appealed to Americans' popular romantic fantasies. In *Uncle Tom's Cabin*, for example, New Englander Harriet Beecher Stowe (1811–1896) characterized a Southern mansion as "built in the Moorish fashion," with "Moorish arches, slender pillars, and arabesque ornaments." This mansion "carried the mind back, as in a dream, to the reign of oriental romance in Spain."[36] Describing a persuasive New England minister in a short story published in 1855, Stowe noted that "the devout poetry of his prayer, rich with Orientalism of Scripture, and eloquent with the expression of strong yet chastened emotion, breathed over his audience like music, hushing every one to silence, and beguiling every one to feelings."[37] By this, Stowe meant the rich mysterious tradition of the East that permeates Western religion.

But it could also refer to something more sinister. In a series of letters compiled as a book titled *Pictures of Southern Life, Social, Political, Military*, the Irish-born correspondent and prolific author William Howard Russell compared southern slavery with its counterpart in the Orient. Confessing "a strange thrill" that he "could, for the sum of $975," buy a black man, Russell recoiled at the prospect. Noting that "there is no sophistry which could persuade me the [black] man was not a man . . . he was assuredly my fellow creature," Russell, who covered the Crimean war a few years earlier, then added: "I have seen slave markets in the East, but somehow or other the Orientalism of the scene cast a coloring over the nature of sales there which deprived them of the disagreeable harshness and mater-of-fact character of the transaction before me." Why? Russell quickly added: "For Turk, or Smyrniote, or Egyptian to buy and sell slaves seemed rather suited to the eternal fitness of things [there] than otherwise." As Russell further noted, "The turbaned, shawled, loose-trousered, pipe smoking merchants speaking an unknown tongue looked as if they were engaged in a legitimate business." But in the American South, Russell noted that it was painful "to see decent-looking men in European garb engaged in the work before me."[38]

The Civil War soon erupted over this and other matters. In discussing the supposedly "Civilizing Effect of Slavery" in another book in 1863, Russell described "some good-looking little negro boys and men dressed in liveries, which smacked of our host's Orientalism."[39] Note that Orientalism here simply means the way things are done in the Orient, and that those things may be perpetually despotic by nature and destiny. The West, on the other hand, should behave differently. Russell's observations suggest a fruitful avenue of study, namely, how American slavery itself was conceptualized, or even excused, as having roots in the venerable East.

As early as the 1830s, some intellectuals had begun to equate the Orient with both the enslavement of blacks and the oppression of women in America. In 1837, as she expounded on the "morals of slavery," Harriet Martineau observed that the increasing independence of men was accompanied by the increased dependence of women. In this, she feared American society was "always advancing toward orientalism." Martineau urged that this "peculiar domestic institution," as she called it, should be overthrown "with an energy and wisdom that would look more like inspiration than orientalism."[40] As Scott Trafton astutely noted in *Egypt Land* (2004), the Mississippi River took on special meaning as "American Egyptomania" spread westward and concerns about slavery intensified. As Trafton put it, "The semiotic and ideological links between the Nile and Mississippi were formative links for the iconography of western expansion."[41]

Then, too, Orientalism could signify something about the way cultures express themselves. For example, James S. Buckingham observed in 1841 that Americans' tendency toward elaboration—to make, as a social critic put it, settling a claim of ten acres equal "the whole discovery of America"— typifies "all the extravagances and the gaudy phraseology which distinguish our western Orientalism." In this case, Orientalism means verbosity and "long harangues," as opposed to the simplicity and straightforwardness that should characterize the United States.

Between 1851 and 1857, Henry Rowe Schoolcraft wrote an elaborate trea-
tise about the origins of Native Americans. Hoping to answer the question, or
rather address the common premise, that Native Americans were "Orientals,"
Schoolcraft compared their culture (as if it were monolithic) to that of many
Asian peoples. Schoolcraft started with a general question: "Are their traits,
opinions, and idiosyncrasies, indigenous or American; or are they peculiar to
the Indian mind as developed on this continent; and not derivative from other
lands?" As was common at the time, Schoolcraft focused mainly on American
Indians' beliefs, philosophy, worship, and languages. Comparing these with
varied Asian peoples, he dismissed some traits as purely Native American.
Others seemed to be well developed in both hemispheres but may have simply
been a result of independent invention. However, still other traits seemed to
be traceable to Asia. Even though, as he put it, "it is difficult to introduce comparisons between the barbarous tribes of America, and the existing civilized
races of Asia" simply because the former were so "undeveloped" and the latter
so "advanced"—there were some fascinating convergences. Moreover, to some
observers, the Indians seemed to represent people who were banished from
the Old World in a state of primitive idolatry—much like ancient Israelites
(Psalms 106:19–31). Furthermore, Schoolcraft contended, there was a relationship between "these pictographic symbols, [and] between the mythology
of the eastern and western hemispheres." Schoolcraft concluded: "Idle, indeed,
would be the attempt, at this day, to look for the origin of the American race
in any other generic quarter than the eastern continent." Schoolcraft believed
the Indians had migrated from the Orient, but was completely unsure as to
when and how this had occurred.[42]

If the material presented in this introductory chapter suggests that cultural identity, like landscape identity, is surprisingly malleable, it further suggests that people from certain parts of the United States did more of that
shaping than did people from other regions. In this regard, New England
stands out as a major source of nineteenth-century Orientalist ideas. It should
now be apparent that Orientalism connotes more than a simple interest in, or
fascination with, the Orient. It also suggests that one is fascinated or interested
enough to act by naming places and peoples after the Orient(als), thus giving
an Oriental identity to the peoples and places encountered. This study further
suggests that the Orientalizing of the West and its peoples was more than
simply aesthetic, for it helped facilitate the process of territorial expansion in
the nineteenth century.

Fascinated by the Orient, those literary New Englanders played an important role in shaping attitudes about the American West. It is telling, perhaps,

that the intellectuals of New England (for example, in Boston) were called Brahmans (or Brahmins). That word itself is Hindi for someone of high caste—a subtle reminder of the growing importance of the philosophical, if still somewhat elitist, writer in America. Coalescing in a broad triangular region stretching from New York to Boston and out into the western frontier of New York State, influences from the New England region helped shape perceptions of landscape and culture as far west as the Pacific Ocean during that crucial time of encounter and settlement in the nineteenth century, namely the 1830s and 1840s. Other areas on the Eastern Seaboard were also involved in the process of Orientalizing the United States. From Philadelphia on the middle Atlantic Seaboard and also in a broad sweep from Virginia to New Orleans, Americans continued to move westward, and as they did, they brought with them, and even refined, references to the Orient.

To see how this Orientalization affected the exploration and naming of parts of the American West and continues to affect it to the present, we must first travel back in time about two centuries and westward into portions of the American frontier just beyond where the nation's most majestic rivers—the Ohio, Mississippi, and Missouri—converge. As it turned out, by moving westward into this frontier, Americans would encounter environments and peoples that were considerably different from what was well known on the Eastern Seaboard. With each day's travel westward, increasingly larger prairies were encountered until finally most vegetation vanished. Here, in an area that was solidly controlled by Native Americans, the newly arriving European Americans imagined that the increasingly strange landscapes and peoples they encountered were as much of the Orient as they were of the New World.

Fig. I-1. Pyramid Lake, illustrated in Emanuel Henri Domenech's *Seven Years' Residence in the Great Deserts of North America* (1860).

Part I

The Frontier West as the Orient (ca. 1810–1920)

Fig. I-2. Hi Jolly Monument, Quartzite, Arizona

1

The American Zahara
Into and Beyond the Great Western Plains

These vast plains of the western hemisphere may become in time as celebrated as the sandy deserts of Africa; for I saw in my route, in various places, tracts of many leagues where the wind had thrown up the sand in all the fanciful form of the ocean's rolling wave, and on which not a speck of vegetable matter existed.

Zebulon Pike, 1806

THE INITIAL ANGLO-AMERICAN MOVE WESTWARD OCCURRED during a time when two ways of viewing the world—either through the ancient authority of the classics or a newer, more personally based romanticism—were prevalent, and sometimes in conflict. For several centuries in Europe, the classical world had been plumbed for its authority and aesthetics. By about 1790, neoclassicism still dominated, but romanticism, which represented a way of experiencing the world through emotion and imagination, now became a factor in the way westerners viewed the world. By emphasizing nature and encouraging individuals to react emotionally to what they experienced, romanticism shaped the way travelers perceived new places. In describing the landscape he experienced on a boat trip up the Missouri River in 1811, for example, Henry Marie Brackenridge noted that the scenery on a particular evening was "beautiful beyond any thing I ever beheld." Disregarding advice to stay close to the boat, Brackenridge wandered off a few miles from it—a risky move no doubt encouraged by his sense of adventure and his secret longing to expose himself to danger. With evening coming on, and "the sky as clear as that represented in Chinese painting," Brackenridge found "the face of the country enchanting." Much like a work of art, everything here—"the flowery mead, the swelling ground, the romantic hill, the bold river, the winding rivulet, the shrubberies, [were] all disposed and arranged in the most exquisite manner."[1]

The observation about two distinct ways of perceiving the world at this time bears repeating: the landscape that people like Brackenridge beheld earlier in the nineteenth century might be viewed as a Chinese painting, but much of the tone had been set by classicism—the tendency to place things in the context of ancient Greece and Rome. From the very earliest times of the New Republic (circa 1775), this fascination with the logic and discipline of the ancient world led to a classicizing of the frontier, that is, imposing a classical order on a scene that might otherwise seem chaotic. Now, however, the element of emotion fueled by romanticism, which is apparent in Brackenridge's use of the word "enchanting," became an ingredient in the mix. Together, they created a potent formula that facilitated the widespread acceptance of Orientalism in America.

The early encounter with the American grasslands was part of the process of Orientalizing the West in that open vistas tended to stimulate the imagination in pivotal ways—namely, by emphasizing vast spaces and distant treeless horizons where the sky descends to meet the skin of the earth unimpeded. The same thing might happen along a shoreline where sand defined the landscape for mile after mile. That shoreline, however, was a linear strip. Now, in the interior of the continent, boundless areas with few or no trees presented a huge canvas that stimulated the traveler to fill in the blanks. The Old World offered many similar seemingly blank spaces filled with danger, intrigue, and romance. One such place was the Sahara Desert—or Zahara as it was widely known after 1815—when American captain James Riley and his crew were shipwrecked off the North African coast, captured by nomads, and sold into slavery. Riley's tale of survival riveted two generations of Americans and reinforced the popular belief that open spaces and adventure go hand in hand.

If this suggests that an encounter with the first truly wide-open spaces of the American West would be fraught with romance, it should be noted that romanticism about wild, exotic locales began in the area far to the east of the western frontier, namely, in upstate New York as related in James Fenimore Cooper's *Pioneers* (the first of the *Leatherstocking Tales*), and it soon spread to the Ohio River country. And yet, by the early 1800s, as American pioneers continued to move westward from the Eastern Seaboard toward interior North America, they traversed a landscape that had already been "classicized" by their parents. The abundance of classical place names such as Rome and Athens in frontier America reflected, and then encouraged, fantasies about the real places whose names they bore. Even a trip down the Ohio and Mississippi Rivers to the Gulf of Mexico in the early nineteenth century kindled the

Classicism vs. Orientalism

romantic zeitgeist of the period. In describing such a trip in 1831–32, British writer Henry Tudor sarcastically observed that in "whizzing along the banks of the Tiber instead of those of the Ohio" on a steamboat, one soon encountered Rome—not the original city in Italy, of course, but one in the American frontier aspiring to the greatness of its namesake. Tudor continued his harangue, "Next in succession came '*Troy*,' and lower down '*Carthage*;' so that, in the space of twenty-four hours, we appeared to have visited the four quarters of the globe; a celerity of movement that left the Arabian enchanters at a boundless distance in the rear." So common were these pseudoclassical communities that they constituted what Tudor called "a geographical jumble and confusion of countries and places on their hieroglyphical chart—the cities and empires of one hemisphere being placed in juxtaposition with those of another . . . as to be highly amusing to the passing traveler."[2] Tudor viewed these places as nearly comical imitations, but Americans took them a bit more seriously. Clearly unimpressed, Tudor observed that "if the adopted names of olden times, dignifying the various localities of American territory, could confer all the treasures of antiquity and literature which they represent, our worthy brethren of the United States would be the most extensive monopolisers of learning, and the most ancient nation in the world." Interestingly, even the process of giving these frontier places classical names embodied more than a hint of a penchant for romanticism.

Tudor mocked this American penchant for one-upping even Arabian enchanters at creating fictional identities by naming new places after ancient ones; however, it reflected a deeper condition, namely, the persistent and increasingly desperate search for classical antiquity in the New World. There was a good reason for this. For minds used to thinking that classical knowledge represented the zenith of culture, the recentness of the American scene must have generated deep insecurities. Moreover, a growing sense of patriotism based on the grandeur and majesty of the American frontier seemed to call for some kind of endorsement. What better way to enable the frontier than to brand it with a deeply historical identity, or authenticity? That even a cynic like Tudor could succumb to the enchantment of the New World was evident when he met his match far to the south near Mexico City. In describing the landscape there, he noted that even though "a 'floating garden' sounds something like eastern romance, and what you would alone expect to find in [an] Arabian story," these were real, and "are still to be seen, though not, as in former times, in a state of cultivation."[3] Tudor had encountered a true engineering marvel in native America, and as his mind searched for an analogue, it naturally drifted toward the Orient. As Robert Irwin astutely observed in *The*

Lust of Knowing, "Orientalism developed in the shade of the much grander discourses of the Bible and of the classics."[4]

The West exerted a strong pull on Americans in the early nineteenth century, well before California and Oregon were touted as new Edens. By the 1840s, however, the appeal of those fair places set the popular imagination to working overtime. For most would-be settlers, however, reaching those fabled areas in the Far West required either a long sea voyage or a trek across a landscape that had not yet been named by them, a place full of Indian names and broad horizons. Stretching nearly two thousand miles from Canada down to central Texas, what we would later call the Great Plains represented a swath of steppelike land several hundred miles wide. The term *steppe* was used for the semiarid grasslands of western Asia, and the concept meshed with what travelers crossing the American plains encountered. Traveling across this belt of open land represented a physical challenge to westward-moving pioneers, but it also tested their imaginations. The interior plains of North America were far from uniform geographically, but one thing about the area—its semiaridity, evidenced by the scarcity of trees—made crossing it a memorable experience for many. Most of the time, traveling here was more emotionally tiring than physically grueling—the typical combination of plodding along worrying if the animals and vehicles would hold up, and if water and food would be available, on the westward journey. On occasion, though, it could be downright exhilarating or absolutely disastrous. It was above all romantic for the growing number of travelers who sensed they were part of a grand adventure.

In crossing a dreary country that was "destitute of trees" near the Missouri River in about 1835, travel writer extraordinaire Washington Irving noted that "the weather was threatening a change, and a snow storm on these boundless wastes might prove as fatal as a whirlwind of sand on an Arabian desert."[5] In equating the dangerous weather and awesome, picturesque landscapes in America with Arabia, Irving held readers spellbound. Again, it is not surprising that he used an Arabian reference for comparison; Irving was already under the spell of Orientalism at this early date and would remain so throughout his life. He, like many of his compatriots, had been weaned on bedtime stories such as *Arabian Nights* in addition to those references to the desert in the Bible. Time and time again, as they traveled westward in North America, writers made reference to Arabian or Persian tales, and with good reason. Those stories from the East provided both the aesthetic and emotional ingredients upon which romanticism thrived.

As Irving's description suggests, the tendency to Orientalize was a result of childhood exposure to fables and adventure stories. In describing American scenery in 1840, for example, Nathaniel Parker Willis noted that the wilderness provided the traveler with "a sense of stillness and solitude, a feeling of retirement from the world, deeper and more affecting than he has ever felt before." The limits of these scenes were "uncertain," and the topography and vegetation "bewildering." As Willis observed, or rather confessed, "thus, in a kind of romantic rapture, he wanders over these plains with emotions similar to those which, when a child, he roamed through the wildernesses created in Arabian tales."[6] This sentiment is worth highlighting, for we will see it come up repeatedly: if traveling into this region was like going back into time before civilization, travelers also turned their own personal clocks back to a time during which they were most impressionable. It is likely no coincidence that both these writers and the American nation were exposed to these stories in their youth. In other words, America, like an impressionable youth, was collectively acting out a youthful fantasy of venturing into the exotic and the unknown.

As Percy B. St. John observed in 1845, this area suggested Arabia as much as it did America. To St. John, it was "a sweeping plain—illimitable, vast, sublime, flat as the Arabian desert—without brush or tree, knoll or hillock, to break its magnificent monotony."[7] In 1855, Baynard Rush Hall also described his earlier travels in the Illinois prairie country in Oriental terms. At that time, circa the1820s, this country was part of the relatively new Louisiana Purchase. As Hall and his fellow travelers found themselves in a forested glade near the prairie, they expected quiet but instead found just the opposite—a cacophonous racket of animal sounds from "bird, and beast, and insect, and reptile, [which] rose at our approach from the bosom of the wavy grass, to break the solitude of the treeless plains." Hall found that this "uproar . . . was deafening! . . . bewildering." Not missing the opportunity to place the scene in context, Hall noted: "How like the enchanted hills and groves of the Arabian Tales!" This glade in the Illinois prairie was a magical experience for Hall, who noted that "the solemn dark of primitive oriental forests, must have suggested to the Magician of the Thousand and One Nights, some of the charms and witcheries and incantations that entranced our first years of boyhood and dreams!"[8]

At its eastern margin, the Great Plains has many of the characteristics of a fair land: copses of trees provide shelter from intense sun, strong winds, and blowing snow, while streams and rivers are dependable. With almost every mile of travel west, however, annual precipitation and relative humidity decrease, trees become fewer and farther between, and challenges mount for the traveler on foot. In the swath of land lying between about longitude 95° and 103° west, average annual rainfall decreases from about 40 inches (ca. 100 cm) to 20 inches (ca. 50 cm). To traverse the plains was literally a slow uphill battle, for one rose in altitude from about 700 feet (213 meters) above sea level to about 5,000 feet (1,524 meters) at the base of the Rocky Mountains. Even though the region appears level to the eye throughout much of this transect, large rivers paradoxically flow through it, originating in the well-watered Rocky Mountains far to the west. In many places, the river channels are wider and deeper than their normal amount of water would imply. These rivers are called "exotic" by geographers because they originate elsewhere and cannot be sustained by the water falling along their lower reaches. They are, in fact, remnants of a time about ten thousand years ago when considerably more water coursed down them. Running water was the culprit here. It carved the land into fantastic features in places and left sandy floodplains in others. Wind also eroded some areas and deposited thick layers of fine loess in others. Thus in many places, the flatness of the plains is interrupted by steep-sided river bluffs and isolated, towering buttes—remnants of the elements shaping a semiarid area. In a land so relatively featureless, these vertical landforms became landmarks to the pioneers, as they no doubt were to the Native Americans who inhabited the region.

To westward-moving travelers, the Great Plains region was the doorstep of the great American West. The increasing aridity encountered here by travelers helped intensify the importance of greenery. It was here, in fact, that two American myths associated with the western frontier came face-to-face. As Henry Nash Smith observed, "The myth of the garden had to confront and overcome another myth of exactly opposed meaning, although of inferior strength—the myth of the Great American Desert." These dry areas were not really deserts, but they conveyed that feeling to people looking for adventure. Because the plains were "inhabited by migratory tribesmen following their flocks and herds"—people who, in essence, "could not be integrated with American society, and were therefore perpetual outlaws"—the native inhabitants here were easy to equate with tribesmen and brigands of the Old World deserts and steppes. As Nash observed, "The analogues were often mentioned—the Bedouins of the Arabian desert, the Tartars of [the] Asiatic steppes."[9] As Peter Mason noted, painter George Catlin often portrayed the Plains Indians as draped Roman orators, and frequently gave them an even more exotic countenance by "setting them in reclining poses reminiscent of Orientalist fantasies."[10] And yet there was something disquieting about traversing this region. As Stephanie LeMenager noted, it represented "the interval" that Washington Irving and other writers recognized as "intractable and resistant to nationalization." Conceptually part of the wider world rather than a part of the nation, the Great Plains was, as LeMenager concludes, "the

West's infamous Great American Desert, the vaguely defined arid region once thought to be a warning that a United States could never fully incorporate western territories into its national domain."[11]

As travel writers reached the American West, they frequently used the term *American Zahara* for what they encountered. Like the Twilight Zone or other fanciful places, however, the American Zahara was not actually associated with any particular place; instead, it referred to what seemed to be the most desertlike regions that travelers encountered in the American West. Rather than having identifiable boundaries, then, the American Zahara was actually a scattering of places. These locales appeared to be—at least to imaginative travelers—much like that fabled, Old World desert that is, in fact, the largest desert in the entire world. The American Zahara kindled both the scientific and literary imaginations during the nineteenth century—a time when science and literary writing (and art) were more closely allied than they are today. These imaginings were likely based on glimpses of the Orient in travel literature and, perhaps, the West's most enduring book about the desert, the Bible. As noted above, however, even current-day encounters with the deserts of the Old World provided plenty of drama, too.

Sometimes a mere glimpse of aridity would start travelers thinking about the Sahara. For example, while traveling across the Great Plains, the aspiring naturalist Fitz Hugh Ludlow (1836–1870) became worried that fellow travelers would think him "a little finical" (that is, finicky). Why? Because Ludlow had purchased waterproof India rubber cloth that could be made into capes to protect the group from the weather, he feared that he "perhaps resembled those Cockney travelers who take marmalade and folding bath-tubs with them across the Sahara." Although the India rubber cloth actually "proved one of the most remunerative purchases of our outfit" because it was so versatile and easy to transport, the point here is that the Sahara served as the standard against which all deserts or desertlike regions would be measured.[12] To judge from their writings, Arabia (which is in reality a continuation of the Sahara) was a very close second.

Although the Great Plains was fairly bleak and commonly called the Great American Desert, it was certainly not as desolate as the real Arabian or Sahara Deserts. It was what scientists would later call a cold desert in that it has a fairly severe winter, while the Sahara is a hot desert. The Great Plains also had a respectable amount of native grasses and brush. Why, then, would seemingly well-informed writers make the claim that it was as barren as Arabia or the Sahara? Drama was one motive. Writers of the period such as Irving by rendering the western American landscape hotter and more arid than it really was also increased their own status in the eyes of admiring and sometimes envious readers. In other words, transforming portions of the American West into the Sahara or Arabia represented both flattery and conceit. If that flattery made the American desert seem even more punishing than much of it really was, conceit made the explorers traversing it seem braver than they really were. In reality, the Sahara and adjacent deserts from Arabia to Afghanistan have no match. They stretch more than five thousand miles, which is at least one and a half times the distance across the entire continental United States. A map of the Sahara in relation to American deserts having similar climatic conditions, which qualify as hot deserts (fig. 1-1), reveals how little of the United States fits that description.

As European American explorers moved even farther west, they increasingly characterized the landscapes they encountered as Oriental. For example, in describing the country bordering the interior American West, Washington Irving noted that Captain Bonneville sought to locate an expedition member named Matthieu, whom he hoped to meet at a winter camp. Accordingly, Bonneville "sent out four men, to range the country through which he would have to pass." To confirm that this was dry, open country, Irving wrote that the "route lay across the great Snake River plain, which spreads itself out like an Arabian desert, and on which a cavalcade could be descried at a great distance."[13] Irving wrote this when the interior American West was gaining a reputation as a place that could be as trying as the Sahara. That name conveyed an almost oceanic expanse that was relatively flat, largely sand-covered, and almost devoid of vegetation, though little of the American West actually fits that description.

There was, however, some truth in the claims made by writers in western America that they had now encountered places like the Sahara. For despite their smaller size, American deserts can at times be as punishing as deserts on any continent. As mountain man James Ohio Pattie noted in 1849, the Indians of the western deserts were well acclimated to the region. As he observed, "They, accustomed to go naked, and to traverse these burning deserts, and be unaffected by such trials, appeared to stand the heat and drought like camels on the Arabian sands." According to Pattie, the Native Americans here were so well adapted to the area's desert climate that they even "tried, by their looks and gestures to encourage us, and induce us to quicken our pace. But . . ." Pattie admitted, "it was to no purpose."[14] These mountain men had met their match in both the native peoples and the weather of the interior West.

The Orientalization of the Great American Desert was, in a very real sense, connected to its novelty as a semiarid landscape and its frontier status in the period 1820–1870. This Orientalizing process began early on the Great

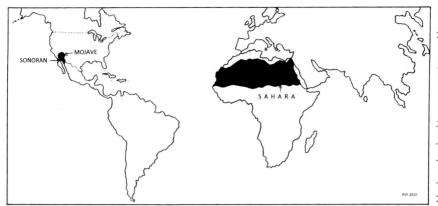

Map by author, based in part on previous world maps showing climate and vegetation

Fig. 1-1. A map showing the Sahara Desert and the only deserts in the United States (Mojave and Sonoran) having roughly comparable climates.

<u>Plains, and scientists had a role in it</u>. As early as 1819, when his expedition moved into the Arkansas River country, botanist Thomas Nuttall noted that in the area near Chickasaw Bluff, the river "was completely choked up by a bed of sand." Here, as Nuttall put it, "we came to for the night on a sand-bar opposite the centre of the island, resembling an Arabian desert."[15]

After trekking through the Great Plains, travelers often continued westward into the Green River country. Here the landscape is even more barren in terms of vegetation and more spectacular topographically. In traversing this region where sedimentary rocks are perched like books of various sizes haphazardly stacked on a table, an imaginative observer such as Fitz Hugh Ludlow could justify portraying the topography, especially the "Church Buttes," in exotic terms. Ludlow's words are worth a closer look, for they reveal an attempt to integrate the region into a national mind-set. Distressed that landmarks like these "throughout the savage interior of the Continent" were neglected because of "their very frequency," Ludlow chastised travelers: "We go out of our way to lavish raptures upon the temples of Yucatan, the mausolea of Dongola, Nubia, and Petrea, the Sphinx, and the Cave of Elephanta, while throughout our own mountain fastnesses and trackless plains exist ruins of architecture and statuary not one whit behind the foreign remains of forty centuries in power of execution, and far vaster in respect to age and size." Impressed by these monumental geological features, Ludlow noted that they should be revered like ancient ruins. To do so, he astutely observed, "there [was] needed an imagination of the means by which nature mimicked art after such faithful fashion, or indeed, at first glance, of the possibility that it could be unassisted nature at all."[16] Ludlow was, in fact, conflicted: the scientist in him sought answers to how the landscape was shaped, but he was aware that the excitement of adventure was needed to stimulate the imagination into fully appreciating the landscape here.

Writing in 1870 when science and art—that is, objectivity and emotion—existed side by side, Ludlow advocated recognizing feelings that "will be awakened in you by natural ruins, statues, castles, temples, [and] monuments." Letting his imagination run wild, Ludlow was admittedly "excited by the ruins of Titanic cities scattered over areas of many grassless, soilless leagues." He confessed that this type of discovery "never lost its freshness with me; it was always a source of child-like terror and delight." Hinting at what was going on in his deeper consciousness, Ludlow noted that "to this day I cannot analyze it, unless on the principle of affording a certain momentary argument for the supernatural. . . ." He encouraged others to consider that argument: "ere you can recover your cold literalism and *modernity,* your logical balance, and your grasp of philosophical explorations." This type of experience, as he put it, "sets you back in your childhood's or your ancestor's marvel-world—shows you how the baby feels, how the ancients felt." Ludlow himself emphasized that word *modernity,* for it was an operative factor in motivating him to seek something more wild, primeval—even frightening—in the western American landscape.[17]

If the majestic sweep of the North American Great Plains inspired many travelers there to wax eloquent about its similarity to the Asian steppe, or even the Saharan or Arabian Deserts, they were not alone. In South America, the llanos and the pampas were equally evocative. As Domingo Sarmiento observed of the Argentine Pampas in the 1860s, "pastoral life [here] reminds us of the Asiatic plains, which imagination covers with Kalmuck, Cossack, or Arab tents." Human society here was "essentially barbarous and unprogressive—the life of Abraham, which is that of the Bedouin of to-day prevails in the Argentine plains." In such areas, Sarmiento observed, "progress is impossible." In this claim, Sarmiento was referring not only to material progress, such as the development of advanced technology, but also to what he called "moral progress, and the cultivation of the intellect, [which] are here not only neglected, as in the Arab or Tartar tribe, but impossible."[18] Such sweeping generalizations were both common and linked to two prevalent European and European American philosophies—the cynicism of environmental determinism and the inherent fatalism of Orientalism. As Sarmiento put it, "Many philosophers have also thought that the plains prepare the way for despotism, just as mountains furnish strongholds for the struggles of liberty."[19]

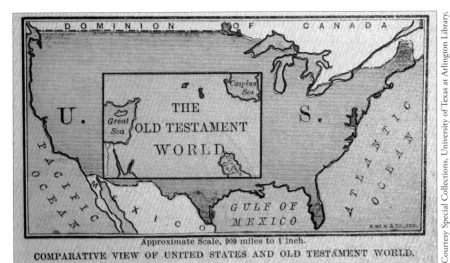

Fig. 1-2. Published by Rand McNally in 1884, this "Comparative View of United States and Old Testament World" superimposed the Near East upon portions of the American Great Plains and Southwest.

In the United States, subliminal references to the Eastern world were made when the geographies were juxtaposed on comparative maps intended to educate the public. In comparing the size of the Old Testament world with the United States in 1884, Rand McNally placed the Old on top of the New (fig. 1-2). Interestingly, the biblical world is here positioned over a substantial portion of the Great Plains. Although it can be argued that this illustration was meant only to compare relative sizes, one subtle effect of this exercise is to also mentally transpose physical and cultural geographies; in so doing, the map viewer can indeed think that more than mere size is a factor. The semi-aridity and cultures of both the American and the Old World locales can also be equated: in this case, for example, the landscape of the Great American Desert blurs with the true desert lands of the Near East; likewise, the Indian tribes in this part of the American West (and Southwest) become, in effect, the wandering tribes of the Bible.

The comparisons, though, were more often literary than literal. The Orient, or rather stories about the Orient, provided despotism and romance aplenty for America's westward-moving pioneers. The frontier was the perfect stage to Orientalize both setting and player. One more example regarding an easily identified, flamboyant historical figure will suffice to show the ease with which identity swapping could take place on the frontier in the nineteenth century. In the 1830s and early 1840s, when much was made of Texas's status as an independent republic, the sultan of the Turkish Empire provided Texas president Sam Houston with a regal Turkish costume. Now, some leaders might simply send a "thank you" note to the sultan and put the thing in a trunk unworn. But not Sam Houston. Given his remarkably transcultural character and his penchant for theatrics, Houston enjoyed wearing the outfit around Texas, prompting one commentator to brand him the "Sultan of the Brazos"—a reference to the river upon which Texas politics was centered at the time. A sketch of the sultanly Houston amused people of the time, but the president himself was unfazed. And why not? Houston was well known and highly controversial as an outspoken supporter of Indian rights and a practitioner of other eccentric behaviors. To the amusement of some and the horror of many, Houston even went native by living among the Cherokees of Texas on occasion. Houston, in fact, personifies the romantic adventurer, an enterprising soul who was remarkably malleable in appearance. Who else would build a home in the shape of a steamboat and live in the contrivance as if it were a normal thing to do?[20] Such cultural experimentation reminds us, though, that the flexibility of the frontier encouraged creative role-playing. That willingness to innovate was a necessary element in the Orientalization process in frontier America.

The Texas prairie was the scene of a more serious role-playing, perceptually speaking. In describing an Indian raid on her west-central Texas farming village in October of 1864, Sallie Reynolds Matthews later recalled that "they came down [upon us] early one morning like the Assyrian host, their cohorts gleaming in war paint and feather rather than purple and gold, with their blood-curdling yells striking terror into the hearts of the little band of settlers along Elm Creek, killing men and women, and taking captive other women and children."[21] This came to be known as the "Elm Creek Raid," and it is noteworthy that the Comanche perpetrators were cast as Middle Easterners. This is yet another reminder of the recasting of Native Americans into terrifying Old World raiders right out of the Old Testament, which describes "Assyrians, warriors clothed in purple" (Ezekiel 23:5–6), and the biblical association of Assyrians with the downfall of women, or rather women's morality, is also noteworthy.

If, as hinted above, South Americans also felt compelled to Orientalize their sweeping llanos, literature and imagination helped. In his classic *Life in the Argentine Republic in the Days of the Tyrants* (1868), Sarmiento further observed that "there is something in the wilds of the Argentine territory which brings to mind the wilds of Asia." Here, Sarmiento claimed, "the imagination discovers a likeness between the pampa and the plains lying between the

Euphrates and the Tigris; some affinity between the lonely line of wagons which crosses our wastes, arriving at Buenos Ayres after a journey lasting for months, and the caravan of camels which takes its way toward Bagdad or Smyrna." The look of the countryside in Argentina was a factor in the similarity, for Sarmiento noted of the pampas that "these outstretched plains impart to the life of the interior a certain Asiatic coloring." But it was also the human element that colored life here as Oriental, for the leader of such caravans here was "like the chief of an Asiatic caravan"—a man who possessed "iron will, and daring to the verge of rashness."[22]

Similar sentiment prevailed in North America. As Washington Irving noted in his wildly popular book *A Tour on the Prairies*, which was published in several editions after its initial run in 1835, "the capture of a wild horse is one of the most favorite achievements of the prairie tribes," and "some fanciful speculatists have seen in them descendants of Arab stock . . . and have pleased themselves with the idea, that their sires may have been of the pure courses of the desert, that once bore Mahomet and his disciples across the sandy plains of Arabia." For his part, Irving conceded that "the habits of the Arab seem to have come with the steed," for the horse "changed the whole mode of living of their inhabitants."[23]

In the 1830s, the prairies of the southern plains in the vicinity of the Texas Cross Timbers attracted the attention of enterprising stock raisers. In describing the landscape here, Adjutant General Hugh McLeod noted that "we saw large droves of Buffalo, & wild horses, by the latter I do not mean mustangs, such as are found in Western Texas," but much better stock. To emphasize the richness of the grassland in this part of the Republic of Texas, McLeod noted that "the Ukraine cannot excel [*sic*] these prairies in the beauty and fleetness of its *wild* horses."[24] To educated observers such as McLeod, the Ukraine represented some of the richest grassland in the world. It bordered on the great steppes of Asia, whose horsemen had become legendary. In the grasslands of the southern plains, the Comanche Indians had also become excellent horsemen in a surprisingly short time, perhaps less than a century, earning the name "Lords of the Plains."

Building on a literary theme that Washington Irving had established a decade earlier—namely, the romanticizing of the "lovely prairies" and their noble, Orientalized peoples—Thomas Bangs Thorpe noted in 1846 that the mustang pony was "adapted to the prairie as perfectly as its sunshine and flowers." These mustangs, or musteños, were wild but their heritage could be traced to the Old World. Not only did "their riders cherish the trappings for them that betray old Spain" but horse and rider perform in a manner in "which may be traced some little of the stately tramp of the Moorish Arabian, exhibited centuries since upon the plains of the Alhambra, and pricked by enormous spurs, that rattle with a tingling sound, of which the mustang's sides, so far from resenting the operation, seem to enjoy it as a dulled taste by luxuries requires mustard and cayenne." Note here a touch of sadism: Thorpe relishes the idea that the horse does not resent the pain inflicted by spurs but is actually invigorated by it, much like the adventurous tongue welcomes spicy—and exotic—food. But if this sentiment seems somewhat sadistic today, that too was an element of nineteenth-century travel romance; it is both metaphorical and sensual in that its Oriental flavor is imparted by the pungent spices mentioned. Of these riders and their horses, Thorpe noted that here on the American prairie, "feats of horsemanship are performed that would delight Bedouin Arabs."[25] Similarly, in 1847, Charles Lanman easily fell into Orientalizing the Native Americans as well as their horses in the northern plains. As Lanman put it, "The Sioux Indians, . . . living as they mostly do, in a vast prairie region, their favorite and principal mode of travelling is on horseback, and away from the larger rivers, you will find them possessed of the finest horses, which they love with true Arabian affection."[26]

Horses, in fact, were a key element in Orientalizing both the American Great Plains and South America's llanos. As on the steppes of Asia, the horse, though introduced only in the 1600s, was in its element here on the American prairie. In describing Texas, which "was but little known to our countrymen, until seen by gallant bands who entered it in aid of the Patriot cause," the Galveston Bay and Texas Land Company raved that "that noble animal, the horse, roves the country in gregarious masses, with all the pride and majesty of his Arabian ancestors."[27] These were wild horses, and the association of the Texas plains with the ancestral home of the unbroken horse is part of the message: Texans, like their horses, are wild and freedom loving.

This equating of the American plains with wild and exotic areas elsewhere was common. Henry Marie Brackenridge called the American antelope "the most swift and beautiful little animal on our continent." As Brackenridge put it, "The description of the gazel in Africa, the favorite theme of Arabian poetry, might be applied to the antelope of Missouri." More explicitly, Brackenridge described this part of the interior American West as "a vast country inhabited only by buffaloes, deer, and wolves, [and which] has more resemblance to the fictions of the 'Arabian Nights Entertainments' than to reality."[28] Little did Brackenridge realize that fiction was exactly what he was writing. Like most Victorian travel writers, Brackenridge was a full-blown romanticist who could draw parallels between the Old World and the New World whenever that Old World offered the right element of drama and excitement.

Danger was a common ingredient in spicing up encounters here. In *The Plains of the Great West* (1877), Richard Irving Dodge describes one of the most unsettling experiences that all pioneers traversing the grasslands feared. At night on the trackless prairie, a group of "emigrants" circles the wagons. Like a resting caravan, they represent civilization. However, their security is threatened by a group of tomahawk-wielding Indians stealthily moving toward the encampment like a pack of wolves. This scenario is in part the basis for subsequent dramatizations of Indians in popular Western movies, but it is based on a more enduring trope—the ever-present, highly mobile, warlike warriors who plunder all travelers crossing the limitless steppe. This is as old and as Asian as Genghis Khan, yet it played out perfectly more than seven centuries later in the American plains.[29]

In another popular book, the Earl of Dunraven advised travelers in the plains about the dangers of traveling in this region. Using wording similar to colonial travel narratives in the Middle East and Asia Minor, he warned: "Never trust an Indian, even though the tribe be at peace, unless you have a very good reason to know that you can do so." To this warning, Dunraven added an enigmatic, misogynistic postscript: "It may seem surprising, but the women are at the bottom of all the mischief." How Dunraven knew this is not disclosed, but he was not the first, nor would he be the last, to speak authoritatively about peoples he barely knew. That included characterizations of women in these tribes as either demonic or noble in a time when women in all societies were regarded with both admiration and suspicion, more often the latter. In this sense, the title of Dunraven's book—*The Great Divide*—was emblematic. It was both a geographic metaphor for the dividing of the waters running to the Atlantic and Pacific, and a cultural metaphor for the division of peoples into civilized and primitive. It was, after all, Dunraven who characterized sunsets in the American prairies as "startling, barbaric, even savage in their brilliancy of tone."[30]

Crossing the plains, many would-be settlers of the Far West first encountered the "real" wilderness and its denizens here as they migrated west. Typically, two types of literature informed them. One was decidedly romantic and Orientalist (for example, the *Arabian Nights*), the other rather more sober—but equally Oriental in origin—namely, the Bible. In an article entitled "California Again!" published in the *Arkansas Gazette* on October 27, 1845, D. G. W. Leavitt encouraged residents to move west much as a minister might inspire a congregation. In addition to bringing to mind a secular world of Oriental despots and marauding Asiatic tribes, many moving west at the time found that the frontier West evoked deeply spiritual feelings that they associated with biblical literature. Leavitt's missionary zeal, which amounted to the assembling of an army of crusaders to move west, predated the popular 1851 slogan "Go West, young man, and grow up with the country" by John B. L. Soule of the *Terre Haute Express* in Indiana. That sentiment was so strong and so persistent that Horace Greeley (1811–1872) used it again in 1865 in his *New York Tribune*. "Go West, young man," which we now associate with Greeley more than anyone else, was also a metaphor for the direction in which young America was headed. In this sentiment, D. G. W. Leavitt freely called upon the spirit of earlier pioneers, namely, those who had first sailed across the ocean to build a new life in a new land. Urging would-be pioneers not to worry about the California Indians or huge distances across the plains, Leavitt noted that the move would require only the same determination exhibited by their forefathers in the 1600s. As he put it: "The Pilgrim Fathers when they first landed on Plymouth Rock, had not a more laudable object in view when they left the mother country, with the ostensible purpose of worshipping God under their own vine and fig tree, and letting others do likewise." Leavitt's reference to the vine and fig tree echoed phrases in the Bible, notably Psalms 105:33 ("He smote their vines and fig trees"); Jeremiah 5:17 ("they shall eat up your vines and fig trees") and 8:13 ("there are no grapes on the vine, no figs on the fig tree"); and Zechariah 3:10 ("In that day, says the Lord of hosts, every one of you will invite his neighbor under his vine and under his fig tree"). Significantly, and very appropriately, these were Old Testament passages that referred to the vine and fig tree as the sustenance of a people. In these references, God oversees what will happen to those vines and fig trees—which is to say people—as they interact with other peoples, the environment, and God. A righteous people, Leavitt's message implied, had nothing to fear from "this contemplated movement to the extreme West."[31]

For American pioneers, traversing the long trail westward across the plains was in part a spiritual journey. New "sublime" vistas and unique landscapes helped generate euphoria among some travelers. In June 1846, Edwin Bryant wrote a friend about his experiences on the Oregon Trail: "For a distance of 300 miles after we left Independence, the prairies presented to the eye a rich and varied landscape, surpassingly beautiful and grand." In seeking to inform his friend about the majesty of this landscape, Bryant continued: "It would almost seem as if the Deity had lain himself out in arranging a garden of illimitable extent to shame the puny efforts of man."[32] Then, too, the experience of traveling west might even encourage a pioneer to change religions—or become religious after lapsing, or "backsliding." In writing to James Frazier Reed while on the way west, James M. Maxey observed that "I will say to you that it made me feel good when I opened your letter and saw that you said Bro[ther] for since you seen me I have become a member of the E M. Church and I think a Christian—I can tell you mor [*sic*] when I see you." Ending his letter with "I remain Your Obt Bro," Maxey had evidently found faith on the trail west.[33] The point here is that for many, perhaps most, pre–Gold Rush pioneers, religion and faith played a role in the westward move. That interest in religion coupled with increasing aridity naturally led people to recall the locations of the original biblical stories.

The landscape of the American West became more evocative and challenging with each day of travel. Where erosion had leveled all but the most resistant of rocks, westbound travelers passed by several awesome spires—Courthouse Rock, Jail Rock, Castle Rock, Chimney Rock, and Scotts Bluff—in about a week's time. This presented them with their first look at landscape features typical of semiarid lands. On his way west across the Great Plains, Horace K. Whitney was one of several Mormon pioneers who took an interest in Chimney Rock and other erosional features. As he looked through a telescope to get a better view of the hulking spires, he noted that "the scene to us was truly one of magnificence and grandeur and almost baffles description." The word "almost" was operative here, for Whitney was a talented writer and not hesitant to try his hand at lavish prose. "The whole scene . . ." as he put it, "was one of romantic solitude and inspired me with singular feelings and reminding [*sic*] me forcibly of the descriptions I had read in my boyish days of the fortified castles and watchtowers of the older time."[34] If the landscape of the West seemed familiar, a revisiting of the adventure stories and tales of youth, it also had powerful religious overtones. And yet something about these landscapes seemed spiritually disquieting. To some, the landscape seemed in disarray, as large, angular boulders littered the slopes and caused travelers to wonder how they came to be placed there. By flood—particularly *the* flood? By fire and brimstone that accompanied volcanic activity? A traveler in the same company described the phenomenon more or less accurately, but then quickly added a spiritual hypothesis when he speculated that these "huge rocks . . . had been rolled out of their natural place by the wash of heavy rains or the convulsive throes of nature at the crucifixion of our Saviour."[35]

The natural wonders of the Great Plains increased toward the base of the Rocky Mountains, where rock strata might be pushed skyward into seemingly bizarre features like Colorado's "Garden of the Gods," in which huge slabs of red sandstone protrude upward at steep angles. The name sounds picturesque, perhaps even playful to us today, but those who named the place recognized its awesome countenance. In describing the varied features of this geological wonderland of sandstone layers, a guide for the Kansas Pacific Railway noted that "its deep chasms and lofty sides, and great stone, of every hue and shape, amaze the beholder." Some of the garden's features are "towering crags and lofty stones set upon end, some inclined like the leaning tower of Pisa, and others erect as was Cleopatra's Needle on Bunker Hill having its own peculiar color." This monumental geological wonder, the guide noted, is "mightier than [the] Chinese wall." In keeping with the popular tendency to view the Native Americans as kin to Asians, especially given the terms *India* (or *Indian*) *red* and *China* (or *Chinese*) *red*, the landscape was easy to anthropomorphize. "The stone fence," as the writer put it, was "a solid wall of red sandstone, very thick in comparison with its frightful altitude." Using a painterly comparison to drive home a cultural prejudice, the writer added: "It was painted red, perhaps that it might endure and gratify the taste of savage red men."[36]

The equating of people and place was common. It is evident in Washington Irving's 1836 description of the Métis, or half-breeds, on America's western frontier. These "new and mongrel races," Irving observed, are "like new formations in geology." Continuing the analogy, Irving considered them to be "the amalgam of the 'debris' and 'abrasions' of former races, civilized and savage, the remains of broken and almost extinguished tribes."[37] Note that Irving here integrates time as well as space in equating this human detritus with the geological debris that veneers the landscape itself. Like the rocks here, which were splintering under the inevitable cycles of freeze and thaw, wet and dry, the native peoples appeared to be fragmenting in the face of western expansion.

Because travelers at this time were familiar with the Bible and a growing travel literature about the Near East, the landscape and peoples along the route took on the character of that distant locale. Even Chimney Rock in Nebraska was given an Eastern countenance as travelers recalled the landmarks of the Near East. As he described "the celebrated Chimney Rock" in the early 1850s, American writer Franklin Langworthy observed: "It is a noted landmark, being visible forty miles each way up and down the river." Although Chimney Rock was seven miles from the road, Langworthy noted that "many travelers go out to survey its curiosities." Why? One reason Langworthy gave stands out:

> The chimney, or column, rises from a pyramid of immense size, as regular in form as those of Egypt. The column rises several hundred feet from the apex of the pyramid, and as to size, is in very exact architectural proportions to the size of the base on which it stands. At a distance, the

chimney has a tall and slender appearance, like the minaret of a mosque, or the smoke-pipe of a steamer. Around the base of the column are inscribed the names of multitudes of persons who have from time to time visited this colossal wonder.[38]

Note, especially, that the language here celebrates rather than denigrates features and accomplishments of the Middle East. Travelers like Langworthy were prone to see ancient ruins such as the spectacular Cleopatra's Needle in the topography west of the Mississippi River. To imaginative travelers, these natural rock columns appeared to be replicas of the famed obelisks of Egypt, some of which had already been transported to cities in Europe.[39]

As cultural historian Neil Harris noted in *The Artist in American Society* (1966), the obelisk proliferated in early nineteenth-century America as a monument to heroic deeds. After a design competition, the obelisk was finally chosen for the Bunker Hill and Washington Monuments because of its simplicity. As an architect put it, the obelisk "was complete in itself." Nevertheless, considerable debate swirled around the obelisk as a symbol. In particular, the virtues of the obelisk and the column were debated in regard to which of these vertical forms was better suited for commemoration in America. Although columns were associated with Greek and Roman classical culture and architecture, the obelisk was of "greater antiquity [and] it also furnished a better surface for inscriptions." Nevertheless, the obelisk was associated with Egyptian architecture, which, as one architect put it, was considered by some to be the "architecture of tyrant kings—of severe and despotic dynasties [and] it therefore can never harmonize with the glorious principles of republican achievement, nor with . . . Christianity." Interestingly, some authorities rather brazenly argued that the obelisk should be used precisely *because* it was Egyptian and would now be employed in a more noble venture—the veneration of American heroes. That, coupled with the notion of the obelisk's great antiquity and singular form, won the day. As a brochure for the Bunker Hill Monument Association put it, with emphasis on height and durability, the obelisk monument *will be the highest of the* [sic] *kind in the world*, and only below the height of the Pyramids." When experiencing it, "no traveler will *then* inquire for the battleground . . . [and] it will endure until the foundations are shaking." The association concluded that "it will stand uninjured to the ends of time." This zeal was deeply connected to a concern about America's inferiority—it was, after all, a young nation with much to prove—and also to a growing sense of American exceptionalism.[40]

These concerns were palpable, in part, because of the grand setting—or challenge—provided by nature on the North American continent. It was,

Author's photograph

Fig. 1-3a. Some nineteenth-century travelers thought the geological formations in the City of Rocks comparable to ancient Egyptian ruins.

as Harris notes, "actually an attempt [by Americans] to come to terms with their gigantic forests and rivers." As one observer put it, nature in America was overpowering, "and so giving a certain *tristesse* . . . and on it man seems not able to make much of an impression." Harris concludes that "with their giant monuments, Americans had made such an attempt: art presented its first statement" in coming to grips with "such power and grandeur."[41] Significantly, an Oriental (Near Eastern) monument was selected.[42]

Farther west, an even grander landscape called for superlatives, for which Egypt would again provide a ready reference. As he traversed the splintered, rocky landscape near what we today call the City of Rocks just south of the Snake River plain in southern Idaho (fig. 1-3a), Langworthy described obelisk-like topographic features with patently Orientalist enthusiasm: "In sight of, and near our road," he wrote, "are two tall and sharp pointed columns, two or three hundred feet in apparent height, their forms being regular and beautifully elongated cones." Whereas the original Egyptian obelisks were about seventy feet high, these would do just fine. Langworthy continued: "Here are monuments erected by the hands of Nature, rivaling in grandeur Trajan's Pillar, or Cleopatra's Needle." He then added another tempting

Fig. 1-3b. An illustration from J. W. Dawson's *Modern Science in Bible Lands* (1889) shows the "Apex of the great prostrate obelisk of Queen Hatasu of Karnak . . . [and] . . . the ruins of a temple of Nubian sandstone."

thought: "Further [*sic*] back on the Fort Hall road, I am told is a succession of these steeples, filling a narrow valley for two or three miles."[43] Like many writers of the period, Langworthy did not reveal how he learned about the ancient ruins he so readily compared to the natural rock formations in Idaho. Illustrations of Old World ruins were relatively rare at this time but would soon become common. It is just as likely that Langworthy and others were inspired by the poetic prose of travel writers, whose words could sufficiently prime a traveler in the West to imagine a connection between the jumbled rock formations here and ancient counterparts strewn along the Nile Valley.

Langworthy's delightful travel writing represents a combination of first-hand experience and hearsay. The very concept of such ancient steeples being part of the natural American landscape evoked pride. Moreover, the prospect of numerous obelisks filling a narrow valley for miles sounds much like American and European descriptions of the rich archaeological treasures littering Egypt's Nile Valley for mile after mile (fig. 1-3b). It is almost as if the western United States deserved to possess such spectacular features that could be observed from the adjacent plains. With so much sweeping natural scenery and so few permanent—that is masonry—Indian villages, the area seemed the right place to imagine such grand artifacts. These could in effect impart an ancient, even noble, quality to an otherwise wild land. Through the process of creating, or rather adopting, their surrogates in nature's wonderlands, obelisks soon graced maps of the frontier West from Wisconsin (where a rock spire called Cleopatra's Needle stands in the Wisconsin Dells), to the interior American West, where the "steeples" that Langworthy wrote about adorn the landscape. By imaginatively transforming these natural features into obelisk-like steeples, the drama of great accomplishments could be reenacted in the American landscape.[44]

The Orientalizing of the American interior served many purposes. One of them involved the new nation's search for identity in relation to other nations. Since the founding of the United States, and especially in the early to mid-nineteenth century, the general belief that "nations are purposive agents in God's historical drama" came to be more specific. It was now believed that God "deduced a special role for the United States." By the late nineteenth century, it would come to mean something even more exceptional, namely, that the United States "was the chosen instrument to move the world toward solidarity and righteousness."[45] With a new frontier expanding outward, American society exhibited "centrifugal tendencies that were essential for the fulfillment of their high missions."[46] Selectively adopting elements from venerable Eastern religious and spiritual traditions helped endorse this impulse.

Religion and spirituality were never far from the mind of the famed British explorer Sir Richard F. Burton. Neither was the Orient. As he reached Kansas on his well-publicized trip across the United States in 1860, Burton began to find himself in increasingly familiar country despite the fact that he had never been there before. Burton described the covered wagons crossing the plains as "those ships of the great American Sahara which, gathering in fleets at certain seasons, conduct the traffic between the eastern and western shores of a waste which is everywhere like a sea and which presently will become salt." In describing the protection worn by the drivers ("rippers") of these wagons, Burton noted that those whose eyes got sore here may "line the circumorbital region with lamp-black, which is supposed to act like the Surma or Kohl of the Orient." [47] In the more arid sections of the western plains, Burton's Orientalism reached a high point aimed at dramatizing the difficulties of travel. The country here had "a burnt-up aspect," and, as Burton put it, for as "far as the eye could see the tintage was that of the Arabian desert, sere and tawny as a jackal's back."[48] Of the Pawnees, whose villages were destroyed by the Sioux, Burton noted, "They are Ishmaelites, whose hand is against every man." However, he also observed that "they and the northern Dokotas can never be trusted" because they were the kind of Indians who, "African-like, will cut the throat of a sleeping guest." By contrast, Burton noted that "most Indian races, like the Bedouin Arabs, will show hospitality to the stranger who rides into their villages, though no point of honor deters them from robbing him after he has left the lodge-shade."[49] Noting that the term *Red Men* was really a misnomer for Indians, Burton observed that "the real color of the[ir] skin, as may be seen under the leggings, varies from a dead pale olive to dark dingy brown" but that "the parts exposed to the sun are slightly burnished, as in a Tartar or an Affghan [*sic*] after a summer march." Burton noted that the Indian's physiognomy "renders it impossible to see this people for the first time without the strongest impressions that they are of the Turanian breed which in prehistoric ages passed down from above the Himalayas as far as Cape Comorin." As if to provide evidence of this Oriental connection, Burton noted that the Indians' fringed leather targes "reminded me of those in use amongst the Bedouins of El Hejaz."[50]

As Burton traveled westward into the high plains, he too encountered the spectacular erosional features along the Platte River. This was familiar country, or at least Burton thought so. "On the far bank of its northern fork . . ." he wrote, "lay a forty-mile stretch of sandy, barren, glaring, heat-reeking ground, not unlike that which the overland traveller looking southwards from Suez sees."[51] International travelers like Burton brought the Near East into the

American West by comparing what they saw with what they had experienced elsewhere. Nebraska's famed geological feature called the Courthouse (now Courthouse Rock), which towered three hundred feet above the area, appeared to Burton not like a courthouse at all. Because it possessed "the shape of an irregular pyramid, whose courses were inclined at an ascendable angle of 35°, with a detached outwork composed of a perpendicular mass based upon a slope of 45°; in fact, it resembled the rugged earthworks of Sakkara, only it was more rugged." Burton thought nearby Chimney Rock was accurately named but then improved on that, calling it a "Pharos of the prairie sea" that erosion had reduced from a towering 150 to 200 feet above its surroundings to a mere 35 feet. As Burton continued traveling west here, the weather also contributed to his Oriental fantasies. It "changed from our usual pest—a light dust-laden breeze—into a Punjaubian dust-storm, up the valley of the Platte." The weather worsened, and soon "the gale howled . . . with all the violence of a Khamsin, and it was followed by lightning and a few heavy drops of rain." Burton noted that the *Mauvaises Terres* (Badlands) were compared by some to Gibraltar, the national capitol, or even Stirling Castle in Scotland; however, as a consummate Orientalist, he "could think of nothing in its presence but the Arabs' 'City of Brass,' that mysterious abode of bewitched infidels, which often appear at a distance to the wayfarer toiling under the burning sun, but ever alludes [*sic*] his nearer search."[52] Still farther west, on the Wyoming plains, Burton observed that "the land became more barren," and dead cattle, their "skins, mummified, as it were, by the dry heat, lay life-like and shapeless, as in the Libyan Desert, upon the ground."[53] Like Burton, many Americans' experiences in the Great Plains plumbed memories of the Old World's semiarid grasslands, though they were more often from biblical or popular literature, or perhaps even Burton's own books, than from firsthand experience.[54]

In searching for Old World analogues in New World deserts, travelers equated what was in fact a relatively small section of arid land—compared to the real Sahara, at least—with the world's largest desert. That process enabled both North America and those who experienced it to undergo a transformation. Travelers convinced themselves that the American experience was similar to Old World exploration. This, as suggested above, both flatters the new (that is, American) locale and empowers travelers here to compare themselves to their counterparts in the Old World. In the case of Sir Richard Burton, the comparison was genuine enough because Burton had experienced both. However, for the most part, these comparisons were yet another way of perpetuating the mysteries of the East in light of a stark reality: the world was running out of places to explore. Nostalgia, then, was a factor in the Orientalization of the West. But just as that nostalgia had its roots in the explorer's childhood, the increasing age and growing maturity of both explorer and industrial society ensured that the sights (and sites) experienced were endangered by the cultural-geographical realization that the world was becoming smaller, and its exotic features endangered, with every mile traveled and described.

Another aspect of these western lands that seemed to link the region with the Middle East was the occasional outbreaks of ravenous locusts. They swarmed, darkening the skies, devouring all vegetation in their path, and bringing to mind the swarms of locusts in the Bible. How devastating were these swarms in the western United States? In 1876, locusts were identified by the US Congress as "the single greatest impediment to the settlement of the country."[55] This, it should be noted, was the same year in which Custer met defeat at the Battle of the Little Bighorn. The reference to locusts resonated with a culture raised on biblical stories, for they darken the sky on occasion in that book, usually either as an omen or as retribution, though locusts and honey suggest yet another connection.

In the nineteenth century, it was common to use the ancient world, especially ancient Egypt, as a reference for what was encountered in the American West. The rivers flowing through the plains were frequently compared with their Oriental counterparts. In 1881, a promotional book about Texas declared, in the bragging manner that would soon characterize Texas overstatement generally: "The Nile has made Egypt famous for her fertility for ages," but in central Texas, "the Brazos and Colorado [Rivers] bring down richer sediments than the Nile." That comparison suggested, or promised, agricultural wealth, but even the countryside or landscape called for comparisons, and Egypt was again the benchmark. The same guide promoting Texas described the landscape of adjacent Indian Territory, namely the "slightly undulating prairie, out of which granite peaks rise in gigantic masses like the pyramids of Egypt."[56] This was no idle or idiosyncratic perception, but one that was widely held.

Historian David Wrobel confirmed that popular attitudes about the American West occurred in several phases. In the first, people tended to see the positive aspects of wild places; thus the Mississippi River could be perceived as the Nile, and towns along it named Cairo (Illinois) and Memphis (Tennessee). As time passed and the settling of the frontier became a reality, however, they tended to romanticize those early landscapes as more barren and harsh than they had really been. That configures the notion of the West, the entire region west of the Mississippi River, as a place that called for a counterpoint to the Arabian Desert, namely, the garden; not just any garden, actually, but rather the mother of all gardens—the Garden of Eden. The terms *garden* and *paradise* were used with such frequency in the nineteenth century that they became clichés. Yet that gardenlike place was based on an interesting and even somewhat conflicted premise about not only the landscape but also the human populations that occupied it.

In fact, the very notion of Eden, a garden where fruit grew on trees that needed no tending, was a double-edged sword to a nation devoted to a Protestant work ethic. One edge of the blade confirmed the ingenuity of the swordsman, but the other left its deep ideological wound on the indigenous peoples of these arid lands. In the 1880s, the Honorable John Runnels, an Iowan, reflected on pioneer times, noting that his state was once a "desolate wilderness," but that it had become as verdant and productive "as the Garden of Eden." However, in the worst sense of Orientalist ethnocentrism, Runnels believed that the American spirit had been the source of the achievement and that peoples of the Middle East could never achieve that type of progress. As he put it, even though "the nations of the East opened their eyes to lands flowing with milk and honey," the people there were "slothful, self-indulgent, and effeminate." Runnels added that "progress was unknown; invention was unheard of, liberty slept and despotism was law."[57]

That suggests that sometime during the nineteenth century, as pioneers were crossing the Great Plains, attitudes began to change. Whereas many of the early pioneers had found what they thought was Eden awaiting their touch (and God's endorsement), they now, in retrospect, reimagined the land they had encountered as a wasteland—wasteland that they had transformed as no other people had, or ever could. This was related to mythmaking about the environment and an inflation of the early settlers' skills. In other words, with the passage of time, mythmaking tended to distance American westerners from their more humble roots as pioneers who were pretty much given the West; now, they viewed it as a hard-earned victory that distanced them both from the more lowly peoples of the East and from the lowly Indians who had possessed it.

Interestingly, Runnels's comment about "effeminate" peoples of the East—meaning their men were weak—is quite revealing. The garden of earthly delights is associated with Adam and Eve and with the latter plucking the apple (fruit of knowledge) from the tree in defiance of God's command. Runnels seems to be saying that it takes, or rather took, a real man to transform the wilderness—and that those men of the East were not up to the challenge. The conflict runs deeper than simple racism, then, and points to fundamental changes in gender relations—namely, the reinterpretation of western

American history as a "man's work." This gendering of the western agricultural landscape as a male achievement runs against a very long tradition, for in reality, while mining and logging (and to a lesser extent ranching) were men's work, women have always had a place in the garden anywhere, be it East or West. As landscape architect Catherine Howett succinctly put it, "One need hardly demonstrate that a mythology linking the feminine with the garden is as old as civilization."[58]

There is considerable evidence that women took part in branding the western frontier as the Garden itself—a role that Annette Kolodny interprets in *The Land Before Her*. Kolodny's subtitle—*Fantasy and Experience of the American Frontiers, 1630–1860*—suggests that considerable mythology was involved in making the western American frontier into Eden. The process was simultaneous with the first arrival of Anglo-Americans. In promoting Texas in 1831, for example, Mary Austin Holley claimed that she had discovered a "land literally flowing with milk and honey," while a decade later Margaret Fuller claimed that she had discovered "the very Eden which earth might still afford." Kolodny calls such open landscapes "the prairie Eden" and links them to deeply embedded notions of a *"promised land* laid out *as an earthly paradise."*[59]

In the vicinity of the hundredth meridian, though, the Great Plains becomes sufficiently semiarid that it is more realistic to tend animals than farm the land. Consequently, ranching became the dominant form of land use here. Significantly, ranching was one of those activities that grafted an Old World identity onto a new land. In his sweeping interpretation of the cowboy origins of the western American, historian Donald Worster reminds us just how eclectic identity can be. As Worster put it, "We ought to begin by getting outside our regional provincialisms, overcoming our insistence on American uniqueness, and trying to situate the cattleman and his ranch in the broad panorama of human adaptation to the earth."[60] We tend to think of cowboys as western American figures, but in fact they derive from the East, more particularly southwestern Asia, where livestock were first domesticated and where nomadic herding is still a significant activity. After all, the hackamore bridle is believed to have originated in the Persian-Arabian world as the *hakma*. From that area, ranching spread throughout the world, transforming the ecology everywhere it became a major activity. For most people, though, ranching is the quintessential occupation in the American West. The ranching culture was surprisingly multicultural, and that helped observers imagine its distant Old World roots.

When W. J. Palmer's wood engraving called *Driving Cattle into a Corral in the Far West* appeared as a stunning two-page illustration in the September 11, 1875, issue of *Harper's Weekly* (fig. 1-4), it codified an image that was long in the making. The engraving's action is what first captures our attention. Palmer positions a whip-wielding wrangler toward the center, and the focus of the whip's attention, a longhorn, hunkers down for the next lashings. Other wranglers likewise crack whips to cajole the stock into the corral, but two additional elements make this scene noteworthy. First, the corral is a series of tall pickets that mirror the verticality of the rugged backdrop of mountains. That backdrop is reminiscent of the broken rhyolite palisades behind Fort Davis, Texas, but might be anywhere (and nearly everywhere) in the West. But then again, the scene suggests something about another land—one far distant where ranching got its start. This, we know instantly from the absolute absence of vegetation and the presence of dust that creates a slight haze everywhere, is a land where water is scarce.

The second element, however, is even more important, and that is the physical appearance of these wranglers. The wrangler at the center of our attention wears what appears to be a military hat, but his facial features, including his full beard, suggest someone who could be Chinese, Mongolian, or even Anglo-American. The place and the job have rendered him both indigenous and exotic. To the left of the engraving, two wranglers reel their ponies around in anticipation of the longhorn's next move. They are likely Indians, but then again their facial features suggest that they could just as easily be from the Asian steppe. At the right of the engraving, a wrangler wearing a hooded vest appears strangely serene, an anchor of sorts amid the swirling action. This man's clothing draws our attention, for he appears to be as much a monk as a cowboy—and would be at home in any desert frontier—the Pecos, Patagonia, or Persia. At the far right, an Indian woman in an intricately patterned dress watches the cattle being driven toward the dust-shrouded opening of the corral. Her dress is exotic, apparently American Indian, but then again reminiscent of the womens' dress in Afghanistan, where tightly woven, abstract patterns also dominate textiles and dress. *Driving Cattle* is remarkable both for the clarity of the delineation of its subjects and for its ambiguity about who these people are.

The truth is, this enigmatic engraving is characteristically western American—which is to say, it reflects a vagueness about ethnic identity by making everyone vaguely ethnic. The cowboy, of course, is much the same. He was in reality as likely to be part Mexican, African American, American Indian, and Anglo-American. It is noteworthy that both a first and last look at this engraving make one wonder about two things: Where in the world is this event taking place? And, who in the world are the people in it? The answer, of course, is that it is both Western and Eastern—and its subjects both western-ers and easterners. That is so because Palmer worked both from real life and from vivid imagination in creating this image. In *Driving Cattle* he provides a masterful look at how ambiguous identity could be on the American western frontier. That ambiguity made it relatively easy to configure the West, and westerners, into an imagined Orient.

In the mid-nineteenth century, the geographic gaze was opening to the West, across sweeping prairies and into the Rocky Mountains. As the doorstep to the American West, the Great Plains resonated as increasingly strange and exotic country to a westward-moving nation. With its aura of wilderness and lawlessness, this part of the western American frontier was easily equated with, and translated into, more dangerous locales. Naturally, the Near East, with its tribes organized under warlords, was a likely candidate for comparison. As the transcontinental railroad moved closer to completion in 1868–69, reporters frequently commented on the "hell on wheels" character of tent camps at the temporary end-of-track. These were places that brought out the worst and most interesting in human behavior. They certainly appalled many observers at the time. Given the near obsession with the Orient at this time, it should come as no surprise that these observers often conflated what they experienced here with what could be found in the Near East and southwestern Asia.

Sometimes this Orientalizing amounted to sermonizing, and it is here we often encounter Orientalism as negative—a demonization of peoples living with less supervision and authority beyond the edges of civilization. Here the control by Judeo-Christian religion seemed tenuous if not altogether absent. As a writer for the *Boston Traveler* put it in August 1868, "The old cities of the plain, Sodom and Gomorrah were as nothing compared with these new cities of the plain." The writer continued, "Everything in the way of society is chaotic, 'and nothing is but what is not.'" And yet moral progress would ultimately arrive here, at least the writer hoped, and "in place of the gambling house and the brothel, we will see the school house and the church."[61]

Of "tent towns" such as Bryan, which was located in the increasingly bleak prairie about eight hundred miles west of Omaha, a correspondent for the *National Republican* reported that "you can find houses that have been put up and taken down fifteen or twenty times." The reporter did not mince words in describing the inhabitants. "The people who live in them," he observed, "are American Arabs." Lest readers think he was merely referring to their mobility, the reporter was very specific: "They are not only nomads, ever on the move, but they can steal and plunder as adroitly and with as little

Fig. 1-4. Containing elements that seem as southwestern Asian as western American, this wood engraving by W. J. Palmer titled *Driving Cattle into a Corral in the Far West* appeared in *Harper's Weekly* in September, 1875.

compunction of conscience as their brethren the Bedouins." These people, he noted, were a "crowd of railroad followers" who, he concluded, "are here to gather up the spoils which pass from the treasury of the company through the workmen into their hands."[62] Note several ironies in this statement. It is the railroad company that provides the opportunity to live here and yet also provides the booty which is ultimately plundered, either by thievery or gambling. The ultimate irony here, of course, is that the "American Arabs" are not Arabs at all but shiftless Anglo-Americans with no permanent employment who live opportunistically.

This characterization transcends race and yet is dependent on it through stereotyping. The racial dimension is palpable in that it seems a perfect metaphor for the colonial coffers overseas that are raided by indigenous, nonwhite nomads; this was an increasingly common theme in news reports about the difficulties in administering colonies in the Middle and Far East. Note, too, that these nomads living along the transcontinental railroad were inherently mistrusted for more than their uncivilized behavior, which is to say they had seemingly surrendered their white European (or in this case, Euro-American) identity. Even though they may in fact have been Caucasian, they had lost that identity by adopting the negative traits of "other" races. This type of accusation, of course, was common in the Victorian period, when good citizenship entailed obedience to the law, loyalty to government and corporation, and good standing in an orderly, permanent community. To fail to achieve this standing was to be, or become, not only nomadic but also ethnic, like the wandering Jew, the ever-moving Comanche, or—as in this case—the footloose Bedouin. It is, in retrospect, probably less racist than it is an indictment of lifestyle.

The Orientalist characterization of nomadic peoples here is somewhat harsher than it would have been in the 1830s, but then again it is based on a more worldly, but increasingly cynical, attitude that occurred when Americans came into contact with not only real Arabs in the Holy Land but also French and British colonizers abroad. For their part, a number of the correspondents in the American West were actually Europeans who were only too happy, but also primed, to discover the barbarism of the exotic foreign land in frontier America along the rails of the Pacific Railroad. This suggests that the outlaw-like "Bedouins" and "Arabs" were fanciful conceits aimed at making the West seem more exotic and more dangerous using literary devices well honed by European explorers and travelers.

From the window of that new wonder of technology—a transcontinental train—much of the prairie and desert West seemed bleak indeed, and one might blame this on expectations raised by the early Orientalists. With other early travel writers in mind, perhaps, one traveler found himself Orientalizing the Great Plains. Expecting to discover, much as he might in Egypt, "that a sphinx and a half score of pyramids were located upon it," he was disappointed to find virtually nothing of interest there.[63] Given the vast expanses of grassland, the few topographic features present were often seized upon as landmarks. With little or no vegetation to conceal them, these landmarks not only stood out but were testimonials to the power of water, frost, and wind to render stone into unique shapes. To imaginative travelers, they could be seen as steamboats and ships, but they were just as likely to become sentinels, ramparts, towers, and other architectural features right out of travel literature. As Lt. E. G. Beckwith candidly noted while exploring the area near the Green River, "Where no sign of vegetation exists, is the appearance of an unfinished fortification, on a scale which is pleasing to the imagination."[64]

Even professional surveyors were not immune from the temptation to succumb to the power of the plains to stimulate the imagination. In 1872, Joseph Nelson Garland Whistler directed the westward survey of the Northern Pacific railroad. This Civil War veteran, who longed for service in the eastern United States but spent many years in the plains, seemed jaded at times. Whistler, though, could appreciate the grandeur of the western scenes he encountered, and the badlands provided plenty to comment on. Whistler noted in his report that "the sight was magnificent beyond anything we had yet seen or hoped to see." Here, where the streams had removed thick layers of sediments that had been deposited over the badlands, strange shapes presented themselves in about 250 feet of multicolored formations. Whistler was impressed by this rugged topography, and the incised route he traveled "so resembled a street that the men were calling [i.e., naming] the different points after large hotels . . . some vast dome-shaped hills rose out of the valley resembling Mosques, [while] others looked like gasometers." By *gasometer*, Whistler meant a burette, which is a graduated cylindrical device used for measuring the flow of liquids or gases. Note how the term *Mosque* is used with other more common words, a reminder of how easily the exotic was integrated with the commonplace in Victorian America. And yet this vivid description relates to the artistic sentiments of the time, Whistler's first cousin being none other than the famous artist James McNeill Whistler.[65]

Travelers moving across, and scientists exploring, the Great Plains found much to ponder at sights like these "*Mauvaises Terres*," or Badlands, where, as geologist Alexander Winchell put it in 1871, "Nature seems to have collected together the relics of a geological age, and buried them in one vast sepulcher" (fig. 1-5). This

Author's collection

Fig. 1-5. This illustration of "Mauvaises Terres, or Bad Lands of Dacotah," which appeared in Alexander Winchell's *Sketches of Creation* (1871), typifies the heavily eroded landscapes that reminded travelers of ancient ruins or minarets.

same Winchell was not only the director of the Michigan Geological Survey and a professor of geology, zoology, and botany at the University of Michigan but also a devout Christian. In his book titled *Sketches of Creation*, Winchell cited the imaginative interpretation of Dr. Evans, "an eminent geologist who almost 'dwelt among the tombs' of the ancient world, as they lie stretched out from the Mississippi to the Pacific shores." Evans noted that "'these rocky piles, in their endless succession, assume the appearance of massive artificial structures, decked out with all the accessories of buttress and turret, arched doorway and clustered shaft, pinnacle, and finial, and tapering spire.'" To add to the poignant element of greatness-gone-to-ruin here in such landscapes, Winchell noted that one could find intriguing fossil bones. These, he observed, contributed to the feeling that the traveler was "walking upon the floor of a long-deserted and ruined vault." Here, as he put it, "skulls, and jaws, and teeth, and thigh-bones lie scattered about," giving the impression that "Death has indeed held a carnival here, and [that] this is the deserted scene of a ghastly repast." Leaving little doubt about the source of inspiration here, Winchell imaginatively characterized such places as "Golgotha"—the site of death and betrayal in the Bible.[66]

The ageless Orient had considerable appeal to Winchell, who characterized the beds of stratified rock from the Carboniferous Period metaphorically. He was so impressed with what these layers of rock could reveal about "world-ideas" here that he stated, "The vaults of the Pyramids recite a history less full of meaning." That, in 1871, was quite a claim, but he went on to explain just how ethereal Earth history could be: "To the soul that holds communion with the visible ideas that dwell about him," Winchell observed, "these rocky walls are vocal with narratives of earthquake and flood, of nodding verdure and of desolating surge; these shales are the tombstones of generations, on which are inscribed chronologies whose minutes are the cycles of the Hindoo."[67] That reference to Hindoo is a reminder that India was recognized as one of the world's most interesting and exotic locales. The reference is not only Orientalist but philosophically significant. At just this time, scholars like Winchell were fascinated by the concept of enduring cycles of birth, death, and rebirth that are so deeply embedded in Eastern religion generally and in Hinduism in particular. It is here that Orientalism again reveals its deep fascination with time. Reference is often made to ruins, past grandeur, and the like. Soon, however, a more strictly scientific community would effectively banish such imaginative interpretations to the realm of art and literature. Romanticism continued to influence people into the early twentieth century, and under its guise a common traveler could inspire others to imagine themselves in a simultaneously timeless and yet very time-conscious scene.[68]

If the open landscape of the semiarid American West suggested the Sahara, Arabia, Mongolia, or other exotic locales, that in turn suggested the more uninhibited sexuality of the barbarians who lived in those distant lands. This too played out in space and time. The increasingly sexualized role of the Orient in the United States has a long history. Whereas the Indian captivity narratives offered by whites on the East Coast were originally portrayed as biblical dramas, by the mid to late nineteenth century, they came to possess more of the Victorian-era obsession with lurid sex. In other words, the latter perfectly coincided with the opening of the far western frontier. Throughout the 1860s and 1870s, the prospect of capture by Plains Indians was associated with sexual enslavement of women. While such captivity became less likely in the 1880s, the fear and fascination remained, as is evident in both literature and art.

But it was the prospect of indigenous female sexuality that also resonated in the steppe and desert areas of the American West. Building on a technique mastered by French painters, American artists and their patrons became enchanted by odalisques (beautiful young women, perhaps from harems) in sensuous poses. In Orientalist paintings such as Frederick Arthur Bridgman's *The Siesta* (1878) (fig. 1-6), a pipe is often placed nearby, yet another suggestion of the pleasures of the Orient.[69] By 1896, when artist Charles M. Russell painted a remarkable image of *Keeoma*, the link between native people and

Private collection, courtesy Spanierman Gallery, LLC, New York

Fig. 1-6. Painted by American artist Frederick Arthur Bridgman, *The Siesta* (1878) builds on the French tradition of depicting a sensuous Middle Eastern odalisque reclining in an exotic setting.

sexuality had become a staple fantasy in American culture (fig. 1-7). Russell, of course, was a prominent painter of western American scenes, but *Keeoma* playfully mixes genres. Languidly lounging like an odalisque in a French Oriental painting, or even in Bridgman's earlier copy of one, the Native American plains woman captures one's immediate attention. In a setting that is otherwise rich in Native American symbolism and looks much like the interior of any tepee, one encounters a woman of Orientalistically inspired appearance and demeanor. Even though she is nominally Indian, her clothing seems more sensuous and lavish than typical Plains Indian dress. Clearly, the woman, or perhaps we should say Russell himself, has taken a cue from the Orientalist painters who found real odalisques so irresistible as subjects. The model for *Keeoma*, however, was none other than Russell's own wife, though her features suggest as much a Middle Eastern woman as a Plains Indian. Note, too, the long, exotic-looking pipe lying next to Keeoma.

In Russell's painting of *Keeoma*, the pipe helps establish an Oriental context. Russell was clearly playing with the Orientalists' clichés here (odalisque in languid pose, pipe at the ready to satisfy or intoxicate) in order to convey a sense of the exotic and the erotic. However, the exotic was none other than the indigenous Native American, who by 1896 had lost much of his or her aura of

Detail from a digital reproduction in the author's collection

Fig. 1-7. Charles M. Russell's painting *Keeoma* (1896) playfully transforms a Middle Eastern odalisque into a Native American woman lounging in a Great Plains tepee.

wildness. The erotic element here is conveyed by a mysterious, sultry woman who is in reality a wife rather than a concubine. Russell, then, is playfully mixing metaphors here, perhaps as a western artist taking a jab at the "Eastern" art establishment. He is also saying, in a sense, that the faux exotic can be found as easily in the American West as in the fabled Orient. The fact that Russell transposed the American Indian and an Oriental subject is noteworthy. It reminds us how strong the lure of the exotic and primitive had become to a rapidly urbanizing and industrializing society. Interestingly, the Plains Indian motifs here are subliminally equated with the mobile peoples of the Asian steppes, possibly the fabled Mongols, in this pastiche on canvas.

At just the time *Keeoma* appeared, people were lining up to see "real" Indians in shows like Buffalo Bill's Wild West. However, as the West became more tame, these Indians were not only more likely to be proudly considered "our" Natives, they were therefore also less likely to be Orientalized because they were now part of our mythic West. Thus, as Americans traveled into the West in the later nineteenth century, they were conflicted. They still expected to encounter endangered exotic peoples, but these same natives had now been brought under control. Rather than being dangerous, these primitive peoples now offered a glimpse of what we ourselves had once been—and had perhaps lost—not very long ago. This represented imperial nostalgia—the process by which the very culture that transforms the lives of indigenous peoples soon longs to recapture those "lost" peoples.[70] In the case of Russell's painting, which appeared in several versions that quickly found their way into art collections and postcards, the sentiment is doubly ironic, for the lounging Keeoma belongs not only to another time but also to another place.[71]

Canada also played a role in Orientalizing the peoples and landscapes of the American frontier during the nineteenth century. Here, as in the plains of the United States and even South America, it was easy to imagine the Indians as Asiatic tribes—a fantasy that persisted until those tribes were subdued. Whereas an American artist like Russell might playfully configure a Plains Indian woman into an odalisque—that is, offer a kinder and gentler domesticated female trope—Canadian geologist J. W. Dawson had something darker in mind in 1889 when he published the popular book *Modern Science in Bible Lands*. Prone to making sweeping generalizations about human physiognomy and Near Eastern history, Dawson described a race of people who had despotically dominated Egypt in ancient times. As part of his research, Dawson consulted a museum artifact called the Head of a Hyksos sphinx (fig. 1-8) to determine that these people were "not Semitic or Aryan, but Turanian." By this Dawson meant a group of warlike people from the land of Tur, a huge, semiarid area that reaches northward from Persia (present-day Iran) into Asia. To Dawson, this artifact resembled "the face of some of the Northern tribes of Asia and Europe," but he quickly added, "and to one familiar with the countenance of the natives of America, it recalls some of these." In noting that the fierce Egyptian face was "altogether different from that of the native Egyptian kings of previous and succeeding dynasties," Dawson observed that it reminded him not only of something closer to home on North American soil but of something equally as barbaric. Leaving little doubt that he had the Plains Indians in mind, Dawson mentioned several of their chiefs by name and also reproduced an illustration of Red Pheasant, "a Cree chief who took part in the Manitoba disturbances of 1885," for direct comparison (fig. 1-9).

Dawson had good reason to mention those "disturbances," which involved loose alliances of Cree Indians and Métis, some of whom had migrated across the border from Minnesota and Dakota Territory. These skirmishes and rumors of skirmishes in the Canadian plains were troubling indeed, for they promised to challenge Dawson's own country's control over that steppelike, rapidly developing, grain-producing region to the west of Lake Superior. Drawing parallels between Canada's Plains Indians and the ancient tribes who

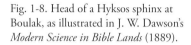

Fig. 1-8. Head of a Hyksos sphinx at Boulak, as illustrated in J. W. Dawson's *Modern Science in Bible Lands* (1889).

Fig. 1-9. The Cree chief Red Pheasant, as illustrated in J. W. Dawson's *Modern Science in Bible Lands* (1889).

had wreaked havoc on Egyptian civilization, Dawson concluded that "no one could doubt" that both of these warlike types represented "the kind of people fitted to trample on the quiet, industrious Egyptians" and, by inference, hard-working Canadian farmers.[72]

After the turn of the century, when Indian troubles were a thing of the past, such comparisons quietly ended. Yet, as ranching and agriculture dominated much of the plains, it was still tempting to equate them with their Old World counterpart. Much like portions of the vast, semiarid region that stretches from North Africa north of the Sahara well into Asia Minor, they featured urban centers surrounded by vast swaths of open country covered with either natural grasses or swatches of Old World grains, such as wheat, barley, oats, and rye, whose origins can be traced to southwestern Asia. By the early twentieth century, it was considered characteristically American, but it also embodied the evolving agrarian landscape of the plains, a timeless Near Eastern tradition of pastoral ranches, small farms, and thriving urban centers. Even though Americans had created a seemingly distinctive landscape here, it too had roots in an area far to the east, namely the Arab world. As historical geographer John Miller Morris concludes, this landscape is still a reminder that "Fez, Morocco, and Lubbock, Texas, have their parallels."[73]

2

In Praise of Pyramids
Orientalizing the Western Interior

> *"Things dread time; time dreads the Pyramids."*

Egyptian proverb

In 1776, an exploring expedition headed by Spanish friars Francisco Atanasio Domínguez and Francisco Silvestre Escalante reached the canyon-carved country of present-day southern Utah. Here, in the rugged, heavily eroded landscape along the Virgin River, they were intrigued by the towering, fantastically shaped landforms that loomed on every horizon. Like many places that European explorers encountered in this western North American wilderness, the countryside here was both awe-inspiring and confusing. These topographical features were so spectacular that the Spaniards named the river along which they were traveling "Río de las pirámides del sulfuro," or River of the Pyramids of Sulfur. The "pyramids" that the Spaniards described were apparently the prominent, dark-colored volcanic cones which remain as landmarks to the present day. To make sense of this rugged and chaotic natural topography, consisting of both igneous and sedimentary prominences, the Spaniards turned for inspiration to something more familiar and man-made, namely the pyramids, towers, and temples erected by ancient peoples. Not surprisingly, the Spaniards named some imposing geological formations after prominent castles in their homeland. These soon bore the name "el Castillo," which persists to the present day in the fairly common toponym "Castle Rock." The Spaniards knew that these features weren't real pyramids or castles, but the mysteriously shaped cones and buttes bore such a close resemblance to these man-made structures, it was easy to imagine that they might once have served that purpose in antiquity.

Nature has long played such tricks on people and still does. Pyramidal features are especially likely to enter folklore as the ruins of ancient advanced peoples. For example, large natural features that exhibit symmetry similar to man-made pyramids recently seduced self-proclaimed archaeologist Semir Osmanagic into claiming that the "Giant Pyramids of Bosnia" are authentic. Similarly, the rectangular block jointing in the shallow water off the Biminis is considered to be the foundations of ancient pyramids representing "remnants of Plato's lost Atlantis." Even more recently, the controversial Gavin Menzies claimed these same features were remnants of Chinese civilization that had reached the Americas in 1421.[1] This rush to attribute a human cause to the shape of natural features serves as a sobering reminder about humankind's tendency to anthropomorphize natural features. The physical properties of landscapes are so much grist for the human imagination—especially when people try to make sense out of not only the physical landscape but also the complexities of human history. The point here is that the human mind has a tendency to search for—and find—similarities between natural features (such as clouds) and human faces; so too does it have a tendency to render natural features into human artifacts (such as pyramids).

The Spaniards' use of the term "pyramids" in southern Utah was natural enough for those rugged prominences of rock that resembled giant pyramids. But which pyramids did they have in mind—the pyramids of Egypt, or the pyramids of Mesoamerica? It could have been either, but given the European fascination with Egypt during the Enlightenment, it was likely that the much more distant location served as a surrogate. After all, as learned men, the Spaniards could have agreed with Herodotus, the Greek historian who set the tone a thousand years earlier when he wrote: "Concerning Egypt itself, I shall extend my remarks to a great length, because there is no country that possesses so many wonders, nor any that has such a number of works that defy description."[2] Of these many wonders, as Herodotus called them, none were more massive or more topographically impressive than the Egyptian pyramids. Towering more than six hundred feet above the Nile River plains, they were one of the Seven Wonders of the World. Significantly, their height was not exceeded by another man-made structure for more than four thousand years. Regrettably, because the Spaniards' report is vague at this point, we will never know if it was Egypt or ancient Mexico that was on their minds when they named the river after pyramids, though the former is likely.

To get that kind of textual detail, we need to consult the journals of later explorers who were far more explicit about why they named geographic features as they did. More often than not, those explorers hailed from a northern

European background. In the early nineteenth century, for example, British explorer David Thompson traversed the semiarid interior of the Pacific Northwest, where volcanic buttes rose starkly. Here, Thompson recalled many years later in his unpublished manuscript called *Travels*, "the imagination may have full play to form to itself the ruins of buildings, temples, fortifications, tables, dykes, and many other things in great variety."[3] Thompson mentions those temples and forts abstractly; to him they appeared to be unnamed reminders of the ancient works of civilizations that are likewise unnamed. As befits any writer seeking to popularize his or her account of travel, Thompson here writes very romantically in an increasingly romantic age. Whether or not he originally fancied seeing temples and forts in the landscape he explored in the first decade of the nineteenth century, we do not know. We do know, however, that by the 1840s when Thompson wrote down his recollections, such romantic sentiments were commonplace among the literary elite. Moreover, an increasingly literate population was influenced by what these educated travelers had to say. With that in mind, let us now consider another expedition to the Intermountain West in the 1840s, more than half a century after the Domínguez-Escalante expedition, when Spain's grip had yielded to Mexican rule; in a few short years that too would change as the United States wrested that region from Mexico.

This expedition was heir to both ancient texts and fairly modern writings that emphasized the age and size of the pyramids. Actual images of the pyramids became increasingly common after Napoleon's scientific and military expedition to Egypt from 1798 to 1801. By the early 1840s, lithographs such as those provided by Scottish artist David Roberts found their way into the United States, where they helped fuel interest in Egypt. Roberts produced numerous sets of lithographs of the pyramids, some beautifully colored (fig. 2-1). Such artwork and associated narratives had more than aesthetic appeal, for Napoleon's victories in Egypt suggested that Europe, and the West in general, had a role in exploring and transforming the modern Orient.

In January of 1844, American explorer John Charles Frémont and his party worked their way into the desert country just east of the rugged, snow-packed Sierra Nevada in today's state of Nevada. Glad to be out of the mountains and at a lower elevation where "the temperature was mild and pleasant," at least by comparison, Frémont and his party moved through the sagebrush-covered landscape at the western edge of a huge interior region he would soon name the "Great Basin." In this desolate area, Frémont and his group were about to become the first Anglo-Americans to create a surrogate landscape in the interior American West, or at least the first to do so and leave a record of it.

Fig. 2-1. Sold as part of a set of hand-colored lithographs by Scottish artist David Roberts in the early 1840s, this evocative view of the Egyptian pyramids captures the romance of Victorian exploration and antiquity.

As the explorers traveled in a southeasterly direction across the desert under Frémont's direction, a large inland lake "broke upon our eyes like the ocean." This, however, was no ordinary lake. In it, they spied a "remarkable rock which had attracted our attention for many miles." Rising out of the waters of the lake, this light-colored rock was large—Frémont's party estimated that it rose "600 feet above the water." The rock's size and height were impressive enough, but it was the shape of the rock that drew their attention from afar and continued to impress them as they inspected it close-up. According to Frémont, the rock "presented a pretty exact outline of the Great Pyramid of Cheops." This is specific enough, but Frémont was not content to let things rest there. He was so convinced about the similarity between this rock and the Pyramid of Cheops that he bestowed the name "Pyramid" on not only the rock but also the entire body of water. Since that day in 1844, the name "Pyramid Lake" honors the rock's resemblance to the prototype in Egypt.

In his reports, Frémont explained the rationale behind his naming of Pyramid Lake. He stated: "Though it may be deemed by some a fanciful resemblance, I can undertake to say that the future traveler will find a much more striking resemblance between this rock and the pyramids of Egypt than there is between them and the object from which they take their name."[4]

When read carefully, this sentence is almost as perplexing as the mysterious sphinx that reposes near the real pyramids in Egypt. What could Frémont have meant by it? Clearly, the first part of his statement reaffirms the similarity between the rock in the lake and the pyramids near Giza. The second part of Frémont's sentence—that there is some discrepancy between "*them*" (the pyramids in Egypt) and the "*object*" after which they are named—appears to be both enigmatic and arcane until we understand something about the actual pyramid in Egypt. Frémont appears to be referring to the fact that Egypt's Great Pyramid, or Pyramid of Cheops, was originally sheathed in white limestone that had spalled away except for its distinctive "cap," which still remains. That cap creates a discontinuity in the otherwise perfect outline of this pyramid. That flaw, if one can call it that, compromises the perfection of the original pyramid. Astute explorers in Egypt in Frémont's day had recently concluded that the original pyramid, which stands 481 feet high, had been about thirty feet higher before elements and vandalism had taken their toll. Frémont's comment reveals his knowledge about the Pyramid of Cheops, and his recognition that the prototype in the Egyptian desert varied from its original—which is to say perfect—form. As geologist J. W. Dawson wrote about forty years later in a statement that Frémont would have understood, the pyramid "has endured in all its magnitude to our time; and, but for wanton destruction, its outer surface would have presented to this day all its pristine beauty."[5] Although there is a ring of conceit about it, not to mention an irony that seems almost postmodern, Frémont believed that his pyramid in the Great Basin was an even better representative of the original than the original. This is noteworthy, for, on a subliminal level, Frémont's emphasis on the pyramid-shaped rock in the Great Basin associates his own enterprising, cannon-toting, semi-scientific mission with the prototype for all such modern incursions, specifically Napoleon's.

Frémont's highly-detailed commentary on pyramids may seem peculiar to readers today, but that is because people nowadays know far less about the pyramids than people did in his time. The Egyptian pyramids today are simply spectacular former wonders of the world that are used as icons in movies and on cigarette packages. True, we popularly recognize the "mystical" powers that went into their design, but we actually know little about the pyramids themselves. For Frémont and his generation, however, the pyramids were an obsession—singular achievements that revealed the greatness of Egyptian culture and held the key to human understanding. Look at any dollar bill and you will see the Pyramid of Cheops, an eye atop it connecting mystically with the heavens. Adopted as a popular icon in the United States by the early

1800s, the pyramid symbolized several things: a greatness to which learned men aspired, a knowledge of construction that was not yet surpassed, and a mysticism that entranced both the American and European publics. Although the pyramids were spectacular ruins by the time Napoleon invaded Egypt in 1798, that bold, imperialistic act by France triggered a wave of interest in the Near East that ultimately affected Europeans and Americans alike. That interest is at the heart of modern Orientalism, and it was so strong that we find it in the wilderness of the North American West well before Anglo-American explorers like Frémont arrived.

Consider the travels and writings of John Lloyd Stephens. As an educated New Yorker, Stephens traveled to Egypt and the Holy Land in 1836, signing the consular book in Alexandria and writing a lively account of his travels that was widely read after its publication by Harper and Brothers in 1837. That book, *Incidents of Travel in Egypt, Arabia Petraea, and the Holy Land*, became required reading for any American visiting, or even thinking about, the Near East. Appropriately enough, Stephens's book begins in Egypt and stimulates the reader's imagination with its tales of discovery from the moment he sets foot on Egyptian soil. Although Stephens could see the pyramids from Cairo upon his arrival there, he had been delayed from actually reaching them for ten days—a situation that only heightened his interest in experiencing them firsthand. As Stephens finally neared the pyramids, he was awed by their size. As he put it, he "saw how very small I was." When he "looked up their sloping sides to the[ir] lofty summits, they seemed to have grown to the size of mountains." Ascending the pyramid, Stephens "realized in all their force the huge dimensions of this giant work." Stephens was personally enthralled by the pyramids and cognizant of the effect that Egyptian history had on modern-day visitors. Speculating about how the pyramids should affect the sensitive traveler, and thus priming all who would subsequently see these wonders, Stephens set up a formula that would be used by the educated traveler. He predicted that "thousands of years roll through his mind, and thought recalls the men who built them, their mysterious uses, the poets, historians, philosophers, and warriors who have gazed upon them with wonder like his own." Like Frémont, Stephens was an admirer of antiquity. The belief that the pyramids were ageless or represented eons of time was especially attractive to the Victorian mind.

But note here that Stephens was also captivated by what the pyramids suggested about brilliant human minds. He described the Great Pyramid in detail, citing impressive statistics and relating efforts by English gentlemen and others to explore its mysterious interior.[6] In other words, the best Western minds were still awed by these accomplishments that stood at the doorstep of the East. To add even more drama to the scene, Stephens also discussed the tragic plight of an Englishman who climbed the pyramid but then carelessly lost his balance and tumbled down its side, shattering every bone in his body by the time he reached the bottom. That fatal accident not only underscored the terrible grandeur of the pyramids and the dangers of travel—it emphasized Stephens's own good fortune, skill, and bravery as he successfully scaled these formidable artifacts.

Stephens's *Incidents of Travel in Egypt, Arabia Petraea, and the Holy Land* was critically acclaimed and widely quoted. Then, as now, a good review could do wonders for both author and publisher. To Stephens's good fortune, his book was praised by Edgar Allan Poe in a twelve-page review that made Stephens's name a household word. Stephens's book sold very well—twenty-one thousand copies in the United States alone within two years. Perhaps even more important, it was not only immediately popular but endured through several generations. *Incidents of Travel in Egypt* remained in print until 1882, a remarkably long publishing run.[7] Stephens's book also sold abroad as well as in the United States. By 1840, learned people on both sides of the Atlantic, including American explorer John Charles Frémont and British explorer Sir Richard F. Burton, were familiar with the type of book that featured a well-educated traveler in the role of modern-day explorer of ancient wonders and exotic places; naturally, *Incidents of Travel in Egypt* appealed to the public in that it combined adventure and education. There were many such writers by the 1850s, as the public had developed a seemingly insatiable appetite for exploration narratives. Using writing techniques developed in the age of exploration, these writers influenced the literature of Europe and the United States in the nineteenth century. More to the point, the self-conscious explorer was a very different kind of writer than the early explorer in that he (and later she) wrote not for the King but rather for the public.

At this time in the early Victorian era, the self-conscious explorer's aims were varied. The geographical motive was to banish terra incognita and expand the reach of colonial power, but the social motive was far more complex. First, the literature they wrote was meant to entertain, educate, and enlighten. That goal squared with a growing belief in the Victorian period that individuals improve their social standing through pursuits that increase knowledge, broaden horizons, and improve prospects for upward mobility. For the Victorian citizen, being widely read was essential. Books graced their libraries and decorated their parlors. The self-conscious explorer was pivotal in this social and educational endeavor. Stephens's *Incidents of Travel in Egypt* revealed how expansive—and irresistible—the Western gaze was over exotic lands. Such authors provided a confessional, personalized look at exotic culture and landscape, often with a moral message delivered either subliminally or overtly. This, it should be pointed out, occurred well before the United States became a major international political force.

As Stephens's book continued to sell very well into the 1840s, John Charles Frémont was involved in his own adventures in the American West. Exploring a large area that was virtually unknown, to the United States public at least, Frémont was getting a grasp on the geography of the Great Basin. This was a time when the public demanded facts and figures as well as drama and adventure. Of Pyramid Lake, Frémont observed: "The elevation of this lake above the sea is 4,890 feet, being nearly 700 feet higher than the Great Salt Lake from which it lies nearly west, and distant about eight degrees of longitude." Frémont made one other observation about Pyramid Lake and that other much larger lake in the Great Basin. Noting what he considered "an object of geographical interest," he observed that Pyramid Lake "is the nearest lake to the western rim, as the Great Salt Lake is to the eastern rim, of the Great Basin which lies between the base of the Rocky mountains and the Sierra Nevada."[8] That one sentence was deceptively simple. In point of fact, it introduces two points of fundamental importance. First, it revealed that the Great Basin was a huge area, spanning a full eight degrees of longitude—about 450 miles (725 km)—from east to west.[9] Second, it suggested that the source of waters for permanent lakes in this region is in the highest mountains, which constitute the eastern and western margins of the Great Basin. With this one sentence, Frémont not only described the new geographic region's hydrology but defined its geographic perimeter for a nation aggressively eyeing the Pacific shore as its western boundary.[10]

Fremont had unwittingly discovered yet another connection between the Interior American West and the deserts of the Old World. Portions of both are endorheic, that is, have areas where any precipitation collects in basins (like Pyramid Lake) rather than reaching the sea. Endorheic regions usually lie far from the ocean, and much of their surface is perennially dry. Fremont realized this as he reconnoitered other nearby desert valleys, which featured playas, or dry lake beds. Further scientific exploration would reveal that these endorheic landscapes are a result of desert climate conditions; if instead there were surplus precipitation, it would fill a valley's basin and ultimately cut a river channel to the sea. Of note here is that in the Great Basin Fremont had discovered a place akin to Egypt's fabled Qattara Depression, a vast area of bone-dry desert west of the pyramids that had long intimidated all but the most intrepid of explorers. Despite its grand name, however, Fremont would have been chagrined to learn that his American Great Basin is small compared to vast endorheic areas of the Sahara, Arabia, and interior Asia (for example, Tibet). In fact, as subsequent exploration would demonstrate, only about five percent of North America is endorheic, while a much larger portion of North Africa and the Middle East is so classified. These are intriguing places indeed, and we still know relatively little about them because they are among the least populated. But that very characteristic—arid desolation—has had considerable appeal.

On his ostensibly military mission into the interior American West, then Frémont did far more than provide geographic information to his superiors; he also provided it to the scientific community, who avidly read his reports. In 1867, as part of the US Geological Survey exploration of the fortieth parallel, seventeen-year-old ornithologist Robert Ridgway studied Pyramid Lake. Ridgway had read Frémont's report and was about to improve upon it in places. In his official report, Ridgway noted that "'The Pyramid' is close to the eastern shore, and appears as a huge rock of a very regular pyramidal shape, rising about three hundred feet above the surface of the lake." Like Frémont, Ridgway noted something else about the pyramid that made it even more perfect than the Egyptian pyramid. As Ridgway noted, "Its base is a nearly perfect triangle, each side being a sheer precipice from the water to the height of a hundred and fifty feet, while only one of the three corners was found to be easily accessible from the boat."[11] Ridgway is here referring to an abstract ideal—the shape of a perfect pyramid, whose bottom as well as sides is triangular-shaped as opposed to square.

Frémont's report also resonated with the American public. Most of the information in it was ostensibly factual—for example, the positions and elevations of geographic features. Some of it, however, transcended facts and engaged mythology. The pyramidal rock in Pyramid Lake again provides a good example. Frémont and his cartographer and illustrator Charles Preuss recorded this feature in several ways. First, they objectified it by revealing its location and its height, which they speculated was six hundred feet. This ambitious quantification they achieved using maps and words. Next, they subjectified the rock not only by associating it with the Pyramid of Cheops in words but by actually illustrating it to substantiate that comparison (fig. 2-2). Frémont believed that Preuss's sketch of the rock was quite accurate, but he longed for something even more convincing. Part scientist as well as romanticist, Frémont tried, but failed, to capture scenes using the newly invented daguerreotype process of photography. The cantankerous Preuss ridiculed

Fig. 2-2. In the section of his 1845 report dealing with Pyramid Lake, John Charles Frémont noted a "striking resemblance" between this rock and the pyramids of Egypt.

Frémont for botching the photography, but the drawing certainly worked well enough to convey a sense of what the expedition members saw and what the public should envision. The image of Pyramid Lake in Frémont's report does more than confirm that geographic feature's presence. It also venerates the feature by associating it with one of the world's great landmarks. Frémont effectively renders a natural feature into a cultural object. In the 1850s and 1860s, expeditions searching for railroad routes would do much the same, as would popular imagery resulting from those reports. These illustrations of the pyramid in Pyramid Lake effectively Orientalized a western landscape feature—that is, associated it with the Near East.[12]

Frémont's Orientalist impulse was closely allied with a broadening engagement of the East in everyday American life. No longer restricted to the intellectual elite, Orientalism had begun to reach into popular culture at exactly the time that Stephens, Frémont, and others wrote for a growing audience. Although Frémont was ostensibly a military man dutifully writing and illustrating a report for the government, he personified the bold self-promotion that would later position him as the first Republican candidate for president of the United States and ultimately compromise his career and sully his reputation.

When the enterprising explorer Frémont coined the name Pyramid Lake in 1844, he also tapped into yet another aspect of American culture that was intimately associated with storytelling and writing—religion. The word *Egypt* today may convey something exotic and erotic; and if religion is thought of at all, it is Islam. However, in the 1830s and 1840s, mention of the word *Egypt* would just as likely be associated with the Jews' slavery there: more to the point, Egypt was associated with deliverance from slavery there by Moses, who led his people to freedom by fleeing into the desert and parting the Red Sea in the process to avoid capture and destruction. It is this religious association with Egypt that resonated so strongly in the popular culture of the nineteenth century. As a place, Egypt embodied two identities at that time. It was on the one hand associated with the ancient Egyptians, but on the other with Judeo-Christian religion. Egypt, then, represented not only pharaonic riches and enslavement but also deliverance by Divine Providence. Egypt thus exemplified many of the classic attributes of the Orient—namely, richness in history, despotism, majesty, poverty, mystery, and spirituality. The Bible mentions Egypt more than six hundred times, and the name was never far from the tongue about twenty centuries later when the American West was being explored. Reaffirming connections to Egypt by configuring natural places in the New World simply reinforced the power of the real place in constructing a new—but actually old—American identity.

The relatively positive view of the Middle East in nineteenth-century America is noteworthy. It explains why Stephens's *Incidents of Travel in Egypt* is so effusive in its praise of the landscape and religious traditions of the Holy Land. Quoting biblical passages from time to time, Stephens thrilled his readers with his travel accounts of places like Petra, of which he wrote: "Nothing can be finer than the immense rocky rampart which encloses the city. Strong, firm, and immovable as Nature itself, it seems to deride the walls of cities and the puny fortifications of skillful engineers." Petra was no ordinary city but was carved out of rose-colored native rock. Although constructed in about the sixth century BCE, Petra remained unknown to westerners until rediscovered by Swiss explorer John William Burgon in 1812. As Stephens observed in a statement about both credibility and faith, "I would that the skeptic could stand as I did among the ruins of this city among the rocks, and there open the sacred book and read the words of the inspired penman written when this desolate place was one of the greatest cities in the world." Stephens then notes that this ruined city could convince even that skeptic: "Though he would not believe Moses and the prophets, he believes the handwriting of God himself in the desolation and eternal ruin around him."[13] Tellingly, travelers half a world away would often use these or similar terms about desolation and ruin to describe the landscapes they traversed on the North American continent.

Many of these observers described ruins in a dramatic, even laudatory, manner. To Europeans and many European Americans, ruins anywhere resonated as romantic and haunted reminders of a past that constantly resurfaced in the Victorian mind. The specter of such a past represented an important aspect of Orientalism. In other words, the Orient was not simply a place (or places) but also a time (or times). Consider, for example, Stephens's and Frémont's encounters with Egypt—the former real, the latter imaginary. Implicit in their prose was the concept of immense time periods that were represented archaeologically. Egypt, like the Holy Land itself, thus had two personalities, or rather two sides, that were irreconcilable. The nostalgia felt for the East represented experience that was palpable, as evident in ruins, but was evanescent in that it could never be recaptured. As the "cradle of civilization," Mesopotamia, and especially Egypt, represented a benchmark that might hopefully be matched through modern technology, but it would never again be repeated.

In the nineteenth century, as a subset of Orientalism in the United States, Egyptomania involved a subconscious desire to imitate the most successful and sometimes arcane aspects of Egypt's past culture. This appreciation is what made Egypt so fashionable among those, like the Rosicrucians, who mysticized the Egyptian past. Founded in sixteenth-century Europe, the Rosicrucians emphasized the mystical teachings of the ancient Near East. By the nineteenth century, Rosicrucians like the black American spiritualist Paschal Beverly Randolph (1825–1875) proposed elaborate "theories of cyclic history, recurring cataclysms, and pre-Adamite races." These theories involved radical shifts in the earth's axis that melted the polar ice caps as well as violent earthquakes that reshaped the stage upon which history was acted out. Such cataclysms, Randolph contended, had caused the sinking of Atlantis, rendering it a "lost" civilization. However, those same forces also yielded fragments of Atlantis, for they "upheaved it again, with a few of its pyramids yet intact, but transforming the happy land into the deserts of the Zahara."[14] More to the point, though, the pyramids represented a glimpse of perfection, the likes of which would never be seen again. Scholars may deride such concepts today, but in the nineteenth century, when intellectuals regularly sought explanations to riddles using combinations of scientific, religious, and spiritual knowledge, they sometimes reached breathtaking conclusions that riveted the public's interest.

To nineteenth-century travelers in the American West, the open desert landscape could also evoke plenty of Orientalist-inspired images. In 1860, for example, as explorer Richard Burton continued his journey across the continent, he left a vivid record of landscape comparisons in what would soon become Nevada. Of a particularly forlorn area here, Burton authoritatively wrote that "the scenery was that of the Takhashshua near Zayla, or the delicious land behind Aden, the Arabian sea-board." The Middle Eastern countryside that Burton compared with Nevada was desolate indeed. Burton continued by observing that this part of Nevada consisted of challenge after challenge for the traveler. Here, as he put it, "Sand-heaps—the only dry spots after rain—fixed by tufts of metallic green salsolae, and guarded from the desert wind by rusty cane-grass, emerged from the wet and oozy plain, in which the mules often sank to the fetlock." In this nightmarish country "the unique and snowy floor of thin nitre [salts], blueish where deliquescent, was here as solid as a sheet of ice." This country could be slippery and slushy after rain and "is blinding by day" and "bitterly cold" at night, attributable to what Burton called, with seemingly scientific authority, "the refrigerating properties of the salt."[15]

Prone to see the Middle East everywhere in the American West—that is, create surrogate landscapes at will—Burton described another scene the next day that also reminded him of Arabia. Traversing the loose sand of an area "scattered over with carcass and skeleton," he came to a place where "broken clay and dwarf vegetation assumed in the dim shades fantastic and mysterious forms." This made Burton think he was "once more amongst the ruins of that Arab village concerning which Lebid sang—'Ay me! ay me! All alone and drear the dwelling place, the home—On Mina, o'er Rijam and Ghool, wild beasts unheeded roam.'" This is Burton the writer referring to both his own earlier experiences and a literary precedent. Significantly, after the ancient writer Lebid that Burton mentions converted to Islam, he no longer wrote such poetry. Instead, Lebid devoted himself to a literary interpretation of the only words he claimed anyone needed to read—the Koran. Burton, however, faced no self-imposed Islamist restrictions on prose.

As he traveled, Burton called upon the words of East and West with near abandon; this is another trademark of the self-conscious explorer. In further describing an Arabian-like scene in Nevada, for example, Burton notes that he and his fellow travelers "were torpid with what the Bedouin calls El Rakl—la Ragle du Désert, when part of the brain sleeps whilst the rest is wide awake." This reference to split consciousness is significant, and perhaps metaphorical for what Burton himself was doing in a literary sense—relying on his own imagination and also the reality of a world already described elsewhere. In this dreamlike scene dusted with blowing sand and obscured by a light haze, Burton described the torturous trek to the salt-rimmed basin of Carson Lake, leaving the reader to wonder just how American, or how

Middle Eastern, the countryside was. The answer, of course, was that it was both, or rather one and the same.[16]

To early travelers, especially those who crossed it on foot or in wagons, the interior West between the Wasatch and Sierra Nevada was so overwhelming and so unusual that it required superlatives. These descriptions often stressed the barren nature of the land, and this land seemed to have only one counterpart. As a writer noted in the *Sacramento Daily Union* in 1867, travelers reported that the region "rivals the Desert of Sahara" in its bleakness, while another noted that "the deserts of Africa or Asia present no more forbidding aspect."[17] Word for word, no part of the American West was more equated with the Near East than the Great Basin. This region made the mind work overtime for several reasons. First, travelers visually considered its barrenness threatening. The use of dramatic prose called attention to the commentator as a person who could brave the wilderness. Equally important, perhaps, was the fact that barrenness, like a blank sheet of paper, stimulated the imagination.[18]

How similar was the interior American West to its Old World counterparts? Mike Davis notes that "Nevada and Utah, for instance, were variously compared to Arabia, Turkestan, the Taklo Makan, Timbuktu, Australia, and so on, but in reality, Victorian minds were traveling through an essentially extraterrestrial terrain, far outside their cultural experience." As Davis puts it, the Victorian explorers "eventually cast aside a trunkfull of Victorian preconceptions in order to recognize novel forms and processes in nature." Geologists in effect "created a new landscape language—also largely architectural, but sometimes phantasmagorical—to describe an unprecedented dialectics of rock, color and light." Davis aptly calls this the "convergence of science and sensibility," adding that it has no twentieth-century counterpart. This convergence "compelled a moral view of the environment as it was laid bare for exploitation" by science, government, and entrepreneurs.[19]

Those who know vegetation very well will recognize differences between western Nevada and, for example, eastern Uzbekistan. However, even someone familiar with both places will marvel at how similar in general appearance they are. Their geomorphology, which developed under similar climatic conditions, and their sparse, low-lying vegetation make it difficult to say which is Uzbekistan and which is Nevada: only after carefully scrutinizing the vegetation by species—the genus *Artemisia* occurs in both—can one be sure.[20] As a map of the world's temperate and cold deserts shows (fig. 2-3), west-central Nevada has far more in common with Uzbekistan than it does the Sahara. Southern Nevada, though, comes much closer to the Sahara, as it is a hot, rather than temperate, or cold, desert.

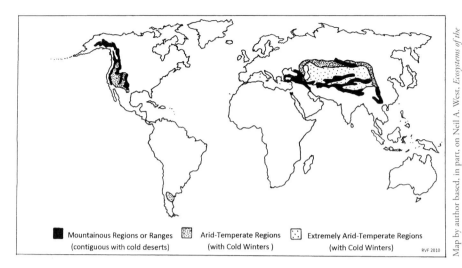

Map by author based, in part, on Neil A. West, *Ecosystems of the World*, Vol. 5, *Temperate Deserts and Semi Deserts* (1983)

■ Mountainous Regions or Ranges   ▦ Arid-Temperate Regions   ▢ Extremely Arid-Temperate Regions
(contiguous with cold deserts)   (with Cold Winters)   (with Cold Winters)   RVF 2010

Fig. 2-3. A map of the world's temperate deserts having cold winters helps explain similarities between the interior American West and portions of Uzbekistan and southwestern Asia.

Comparisons between Old World and New World deserts are further complicated by human historical influences, notably the actual spread of plant species like *Salsola* ("tumbleweed") and tamarisk ("salt cedar") from the Old World to the New World since about 1500. So similar are the basic environments that these plants have found a niche comfortable enough to spread like wildfire; they are branded invasive species but are considered somehow natural because of the ease with which they dominate.[21]

Portions of the American West where dunes shift about are relatively rare, but they were especially evocative. They readily brought to mind the vivid descriptions of early desert travelers. Consider, for example, Marco Polo's descriptions of the sand dunes near Dunhuang, China, where the Caves of the Thousand Buddhas are located. These dunes were known for the mysterious sounds they produced. "Sometimes . . ." Polo related, "you shall hear the sound of musical instruments, and still more commonly the sound of drums." Like many of Polo's accounts, this was regarded with skepticism. However, science has proven Polo correct: some dunes are "musical" indeed. These sounds have been heard in dunes elsewhere and are the substance of legends. The Arabs fancy them to be the bells of a subterranean convent,[22] while to Native Americans in the West they were yet another indication that the landscape was alive and populated by spirits. More recently, they have been called "booming" dunes—testimony that differently trained peoples may interpret the same phenomena differently.

Dunes that make such sounds are also found in the American West, for example, at Dumont Dunes in the Mojave Desert and at some locations in the Great Basin of Nevada. The actual mechanism by which dunes boom is not known, but researchers deduce that the booming dunes have an upper layer of dry sand about six feet in thickness that lies over a harder, cemented surface. The sound is emitted when the sand grains, which are ideally of similar size, strike each other and emit about the same frequency. When the sand grains collide with each other, their sound resonates against the underlying, harder surface. Tall dunes with steep slopes are most likely to emit these sounds. These singing dunes impressed Nathaniel Curzon, who wrote about them in *Tales of Travel* (1923). A romantic at heart, Curzon called the sounds they make "the voice of the desert." Although some people describe these dunes as sounding like marching soldiers or volcanic eruptions, most compare them to music. To Curzon, the sand dunes seemed to be "speaking in notes now as of harp strings," or "as of trumpets and drums." He too recognized that the dunes created a "mystic fascination to which no one can turn a deaf ear." In his book, Curzon noted that he had found only one "Singing Sand-dune, analogous to the Asian and African cases which we have been discussing," in North America. This dune was located in Churchill County, Nevada, and "is said to be 100–400 feet in height, and four miles long." Curzon added that "when agitation of the sand starts it sliding a noise is produced like that from telegraph wires fanned by a breeze." [23] That singing hum resonated as a kind of harmonic "Asian" note.

In searching for surrogate landscapes between the Near East and the Far West, we need look no farther than the dunes of sand that occupy portions of these desert landscapes. Whether they "sing" or not, sand dunes are especially prone to being mythologized: composed of inert geological material, they can move; situated in the quietest of deserts, they can hiss and, yes, even emit musical sounds or roar at times; part of a hard, rock-ribbed desert land, they embody softness; significantly, in the most masculine of desert landscapes, they introduce an element of the female. Writer Terry Tempest Williams, for example, describes the sand dunes near Utah's Great Salt Lake as undeniably "female." As Williams put it, they possess "sensuous curves—the small of a woman's back. Breasts. Buttocks. Hips and pelvis."[24] These dunes are visually evocative, but they form part of something even more profound. They are not only landscapes but also soundscapes—that is, places characterized by words for the sounds that describe them—in this case the hissing, shifting, singing, sliding, smooth sandscapes of the desert.[25]

In a literary and folkloric sense, this linguistic effect is as profound as the visual in conveying the nature of this type of landscape. These dunes are, so to speak, sinuous, slippery, sensual, seductive, and sexual in their connotations. Small wonder, then, that dunescapes provided the setting of such Orientalist romances as *The Sheik*, which bring Western popular culture face-to-face with the seduction of the "other" as lover. The very looseness of sand underfoot suggests that we may lose both our bearings and our balance, by being seduced. The metaphor is even more potent when, in the midst of that sensuous sandy skin of the desert, we arrive at the oasis—a fertile, moist place where protection and rejuvenation await.

The power of landscape in this drama between East and West should not be underestimated. In 1880s Nevada, travel writer Phil Robinson observed that the landscape beyond the Humboldt River valley was as dismal as any desert on the face of the earth. He characterized it as "desert again with the surface of the alkali land curling up into flakes, and the lank grey greasewood sparsely scattered about it." Robinson then quickly and authoritatively informed the reader that "the desolation is as utter as in Baluchistan or the land of Goshen." Those references to two desert places in the Old World position Robinson as not only a traveler to real places but also as a reader of the Bible. Continuing the description, Robinson finds a cultural comparison irresistible, adding that in this forlorn locale, "instead of Murrees there are plenty of Shoshonees to make the desolation perilous to travellers by waggon." Murree refers to a rugged area in the province of Punjab, Pakistan, and its residents, including the city of Islamabad. As if this comparison were not poignant and dramatic enough, Robinson could not resist commenting on the enigmatic, mysterious nature of the Indians. "I do not think that in all my travels," he observed, "I have ever met a race with such baffling physiognomy." After declaring that it is impossible to determine what, or even if, an Indian is thinking, Robinson concludes "they are hieroglyphics altogether, and there is something 'uncanny' about them."[26] That reference to "hieroglyphics" transforms the Indians into objects, but it is also a metaphor for Oriental inscrutability. Hieroglyphs can also symbolize something natural as well as cultural, however, as when Robinson earlier characterized a desert landscape in Utah as "sage-brush and sand, with occasional patches of tiresome rock fragments and unlimited lizards." These, as he put it, were "nature's hieroglyphics for sultry sterility—[which] were the only features of the journey."[27] In either case, the reference to hieroglyphics Orientalizes both the Nevada landscape and the peoples who occupied it as mysteries needing to be decoded.[28]

And yet despite its novelty, the desert experience touches a universal chord in all humankind, as Mark Twain observed when he witnessed his Western town-bred fellow travelers in the Middle East adjusting to the "free life of the camp and the desert," as he called it. This lifestyle, as we have seen, was easy for some European American travelers to despise, but Twain understood something grander about humankind. As he put it, "The nomadic instinct is a human instinct; it was born with Adam and transmitted through the patriarchs, and after thirty centuries of steady effort, civilization has not educated it out of us yet. The nomadic instinct . . ." Twain concluded, "can not be educated out of an Indian at all."[29] That, in a sense, helped conflate nomadic Indians in the West with existing examples of the world's most celebrated nomads—namely, those of the Near East and Mongolia.

Although it now had a pyramid, sand dunes, and even nomadic peoples that suggested the Near East and adjacent southwestern Asia, the interior West lacked one essential ingredient—the camel. That, however, would soon change, as the US military began to import them by employing the skills of a Syrian camel driver named Hadji Ali—or "Hi Jolly" as he became known to Americans prone to simplifying, or Anglicizing, names. Bringing camels to the arid American West was the brainchild of Jefferson ("Jeff") Davis, then secretary of war and destined to play a major role in the military exploration of the West. Davis was always on the lookout for efficient methods to reconnoiter the southern Interior West, including the Mojave and Colorado Deserts. This episode brought Americans face-to-face with the Orient as well as transporting camels from that exotic part of the world to the American West.

On May 10, 1855, Davis ordered Major Henry Constantine Wayne to "proceed without delay to the Levant" in order to import camels "for army transportation and for other military purposes." Davis correctly noted that Wayne might first find, in France and England, connections to those individuals experimenting with using camels in military service. These were appropriate locales, as they were centers of European Orientalist thought. Davis was also aware that Barbary camels were being bred to improve their size and strength. Wayne carefully followed Davis's guidance. At the beginning of his journey to the Middle East, Wayne stopped in London, where he visited the zoo to view the camels there. As planned, Wayne next visited France. In Paris, he conducted more research on camels, always keeping in mind Davis's advice that superior breeds of Persian camels were said to exist in Salonica.[30]

Wayne was joined by Dixon Porter, and both were about to learn a good deal more about camels and about Middle Easterners than they had ever imagined. Upon arriving in the Middle East with ample cash that they flashed around openly, Wayne and Porter were at the mercy of people who hoped the Americans would buy anything they offered. Many people, in fact, were amazed that Americans would want to buy a camel at all. When a Turk asked incredulously, "Have you no camels in America?" Porter answered "No," upon which the Turk exclaimed, with pity: "My, you must be many years behind the times."[31] This cultural bantering was typical of the period, as was stereotyping on both sides. For example, Porter observed that "the Egyptians, most inconsiderate and cruel camel-masters in the world, have the most wretched-looking beasts, while the Turk, more humane in disposition, keeps his flock in fine order."[32] The Turks, like most Middle Easterners, used the single-humped dromedary camels that were so well adapted to that region's hot deserts (as opposed to the Bactrian camels, two-humped creatures with heavier fur that were native to colder Central Asia).

If Wayne and Porter were regarded somewhat skeptically by the locals in the Middle East, their exploits drew intense interest back in the United States. In October 1857, a reporter for *Harper's Monthly Magazine* vicariously rhapsodized about the search for camels. In a passage that referred to the founder of Islam, he wrote: "It is the one-humped, or Arabian, camel that we have in our mind's eye when we read of the prophet's mild-white darling." The Americans here had their choice of many kinds of camels—"the camel squadrons of Semiramis, and Xerxes's simoon of hedjins—of the proud Mahri stallion, exulting in his pure lineage—of the wind-challenging Nomanich, the never-failing Bicharieh, the wondrous Ababdeh hedjin, such as he that went from Cairo to Mecca, nine hundred miles, in nine days, nor paused to eat or drink." It was, however, "the caravan camel, the merchant-ship of the Sahara, first in the song when the night-bound drivers sing of sand—of the true war-ship of the desert"[33] that was selected. Although confused readers back home evidently scurried to dictionaries and atlases in order to comprehend exactly what they were reading about exotic lands, the story confirmed that the camel was capable of traveling great distances with little food or water, that is, it was perfect for the arid interior West.

After negotiating, the Americans found what they were looking for, and soon the camels were headed back to the United States on a steamship. Arriving in the bustling port of Indianola, Texas, the camels excited much interest. Some people regarded them with skepticism: Could the camels really measure up to the rigors of the West? The answer was yes—and no. Historian Harlan Fowler observed that "the truth was, the soldiers did not take too well to the camel." That was an understatement. The soldiers found in this odd-looking beast "none of the lovable qualities that the Arabs imputed to him."[34] Camels were considered to be smelly, ill-tempered, and even dangerous. They were difficult to ride at high speeds without most riders becoming, well, "sea-sick"—the term they often used for the jostling provided by these ships

Fig. 2-4. As suggested by this illustration of "Camels in Nevada," which appeared in *Harper's Weekly* in 1877, the importation of these "ships of the desert" helped impart an Old World character to the arid American West.

of the desert. Plus, it was believed that camels held grudges! As proof of this latter claim, it was said that when an Arab was the focus of a camel's ire, he would put his clothes nearby, and the camel would ferociously attack them, after which the camel and the thankful Arab would call a truce. Despite these alleged character flaws, government explorer Lt. Edward Fitzgerald Beale claimed that camels could "live on anything and thrive," and go long periods without drinking. Beale added that "I have never seen or heard of one stumbling, or even making a blunder." Whereas mules were desperate for water after a long trek, Beale humanized the camels by claiming that they seemed to view the mules' distress "with great contempt."[35]

Through stories and news dispatches, readers soon learned that camels were used in a number of desert areas across the American West. These became part of the folklore of the West and added to the region's mystique. An evocative illustration of "Camels in Nevada" (fig. 2-4) was published in *Harper's Weekly* as part of a series about the West that ran in the 1870s. In it, the gangly-looking creatures saunter through the desert guided and ridden by modern day "Bedouins" in the vicinity of Death Valley. Although this image seems Middle Eastern enough, with a rider perched high atop the camel, reports from this expedition reveal that the camels were used to haul supplies and equipment only, not for riding.[36] Those on the expedition had evidently learned by this time that riding a camel, either in the Middle East or in the Nevada desert, was no easy feat; most of the riding was done on the backs of trusty mules, and many simply preferred to walk rather than ride the cantankerous camels.

As historian Arthur Woodward noted, the camels used on the Nevada-California Border Survey of 1861 proved valuable transporters of all types of cargo in one of the most arid portions of the Intermountain West. Camels also found other uses and other owners, too. A telegraph operator reported that camels "owned by some Frenchmen in Virginia [City] . . . are now transporting salt from Humboldt [Nevada] to that place."[37] Camel mania gained strength during the 1860s. No sooner had the transcontinental railroad been completed than Costello's Great Show Circus Menagerie and Abyssinian Caravan arrived at Corinne City, Utah. The centerpiece in the show's advertisement was an Arab-garbed man holding the reins of a towering two-humped camel—about as fine a symbol for the exotic as could be imagined[38]—even though Arabs were (and are) more likely to ride dromedary camels instead.

But alas, despite this popular widespread interest in camels in the American West, they were met with opposition by many. As historian Woodward observed, camels "were cordially hated by owners of mule, ox, or horse drawn vehicles." He suggests this was because those frightened animals "took off across country in every direction when they caught a whiff of camel odor or met the ungainly creatures face to face unexpectedly on the road." Other factors for the camels' demise in the nineteenth-century West included the outbreak of the Civil War, lack of training on the part of those who took care of them, and "the inhumanity of man and his intolerance toward innovation plus the ready trigger fingers of the angered teamsters."

A look at legislation in the interior West confirms that the teamsters' concerns and threats were not idle. They badgered the Nevada legislature so effectively that the Silver State passed a measure making it "unlawful for the owner or owners of any camel or camels, dromedary or dromedaries, to permit them to run at large on or about the public roads or highways of this State." The law passed but was ultimately repealed in 1899, possibly to permit the camel races in Virginia City to be held.[39] This change of heart confirms the growing power of tourism in the West more than a century ago.

Despite their relatively short time in service, the camels of the West live on in legend. As some of them escaped captivity, reports of them were heard for many years. From Nevada and Utah to southern Arizona, miners and others rubbed their eyes (or put down their whiskey bottles) to see an astounding sight—wild camels sauntering across the American desert. Among the most interesting sightings, if it can be called that, is a Chemehuevi Indian basket featuring a single-humped Arabian camel—an interesting example of how an exotic element can become part of traditional crafts. A circus even rounded up some feral camels near Flagstaff, Arizona, in 1880 and put them to work under the big tent.[40]

Although unsuccessful, the camel experience in the interior West represented an effort to Orientalize the American West. Ironically, the only remaining physical evidence of the camels themselves in the West today exists in a museum that has the skeleton of the male camel named Said (sometimes written as Seid), who was killed by an older and evidently more ferocious camel named Touli in Los Angeles in 1861.[41]

Before leaving the western portion of the Great Basin, it is worth noting that near Frémont's pyramid is yet another symbol of Egypt, namely, a slightly less distinct feature that is interpreted as a sphinx by some. That patiently crouching creature, seemingly part human and part feline, is an enduring symbol of the power of ancient Egypt. In popular culture, the sphinx can signify any enigma or riddle. Some mysterious people can be enigmatic enough to warrant characterization as sphinxes, and when they are associated with the desert, that makes the association even more apt. In this regard, no denizen of the Nevada-California desert borderland was more enigmatic than Death Valley Scotty, the eccentric desert prospector and entrepreneur who bewildered America about a century ago. Always in the spotlight, Scotty was perennially involved in showy stunts and mysterious schemes, a number of them involving lost mines. When it was reported that Scotty's lost mine had been found, a *New York Times* editor was saddened because "once located on the map . . . it would quite likely be found that its treasure had a limit—that it was not the vestibule of Pluto's bullion chambers or propylaea of God Mammon's vaulted crypts, but just a hole in the ground, capable of petering out like the rest of them."[42] Actually, Scotty's own demystification was far less noble. As it turned out, his fortune was about to be revealed as a pyramid scheme. When the already legendary Scotty was exposed for his involvement in a fraudulent mining scheme, the *Los Angeles Evening News* could not resist satirizing him as the sphinx whose mystery had been solved, though even that bad publicity did not diminish his appeal among gullible investors (fig. 2-5).

Given Scotty's reputation as a wheeler-dealer in America's hottest and driest desert region, this cartoon's association of Scotty with the desert sphinx was

"SCOTTY" NO LONGER IS A MAN OF MYSTERY

Fig. 2-5. On March 19, 1906, the *Los Angeles Evening News* featured a cartoon showing Death Valley Scotty as the sphinx, complete with a vulture perched ominously on his hat.

perfect. It conflated the American West with Egypt by rendering one of the West's own most colorful characters with what is arguably the world's most ancient figure. By the turn of the twentieth century, then, this most arid and inhospitable section of the West could still claim a connection, albeit sometimes satirically, with ancient Egypt.

3

Chosen People, Chosen Land
Utah as the Holy Land

"Joseph Smith had a vision . . . was possessed of a vision, an expanding one of breathtaking scope and ambition for a chosen people."

Philip L. Barlow, 2007

To appreciate the power of Orient-inspired religion in John Charles Frémont's time, consider yet another part of the interior West—the eastern edge of the Great Basin, where the Great Salt Lake forms one of the West's most prominent landmarks. In the early 1840s, the entire Great Basin was the home of Native Americans, and no whites lived there. At exactly this time, however, this huge, stark, interior region was poised to become a place of refuge for a religious group seeking deliverance from tribulations more than one thousand miles to the east. They too would Orientalize the landscape. In the mid to late 1840s, Frémont's reports played a role in bringing the Great Basin to the attention of the public. Thousands of people read Frémont's reports and studied Charles Preuss's accompanying maps, but none more avidly than the Mormons.

The year in which Frémont named Pyramid Lake, 1844, was a tumultuous one for the Mormons. Despite their peripatetic, westward-moving nature, the Mormons had still not settled very far west of the Mississippi at that time. Controversial since their establishment of the Church of Jesus Christ of Latter-day Saints in 1830, the Mormons now settled into the heart of the North American continent, namely Missouri and then their new community of Nauvoo, Illinois, by 1840. They were part of the most successful and controversial religious drama on the American frontier—and in all of American history, for that matter. It began in the 1820s when a teenage boy scoured the Bible and his native New England for inspiration. Distressed by what he perceived to be organized religion's failures, Joseph Smith created his own; his vision had broad geographical consequences. Within fifteen years, Smith created a new church whose roots ran deeply into two different geographic locales: the fertile loam of the American frontier and the stony semiarid soil of the Holy Land. In his insightful book, *Joseph Smith: Rough Stone Rolling*, biographer Richard Lyman Bushman observes that Smith was more like a biblical-style prophet than any other religious figure America has ever produced.[1] That biblical style of leadership involved many references to Old World precedents, but this new religion was characteristically American in other ways—namely, its production of a new literature, its millennialism, and its near obsession with order and progress.

In his presidential address to the Mormon History Association in 2006, historian Phil Barlow noted that "Joseph Smith pre-empted Steven Spielberg by going 'back to the future' and then pulling it into the present." By this, Barlow meant that Smith was prone to interpret phenomena as "the ancient order of things"—an idea not original to Smith, but one associated with his religious beliefs. As Steven LeSueur observed, if Smith were given an "ancient manuscript," he would interpret it as "the writings of the ancient prophet Abraham." Similarly, Smith might interpret a human skeleton as "the skeleton of an ancient Nephite [one of the Israelite families of the Book of Mormon] warrior," a new place of settlement as "the Garden of Eden," and "a pile of stones" might be "an altar built by Adam to offer sacrifice to God."[2] Note that Smith could effortlessly shift things and places between hemispheres through this process. To Smith, the American landscape was haunted by the memories of Old World peoples who ventured here more than two thousand years before Columbus. The American frontier thus became the Near East, with its Garden of Eden, altars of Abraham, and the like. On the one hand this might seem to devalue America as a place. However, looked at in another light, it dignifies America as being the site where ancient events transpired. America, in other words, was the place where God spoke to man and, according to the Mormons, still does.

To the Mormons, the Garden of Eden figures in frontier American history. In trekking westward, the Mormons were fleeing oppression, but they had yet another goal. According to Joseph Smith, the place called Adam-ondi-Ahman was literally the Garden of Eden. Its location? Not in the Middle East, but rather in frontier Missouri! This Mormon belief that the site of the real Garden of Eden is located in America is significant for several reasons. It reaffirms and underlies the Mormons' belief that America was, and is, a special place where sacred biblical events took place. Then, too, it reaffirms the Mormons' nearly genetic patriotism—a belief in American exceptionalism that reaches to the core of their religion.

But it is the Mormon presence in Utah that will concern us here, for in a remarkably short time they would transform that area adjacent to the lofty Wasatch Range into both the Holy Land and New Zion. Even though the nineteenth-century Mormon appropriation of the North American West as a chosen land for a chosen people occurred quickly, it was a geographic metaphor long in the making. In fact, more than two centuries before the Mormons began moving west, metaphors equating North America with the Holy Land were common. They were especially well established in areas along the Eastern Seaboard—another reminder that the northern Europeans' Orientalization of the American West depended on the earlier acceptance of Orientalism in the American East. The foundation of the America-as-Israel myth can be traced to the early Puritans, many of whom interpreted their transatlantic voyages as analogous to the Israelites' miraculous passage through the parted Red Sea. This placed the British subjects who founded the American colonies in the 1600s in an ancient and heroic role. That process, of course, required specific places in which the drama could be enacted, or rather reenacted. Further building on the metaphor, American colonists conflated their new wilderness as a "desert" that could be transformed into "a land of milk and honey." The desert here on the East Coast was obviously metaphorical and not physical, for they had settled in a humid, forested land. Nevertheless, they were prone to see geographic parallels between the Eastern Seaboard and the Holy Land. This was largely based on that area's similar latitude to its Old World counterparts. Although the Eastern Seaboard's geographic parallels to the Holy Land were not strong, it was widely believed that North America itself was the New Zion. That belief was widespread in the new colonies, but no American region acted on it with more conviction than New England.[3]

From the outset, New England had a special character linked partly to the mind-set of its early settlers and partly to its peripheral geographic location. Biblical scholar and explorer Edward Robinson implied that New England had been branded with a biblical identity that kindled its religious zeal at every turn. As Robinson's biographer notes, "His yearning for the specific places mentioned in the Old and New Testaments derived from the ways in which his childhood in Connecticut was infused with an imaginary knowledge of Palestine and its neighbors, Syria and Egypt, so essential in the unfolding of sacred history."[4] The two things that stirred Robinson's imagination and intellect were a spate of biblical place-names on the land and New England's palpable heritage of Puritan religious history.[5] As a testimony to the belief that

Americans were creating a New Zion, place-names of biblical origin—Mount Zion, Bethlehem, Mount Horeb, Canaan, Salem—soon proliferated.

The Holy Land's past was appealing in this America-as-New-Zion myth, but it was the American future that offered particular appeal to a country inventing itself, or rather reinventing itself. By the early 1800s, in the Second Great Awakening, upstate New York's "Burned over District" became the nexus of considerable Protestant zeal and utopian thought. The district was perfectly positioned as a funnel through which a zealous New England culture would spread westward toward the Great Lakes. The western New England frontier was the birthplace of an American religion that would ultimately transform much of the Intermountain West into Zion. Created anew on an American stage and solidly based on Holy Land history and mythology, the Church of Jesus Christ of Latter-day Saints was strategically positioned in the nation's westward move. The Mormons' sequential migration from New England, to Ohio, to Missouri, and then to Illinois reveals their restless search for a promised land free of persecution.

Given Joseph Smith's passionate espousal of the new religion, which challenged the belief that the Bible was the final word of God, animosities increased, especially when non-Mormons began to resent the Mormons' growing political clout. In 1842, John C. Bennett offered a scathing, anti-Muslim-inspired opinion of Mormonism. In noting that "it is unnecessary to do more than to allude to the well-known history of Mohomet [sic], who, fatally for mankind, was enabled to carry out, to the fullest extent, schemes similar to those I have mentioned above," namely those of the Latter-day Saints, Bennett linked the Mormon faith with Islam. "There is no doubt," Bennett concluded, "that Joe Smith would, if he possessed the capacity, imitate the great Arabian imposter, even in his wars and conquests."[6]

This virulent prose was part of American Islamicism, which essentializes and oversimplifies Muslims and their faith.[7] Such prose not only Orientalized Joseph Smith and his followers but added fuel to the fire of anti-Mormon passions. Smith, now a charismatic presidential candidate, was jailed in June of 1844 for destroying the printing press of a rival newspaper.[8] Passions became incendiary, and a mob murdered Joseph Smith and his brother Hyrum by storming the jail in which they were being held. Significantly, that violent incident led to Smith's martyrdom and helped link his fate with that of other prophets, including John the Baptist and Jesus, who had died for their religious beliefs in the Holy Land.

Shortly thereafter, Brigham Young became president of the Mormon Church. A poorly educated man who possessed incredible talents as a leader and colonizer, Young sought a place where the Saints could worship and build a religious empire unmolested. Young and his fellow strategists considered a number of locations, including Texas, but words allegedly spoken by Joseph Smith before his own death—prepare to take the Saints to the fastness of the Rocky Mountains—placed the Far West at the top of the list. In 1847, just three years after Smith's death, an advance guard of the Saints reached the Intermountain West. Their long trek to the mountainous West across the Great Plains was interpreted as the Jewish Exodus.[9] Although that comparison was not altogether alien as applied to non-Mormon migrants either, the Mormons were not traveling as individuals. Rather, they were consciously traveling west as a people, and that makes their experience decidedly different from the typical frontier American experience. The collective nature of their migration burns it into the pages of history as a broader cultural drama—namely, a diaspora.

By July of 1847, the Mormons claimed almost the entire interior American West as their home, which they called Deseret, and they immediately began to put their distinctive stamp on the landscape.[10] Not coincidentally, one source of their information about this region came from none other than John Charles Frémont's 1845 report, which described what little was known about the geography of the Great Basin. Despite, or perhaps because of, Frémont's proclamation of the area as "desolate" and home to "miserable" Indians, the Mormons found the place attractive. Shortly after they first laid eyes on the Great Basin, it effectively became the center of their religion. Under Young's leadership, the area grew rapidly and was transformed in the popular imagination from "wilderness" into "Mormon Country" within a few short years.

Utah's physical landscape, particularly the topography of the area surrounding Utah Lake and the Salt Lake Valley, played an important role in the process of Orientalizing the Intermountain West. The desert-mountain setting here was so visually compelling that it became part of the equation. Traveler and convert alike usually reached the area by crossing a portion of the Rocky Mountains, which afforded a stunning view of the Great Salt Lake valley as their long journey neared an end. Psychologically, the juxtaposition of mountains and valleys—which is to say the embrace of the valley as a final destination framed by the inspirational heights of the mountains—was a perfect combination. Brigham Young himself is said to have seen the area in a dream before he arrived with an early party of Mormons in July of 1847. His certainty about the location seemed foreordained and hence prophetic, much like a verse in the Bible: "Go forth from your native land, and from your father's house, to the land that I will show you" (Genesis 12). This was a land seen in a vision, and by moving here, Brigham Young did more than claim a lightly populated place for the Latter-day Saints. He also gave an ethereal dimension to a physical landscape and by so doing rendered wilderness into home.

Upon reaching Salt Lake City about a dozen years after the Mormons had first arrived, British explorer Richard F. Burton remarked that "every meridional street is traversed on both sides by a streamlet of limpid water, verdure fringed, and gurgling with a murmur which would make a Persian Moollah long for improper drinks."[11] Burton could also write seriously about his emotional reactions to what he saw in Utah. Emotion and mysticism are important elements in a phenomenon like Orientalization, for romantic movements rely more on the heart than on reason. When even the normally objective Burton reached the point overlooking the Great Salt Lake valley in 1860, he confessed that he was moved to tears, as had been migrating Mormons, when his party gazed upon the valley below. By 1861, Burton had helped to spread the word about Utah's similarity to the Holy Land via his popular book *The City of the Saints*. This is remarkable, for it suggests that it took only about a decade for the new environment of Utah to be rendered, on both sides of the Atlantic Ocean, into its Old World counterpart. In other words, the Utah landscape took on the cachet of a sacred place as folkloric imagination became accepted history through the words of "witnesses," including writers, who confirmed its power as the Mormons' Promised Land.

This happened in steps. In 1849, Mormon apostle Orson Pratt prepared a tract for prospective converts in England who wanted to relocate to this new Jerusalem in the American West. Mormon leaders were no strangers to the real Holy Land, apostle Orson Hyde having visited Jerusalem in 1841. References to the Holy Land were evident in Pratt's publication *The New Jerusalem; or the Fulfillment of Ancient Prophecy*. Pratt claimed that the words in Isaiah—"O Zion, that bringest good tidings, get thee up into the high mountain" (40:9)—prophesied the Saints' move to Utah, which Pratt tellingly claimed was "one of the most wild, romantic and retired countries on [*sic*] the great western hemisphere." As historian Ernest Lee Tuveson observed, "The idea of 'retirement'—that Zion must establish itself and prepare for its work in complete isolation—supersedes any hope that the Saints would decisively influence the course of political affairs in the great world" despite the Mormons' earlier high profile in national politics. It was, after all, Joseph Smith who felt so strongly about outlawing slavery in the new western lands that as president of the United States he would have granted a petition to "possess the Territory of Oregon, or any other Contiguous Territory . . . that they might extend the mighty efforts and enterprise of a free people from the east to the west sea, and make the wilderness blossom as the rose." As fate would have it, not just any people, but the Mormons themselves, would take up that charge with religious zeal.[12]

The timing and geography here were pivotal. The millennial zeal that was felt nationwide in the early nineteenth-century United States coincided with both the westward-moving frontier and the Mormons' peculiar role in it. But an important distinction needs to be made. Although mainstream America's belief in Manifest Destiny evidently had strong religious underpinnings, its motivations were largely secular. However, the Mormons as a unified group acted it out in a religious context on the frontier. Their move to the Rocky Mountain West in the late 1840s was a singular event in not only American but world history.[13] The wholesale movement of this one Christian religious group reenacted the Jews' flight out of Egypt. By so doing, the Mormons recast a large portion of the American West as the Near East almost overnight.

In Utah, the Mormons found, or rather helped create, the perfect surrogate landscape in which to act out this drama. As art historian John Davis observes, "The singular landscape features surrounding them—such as the Great Salt Lake, with its evocation of the Dead Sea, or the ever present desert, which inspired such town names as Moab, Utah—only reinforced the connection and aided in the creation of their own 'sacred' space."[14] As sociologist Thomas F. O'dea observed more abstractly half a century ago, the Mormons "feel the West to be their own peculiar homeland, prepared for them by the providential action of Almighty God, and its landscape is intimately associated with their self consciousness and identified with their past."[15]

The Mormons are associated above all with making the desert blossom like the rose. This sentiment and phrasing is of course from Isaiah, but such a transformation is also described in Isaiah-like prose in the Mormon book Doctrine and Covenants: "And the Lord, even the Savior, shall stand in the midst of his people, and shall reign over all flesh. . . . And in the barren deserts there shall come forth pools of living water; and the parched ground shall no longer be a thirsty land."[16] Like Isaiah, the Mormon passage reveals that parched land will become well watered. Note, however, a significant difference between Isaiah and the Mormon version. To begin with, the Mormon version is millennial; that is, it references the presence of a savior. Note, too, that the Lord's people are also mentioned in the Mormon passage. By these additions, the Mormon version of Isaiah is updated into the latter days and becomes very specific as to the actual people who will be affected. It is, in other words, a prescription for Mormon empowerment in the Intermountain West yet was written well before the Mormons ever migrated there. That alone gave it the ring of prophecy to the Mormons.

At first, the Saints interpreted this passage as metaphorical, but after they arrived in Utah, it became literal. In April of 1853, Orson Hyde delivered a prayer just after the northeast cornerstone was laid at the Mormon Temple in Salt Lake City. Hyde began the prayer with a reference to the spiritual importance of the temple itself but soon focused on the geographical setting. He thanked God for "thy manifold blessings and mercies extended unto us—that since we have been compelled to flee to the valleys and caves of the mountains and hide ourselves in thy secret chambers, from the face of the serpent or dragon of persecution, red with the blood of the Saints and martyrs of Jesus, thou has caused the land to be fruitful—the wilderness and desert to rejoice and blossom as the rose."[17]

In 1865, George Albert Smith delivered a speech in St. George, Utah, in which he noted that "flood water" could irrigate crops, including wheat fields and new vineyards. Late in this speech, Smith observed that the Mormons in St. George, despite settling a barren desert environment, had "the place looking like the Garden of Eden." Smith also agreed with Elder Snow that "a people possessed of such great energy aided by the ready co-operation of their brethren in the north, are bound to conquer that desert and not only make it blossom as the rose, but make it one of the most delightful regions of the earth."[18] Here again the words of Isaiah are effortlessly applied to the Mormons' Great Basin setting. The Latter-day Saints are the beneficiaries of both a literary tradition and a work ethic, and God has paid them handsomely for their belief.

Just two years later, in 1867, Orson Pratt observed that although the ancient church had failed to fulfill prophecies, the Latter-day Saints were already doing just that. They were, in Pratt's words, fulfilling both ancient and latter-day prophecies—commanded by God to "go from all these nations [of the Old World] to the great western hemisphere, locate yourselves on the high portions of the North American Continent in the midst of the mountains, and be gathered into one." Leaving little doubt as to which book in the Bible had been the catalyst, Pratt added: "The Prophet Isaiah, in the 35th chapter, says 'The wilderness and the solitary place shall be glad for them, and the desert shall rejoice and blossom as the rose.'"[19]

By 1870, Pratt reflected on the changes that had occurred since the Latter-day Saints first arrived in Utah a generation earlier. Again referencing Isaiah, he observed, "After we are gathered, the desert is to rejoice and blossom as the rose," adding that he often thought of this passage as he witnessed Utah's many orchards and gardens blossoming in spring. As Pratt put it, "Every one knows that fruitful as it now is, when we came here it was called a desert." Sensing that some might doubt this, Pratt cited two types of evidence. First, he urged people to "go to the old maps, and you will find this section of the country laid down as 'The Great American Desert.'" Second, he cited the actual level of the Great Salt Lake, whose waters had risen "some ten or twelve feet above the surface as it existed in 1847, when I first saw it." As it was prophesied, Pratt added, "Streams have broken out in the desert, and waters in the wilderness." This may be connected to the secular mid-nineteenth century myth that "rainfall follows the plow," but Pratt recognized this as part of the predictions that Isaiah and David mention, adding, "the waters, rivers and springs that should break out to water the barren, thirsty land! The parched ground shall become a pool, and the thirsty land springs of water."[20] As geographer Richard Jackson noted, the Mormons here appear to be revising history to make their act of settling this part of the West more heroic.[21] Throughout the 1860s and 1870s, Mormon leaders used similar language to claim that the Latter-day Saints were becoming successful, thereby confirming their status as the chosen people.[22] These chosen people had thus transformed the desert wilderness into their promised land, a veritable Garden of Eden. The fact that this occurred about three millennia *after* Isaiah likewise confirmed not only the Latter-day Saints' geographic mission but also their actions in a preordained time—the actual latter days themselves.

The Mormons almost instantaneously branded Utah as the Holy Land, and place naming was part of the process. It is ironic that the details surrounding Brigham Young's proclamation "This is the place" are known (and often recited) for the general site of Salt Lake City, but there is no record of exactly who named the river connecting freshwater Utah Lake with the waters of the Great Salt Lake the "Jordan." An early reference to Utah's Jordan River is found in an official message that was provided to Mormons in England and Council Bluffs, which is to say, those Saints bound for the Great Basin. The message noted that the area "will require irrigation to promote vegetation, though there are many small streams emptying in from the mountains, and the western Jordan (Utah outlet) passes through from south to north."[23] The term "western Jordan" certainly confirms that the Mormons imagined the Utah river in terms of its eastern counterpart. The ultimate source, of course, is biblical. Utah's Jordan River does much the same thing as its namesake, which connects the fresh waters of the Sea of Galilee with the salty waters of the Dead Sea. The Bible mentions the River Jordan and its valley about two hundred times, mostly as a border between peoples. Moreover, the border also separates a relatively well-watered land to the west and the much drier lands (Canaan, for example) to the east. The Mormons must have been aware of that geographical distinction as they looked westward over the valley from their relatively well-watered site at Salt Lake City to the rather barren slopes of the Oquirrh Mountains. To those living an almost biblical drama, that river would logically be called the Jordan. Across it lay an absolute wilderness, while on the Salt Lake City side, which is to say the Jerusalem side, the land would be bountiful, as confirmed by the denser vegetation on the slopes of the Wasatch Range.

But the river serves not only as a landmark but also as a source of water, and that water has two very different purposes. First, it is a source of life, as people, animals, and crops depend on it. Second, and equally important for peoples of faith, the Jordan River serves a spiritual purpose. Like its prototype in the Holy Land, which had been used for Christian baptisms since the time of Christ, and later during the Crusades, immersion in this new Jordan River represented spiritual renewal. Early descriptions and photographs reveal that Utah's Jordan River served a similar purpose to that of the River Jordan. Although baptism in rivers was common in the United States, in this case it likely helped further equate the river in Utah with its counterpart in the Holy Land. Moreover, the fact that this river was in America—a land sacred to the Mormons as a location where Jesus had once actually preached—endorsed it as part of the *New* Zion.

In addition to sacred waters, topography itself branded the Mormons' new homeland as sacred ground. In the 1840s and 1850s, with persecution such a dominant theme, the mountainous setting sequestered the Saints from their sometimes violent detractors. So, too, did the desent itself. Speaking in Utah, Mormon leader George A. Smith revealed how the Mormons' identification with Israel perfectly matched their new home in the Intermountain West: "I thank the Lord for these deserts, rocks and mountains, for they may be a protection to us." Quoting, or rather paraphrasing, the Bible, Smith continued, "And while our enemies are trying to exterminate us, Israel dwells safely in the tops of the mountains."[24] As the Old Testament had prophesied: "The house of the Lord shall be established in the top of the mountains."[25] This difference was acted out as a separation from non-Mormons, who were labeled Gentiles.

The Mormons themselves used this theme throughout much of their nineteenth-century history.[26] As early as the 1840s, they "took on the role of fostering the Jewish revitalization of Jerusalem, the other heavenly city." There was, of course, an ulterior motive here that related to scripture: "Like many dissenting religious sects, they [the Mormons] felt that the restoration of the Jews to the Holy Land was a necessary prelude to the return of the Messiah."[27]

And yet something else was also occurring. Through the process of cultural identity formation, the Mormons became surrogate kin to the Jews of the Old World. That primal Judeo-Christian tribal identity is more than folkloric, in fact, because the Mormons, like all Christians, can ultimately trace their cultural roots and religious ideology to a source in the Middle East. But the early Utah Mormons went further into the Holy Land for inspiration than most Protestant sects. That the Mormons felt themselves to be divinely inspired to live out Exodus as recipients of the Promised Land in the Intermountain American West is quite instructive. It reminds us of the power of the human mind to draw comparisons to sacred places that linger in the memory and are resurrected, first through human imagination, and then through the application of considerable labor, in lands far away from their originals. Another geographic factor helped the Mormons make the transition. The Mormons' Israel is associated with the wilderness—that is, a place like that remote location where Moses and other prophets were both inspired and tempted. It is this connection that made the desert frontier the perfect place for Mormons—and Mormons the perfect people for the desert frontier.

The Mormons moved west with an almost insatiable zeal for new experiences in lands that were increasingly distant from their birthplaces and alien to their experiences. They viewed themselves as "pilgrims marching to a promised land, the center of which is a Zion, a New Jerusalem."[28] The search for a place of perfection, a place that God can look upon with pleasure, is deeply embedded in Mormon ideology. That place would be a holy city, or rather many holy cities, but there would be one crowning city at the center of that empire. Ironically, however, once that city was founded, it would become "a kind of world center to which the scattered peoples of Israel (more strictly, of Judah—that is, Jews descended from that tribe) were to return."[29]

This connection plays out in an interesting way when Native Americans are brought into the picture. If, according to Mormon ideology and the beliefs of many other nineteenth-century observers, Native Americans were actually remnants of the Lost Tribes of Israel, then that cast them into the role of Orientals. On the American frontier, the Mormons moved westward only to find the East, in a manner of speaking, when they got there. American Orientalism, in other words, is not only a transoceanic phenomenon but also a characteristically nativistic phenomenon. By reaching the continental interior (either the Garden of Eden site in Missouri, or later the Salt Lake Valley as the New Zion), a group of Americans found a surrogate not only for the landscape of the Middle East but also for its native peoples.[30]

The belief that Native Americans represent lost tribes who scattered across the earth following the Diaspora was an idea whose time had come. The belief reveals that Americans were engaged in a dialogue about the origins of a people who seemed exotic as well as familiar.[31] Who were these Indians? More to the point, how and where did they originate? In words that seemed right out of the Bible in some places and yet radically different and new in places, the Book of Mormon answered questions about racial makeup and migration. It claimed that the Indians were descendents of the Lost Tribes who left the Holy Land in about 600 BC and traveled for thousands of miles, finally landing in America. Mormons called these people Lamanites. With this declaration, the Mormons solved a long-standing theological dilemma. The Mormons, however, were not the first to draw such conclusions. As early as the 1520s, the Spaniard Pedro Mártir de Anghiera had concluded that the Indians had been sent to the New World by King Solomon, while later in the century Juan Suárez de Peralta stated that they were remnants of the ten Lost Tribes of Israel.[32] Robert F. Berkhofer Jr. addressed "Christian Cosmogony and the Problem of Indian Origins" in his seminal work *The White Man's Indian* (1978). As Berkhofer concluded, "A scriptural solution to the problem of origins demanded efforts to plug up the loopholes left in the Mosaic account."[33]

In the nineteenth century, many people saw similarities between the Indians and people in the Middle East. Their dark skin color and different dress may have been reasons why the American Indian was often conflated with tribal peoples of the Middle East. As early as the 1830s, John Lloyd Stephens commented that a Bedouin chief he met in Arabia reminded him of a "wild, savage, and lawless" Native American.[34] If Stephens could opine about such things in the 1830s, why couldn't Mark Twain three decades later? In his classic *The Innocents Abroad* (1869), Twain described Arab women and children as "worn and sad, and distressed with hunger." As Twain succinctly put it, "They reminded me much of Indians, did these people."[35] Twain was in a good position to use this analogy, for he had considerable experience with Native Americans from his sojourn in the Intermountain West earlier in the decade.

In times of frenetic mobility and changing social relationships, including increasing democratization, answering troubling questions about the origins of Native Americans was not an idle pastime but an essential endeavor. According to the Book of Mormon, Native Americans had a direct line of descent from the house of Israel. However, having fallen away from the values of Judeo-Christian religion, the Indians lost their fair features. Nevertheless, these same Indians could be forgiven if they embraced the Mormon faith. In one fell swoop, then, such beliefs explained race (the Indians had lost their physical traits by being exposed to a harsh environment but could now get their whiteness back), reconstructed a genealogy for the first Americans, and also redeemed the word of God (who had sent colonists westward to bring that word to these pagans). One of the Lamanites who became a Mormon was Wakara (aka Walkara or Walker), a Ute who served as a military leader to his people. In addition to being known as "Napoleon of the Desert," Wakara was also called "Soldan [Sultan] of the Red Paynims."[36] In the Mormon view, Indians are conceptualized as being from the Middle East originally—hence, they are vestiges of Eastern tribes. If this has a ring of irony, it should, for it means that Anglo-Americans are actually kin to the Native Americans, and that the latter can become the former through the process of cultural assimilation. Moreover, Native Americans purportedly have a more direct line of descent from the house of Israel, so ironically, less pure-blooded people (European Americans) redeem the purer through assimilation.

Mind-boggling? Actually, it becomes even more intriguing when one realizes that the Mormons themselves were figuratively transformed into peoples from, or of, the Middle East (Israel). By adopting the identity of Israelites, the Mormons become the Oriental "other" despite the fact that they were white northern Europeans—and Christians. As if this were not complex enough, consider this: if, as is often noted, the Mormons assumed an Israelite identity so completely that they transformed Jews into Gentiles, that occurred because they so effectively transformed themselves into ancient Israelites.

The Mormons' increasing talk of resistance to US authorities, coupled with their practice of polygamy, made them an easy target. Such determination gave Mormons an Old Testament (and even Koranic) quality of ancient desert patriarchs. When critics complained that the Mormons enslaved their women, they used the same logic as Stanley Lane-Poole, who wrote that "the degradation of women in the East is a canker that begins its destructive work early in childhood, and has eaten into the whole system of Islam."[37] Even that admirer of the Mormons Richard Burton observed that "'Mormon' had in fact become a word of fear; the Gentiles looked upon the Latter Day Saints much as our crusading ancestors regarded the 'Hashshashiyun,' [i.e., assassins] whose name indeed, was almost enough to frighten them." Deftly weaving Mormon patriarchs into an Old World desert kingdom tapestry, Burton further noted that "Mr. Brigham Young was the Shaykh-el-Jebel, the Old Man of the Hill redivivus, [while] Messrs. Kimball and Wells were the chief of his Fidawin, and 'Zion on the tops of the mountains' formed a fair representation of Alamut."[38] In Burton's mind, the Mormons had essentially become Arab Muslims.

Small wonder that the Mormons were so easy for other non-Mormon peoples to Orientalize. Frontiers are traditionally places where identities are in flux, and this conundrum of Mormon-as-Israelite (or Muslim) proves that maxim several times over. Oleg Grabar observed how complex things were becoming in the nineteenth century as American Orientalist identities were being created. As he put it, "The complexity of modern American culture is such that there are many 'others' in its psychological makeup and that the 'others' of some are the 'us' of others."[39]

The process of Orientalizing the American West required that both the physical landscape and its peoples be rendered as exotic. One pro-Mormon observer used vegetation to describe the Mormons and Indians metaphorically. Although he despised the extensive cover of sagebrush and other native desert vegetation in the Great Basin, British travel writer Phil Robinson rhapsodized about lucerne, which was (and is) also known by its Arabic name *alfalfa* in the American West. Robinson noted that the Mormons cultivated this forage crop with considerable skill. It enabled the Saints to raise fine livestock that provided meat and cheese. "Indeed," Robinson observed, "as the Mormons say, the territory could hardly have held its own had it not been for this wonderful plant." Robinson was not content to stop with the economic aspects of alfalfa, however, for he fancied a racial comparison here that he employed with abandon: "Once get it well started (and it will grow apparently anywhere) the 'alfalfa' defies the elements [because it] becomes aggressive, and, like the white races, begins to encroach upon, dominate over, and finally extinguish the barbarian weeds, its wild neighbours." As if this were not explicit enough, Robinson then added that "fences and such devices cannot of course keep it within its bounds, so the Lucerne overflows its limits at every point, comes down the railway bank, sprouts up in tufts on the track, and getting across into the Scythian barbarism of the opposite hill-side, advances as with a Macedonian phalanx to conquest and universal monarchy." This is Robinson at his most effusive, florid, and Orientalist, making allusions to not only clashes of cultures but ancient Near Eastern history. So rapt was Robinson about the dominance of lucerne over barbarian weeds—which is to say Mormons over natives—that he confidently but erroneously predicted that Utah "in time . . . will become the Lucerne State."[40]

Robinson's *Sinners and Saints* (1883) reveals much about the process by which both landscapes and peoples of the New World were Orientalized. Sometimes Robinson's references are direct; for example, he describes the barren countryside south of Manti, Utah, as "white with desperate patches of 'saleratus,' the saline efflorescence with which agriculture in this Territory is for ever at war, and resembling in appearance, taste, and effects the 'reh' of the Gangetic plains." Note that Robinson here relies on more than one sense (appearance, taste, and so forth) to describe the countryside, a not so subtle way of reminding the reader that Robinson himself has personally experienced the original place and is thus qualified to comment. "Here, as in India," Robinson continues, "irrigation is the only known antidote, and once [the farmers] wash it out of the soil and get crops growing . . . the enemy retires."[41] In other places, Robinson describes the beauty of the landscape using that same comparative and Orientalist model. For example, in describing the hilly country along the Sevier River's "curiously fantastic path," he notes that the dry landscape changes as "verdur creeps over the plains, and vegetation steals on to the hill-sides, and then suddenly as if for a surprise, the complete beauty of Long Valley bursts upon the traveller." This area, Robinson exclaims, "rivals in its beauty the scenery of Cashmere."[42] The reader here senses that Robinson has seen the real Cashmere (Kashmir), and is thus qualified to make that comparison.

Although there are many geographic and cultural differences between the Holy Land and Utah, a culture eager to seek Old World connections found it easy to blur these. Consider again how vegetation could serve as a metaphor for a religious figure from the Holy Land. In the southern Great Basin and Mojave Desert, the bristly *Yucca brevifola* tree was often mistaken for more familiar types of vegetation. For example, it was commonly called a "Prickley Pine" by early Mormon travelers. Addison Pratt described it in 1849 as "a Solitary looking vegitable [*sic*], of the prickley pear order, called prickley pine, that are scattered over those deserts, growing from 3 to 30 feet high." In that same year, George Q. Cannon noted that his group encountered "Prickly Pine as large round the butt as a man's body," adding that "it resembled Pine apples [in] the leaves [and] the bark was a good deal like oak bark."[43] Many people in the nineteenth century, however, considered them to be palm trees or even palmettos. As late as about 1930, a postcard noted that "the Joshua Palm abounds throughout certain sections of the Great American Desert, and once seen, is a sight rarely forgotten."[44]

There is nothing remotely like this plant in the Middle East. And yet in a widely told story, the American yucca tree was transformed into a biblical character through a process involving both folklore and popular culture. Mormon missionary Elisha Hunt, traveling across the Mojave Desert in 1851, is said to have told his followers, "Look, Brethren, these green trees are lifting their arms toward heaven in supplication. We shall call them Joshua Trees!"[45] (fig. 3-1). The Mormons appear to have named the Joshua tree, but this act

Photograph by Garry Blake

Fig. 3-1. Native to the Mojave Desert, the Joshua tree (Yucca brevifolia), or "Praying Tree" as it was sometimes called, conflates prickly desert vegetation with a biblical prophet.

by Hunt is likely apocryphal. It first came to us in the twentieth century, reinforced by Maureen Whipple's *The Giant Joshua* (1942).

In her later book *This is the Place: Utah* (1945), Whipple observed that Mormon country had an Old World religious stamp, what she described as the "Biblical peace of tiny green oases set against the savage violence of the hills."[46] The reference, of course, is pure Old Testament, wherein the desert and its wilderness challenges contrast with the order of the sedentary oasis.

If Salt Lake City represented New Jerusalem to many people, then a new Sodom and a new Gomorrah had to be nearby. In Utah, that equivalent of "sin city" was located near the shore of the Great Salt Lake in much the same position as the fabled Sodom and Gomorrah bore to Jerusalem. That place was Corinne, a veritable den of iniquity. How did such a place arise in Mormon Utah? Generally, mining towns might fill the bill, but in this case the railroad was the facilitator. As the transcontinental railroad neared completion in 1869, Corinne blossomed several miles northwest of patriarchally named (and all Mormon) Brigham City. Corinne was named after a woman with that name, but exactly who she was remains a mystery.[47] Railroad historian Lucius Beebe called Corinne "the new scarlet woman of the Utah desert." Certainly, Corinne had earned its wicked reputation, for it was a far more "wide-open" town than Salt Lake City. Another historian calls it "The City of the Ungodly." Actually, some observers believed that Corinne's strategic location positioned it to be "the Queen city of the Great Basin," perhaps even the capital of Utah. That, however, was not in the cards.[48] Although Corinne never grew to become the prominent city hoped for by its promoters, neither did it meet the wholesale destruction meted out by God to Sodom and Gomorrah. As a reminder that all things change, though, Corinne ultimately became a predominantly Mormon town and today presents a completely bucolic image. In other words, the "sinner" became a "saint"—in more ways than one.[49]

To many observers, Salt Lake City in the early 1880s represented both the West and the East. The Mormon city was, according to Phil Robinson, "Oriental in its general appearance, English in its details." But some of those details could have an Eastern quality, as some perceived them. When the Mormons encountered a scarcity of building materials for their new homes in Great Salt Lake City, they used adobe. As George A. Smith put it, because "the children of Israel built of sun-dried bricks we have done the same."[50] Building on the Oriental theme in words reminiscent of Burton's flowery Orientalist prose, Robinson observed that Salt Lake City was "the young rival of Mecca, the Zion of the Mormons, the Latter-Day Jerusalem." Not content to end his comparisons there, Robinson added that Salt Lake City was a place where "Shepherd Kings" governed "the place of the tabernacle of an ancient prophet-ruled Theocracy." Affected by the Orientalism of his times, Robinson recognized that the Mormons' difficulties with Gentiles placed Salt Lake City as "a beautiful Goshen of tranquility in the midst of a troublous Egypt."[51]

In another example of just how quickly landscapes as well as peoples may become surrogates for their originals elsewhere, the comparison of Salt Lake City with Jerusalem was made very soon after the Mormons arrived. It was

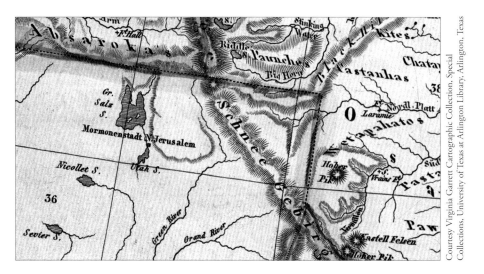

Fig. 3-2. In this detail from F. W. Streit's map titled *Die Vereinigten Staaten von Nord-Amerika* (Leipzig, 1851), Mormonstadt, the "Mormon City" (Salt Lake City), is also called "New Jerusalem."

made in writing and in images, including maps. On the German map entitled *Die Vereinigten Staaten von Nord-Amerika* by Dr. F. W. Streit (Leipzig, 1851), Salt Lake City is indicated as "Mormonenstadt N[eu] Jerusalem"[52] (fig. 3-2). The "Mormon City" lies west of the Schnee Gebirge (i.e., the Snowy [later Rocky] Mountains), and the Gr. Salz. S. (Great Salt Sea, i.e., Great Salt Lake) lies to its northwest. The word *sea* here may suggest this body of water's similarity to the Dead Sea far better than *lake*. However, that reference to New Jerusalem is particularly evocative for several reasons, not the least of which is Jerusalem's central location in Judeo-Christian religion. As a community steeped in religious history and mysticism, Jerusalem had been visited by Christian pilgrims since the second century AD. Small wonder that it resonates as strongly to Christians as Mecca does to Muslim pilgrims. Both represent birthplaces, so to speak, in the lives of religions.

In describing Utah in terms of the Holy Land, many travelers were influenced by popular literature about that region. Consider, for example, the scientist Howard Stansbury. After months of experiencing the desolate area around the Great Salt Lake in 1849, Stansbury sought a way to declare that Salt Lake City's setting, or "studding" as he called it, was a joy for the weary traveler to behold. Stansbury claims that "this beautiful city with noble trees, will render it, by contrast with the surrounding regions, a second 'Diamond of the Desert,' in whose welcome shade, like the solitary Sir Kenneth and the princely Iderim, the pilgrim, wayworn, and faint, may repose his jaded limbs and dream of the purling brooks and waving woodlands he has left a thousand miles behind him."[53] For those familiar with Stansbury, this is about as poetic as he ever got. Note, however, that the sobriquet "Diamond of the Desert" that Stansbury used is a literary reference to a life-giving spring in the Holy Land encountered by Sir Kenneth and Iderim—two of Sir Walter Scott's memorable characters in the popular novel about the Crusades called *The Talisman* (1827). Here, in Scott's own words, is the prototype description that influenced generations of writers:

> The Christian Knight . . . said to his pagan associate of the journey, 'I would I knew the name of this delicious fountain, that I might hold it in my grateful remembrance.'
> 'It is called in the Arabic language,' answered the Saracen, 'by a name which signifies the Diamond of the Desert.'[54]

With this literary reference, we see the power of a writer of fiction to influence Stansbury the writer of scientific literature. Significantly, John Lloyd Stephens had also used and credited Scott's term "Diamond of the Desert" in describing how he longed for relief from "the intense heat and scorching sands" in Egypt.[55] Through Scott's and Stephens's passages, we better understand the process by which Stansbury the scientist came under the spell of both the real Mormon city and the fictional and travel literature about the Holy Land. Like the prototype Jerusalem, the Mormons' Great Salt Lake City was an oasis adjacent to burning desert.

By the 1850s, Mormon settlements had spread to a large portion of the Intermountain West. Salt Lake City was now the hearth of Mormon culture, but the Saints' presence was felt as far away as San Bernardino (California) and Genoa, a small community near present-day Carson City, Nevada. Nineteenth-century travelers to Utah not only commented on how effectively the Mormon settlements utilized scarce resources but also cast those settlements in the context of another arid region—the Middle East—that was never far from their thoughts. Comparisons between the Mormon West and the Holy Land were inevitable for several reasons. First, many had read about places of stark desert and rugged topography in the Bible and thought the Mormons' new homeland a natural fit.

Second, as explorer Burton had observed, the Mormons' polygamy, temple worship, and desert setting conspired to impart both an Old Testament and an Islamic character to people and place here. Burton made the connection from his extensive travels in the Middle East and his whirlwind tour through the Victorian West. As a renowned explorer, Burton spoke, or rather

wrote, with considerable authority. In 1861, for example, Burton noted the
Mormons' belief that Salt Lake City was, as he put it, "New Hierosolyma, or
Jerusalem, alias Zion on the tops of the mountains, the future city of Christ."
With the Orient he knew so well firmly in mind, Burton noted that Mormon
"pilgrims" traveling to this city, "like the Hajiis of Meccah and Jerusalem, give
vent to emotions long pent up with their bosoms by sobs and tears, laughter
and congratulations, psalms and hysterics."[56] The place was sacred enough that
it made an impression on people coming and going. Leaving Salt Lake City
in the 1850s, Mormon leader Hosea Stout observed that a "light cloudy fog
rested on it, in which we could see President Young's House, like Solomon's
Temple in the midst of the glory of God."[57]

Burton, of course, was at the forefront of this Orientalist trend. During
his travels in the Middle East, Burton went undercover to better understand
Islamic traditions and tenets. Like many Orientalist-inspired European travelers of the period, Burton often dressed in the style of Middle Eastern desert
dwellers; covering himself with flowing garments, he wore sandals and armed
himself with the same weapons used by natives. Photographs and paintings of
Burton show him as almost indistinguishable from a Middle Easterner. In one
image, he is called El-hadj Abdullah (The Pilgrim Servant of God), no doubt
a reference to his very risky trip to Mecca disguised as an Arab. In others, he
is dressed like a half-Arab and half-Persian, further adding to his mystique
and authority. It was, after all, Burton who famously—or rather infamously—
endorsed polygamy as a viable form of marriage (fig. 3-3).

American writers also had plenty to say about the Mormons' "peculiar" type of marriage. Mark Twain, who had considerable experience with
the polygamous Mormons, drew a snide East-West allusion in *The Innocents
Abroad*. As only Twain could, he noted that although polygamy was prohib-
ited for the common man in Turkey, "they say the Sultan has eight hundred
wives." This, Twain opined, "almost amounts to bigamy." Not content to let
things rest there, Twain added that "it makes our cheeks burn with shame to
see such a thing permitted here in Turkey" while "we do not mind it so much
in Salt Lake, however."[58] For his part, the ever-humorous Twain stated that
Mormon men should actually be commended for marrying so many wives.
Why? According to Twain, Mormon women were so homely that a real social
service was being performed by these brave Mormon men who married them
when, presumably, no one else would.

Mormons took much criticism in the mid to late nineteenth century.
Some writers criticized the Mormons caustically, while others tried humor
to get their point across. Of all the Europeans who cast the Mormons in an

Author's collection

Fig. 3-3. In this hand-colored image of renowned Orientalist Richard
F. Burton, ca. 1848, the British explorer wears the turban and robes
of a half-Arab and half-Persian from Bushire.

Orientalist light, the Frenchman Albert Robida (1848–1926) was one of the
most humorous. Robida was an adventure and travel writer as well as an illustrator. His *Voyages très extraordinaires de Saturnin Farandoul* (1885) features
an image of a train carrying sailors departing for the city of the Mormons that
is rendered with classic Orientalist flourish (fig. 3-4). As the passenger train
careens across a tall, curving trestle, sailors clad in Middle Eastern style costumes lounge on the cars' roofs as they casually smoke long pipes in the fashion of the Orient. This is one of the scenes in an absurd tale about the adventurous Farandoul, who learns about the Mormons' polygamy and decides
to become a Mormon in order to marry several women who will be provided to him by Brigham Young. Farandoul has a political as well as personal
motive. He claims that Turkey had declined after polygamy was denied to

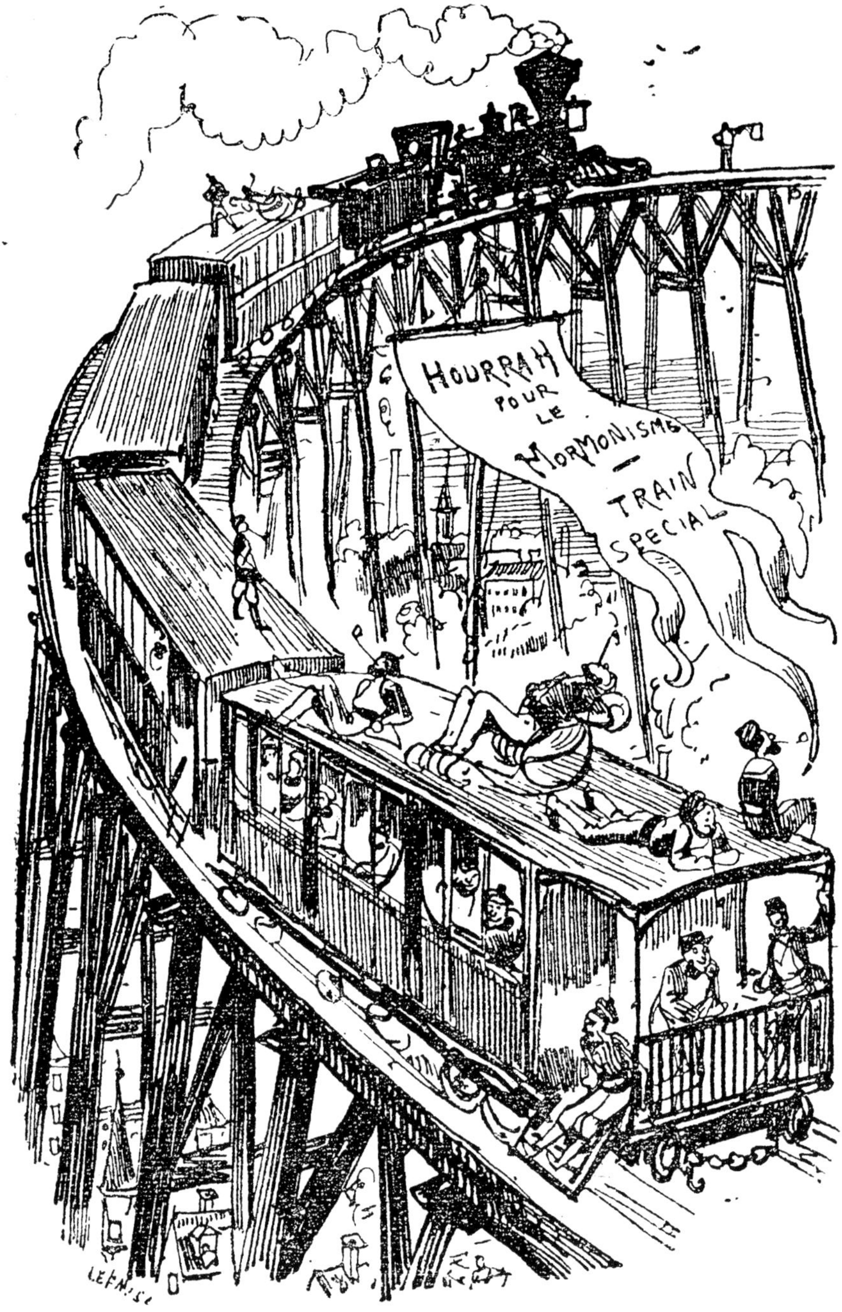

Author's collection

Fig. 3-4. This humorous illustration of a train departing for the city of the Mormons appeared in Albert Robida's *Voyages Très Extraordinaires* (1885).

all men except "the great statesmen, the pashas and the sultans." The women Farandoul marries are from different ethnic groups and constitute a nearly perfect multicultural harem. The list includes French, Polish, American, Parisian, Mexican, Peruvian, German, Russian, and Chinese women, and even one "Negress, age and place of birth unknown." Surrounded by these beautiful, adoring women, the ecstatic Farandoul finds immediate—though short-lived—bliss in Utah.[59]

Voyages très Extraordinaires is delightfully satirical, and it joins a long list of writings that poked fun at the Mormons and denigrated their seemingly Old World Eastern beliefs. And yet, for all the detractors and humorists who criticized Mormon decadence in Utah, the Mormons had their supporters. Burton was one of their admirers, and even the usually caustic Phil Robinson praised them on occasion. Other observers noted the Saints' honesty, integrity, spirituality, intelligence, and so on. It is safe to say that the Orientalists who wrote about Utah were—like all Orientalists—of varied backgrounds and had varied agendas. Sometimes even the same writer could be positive or negative about the Mormons depending on which trait he or she selected for scrutiny.

But the Mormon presence above all positioned the Intermountain West as a place where Old World religion was thriving, and this calls for a brief digression into how Orientalism generally builds on religious themes. The tendency to experience the American West as the Near East is closely related to the way Europeans and Americans conceptualized the real Near East as sacred ground. Art historian Brian T. Allen observes that nineteenth-century "American treatments of the Near East and Middle East, amazingly diverse in subject matter, were generally very positive and so various that it is difficult to tag them as ideological." As Allen put it, "American Orientalism was a distinct phenomenon with some European currents but ultimately unresponsive to formulas based on the schemes of domination or denigration first identified by [Edward] Said." As proof, Allen identifies several themes in American Orientalist paintings, most of which emphasize the continuity between America and the Bible lands. An important theme in paintings by Frederick Church, for example, is similarities rather than differences, with, as Allen put it, "the similarities arising from the American world's descent from an older order of chosen people."[60] Allen concludes that American Orientalists' "basic impulse seems to have been to make the Islamic world more familiar rather than more exotic or even inferior through their concentration on its connection to American spiritual traditions and their view of Islamic subjects through the lens of American iconographic traditions."[61]

The process by which Utah's physical landscape was configured into the Holy Land by those who experienced it about a century and a half ago depended in large measure on their seeing analogies between this new place and the familiar places in the Bible. Gold Rush–bound travelers like Franklin Langworthy were well aware that by entering Utah Territory, they were experiencing a drama that was both very new and very old. As he observed the Great Salt Lake, he wrote that this huge body of salty water "in some of its characteristics, bears a striking resemblance to the Lake of Asphalts, or the Dead Sea in Palestine, upon which once stood the cities of Sodom and Gomorrah."[62] The comparison of the Great Salt Lake with the Dead Sea was very common, as writers often drew comparisons between both "brooding" and "dead" bodies of salty water. In his diary entry of August 5, 1864, Howard Stillwell Stanfield noted that "I had set this day apart for the especial purpose of using it for taking a trip to Salt Lake the dead Sea of the Saints."[63]

To better understand this, we can deconstruct the poetic prose of Emmanuel Henri Domenech. Born in France and ordained as a Catholic priest in Texas in 1848, Domenech claimed that he traveled extensively in the West, as documented in his popular book *Seven Years' Residence in the Great Deserts of North America* (published in London in 1860). Two years later, likely as a result of its success in both England and the United States, Domenech published a French translation called *Voyage Pittoresque dans les grands déserts du Nouveau monde* (1862).[64] Of the Great Salt Lake, which is one of the numerous aquatinted images in his beautifully illustrated book (fig. 3-5), Domenech had much to say. He observed, or rather intoned, that "the malediction of heaven seems to weigh heavily on this solitude, which reminds one of the desolate shores of the Dead Sea, where Sodom and Gomorrah were destroyed."[65] Not content to merely draw this biblical comparison, Domenech explained that two factors— the topography and the atmosphere—gave the Great Salt Lake its ominous demeanor. He noted that the mountains to the east "appeared inaccessible . . . whilst thick vapours moved above their summits." In one of the most haunting descriptions of the Great Salt Lake ever written, Domenech noted that

> light mists, produced at twilight, hovered amidst its vague glimmer, and danced over the waters, looking like crepe tinged with the most lovely pink . . . a transparent veil that shed upon nature the charm of a faint light, which, as it gradually rose to the summit of the mountains, assumed a more somber hue, an indescribably dismal appearance, that filled the soul with sadness and the eyes with tears. The immense valley, of a lugubrious and funereal aspect, recalls to mind that of Jehoshaphat, the valley of graves.[66]

The Dead Sea itself was the subject of considerable poetic and scientific discourse at this time. Domenech's illustration of the Great Salt Lake owes much to American scientific reports (e.g., Stansbury) and also to similar illustrations of the Dead Sea, which drew scientists anxious to unlock its geological and hydrological secrets. Evocative illustrations of the Dead Sea were common in the popular guidebooks used by pilgrims and tourists in the nineteenth century (fig. 3-6). Ultimately, Domenech was a moralist rather than a scientist, and his description of the Great Salt Lake was based on cultural history as well as similarities in physical geography. Further drawing the Dead Sea comparison like a tightening noose around the Great Salt Lake, he states that "an imposing silence continually reigns around this deserted lake, which might well be called the 'Lake of Death.'" Note here the not so subtle reference to the original Dead Sea. This is a remarkable description made all the more so by the fact that Domenech may never have actually seen the Great Salt Lake.

Domenech had now primed readers for the final judgment, and he was quick to deliver it. Ever imaginative and judgmental about the Indians who had fallen from God's grace, Domenech posited a reason for this dead lake's gloomy, sepulchral quality: "One would say that God, in a day of wrath, had cursed these solitudes on account of the crimes of their inhabitants, whose ashes lay moldering for many centuries beneath the sands of the desert."[67] These "ashes," one assumes, serve much the same purpose as the salt pillar into which Lot's wife had been transformed for her disobedience to God. That horrific retribution had occurred on the shores of the Dead Sea in the vale of Siddim (Genesis 19:26). This large lake in Utah made such a strong impression on Domenech and other travelers that it brought to mind another of God's actions—this one in the future; Domenech's reference to Jehoshaphat recalls the biblical prophecy of the place where the terrible battle of Armageddon will take place.

What lay behind Domenech's harsh statements about the native peoples' past lives? Taking a cue from the Mormons, perhaps, Domenech considered Native American tribes to be descendants of lost tribes from the Old World. Unlike the Mormons, however, he held little hope that these "savages" could ever be reclaimed. In condemning both the Indians and the environment, Domenech worked himself into an intellectual quandary that he himself was unaware he had created. He claimed that the Indians had fallen from grace and gradually assumed distinctive racial qualities, including a copper-red skin color, as a consequence of being cast into this hellish environment—much like something cast into a furnace. Yet he also stated that the Indians themselves could be blamed for actually creating that degraded and moribund character

Fig. 3-5. The Great Salt Lake, illustrated in Emmanuel Henri Domenech's *Voyage Pittoresque* (1862).

that had transformed the environment—a paradox of the first order generated by the prevailing environmental determinism and the ideological racism of the nineteenth century.

But it was the environment of the Great Salt Lake that so impressed Domenech as forlorn and dejected. Like a somber symphony full of minor chords, Domenech's passage about the lake employs dark imagery. True, the passage begins with a "glimmer" of hope as mists dance over waters tinged with lovely pink—the glow of life. However, the adjectives "somber," "dismal," and "lugubrious" are carefully placed to accentuate the real message here, which is revealed by the words "crepe," "funereal," "sadness," and "tears." Whereas the countenance of the Great Salt Lake does change depending on weather conditions, Domenech emphasizes its darker moods. To him, this lake is dead in several meanings of the word. Unaware of the lake's brine shrimp and other organisms, Domenech thinks it to be completely devoid of life. To him, it is not only lifeless, but moreover capable of inducing depression of both mind and soul. It is, in a word, a metaphor for the ephemerality of all life and the wrath of God's final judgment.

Domenech was not alone in possessing such a morose mind-set. About a decade later, another French traveler, Eugene Buissonet, traversed this same area in December of 1868. Buissonet's diary entries from the vicinity of the Great Salt Lake convey a common sentiment about the area that we might

Fig. 3-6. As seen in this evocative lithograph, ca. 1900, the Dead Sea was commonly illustrated in European and American travel guidebooks of the Near East.

today attribute to psychological depression. Like others traversing the huge and desolate desert region west of this formidable body of water, Buissonet observed that the mountains were stark and bare, "and the plains are covered by alkali sheets which are not thick but very spread out, which makes this countryside look even more sterile and sad to behold."[68] Buissonet's exact words—"de plus triste a contemplar" are difficult to translate exactly; one might also say he felt they were *too sad to contemplate* without a feeling of depression because they reminded him of what Domenech would call the physical world's ultimate fate.

Utah was rich in landscapes that suggested biblical places. When Union Pacific Railroad surveyors entered the Great Basin in 1864, they encountered fascinating topographic features. When tasked with drawing these landforms for their report back to the railroad's headquarters in Omaha, they faced a quandary. Although their scientific impulse was strong, their tendency to romanticize was even stronger. Consider, for example, *Point of the Mountain, from Camp 2*, drawn by A. J. Mathewson under the direction of Union Pacific division engineer S. B. Reed (fig. 3-7). Although the real Point of the Mountain in Utah is a distinctive topographic feature, it became even more so under Mathewson's fanciful pen strokes. Most people who glimpsed Mathewson's illustration must have experienced déjà vu. This Point of the Mountain seems to be more of an archaeological ruin than a geological feature. If Mathewson's

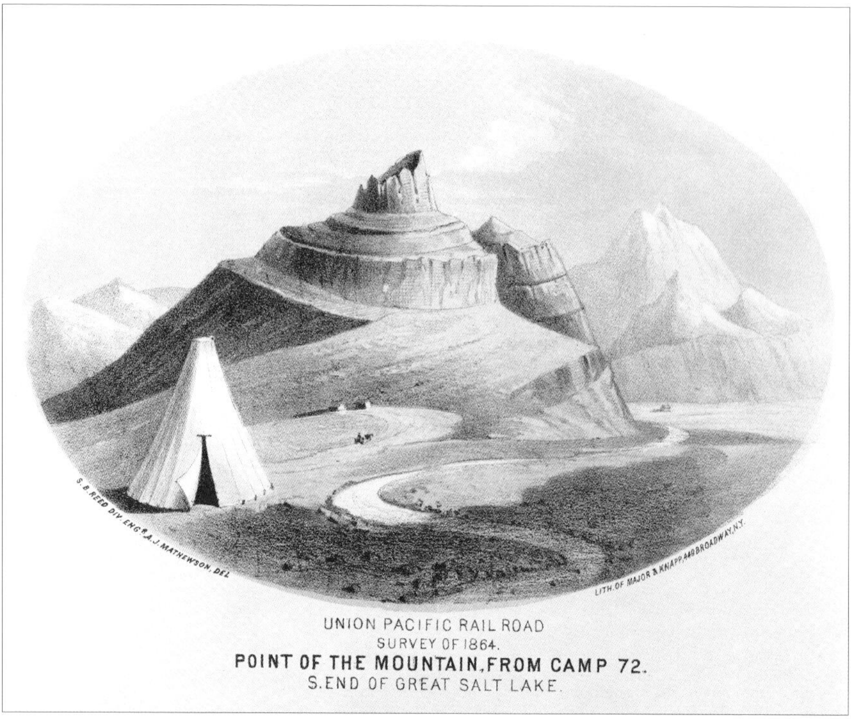

Courtesy Utah State Historical Archives

Fig. 3-7. In this illustration from the Union Pacific Railroad Survey of 1864, the topography at Point of the Mountain, Utah Territory, appears to be as much an ancient ruin as a geological feature.

rendition of Point of the Mountain calls to mind the Tower of Babel, there is a good reason. As the subject of artists since the Middle Ages, who envisioned the Tower of Babel as a huge conical feature ascended by a ramplike spiral staircase, it was a familiar icon to artist and public alike. In 1563, Pieter Bruegel (circa 1525–69) depicted the tower as a ruin ascended by a spiral ramp in at least two paintings. By the time Mathewson rendered Point of the Mountain, other artists rendered the Tower of Babel with much less architectural detail, giving it the appearance of a stack of stratified but tilted rock layers. A comparison of Mathewson's *Point of the Mountain* with Gustave Doré's dramatic *The Tower of Babel*, also called *The Confusion of Tongues* (1865–66; fig. 3-8), reveals a remarkable convergence. Both images are so architectonic—and romantically geological—that they mirror the blurring between science and art—and geology and archaeology.

The opening of the transcontinental railroad provided plenty of opportunity for writers to speculate about the austere landscape that they experienced in Utah. Not surprisingly, they too often used Orientalist language to describe

Fig. 3-8. Gustave Doré's dramatic painting *The Confusion of Tongues* (1865–1866) builds on the venerable European artistic tradition of rendering the Tower of Babel as a conical spire with an inclined stairway.

the Great Salt Lake. After 1869, travelers on the recently completed transcontinental railroad could not resist drawing parallels between what they saw in Utah and what their biblical training as well as their actual travel experiences had taught them about the Holy Land. For example, travelers were awed by the cloud of vapor that rose from the hot springs along the Wasatch Front north of Ogden. Searching for ways to describe this phenomenon, they turned to their knowledge of the Bible. As a travel writer put it in the 1870s, "The chief feature of interest here is the Hot Springs, whose clouds of vapour rise far away at the foot of the mountains, reminding one of the 'cloud' which protected the Israelites by day on their march through the weary wilderness."[69]

In another example, one of Nelson's *Pictorial Guide Books* describing scenes along the Central Pacific Railroad (1871) notes that as the train moved westward beyond Promontory Summit, "the air is impregnated with alkaline and saline odours from the Salt Lake." Here, the writer observed that "Monument Point is a grassy promontory, stretching far out into the waters of the Dead Sea of the West."[70] This reference is more telling when we recall that Corinne, at the northern edge of the Great Salt Lake, was often cast as Sodom and Gomorrah—sinful cities that were destroyed on the shores of the Dead Sea.

It is here that physical and cultural features of the area become confused. We know that not everyone who visited Utah held the Mormons in high regard; some even suggested that Salt Lake City itself was the new Sodom, no doubt because of the Mormons' practice of polygamy. In the early 1850s, Franklin Langworthy seamlessly linked the Latter-day Saints and the physical environment they inhabited to biblical history. Traveling along a road at the southern edge of the Great Salt Lake, Langworthy speculated about geology and vengeance:

> It would seem that this whole region rests upon subterranean volcanoes, and at some future day a fiery deluge may fill the entire valley of Salt lake with a sea of molten lava. This would be to the modern Sodom a fate like that which we are told in ancient times befell [sic] the cities of the plain. If such a catastrophe should happen, and if in their flight, any Mormon should look behind, he might easily be turned to a pillar of salt, if he should chance to fall into certain springs along this road.[71]

Here Langworthy is both dramatic and judgmental. As an exemplary anti-Mormon, he found little to praise about the Saints, and one senses that he wishes just such a fate would befall the Mormons before they, as he put it, "transform this free Republic into a despotism, with some Mormon prophet for an autocrat."[72]

Subtle and sometimes not so subtle comparisons of Utah with the Middle East bring to mind two remarkable illustrations that make the comparison very explicit. By the late nineteenth-century, when the railroads sought aggressively to promote Utah, they employed landscape images and maps. For example, in 1886, a promotional pamphlet on the Great Salt Lake called this geographical feature "the Dead Sea of America," Employing a stunning color lithograph to make the comparison (fig. 3-9a). A decade later, the Rio

Grande Western railroad published a promotional brochure called *Pointer to Prosperity*. That informative brochure lauded the amenities of the new state of Utah, and its back cover featured "A Striking Comparison" (fig. 3-9b). Drawn from a "Bird's eye" perspective as if the mapmaker were high above the earth, this ingenious map juxtaposed a portion of the Holy Land with Utah's Wasatch Front. This comparative map reveals that the general configuration of the areas adjacent to Jerusalem and Salt Lake City are very similar. To many people of a century ago, this map's Utah-as-Holy Land comparison was not only physically "striking" but culturally significant: after all, the Mormons had settled their new Zion creating what the map calls a "Promised Land" that was reminiscent of the Jews' homeland (today's Israel, Palestine, and adjacent parts of Jordan). Thus this "striking comparison" map suggests more than a simple topographical comparison: it also implies a strong historical and geographical connection between the Holy Land and its Utah counterpart.

Statements by the Mormons themselves helped cement their identity as an Old World people living in a new land. Moreover, at this time, the term *Promised Land* is heard in light of the Mormons' aggressive and successful colonizing of the desert between the mountains. Significantly for both the ancient Jews and the earliest Mormons arriving in Utah, that Promised Land was lightly settled and between two major empires—Mesopotamia to the north and Egypt to the south. Similarly, the Mormons' Promised Land was essentially unclaimed, lying between the United States and the more populous shores of Mexican California.

The publication of this "striking comparison" map illustration could not have been better timed. In 1896, the national economy was rebounding after the financial panic three years earlier. Significantly, the railroad that commissioned the *Pointer to Prosperity* pamphlet was undergoing a transformation, as was Utah. Originally built as a narrow gauge line from Denver to Salt Lake City, the energetic Rio Grande Western was being converted to standard gauge at just that time. This meant that the rolling stock of any railroad could pass over its line via interchange—which is to say that the Rio Grande Western was now in league with a nationwide rail network. Similarly, with the polygamy issue essentially resolved and Utah now part of the Union in 1896, entrepreneurs could feel less apprehensive about investing in the Beehive State. Had the "striking comparison" map been created two decades earlier, that Promised Land would have seemed more like a contested but largely Mormon-controlled kingdom rather than a land open to all comers.

Ironically, then, this "striking comparison" map is a modern device that builds on an ancient biblical prophecy updated after centuries of westward

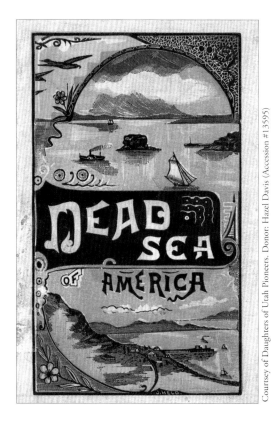

Courtesy of Daughters of Utah Pioneers. Donor: Hazel Davis (Accession #13595)

Fig. 3-9a. A pamphlet published by the Utah & Nevada Railway in 1886 portrayed the Great Salt Lake as the Dead Sea of America.

migration, originally across the Atlantic, and then overland to the Pacific. That such an ancient text is called upon so effectively reminds us that slogans are as malleable as identities. Above all, the "striking comparison " map instills nationalism as well as encourages the growth of an individual state. Through its use as an iconic device, the striking comparison equates a part of America with the Holy Land in order to reaffirm that the promise of success is inevitable through wise investment, hard work, and the blessings of Divine Providence.

In 1897, on the golden anniversary of the Mormons' arrival into the Great Salt Lake valley, a special event called "the wedding of the waters" witnessed "the Baptism of the Jordan River." Whereas that Utah river had long served as a locale for baptisms—in recognition, perhaps, of its namesake in the Holy Land serving the same purpose for nearly two millennia—this baptism was more public and promotional. A container of water from the "real" River Jordan was "merged" into the Utah river. This ceremonial merging of the waters of the two rivers Jordan was both symbolic and cathartic and made real the persistent belief that these waters were natural counterparts.

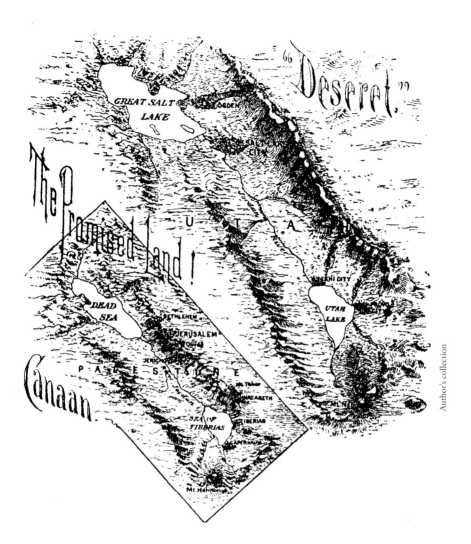

Fig. 3-9b. This map in the Rio Grande Western Railway's promotional brochure titled *Pointer to Prosperity* (1896) shows "A Striking Comparison" between the topography of the Holy Land and Utah.

The Mormons not only recognized the similarity between their new homeland in Utah and their ancestral homeland in the Middle East but also helped reinforce it by transforming the edge of the Great Salt Lake into the Intermountain West's first Orientalized tourist mecca—Saltair. Although the Great Salt Lake presented a somber, Dead Sea–like spectacle in the 1850s and 1860s, things began to change as the railroads revolutionized travel. By the early 1890s, when the Mormons began to assimilate or Americanize (for example, by

disavowing polygamy and deemphasizing collective enterprises), the shore of
the Great Salt Lake presented an opportunity to enrich the previously inward-
looking Mormon culture. Whereas early travelers had complained about the
harshness of the lake's salty waters, now the unusual nature of this lake, namely
its hypersaline waters, actually lured people. Realizing the lake's potential as a
tourist destination, the Mormon Church built a huge recreation pavilion there
in 1893. Reached by a fifteen-mile-long railroad running in a straight line due
west of Salt Lake City, Saltair represented "an effort to provide a wholesome
place of recreation under church control for Mormons, particularly families
and young people." Ten years earlier, the *Deseret News*, which was owned by
the LDS Church, had expressed a concern to parents about the dangers of
typical pleasure resorts: "To allow children of either sex of tender years to
go unprotected to pleasure resorts where all classes mingle indiscriminately is
criminal." The paper was especially concerned about "practiced voluptuaries"
and rough elements who provided a bad example for Mormon youth.[73]

Given the Mormon Church's concern, it is interesting that the architectural style chosen for the huge Saltair pavilion was Moorish. The Mormon-
owned *Deseret News* described the stunning effect the building created at
lakeside as follows: "The magnificent pavilion, rising, Venice-like, out of the
waves in stupendous and graceful beauty, deepened in its semi-Moorish architectural lines, the suspicion that what one saw was not firm structural reality
but a rather delightful oriental dream." That is not surprising considering that
Saltair's lavish eclectic design expressed the high Oriental style so common in
pavilions and amusement parks elsewhere. Note that the term *Oriental* is used
positively here. The Orient was associated with lavish and beautiful spectacles
that could enchant, so why not employ its architecture for just that purpose?

Saltair was a magical place indeed. About the size of the Mormon
Tabernacle in Salt Lake City, the Saltair pavilion was huge. Its dome was a
characteristic central feature, but it was complemented by six-sided domes at
each corner of the 140' x 250' building. Moreover, at the ends of two sprawling, ornate wings that flanked the pavilion, bud-shaped domes rose to add to
the architectural spectacle. Tall towers resembling domed mosques rose from
the middle of each wing, so that the entire design did indeed seem like something out of the *Arabian Nights*.[74] Saltair was built just at the time when a new
and more sensual aspect of Orientalism swept the United States and Europe.
Emphasizing the exotic aspects of bazaars in the Muslim world as well as portions of Asia, Saltair itself was majestic, and its setting at the edge of a huge
body of water in the desert provided a surreal quality. Note, however, that it
was built in a lavish Moorish style and yet intended to serve as an antidote

BATHING IN GREAT SALT LAKE, SALTAIR BEACH.

Author's collection

Fig. 3-10. Postcard titled "Bathing in the Great Salt Lake, Saltair Beach" (ca. 1909) shows the spectacular Moorish-style Saltair pavilion, which was built by the Mormon Church to provide wholesome entertainment.

to moral decadence—a subtle reminder that *Oriental* was not universally regarded as negative in American popular culture. A lantern plate image of the Saltair pavilion with a small steam launch tied up to the huge Moorish hulk of a building suggests some of the grandeur of Venice, Italy—a city we think of as European or Italian but which owes much of its appeal to its trade with, and copying of buildings from, the Oriental cities of the Middle East.[75]

Colored postcard views of Saltair reveal how impressive this Orientalized pavilion appeared in the early twentieth century. One popular postcard, "Bathing in Great Salt Lake, Saltair Beach," published about 1910, features bathers, some standing, some evidently bobbing like corks in the lake's salty water (fig. 3-10). Behind them rises the magnificent Saltair pavilion, whose four towers crown a spectacular sructure that epitomizes America's romanticized version of Near Eastern architecture. In this view, the postcard colorists tinted the bulk of the building ocher, the main domes slate purple, and the turrets crimson. These color combinations, so popular among Orientalist revival architects, heighten the building's ornateness and further add to its exotic and sensual quality.

Oriental-style buildings such as Saltair are based on antiques, which constitute what the late French philosopher Jean Baudrillard called "marginal objects." Rather than functioning as the originals, they "answer to other kinds of demands, such as witness, memory, nostalgia or escapism." Although inspired by mosques, palaces, or other buildings in the Near East, they have a different meaning in the American West. Their presence has atmospheric and symbolic value but is suspect. Likening a fascination with such objects—Oriental rugs, Oriental-style buildings—to imperialism, Baudrillard cautions that these "ancestral objects, sacred in essence but desacralized . . . are called upon to exude their sacredness (or historicalness) into a history-less domesticity."[76]

Although the type of criticism rendered by Baudrillard is widely shared by academicians, most people do not live their lives pondering the deeper meanings of (in)authenticity. They easily succumb to the magic of such imitations. In a remarkably candid retrospective article titled "Xanadu by the Salt Flats—Memories of a Pleasure Dome," western writer Wallace Stegner (1909–1993) recalled Saltair in the 1920s as "an enchanted palace whose onion domes float on the desert afternoon, and whose halo of light at night pales the stars." In addition to the sound of "gritty salt underfoot, or the sight of potted palms glittering with salt like tinsel," Stegner was impressed by the smells of the place. Here, at "the great Moorish pavilion that rose on pilings out of the lake," Stegner cooked burgers and hot dogs during the summer. These smells seared themselves into his memory. As Stegner put it, the "incense of hamburgers and hotdogs" made him "rise on my hind legs with a spatula in one hand and a bun in the other and give voice to an atavistic howl, a nasal, high, drawn-out ululation like that of a muezzin from a minaret or a coyote on a river bluff."

That reference to the minarets of Islam as well as the coyote reveals the power of Stegner's youthful imagination to transform Utah into the Middle East. Significantly, though, Stegner was aware of Saltair's ephemeral nature, for the magical place was continuously assaulted by the corrosive brine of the Great Salt Lake and pummeled from time to time by winds. Culture and economy likewise would prove unkind to Saltair. Sequestered in Stegner's memory, though, Saltair became a place sacred enough that he remembered it "like lost Eden." That Eden is in part metaphorical, for Saltair was a place that had a seedy, earthy side that challenged Stegner's youthful innocence. This is revealed by the stories Stegner's older brother told him about the goings-on there—"most of which I could not believe but would have liked to." Stegner's and the nation's morality were changing with age, but the point of his entire essay is that his time there was sacred and never to be repeated. Like Xanadu, this "pleasure dome was never built" but rather "was decreed, [and] it rose like an exhalation." *Apparition* is as likely a word, for Stegner's Orientalist dream suggests the inseparability of times and places that are simultaneously real and make-believe.[77]

At the same time Saltair was booming and Stegner was about to come of age, Utah was changing into a more cosmopolitan state, but it would forever owe a debt to the early Mormons' transformation of wilderness into Zion. In his inaugural address on January 1, 1917, Utah governor Simon Bamberger reflected on how effectively the Mormons had settled the Salt Lake Valley seventy years earlier. Using words that must have resonated with his own Jewish background, Bamberger declared: "This valley lying before us, such a short while ago but a bare plain with here and there a little stream of water, along which a few willows and rushes, and here and there a clump of sage brush, has indeed been made 'to blossom like the rose' and we can truly say, 'This is the Place.'"[78] Like the earlier words that Abraham heard decreed, Bamberger's speech empowered the chosen people while not even mentioning the others who occupied the land. This convergence of geographic locale and providential decree can be identified as specifically in time and place as any seminal act in religious history. Bamberger's speech references the most significant four words in Utah history—Brigham Young's "This is the place" declaration made on July 24, 1847. But as we can sense in Governor Bamberger's declaration, this place was not only geographically correct but also metaphysically perfect to position the early Latter-day Saints and ultimately all of their descendants as the rightful inheritors of this land.

That land itself took on new meaning with the building of the San Pedro, Los Angeles and Salt Lake Railroad in the early 1900s. Now, Los Angeles and Salt Lake City were finally connected by a direct line, and the remote but spectacular landscape of southern Utah was accessible to tourists. Mormons and the National Park Service had a role in opening up this area to visitation. In the first decade of the twentieth century, the SP, LA & SL railroad became part of the Union Pacific Railroad, whose shareholders included a high percentage of Mormons. For its part, the National Park Service had a long record of working with railroads to develop national parks (for example, Yellowstone). Working in harmony, Mormons and Park Service officials opened up the awesome ramparts of granite that would come to be known as Zion National Park in 1919. This name *Zion* was natural enough, given the presence of the Mormons nearby. The Union Pacific Railroad ran trains to Cedar City, from which buses transported park visitors into the wild canyons, which featured "fair cities in painted stone," as a Union Pacific brochure put it. The Utah Parks Company, which was a subsidiary of the Union Pacific Railroad, was incorporated in March 1923 for the express purpose of building the camp and hotel facilities at Zion National Park and operating the bus tours to the other spectacular parks in the area, including Cedar Breaks, Bryce, and even the north rim of the Grand Canyon.[79]

Author's collection

Fig. 3-11. The Temple of Osiris in Bryce Canyon National Park, Utah, uses the name of an ancient Egyptian ruin to characterize a natural feature in the landscape. Colortone postcard by the Deseret Book Company of Salt Lake City, ca. 1930.

The spectacular rock-ribbed landscape of southern Utah has resonated as distinctive country since the arrival of the Spaniards in the 1770s and was likely so to the Indians before them. However, as we have seen, the Europeans, and later European Americans, found it easy to equate such country with landscapes of the Old World. What especially impressed travelers in this corner of Utah was the labyrinthine nature of the landscape; deep canyons flanked by austere, nearly vertical walls of stone. In point of fact, only a few places in the Holy Land approach this grandeur, but the operative factor in rendering these western lands into biblical places was the human imagination, and the fact that both writers and artists tended to exaggerate it. Then, too, the solitude here—it was always lightly populated—added an element of drama.

Although the seemingly modern Mormon presence was a fact of life in this part of the West, the theme of Old World religion carried over to particular features in Zion and other nearby parks. Consider, for example, the fabulous "Temple of Osiris" in Bryce Canyon National Park (fig. 3-11). It represents a series of statuesque columns that simultaneously appear recognizable as architectural features, or rather architectural ruins, and a surreal fantasyland of spires. The stratified rocks here range in color from greenish to pink, orange, and buff. To the imaginative visitor, the Orientalist-inspired names of these features served to make these varicolored rock units appear much like

Fig. 3-12. The evocative name Walls of Jericho in southern Utah's Cedar Breaks associates a natural geological feature with an event in the Bible. Postcard by the Gray News Company of Salt Lake City, ca. 1930.

the polychrome columns of the famous temple of the same name in Egypt. That underscores the enduring power of Egypt to stimulate the imagination and reinforce the popular cultural perception of the West as a wonderland possessing scenery rivaling the wonders of the ancient world.

In nearby Cedar Breaks National Monument, the evocatively named "Walls of Jericho" (fig. 3-12) bring to mind the blowing of trumpets and the shouting after which the city of Jericho was "utterly destroyed," as described in Joshua (6:2–21). The "Walls of Jericho" is actually a natural bridge, which is to say a testimony to the erosional power of running water. This spectacular rock feature is solid enough, but that gaping hole needed some explaining. As translated into biblical story, in which the wall simply "fell down flat," the hole suggests something miraculous. It reminds visitors of the power of God to destroy the enemies of Israel, in which, as the popular gospel song claims, "the walls came tumbling down." In contrast to the Temple of Osiris, Jericho's tumbled-down walls were known only from the biblical narrative; and yet the passage in Joshua was so evocative that early travelers (and later, park employees) perpetuated the story in stone here. Two forces operate in this type of landscape promotion. The first instills appreciation; the second stimulates visitation to the area via tourism. With this one-two punch, the iconizing of Utah's natural environment as spiritual place was firmly fixed in the popular mind.[80]

4

Finding New Eden
The American Southwest

". . . the Southwest is America's Orient."

Barbara Babcock, "A New Mexican Rebecca" (1990)

Tʜᴇ ᴇᴀʀʟɪᴇsᴛ ᴘᴀʀᴛ ᴏғ ᴡᴇsᴛᴇʀɴ Nᴏʀᴛʜ Aᴍᴇʀɪᴄᴀ to be Orientalized was what Anglo-Americans now call the Southwest and Mexicans call "el norte." However, it was the Spaniards, not the Anglo-Americans, who deserve credit as the first Orientalizers of the region. We must go back in time nearly five centuries to see how this occurred. The Orientalization of the entire North American continent appears to have begun with Estevanico (circa 1500–1539), who was called "the Moor" by those in the Narváez expedition of 1528. That name Moor—a more or less reflexive Spanish figure of speech for someone dark and different—effortlessly linked exotic person and exotic place. Shipwrecked on the Texas coast with Álvar Núñez Cabeza de Vaca, Estevanico the Moor was a North African slave who trekked back to Mexico with Cabeza de Vaca by traversing much of the southwestern borderlands in the early 1530s. Although much of North Africa is not universally considered to be part of the Middle East, the spread of Islam throughout that area and into Spain closely links the Moors—and, by association, Estevanico—to it. By many accounts, Estevanico's skin color was dark, or at least brown. Estevanico was likely the first non-European ethnic visitor to the region, and he brought considerable cultural baggage with him. To Spaniards, the name Moor also suggested distant origins and Islam, but the Native Americans regarded him with awe. Unfortunately, the Moor earned the dubious distinction of being killed by natives on a later expedition into the Southwest—the first "Oriental" victim of violence in a land that would experience a good deal of interethnic warfare in the next several centuries.

126

That violent act, interestingly, is often attributed to Estevanico's tendency to charm, seduce, and bed native women. If the story is true, those southwestern Native American women may have been the first Americans to be seduced by the East, or a representative of it. Their husbands, however, evidently viewed things quite differently, reacting with startling and lethal force. This story's content, rather than its veracity, is most important here. If the story is true, Estevanico is the first, but far from the last, of the sexualized Oriental seducers on the American continent. There may be a lesson here. Estevanico's mixed reception as accepted lover and executed interloper can serve as a warning that the Orient and its peoples could—and would—be viewed with alarm and apprehension by peoples living in the Americas.

Another early reference to the Orient is Francisco Vázquez de Coronado's use of the term "the Turk" (el Turco) for a Pawnee Indian in 1540. El Turco was a native guide who led, or rather misled, Coronado's expedition toward the fabled realm of Quivira to find the riches they sought. Coronado evidently named this Indian slave "el Turco" for several reasons. Among these were his appearance, his lower status, his non-Catholic faith (the Spaniards of this period having a strong disdain for Muslim "infidels"), his knowledge of the far-ranging, exotic-appearing countryside and its peoples, and his deviousness. After leading the Spaniards on a weeks-long, rambling journey into the Great Plains, el Turco finally confessed that he had deliberately led them astray. When asked why, el Turco answered that the people of Cicuique (or Cicuyc) begged him to do so in hopes that the Spanish interlopers would die without food or water on the plains. This, el Turco noted, was simply a way of paying the Spaniards back for their abuses to the Indians.

Needless to say, this explanation infuriated the Spaniards, who resented this affront to both King and Conquistador; probably, however, the Spaniards were even more upset because of the danger in which they had been placed—as well as their being led to a place that possessed none of the riches they sought. As payback, the Spaniards garroted el Turco on the spot. It is posited by some that the name *el Turco* was provided after the Turk's lies were revealed, and that "under this suggestion, he was seen as 'evil' like the Turks, enemies of the Christians of the time."[1] There is no evidence for this, however, and it could be speculation by a generation of scholars weaned on politicized Orientalism. Regardless, this incident is of interest because it reveals how a native of the New World was Orientalized long before the arrival of the British. By calling him "the Turk," the Spaniards in effect reenacted European encounters with the East in an entirely new setting. This unfortunate incident represented the second widely recorded association of the western American frontier and its peoples with the Orient.

Throughout the long period from 1598 to about 1810, the Spaniards occasionally referred to the Pueblo Indians using Orientalized terms. The holdouts at the Sky City of Acoma, for example, were sometimes equated with the Jews who held out against the Romans at Masada. Like that incredible stronghold overlooking the Dead Sea, the Indian city was perched high up on a mesa and seemed impenetrable. Another aspect of material culture equated Indians and Turks. The Indians' use of mineral turquoise was based on the blue stone's similarity to the sky. It was a stone of spiritual significance to the natives. We use the term "turquoise" today as a result of the Spaniards, who named it *turquesa* because of the stone's original association with the Turks.[2]

Perhaps Spaniards were influenced by Islam as they now zealously spread Christianity to infidels in the New World, much as the Moors had spread Islam into the Iberian Peninsula. Despite their strong Islamic traditions, Spaniards soon came to despise Iberia's Moorish heritage. In the New World, it was easy to classify the Native American "other" as a Muslim. As Nabil Matar observed, and Robert Irwin more recently concluded, "The [Spanish] literature of the period frequently compared the barbarous, pagan American Indians to the Muslims and both were regularly accused by Christian writers of idolatry, sodomy and indolence."[3] It was, after all, the Moors who had forged a new identity in Spain, creating in effect two societies, dominant Muslims and minority Christians, the latter becoming second-class citizens. Even today in Mexico and the Southwest, that dish of brown beans and white rice is called Moros y Cristianos (Moors/Muslims and Christians)—a seemingly innocuous meal and name that represents the darker Moor and the lighter Christian; interestingly, the bean itself is a native of the New World, while rice (symbolizing the whiter Christian) originated in the Old World. The indigenous bean's becoming the infidel Moor reminds us how easily the Native American Indian could be placed in that Moorish role.

By the time European Americans began to arrive in the West in the early nineteenth century, they too were primed to view both landscape and people through the lens of Orientalism. In an early nineteenth-century book of various titles, including *Travels and Romantic Adventures of Monsieur Violet*, Frederick Marryat contended that "the Shoshone women, as well as the Apache and Arrapahoe, all of whom are of the Shoshone race, are very superior to the squaws of the Eastern Indians." By this he meant that "they are more graceful in their forms, and have more personal beauty." This, of course, is sexist, but as Marryat put it, "I cannot better describe them by saying that they have more similitude to the Arabian women than any other race." By this, Marryat meant "they are very clean in their persons and in their lodges; and all their tribes having both male and female slaves, the Shoshone wife is not broken down by hard labour, as are the squaws of the eastern tribes." These women, as he put it, "ride as bravely as the men, and are very expert with the bow and arrow." Marryat seems smitten. These Shoshone women are not only attractive and brave but also faithful to their husbands. As Marryat observed, perhaps with mixed appreciation and disappointment, "I really believe that any attempt upon their chastity would prove unavailing."[4] Note here that Marryat's romantic view has a touch of the ethnographic: as he compares Native Americans to each other, some come out losers and some winners. Note, too, that the term "Arabian" is used in a positive sense.

When seen by Americans traveling in the mid-nineteenth century, communities in the Mexican borderlands possessed particular "charms," as some put it, and this often had sexual overtones. This simmering sexuality accompanied US military personnel who entered the region during the 1846–1848 US-Mexican War. American soldiers, who almost invariably mention the mysterious, sensual quality of Mexican women, were especially susceptible to the region's charms. Both the cultural landscape and the women here seemed exotic enough to enchant troops bent on conquest—that is, making the area part of the United States. In these comparisons, Mexican males did not fare particularly well. The tendency for Anglo-Americans to see ugliness in Mexican men and beauty in Mexican women is noteworthy. As Henry Howe put it in describing New Mexicans in 1853, "The males are generally ill-featured, while the females are often quite handsome." Moreover, Howe added, there is a "wide difference in the character of the two sexes." By this he meant that their behavior differed markedly. As Howe put it, "While the men have often been censured for their indolence, mendacity, and treachery, and cruelty, the women are active, affectionate, and open-hearted." These women, he concluded, possess "a natural sympathy for every suffering being, be it friend or foe; which compensates, in some degree, for the want of a refined education."[5]

The ability to charm extended easily from people to landscape and lasted for generations. Writing in 1919, more than half a century after the US-Mexican War, historian Justin Harvey Smith noted that American soldiers during the war found San Antonio, Texas, to be a fascinating, if somewhat decadent, community that easily charmed them. As Smith noted using Whitmanesque language, "The moss-covered walls of the Alamo, pitted by Santa Anna's cannon balls—looked in their eyes like some ancient oriental city 'just dug up,' as one of them said; and the cactus, the live-oaks, the mockingbirds, the pellucid river and the many varieties of grapes extinguished soon the memory of past fatigues." Smith's term "oriental city" was noteworthy, as it suggested antiquity and mystery.[6]

The realities and seductions of war led American troops far south into the heart of Mexico. With every mile of southward trekking, they encountered cities that cast an even stronger spell based in part on romantic Orientalist literature and art. For American soldier Sam Chamberlain, words were not enough to describe the charm of Mexico. Chamberlain painted scenes rich in color and seduction, including one of himself in bed with two Mexican women—a reminder that the forbidden pleasures of the Orient could also be found on the North American continent. For beleaguered troops inclined toward the painterly, the landscape offered considerable appeal. As one of them noted, "Another comfort was to gaze from a safely remote hill at Vera Cruz, which looked—the soldiers agreed—so oriental, with airy palm trees visible over the white wall, hundreds of buzzards floating in wide circles far above, the dark bulwark of Ulúa set in waves of purple and gold on the left, a forest of American spars and masts on the right, piercing the misty splendor of the yellow beach, the bright sails of fishing boats in the middle distance, and the vast, blue, cool Gulf beyond it all."[7] These Mexican communities were exotic, and by such fantasizing, the troops imagined that they were on even more remote foreign soil than the American continent, namely the Orient.

Consider next how even scientific expeditions along the newly created US-Mexico border helped transform the Southwest into the Orient. In the Victorian period, Asia exerted considerable influence on American artists, a number of whom went to the Southwest on government-sponsored expeditions. The scientific illustrations in William Emory's impressive three-volume *United States and Mexican Boundary Survey* (1857)[8] are worth a closer look in this regard. Whereas the scientific drawings of specimens such as fossils, snakes, and cacti are close to photographic in their accuracy, the southwestern landscape drawings by James David Smillie (1833–1909) are clearly romantic, even Asian, in their use of contorted vegetation and silhouetted topography. Smillie later became a well-known landscape painter, but he sketched landscapes for Emory's report when he was in his early to midtwenties, an impressionable age indeed. One of his drawings—*View From Monument XVIII, in the Puerto de la Sierra del Pajarito, looking West Towards Monument XVII on the Cerro de Sonora* (fig. 4-1)—deserves closer scrutiny. Its title sounds clinical enough, but one should note that the method used by Smillie to depict the gnarled tree and shrub in the center foreground speaks volumes about artistic and cultural influences. If that drawing reveals an uncanny resemblance to Japanese (and Chinese) paintings, it is likely because Oriental painting was in vogue at the time. True, that may be a gnarled manzanita bush in the lower center of the drawing, for the manzanita does possess twisting branches

Fig. 4-1. A mid-nineteenth century drawing showing a portion of the US-Mexico border in Arizona Orientalizes aspects of the landscape.

somewhat like the plant that Smillie drew. However, the drawing has an undeniably Asian quality due to the actual style of rendering. Moreover, even the agave (century plant) and other vegetation reveal similar stylistic liberty. Smillie rendered the mountain background with a stylized looseness more characteristic of Asian art than American scientific illustration. Was Smillie influenced by the paintings and drawings by Asian artists? Or was he inspired by fellow artists who had traveled to the Far East in search of inspiration? If the West's rugged landscapes could be softened by artists using the popular Hudson River school style of painting, then there is no reason that those same landscapes could not be rendered in the increasingly popular Asian style by American artists—even those on seemingly scientific missions.

If, as noted earlier, impressions of places are based on both landscapes and inhabitants, then more needs to be said about the Mexican people encountered in this region. Underlying the fascination of Mexican women was their *mestiza* heritage, for many were part Spanish and part Indian. To better understand Anglo-American perceptions of Native Americans, we should consult S. W. Cozzens's *The Marvellous Country* (1875). In words and images, Cozzens's book beautifully reveals how landscape and people fit into the process of Orientalization. As he traveled through New Mexico's Mesilla Valley, Cozzens stated with disarming sincerity: "Could a person familiar with

Bible history be suddenly transported and set down in the Mesilla Valley, he would certainly imagine himself among the Children of Israel, so primitive are the habits and customs of the people."[9] Cozzens here references not just the Indians, for Spaniards (in becoming Mexicans) had so thoroughly mixed with natives that they often had much the same identity to visitors here. However, Cozzens is more specifically referring to Indians when he later discusses the fabulous Acoma Pueblo. In characteristically Victorian fashion, and not unlike Frémont's introduction to the distant view of Pyramid Lake that becomes focused on the familiar, Cozzens translates American Indian settlement and landscape in terms of the Old World:

> We could have witnessed no more beautiful or enchanting sight than the sunrise which burst upon us ere we were half a dozen miles from Acoma. Before us rose the peaks of the Sierra Madre one above the other, each of an entirely different hue, reminding us of the ladder which Jacob of old saw set up between the earth and the heaven [sic], or of some vast staircase constructed by the Afreets [supernatural demons in Arabic and Islamic culture], to enable them to ascend to the very gates of Paradise.[10]

Thus it is that Indians, especially Indians of the western United States, become dwellers in a land that was read as biblical. Small wonder then, that the American Indian was characterized as (and believed to be) the Israelite in the New World.

This conflation got underway early and as destined to endure. Anglo-Americans arriving in the Southwest in the 1850s were prone to see similarities between the Indians and southwestern Asians. Some of these Indians were extremely helpful to early-day travelers, and they were likely to be called "good" Indians. Among these were the Pima-Maricopa peoples of central Arizona, who were a godsend to California-bound travelers in about 1850. In their villages not far from present-day Phoenix, they cultivated gardens and provided much-needed supplies for the travelers, many of whom were in dire straits by the time they reached this location. To help travelers who might otherwise perish of thirst, they dispatched what the travelers called "Good Samaritans of the desert." These Indians carried "gourds of water, roasted pumpkins, and green corn." William Emory observed that the Pima, who "surpassed many of the Christian nations in agriculture, [were] little behind them in the useful arts, and immeasurable before them in honesty and virtue." Putting it more bluntly, the Quaker forty-niner Edward Pancoast stated that the Pimas were "the best type of Indian on the Continent."[11]

That concept of the Good Samaritan, of course, was, and is, used for anyone who helps someone in need; it originated in the Bible, wherein Jesus fondly describes a man from Samaria who helps a man in need who had been robbed and beaten (Luke 10:33–35). This biblical reference helps place the original Good Samaritan in the desert wilderness—much as these Indians in Arizona were positioned to help mid-nineteenth century travelers crossing a seemingly similar and equally dangerous arid region. The Simpson Kern expedition typified this tendency to find the Old World, especially the Near East, in the far Southwest. At this time, the adobe pueblos were especially likely to be equated with the dwellings of the Middle East. These pueblo dwellers were considered to be civilized (i.e., "good") Indians, as they were sedentary agriculturists.

However, the other types of Indians living in the region were nomadic tribes such as the Comanche and Apache. When these Indians were on horseback, they were equated with Mongols, Tuaregs, or other Asian and Middle Eastern tribes. Regardless of their origins, these nonsedentary Indians, like their mobile counterparts in the Orient, were perceived to be the most dangerous, duplicitous, and cruel of the Native Americans. They struck absolute terror in pioneers from Texas to Arizona.[12]

Some fears, however, were deeper than others—the fear of abduction being the most disquieting of all. The fear and reality of abduction by Indians and captivity in their hands had a long history on the Eastern Seaboard. Captives in the 1600s and early 1700s were likely to relate their experiences in terms of biblical narratives, but by around 1830 to the 1880s, they were far more lurid—a fact that coincided perfectly with the Anglo-Americans' arrival in the Far West. In addition to the fear of outright physical harm, the strongest fear was that the white person abducted would actually identify with the Indians and stay with them voluntarily—something that happened fairly frequently. Far more rare, but nevertheless written about rather frequently, was abduction followed by sexual abuse. Fears of sexual mutilation on the part of males and the fear of rape on the part of women were common themes. In this, the desert or wilderness had a role, for such sexual depredations were considered more likely in areas far from civilization. With every mile from civilization, it seemed, those fears increased exponentially.

Nowhere was this fear more apparent than in the desert Southwest, but for Anglo-Americans it began farther east in the Great Plains. In migrating across that region to the Intermountain West in 1850, Susan Ellen Johnson Martineau recalled a narrow escape when a young Indian man expressed an interest in trading horses and other things for women—her in particular, with whom he seemed quite smitten. In a classical lead-up to captivity drama, the pioneers refused but the Indian persisted, attempting to dash away with her after dark. He waited, as it was later related in her husband's diary, "till the night became as dark as Egypt, then brought his horse up near the tent, and waited for a favorable moment" to carry her away. Note how dramatic this description is; it is as much a passage from an Orientalist desert novel as a factual account. Note, too, how quickly and satisfactorily it ended: the woman's screams "instantly brought her help, as she leaped from the horse, while her dusky lover—disappointed and baffled in his daring scheme—dashed away down the [river] bank into the thicket and was instantly lost to sight."[13] Later, in Arizona, Susan asked her husband, James, to kill her if she were about to be captured by Apache Indians for, as he put it, "I knew, too, that quick death at my hand would be a thousand times more merciful than such tortures as the Apaches had already inflicted upon many women and children." Martineau agreed to Susan's macabre request, adding, "But, Oh! What a dreadful thing it is to be obliged to make so fearful a promise!"[14]

It is significant that these Apache-themed dramas took place in the hot, arid sections of the American West. "The desert . . ." as feminist scholar Ella Shohat observes, "functions narratively as an isolating element, as sexually and morally separate imaginary territory." This sexualized desert is fascinating and dangerous country. It is here, as Shohat put it, that "the real dramatic conflicts take place." By this, Shohat means the desert is psychologically far away from the origin point of the white woman, who seems especially vulnerable here. Putting this in Orientalist terms, this is "the desert where women are defenseless and [where] a white woman could easily become the captive of a romantic sheik or evil Arab." Shohat further suggests that this type of "isolated desert locale gives voice to a masculinist fantasy of complete control over the Western woman, the woman 'close to home,' without any intervening protective code of morality." This formula later served Hollywood well as a way to "censure female adventurousness and the male tyranny of harems and rapes—but only, paradoxically, as a way of gratifying Western interracial sexual desires."[15]

The contrast between sedentary, well-behaved peoples and unsettled, nomadic barbarians is one of the basic elements inherent in Orientalism. It certainly played out in the Old World as clashes between agriculturists and herders. Colonialists admired those sedentary and ostensibly well-behaved peoples more than their archenemies—the raiding nomads like Genghis Khan. In the New World, this translates into the good Indian-bad Indian syndrome, the "good" Indians being those well-behaved sedentary agriculturists (like the Hopis and Pimas), and the "bad" Indians being the mobile nomads (like the Apaches and Comanches), who could raid settled places with impunity.

In describing why the valleys of Arizona were still unsettled despite the fact that they "are not surpassed for fertility and beauty by any that I have seen, and that includes the whole world," Charles D. Poston of the newly created Arizona Historical Society noted in 1894 that Apaches had been "a continual source of dread and danger." There were, however, "evidences of a still more remote and mysterious civilization by an aboriginal race, of which we know nothing, and can learn but little by the vestiges that they left upon the earth." We now know these indigenous peoples as the Hohokam, but to Poston they were nameless. He did know, however, that "the engineering for their irrigating canals was so perfect as that practiced on the Euphrates, the Ganges, or the Nile." These Middle Eastern and southern Asian cultures exemplified the highest order of cultural organization, the progenitors of our own culture in the broadest scheme of things.[16]

In the West of the nineteenth century, travel writers took part in the wholesale casting of Indians into roles straight out of literature. It was widely believed that the western Indians were not only skilled torturers but also depraved cannibals. Moreover, when this alleged barbarism was coupled with the prospect of sexual licentiousness, it was both titillating and horrifying. As a German traveler reported, or rather bragged, "A number of young Indian girls fell upon me, ripped at my clothes and allowed themselves the most embarrassing grasp of hands." Historian Ray Allen Billington laconically noted that this man had "barely escaped with his honor." Given the rich tradition of travelers embellishing the truth, of course, the encounter may have been more the product of fantasy than anything that actually happened. However, it offered a lesson regardless of veracity. The perpetrators of this licentious act were wanton, for this was not the way that proper people behaved. As Billington concluded, "Such liberties were not allowable in Victorian Europe."[17]

There is evidence that this fascination with the exotic-as-erotic was part of the southwestern American experience, and that it often played out in an Orientalized way. For example, in his military reconnaissance of the Southwest (1846), the "soldier-scientist" William Emory described an encounter that took place near Santa Fe, when Emory's entourage spotted a group of Apaches. One of the women on horseback not only interfered with army business but was evidently something of an exhibitionist. Emory, himself an archenemy of the Orientalism-prone John Charles Frémont, couldn't resist describing this woman in great detail in a way that brought to mind Orientalist sexual fantasies. The woman, Emory notes, "had on a gauze-like dress, trimmed with the richest and most costly Brussels lace, pillaged no doubt from some fandango-going belle of Sonora." So far, she is simply characterized as one of the wild Indians who preyed on the Spanish nobility, an interesting contrast in itself given Emory's task of taking the northern portion of Mexico for the United States. As if Emory's description weren't fascinating enough, however, he quickly notes that "she straddled a fine grey horse, and whenever her blanket dropped from her shoulders, her tawny form could be seen through the transparent gauze." Emory's readers now imagine that dusky native woman's body astride the steed, at which point things become even more interesting. To show off her horsemanship in front of the troops, "she charged at full speed up a steep hill." However, in the commotion of undertaking this spectacular feat of horsemanship, "the fastenings of her dress broke, and her bare back was exposed to the crowd, who ungallantly raised a shout of laughter." To leave little doubt that she was not intimidated by this calamity, the woman "wheeled short round with surprising dexterity, and seeing the mischief done, coolly slipped the dress under arms and tucked it between the seat and the saddle." At this point, we can imagine a vixen as brazen as Lady Godiva, for Emory concludes that "in this state of nudity, she rode through the camp, from fire to fire, until, at last, attaining the object of her ambition, a soldier's red flannel shirt, she made her adieu in that new costume."[18]

The image of a naked (or nearly so) woman going from campfire to campfire suggests a camp follower, but the idea of her desiring a man's flannel shirt appears to suggest less gender swapping than a kind of intimacy wherein the garment worn close to the body of a soldier now clothes a native. Although on the surface there is nothing to identify this as an Orientalist fantasy, the notion of a pillaging, shameless, horse-bound woman certainly recalls descriptions of the tribes of the Asian steppe. On one level, Emory is feigning humor—that is, poking fun at this woman. On another, he reveals that he not only admires but perhaps also desires the abandon she represents.

Recounting his early 1860s travels through the Apache country of southern Arizona in his popular book *Across America and Asia* (1870), American geologist Raphael Pumpelly related the case of a "poor woman" who had been abducted by Apaches. When she was barely able to keep up with the Indians, who kept "prickling her with lances to prevent her falling behind," they finally "lanced her through and through the body" and threw "her over a ledge of rocks, left her for dead." Rather than perishing, however, the tough woman plugged her own wounds with rags and dragged herself home, a painful process taking several days as she subsisted on roots and berries. Even the normally nonjudgmental Pumpelly called these Indians "savages." He noted how much terror they struck in the local settlers, and in him, as he crossed Arizona. Here, especially during the night, when "fancy gives life to the blackened yucca, and transforms the tall stem of the century plant into the lance of an Apache," Pumpelly stated that the traveler takes "every object within fifty yards for the lurking-place of an Indian."[19] This description is similar to those written about "ruthless" or "barbaric" tribes in Arabia and portions of southwestern Asia in "travel accounts" by careful observers such as Richard F. Burton, or in the work of imaginative novelists such as the German Karl May, whose *Oriental Odyssey* contained riveting passages about the Middle East, for example, "these mountains reek to this day with the blood of those who fell victim to racial hatred, wild fanaticism and the desire for rape or bloody vengeance."[20]

Undermining civilized colonial order at nearly every turn, except when it was in their favor to cooperate, these American Indian "barbarians" were troublesome but secretly admired by many Europeans. As they moved about the American West, some well-traveled Englishmen compared the fate of American Indians with that of the "Natives" in the British colonies in the Orient. In most cases, they felt the American Indians fared worse. As the Earl of Dunraven put it in traveling in the American West in 1874, "The tribes exclusively inhabiting the United States have suffered more than their brethren who partially or altogether live in British possessions, for they have come more into collision with the superior race."[21]

The widespread belief that the American Indian was disappearing made Orientalist comparisons all the more poignant and heightened nostalgia for a "vanishing race." This belief was among the many factors that led Americans to question whether a more humane Indian policy wouldn't be more advisable— but only after most Indians in the West were either on reservations or had fallen victim to land encroachment by settlers and resource users like loggers, miners, and ranchers. But the colonizers were ambivalent about the process, seeking a tamed (that is, controlled) frontier while increasingly romanticizing the "free" way of life that was lost in the process. That tortured sentiment, of course, is another example of imperialist nostalgia—the lamenting of the noble things lost through colonization, provided that the successful colonizers are the ones privileged enough to do the lamenting.

By now it should be obvious that the Spaniards were not alone in seeing parallels between the Orient and what they experienced on their northern, Indian-dominated frontier. For their part, the Anglo-Americans also tended to view parts of the American Southwest as Middle Eastern well before the Southwest became part of the United States after 1848. The Anglo-American Orientalization of the region may have begun in Texas. In 1839, for example, John Leonard Riddell observed that San Antonio "reminded me of Tadmor in the desert mentioned in the Scriptures."[22] As they traveled deeper into the

Southwest, Anglo-American observers commonly confused Hispanic and Middle Eastern architecture. For example, again quoting S. W. Cozzens's popular book *The Marvellous Country*, Arizona's mission San Xavier del Bac was portrayed as "the most beautiful, as well as remarkable, specimen of Saracenic style of architecture to be found in the country." It should be noted here that this was a complimentary statement, for Cozzens quickly added, "Nor have I ever seen a building in such perfect harmony with its proportions as is this."[23]

Located at the end of the long trail from Saint Louis to New Mexico that bears its name, Santa Fe was frequently cast in exotic terms. In 1866, a traveler described Santa Fe as a nearly "pure Mexican" community of about five thousand, observing that "the houses are of adobes, or mud brick, one-story high, with but two or three exceptions." Not content to end the description there, the writer declared that "the material and mode of building are precisely the same as adopted by the ancient Assyrians." Moreover, he observed, "You may find the perfect counterparts of the common adobe houses to-day, on the banks of the Euphrates and the Nile." Santa Fe's adobe buildings likely resulted from cultural diffusion: "The Spaniard in Mexico built his adobe as he had it in Andalusia, whither it was brought by the Moors from Africa, who, in their turn, had received it from the East." Small wonder that viewing the landscape of Santa Fe was at least in theory much the same as experiencing its original in the Near East.[24] After all, the word "adobe" itself is Egyptian Arabic (*adobar*) for sun-dried brick.

In fact, Santa Fe has also been considered partly Moorish due to its Spanish architectural roots. Few writers captured the connection between Moorish and Spanish heritage better than Ralph E. Twitchell, who wrote for the Santa Fe Railway, which built its line through northern New Mexico: "Something of that intangible air of mystery that the Moors brought from the Far East to Granada," Twitchell wrote, "was transplanted to American soil by the conquistadores." Here in New Mexico, as Twitchell put it, "among scenic surroundings that must have reminded them of their Iberian home, blossomed the City of Holy Faith, the capital of the Sunshine State."[25] This conflation of the New and Old Worlds venerated Santa Fe, adding to its cachet as an "ancient" city. It also helped transform a locale in the Americas into something far more exotic, namely an Oriental-appearing place in the American Southwest.

As the locale of considerable military activity in the US-Mexican War (1846–1848), the Southwest was astride an early route of migration to Southern California along which pioneers experienced "ancient ruins, magnificent landscapes, and exotic peoples." As Lea Dilworth observed, their "regionalist (and nationalist) rhetoric was often similar to the discourse of Orientalism."[26] In a process that Marta Weigle astutely calls "Southwesternism," the American Southwest answered Americans' need for an Orient. "Unlike the Plains Indians, who were usually represented as savage (though sometimes noble) warriors, the Pueblos were a 'semi civilized' self-sufficient, settled, and agricultural people who lived in houses and produced attractive handicrafts."[27] Artist Henry Cross depicted the Hopi Indians as an "oriental curiosity."[28] The classic images of the "olla maidens"—women with pottery jars balanced on their heads—gave the region an exotic, Asian quality. According to Barbara Babcock, this image was the most common icon for indigenous southwestern women. It was well developed by the late nineteenth century, but the Orientalization of natives in the Southwest by Anglo-Americans began more than half a century before that.

The Southwest-as-Near-East also relies, in part, on the lifestyles associated with certain Indians. As in the Middle East, some indigenous peoples here are sedentary, while others are nomadic. In both places, it should be noted, even nomadic peoples might live in one location for a season or more. Yet they conveyed the popular impression that they were constantly on the move. Then, too, in the seventeenth and eighteenth centuries and well into the nineteenth century, portions of the area resembled the Near East, as a thriving slave trade existed here. Those Indians who raided communities and took captives as slaves usually hoped to ransom some and thus improve their status vis-à-vis the European Americans. This, as historian James Brooks notes in *Captives and Cousins*, was a time-honored tradition among certain American tribes before Europeans arrived. However, it was also reminiscent of Muslim-Christian interaction in Spain circa 1200 AD. As Brooks noted, "A broadly held code of male honor superseded ethnic and religious differences in Early Modern Spain, providing the moral framework within which contests for honor, territory, subjects, and women took place." The symbolic drama of "los moros y cristianos," reenacted annually for more than two centuries in the Southwest as "Los Comanches," reflected the varied ways of life here. This event was a simulated taking of a virgin Spanish or New Mexican girl by Indians. The girl would in turn be ransomed as a way for both societies, Indian and European, to interact and save face. As Brooks concludes, the phenomenon of seizing a captive who will then be returned through *rescate*, or ransom, "had parallels in the 'Old World' that would prove more meaningful when both worlds met in the Southwest Borderlands."[29]

Given the tendency to see or, rather, imagine concrete connections between this part of North America and the Middle East, it is understandable that Jicarilla Apache Indians were given the title of Faraónes—or Pharaohs—by

A NATURAL SANDSTONE FORMATION.

Fig. 4-2. As illustrated in Cozzens's *The Marvellous Country* (1875), a natural geological formation in the American Southwest appears to be an ancient ruin, complete with walls and towers.

the Spaniards. Like the ancient Egyptians, the Jicarilla Apaches kept slaves. The upshot of this is that the Indians' behavior seemed familiar indeed. Much like the Moors and Arabs, their cultures used captives as a natural part of the social interaction process; small wonder, therefore, that Indians were frequently equated with Turks, Berbers, and the like by travelers. Interestingly, this propensity to barter with captives in the Muslim world seems somehow barbaric and ancient to westerners today, yet it is a deeply rooted tradition in that part of the world. Small wonder, too, that American military action in the Middle East today is characterized as something out of the Wild West, where natives not only use unconventional and seemingly barbaric military tactics but seize hostages whom they literally view as pawns that will be exchanged for valuable players—their own seized warriors.[30]

Cozzens's florid narrative in *The Marvellous Country* deserves closer examination because it is quite instructive regarding how natural features in the Southwest were, through vivid imagination, turned into turreted, domed, and otherwise Oriental cities. Traveling through southern New Mexico, Cozzens and his fellow travelers found themselves staring at "some remarkable sandstone formations" that appeared to be an ancient city. As Cozzens put it, "We found about forty columns, worn by the winds and rains into most singular shapes. Some looked like churches, towers, castles, or barracks, and others very like human beings of colossal proportions. So striking were these resemblances," Cozzens added, "that it was hard to believe [that] the hand of man had nothing to do with their formations."[31] As Cozzens's book illustrated these natural features (fig. 4-2), they are given a clearly architectural character. This, of course, is as much artistic sleight of hand as Cozzens's enthusiastic description.

But things became even more architecturalized the farther Cozzens and his companions traveled in the vicinity of the Organ Mountains. Always up for diversions of interest to share with his readers, Cozzens noted that his guide urged them to visit an even more spectacular, fantastic sight. Near a series of lakes in the mountains, the guide told Cozzens about "a very peculiar sandstone formation, well worth seeing." Pondering the word *peculiar*, Cozzens agreed. Moving in that direction, Cozzens spied something in the distance. "Bringing our glasses to bear upon that portion" of the countryside, he noted, we "saw what seemed to be a large city, with its spires and domes and towers glittering in the bright sunlight, and rivalling in splendour even the creations of the genii conjured by 'Aladdin's wonderful lamp.'"[32] As one of the stories related in *The One Thousand and One Nights*, (or simply the *Arabian Nights*), "Aladdin and the Magic Lamp" was read by an avid public in both the United States and Europe. Its blend of magic and intrigue epitomized Orientalist tales. A landscape that seemed out of that story was irresistible. Naturally, Cozzens and several others hiked closer to get a better look (fig. 4-3). Not content to leave the reader only intrigued, Cozzens then explicitly described the sight that greeted him the next morning. In one of the most vivid passages ever penned transforming natural objects into architectural forms, he wrote:

> The next morning the guide called us to behold the wonderful effect of the rising sun upon the city of enchantment that we had seen from the mountain the day before. As we approached this marvellous architecture of the elements, we could not repress our exclamations of wonder and delight. Streets were plainly visible; massive temples with their spires and domes; monuments of every conceivable shape; castles of huge proportions; towers and minarets, all formed of pure white silica, which glittered in the sunlight like walls of crystal. It was hard to persuade ourselves that art had had no part in forming these graceful testimonials to the wonders of nature.[33]

Note here the use of terms like "temples" and "minarets," a way of further distinguishing the towers and castles as Near Eastern, which is to say Oriental. To place this awesome location in the context of his group's members, Cozzens revealed the general incredulity about this city of stone. "'Surely,' said Dr.

Fig. 4-3. This illustration of "A City not made with Hands" in Cozzens's *The Marvellous Country* (1875) transforms New Mexico's Organ Mountains into a magical cityscape of towers and minarets.

Parker, 'this must be a city.' 'Yes,' replied I, 'a city, but not made with hands.'"[34]

In this exchange, we witness Cozzens doing something that represented an increasingly common trend, namely, endowing the American landscape itself with a kind of spiritual quality that ostensibly transcends culture. How did this spiritualization of the landscape work? First of all, Cozzens had to find some way of showing the greatness of this majestic landscape, and so he went to considerable effort to show that nature herself had created a spectacle that could mock the most majestic works of man. That those works belonged to the Old World, and particularly to the Orient, reveals a sense of appreciation, even reverence, for that original landscape. However, Cozzens was part of a trend that would ultimately change the way we would view landscape—no longer in the context of works of man but of works of the Great Creator. In that sense, Cozzens was yielding to a more naturalistic philosophy, including that held by Native Americans, rather than that espoused by the patriarchs of old. Such views were more typical of radical Walt Whitman than conservative prophet Brigham Young. For our purposes here, however, the thing to remember is that this more natural philosophy would ultimately undermine Orientalist appreciation and lead to a new way of describing and promoting regional identity, namely, as exceptionally American in nature.

Historian Anne Farrar Hyde noted that people in the nineteenth century tended to find "the far away nearby"—as did Frederick Dellenbaugh, who explored the Grand Canyon with John Wesley Powell and saw in a rock formation "the airy structures evolved by the wonderful lamp of Aladdin." Hyde notes that Major Clarence E. Dutton, who also explored the Grand Canyon with Powell, was a masterful describer of the unusual landscapes here. Dutton observed that travelers whose experience was with the eastern United States or Europe "would enter this strange region with a shock" because they had seen nothing that could compare with the bizarre landforms of the Southwest. Nothing, however, may be too strong a word, for art and literature provided many examples that would fit. Although Dutton used many abstract terms in describing and naming topographic features here, he clearly succumbed to the Orient on a number of occasions. As Hyde put it, Dutton "often chose references to the Far East to express the alien and exotic quality of the landscape." It was Dutton who "filled the depths of the Grand Canyon with shrines, temples, thrones and castles lived in and sat upon by Woton, Shiva, Vishnu, Isis, and even King Arthur."[35]

The important point to remember here is that the combination of people and setting work to substantiate place and at the same time create new places in the imagination. As two southwestern anthropologists recently put it, "Landscapes and people cannot be separated; one entails the other."[36] This is evident in a placid scene that was used to illustrate Lee C. Harby's article titled "Texan Types and Contrasts" in the July 1890 issue of *Harper's New Monthly Magazine*. The artist is Frederick Remington, and the subject is simply titled "Woman Vending Fruit on a Street Corner" (fig. 4-4). Remington made this photo engraving of a street scene in El Paso, Texas. That explanation seems straightforward enough, but consider again this scene's timelessness and, if you will, placelessness. In scrutinizing this engraving, one cannot tell the time period it represents (for it appears to be devoid of modern technology) or where it was encountered (that is, in what hemisphere Remington encountered it). In reality, this scene could be in Tangier or Texas. The background helps a bit, for those adobe buildings with their viga beams suggest the Southwest or Mexico, but in truth the scene's architecture appears to be as much from North Africa or Asia Minor as it is "southwestern." Placelessness, though, may not be quite the correct word here, for the locale is indeed generic, conveying places in both the Orient and the West that look similar enough to be confused. Timelessness, too, may be incorrect because the scene represents a place where an indistinct period of time—that is, tradition—trumps modernity. Then, too, the woman's profile, her covered head, her dress, even her wares, might be as Middle Eastern as they are Hispanic Texan. Remington paradoxically portrays a southwestern American subject that could be southwestern

Fig. 4-4. Although depicting the American Southwest (El Paso), Frederick Remington's *Woman Vending Fruit on a Street Corner* features a subject and locale reminiscent of North Africa, the Near East, or Asia Minor.

Asian. That ambiguity, again, is part of the seductiveness that occurs when new regional identities are created by building on old ones.

In the late nineteenth and early twentieth centuries, the Santa Fe Railway played a major role in promoting and Orientalizing the southwestern pueblos. Their route from Chicago to Los Angeles ran near some of the pueblos and directly through one, namely, Laguna Pueblo in New Mexico. Ever aware of opportunities to increase revenues as well as increase the support of the native peoples here, the railroad stopped passenger trains to enable passengers to purchase handmade items from the Indians. It also sponsored art contests to encourage artists to render the indigenous landscapes and peoples. Many of these artists did just that, using the Orientalist motifs prevalent at the time.

Moreover, the Santa Fe also worked closely with the Fred Harvey Company, which supported ethnographic research enabling them to more effectively promote the "authentic" heritage of the region—and to market that heritage. The Santa Fe Railway created a corporate identity around the Southwest and its indigenous peoples, as did the Southern Pacific railroad that crossed the region closer to the Mexican border.

Along its more southerly route across the Southwest, however, the Southern Pacific had none of the spectacular pueblos, although it did run close to the ancient, multistory adobe "apartment house" called Casa Grande. This part of the region also had the "civilized"—that is, peaceful—Papago or Tohono O'odham Indians. But those civilized Indians had a singular counterpoint: also in Southern Pacific country were the Apache Indians, whose reputation for wildness and cruelty was well known as early as the mid-nineteenth century. The railroads took advantage of the literary fascination with the region, incorporating both fictional and real historical identities into their advertising. Of all railroads operating in the American West a century ago, however, only one actually incorporated the name "Orient" in its official title. That railroad was the Kansas City, Mexico and Orient (KCM&O), a line built southwestward from Kansas City through Oklahoma and Texas into Mexico on its way to the port of Topolobampo. That exotic-sounding port was the Orient railroad's destination, to establish a presence on the shores of the Pacific Ocean. However, the ultimate goal of the "Orient," as it was called, was the Far East.[37]

The railroads and other corporations, including townsite developers, were highly influential in this region. They exercised considerable power in creating both a southwestern, and a romanticized Oriental, heritage here. There is an implication of rejuvenation or rebirth in the Southwest, especially for jaded easterners. Consider Phoenix, Arizona, which still enchants some visitors with its date palms and dry air, especially those willing to overlook its gridlocked traffic and deteriorating air quality. The name *Phoenix* became quite common in the United States in the nineteenth century, and it then had an "Oriental" quality in the popular mind. The phoenix is a legendary bird portrayed in Egyptian stories as native to Arabia. The phoenix lives for a thousand years and then dies after singing a beautiful song and sacrificing itself on a funeral pyre. In a miraculous act, the phoenix is then reborn to live another thousand years after it rises from the ashes. This legend, which is Middle Eastern in origin but is also found in Greece and farther east to southwestern Asia, reminds one how readily Americans incorporated what were originally Oriental motifs into place naming. Naming a community after the phoenix implied that it too would not only be reborn, but would be reborn even stronger and better than the original. In the case of Phoenix, Arizona, settlers in the 1860s and 1870s were well aware of the evidence of an "ancient" culture, the Hohokam, which left an elaborate irrigation system of impressive ditches but had otherwise vanished by the nineteenth century. As both pragmatists and romanticists, these latter-day settlers realized the name *phoenix* resonated as something legendary, irrepressible, and magical—just the qualities that the new, but also very old, city of Phoenix, Arizona, would possess. This may seem fanciful and even more than a little naive today, but it represents the romantically inspired boosterism of the time.[38] Speaking of latter-day settlers, the Mormons were also part of the growing European American population, but added another interpretation: they considered some of these Hohokam earthworks near Phoenix to be the fortifications of ancient Book of Mormon people.

The fabled Phoenix was not the only ancient symbol appropriated by southwestern developers and image builders. In what came to be called "the Valley of the Sun" near Phoenix, the developers used other symbols, including the camel, to connect the new city with the ancient Near East. A revealing advertisement in the 1914 issue of *Progressive Arizona* magazine shows a man clad in Middle Eastern garb overlooking the valley near Phoenix, while his camel nearby also ponders the scene. This advertisement by the Scottsdale Investment & Land Company uses explicit symbols, but some could be more abstract. Consider, for example, the swastika, which appears to be rather universal in that it was known in both the Old World (especially South Asia) and the Native American Southwest. Railroad and mining companies appropriated the swastika in the early twentieth century as a characteristically southwestern symbol. The swastika's adoption is easy to understand. This symbol stood for good luck or good fortune and integrated the four directions of the compass into a potent design. In the period from about 1910 to 1920, the Swastika Coal Company in New Mexico used that symbol on its logo, or herald. Similarly, the Pecos and Northwestern Railroad used the swastika on its logo. This railroad emblazoned the swastika on its locomotive tenders as well as its coal-carrying gondola cars. In the early twentieth-century industrial Southwest, then, it was not unusual to see the swastika in both Native American and Anglo-American contexts. Such iconography naturally vanished by the late 1930s as Adolph Hitler rose to prominence in Germany.[39]

This use of the swastika represents the simulacrum, which on one level simply means an image or representation of something, but on another demands scrutiny as an insubstantial form or semblance of something that insinuates itself broadly and deeply into a culture. The forms or images can be repeated ad infinitum, becoming, as Jean Baudrillard calls them, "second order simulacra." To Baudrillard, these are in essence forgeries that were born out of the Renaissance and manifested in a wide range of objects, "from the deceptive finery on people's backs" to "Baroque theatrical scenery."[40] This again represents a critical view, but people often readily adopt such imagery as part of the process of romanticizing past peoples. Although it involved counterfeiting others—other peoples, other places, other objects—the predisposition to imagine the Orient enabled the East to possess the Southwest.

There was a lot to start with here. The design of the original pueblos greatly contributed to the "Oriental" impression because their cubic form and adobe construction had strong similarities to settlements in parts of North Africa and the Middle East. This imagination-inspired perception also dates from Spanish times here. Explorers from Coronado's time imagined the Indian pueblos they spied from a distance to be fabulous cities that rivaled or eclipsed cities in the Old World. On closer examination, the cube-shaped adobe buildings of both the Native Americans and Spaniards were often considered by travelers in the nineteenth-century Southwest to be duplicates of Old World structures. Scholars too noted the similarities, despite the fact that the two styles of architecture originated in two widely separated but similarly arid regions of the world. In northern Mexico, for example, geographers Robert West and John Augelli attributed the design and exterior appearance of such houses to both Berber and Native American building traditions.[41] Small wonder that the Spaniards felt so at home here, though the Indians often took a different view of their presence.

As historian Jerold Auerbach demonstrated, soldiers and writers were not alone in their tendency to see the Orient near, or south of, the US-Mexico border. By the 1880s, ethnographers were also among those who Orientalized the Southwest and its peoples. Primed with a solid dose of Orientalist thinking from Europe, as well as his own creative imagination, ethnographer Frank Hamilton Cushing saw similarities between the Near East and the southwestern tribes. As Cushing put it, "How strangely parallel have been the lines of development in this curious civilization of an American desert, with those of Eastern nations and deserts." By Eastern, of course, Cushing meant southwestern Asia and the Middle East. Cushing seemed especially enchanted by the "eastern" aspects of southwestern Indians. As natives moved through the region on burros, Cushing mused that he was instead observing "a caravan crossing a desert waste."[42] Moreover, it was not just any Eastern people Cushing encountered here in the Southwest, but a decidedly biblical people. To him, they evoked "a Scripture-like scene" on the one hand, while their religious ceremonies, he

Author's collection

Fig. 4-5. This illustration from *The Illustrated Police News* (1886) of Matilda Cox
Stevenson confronting a Hopi Indian man at Oraibi, Arizona, personifies colonial
authority and indigenous submission.

contended, were "strangely like those of the ancient Egyptians and Greeks."[43]
This reminds us that although the religious component of Orientalism may
have weakened by century's end, it was never completely erased.

Cushing was not alone. His colleague, ethnologist Matilda Cox Stevenson,
was also prone to romanticize the Southwest, as were others, who observed
that the settlements of the Southwest were similar to "the villages of ancient
Egypt and Nubia, Nineveh and Babylon," and that "we must cross deserts
and scale mountains till we reach the Eden of the West."[44] Few images better
reveal Victorian-era prejudices and stereotypes than one showing Stevenson at
Oraibi, in 1886 (fig. 4-5). Stevenson, who began her career studying women
and children, arrived with her husband, James, in that Arizona Hopi Indian
village expecting to be warmly welcomed by the natives. Her goal, after all,
was to study the natives under the auspices of the Smithsonian Institution.
Upon arriving at Oraibi, however, the Stevensons "encountered stiff resistance
to their being in the village, an incident sensationalized some months later by
The Illustrated Police News."

This illustration shows the two ethnographers standing amid the Hopi
Indians, but it is Mrs. Stevenson who commands our attention as she upbraids

a resistant Indian man. As depicted in the scene, Mrs. Stevenson is in full Victorian dress—a symbol of propriety and order—and seemingly in full control. She leans menacingly toward the Indian man, who has evidently fallen or been pushed back against the wall. For our purposes, the Indian is the consummate "other"; true, he is a native of the Southwest, but he might just as well be from the Asian steppe or India itself. In the racist wording of the time, the illustration is derisively titled "cowed by a woman," and provides nominal proof that Indian men—like children—can be disciplined and controlled even by the fairer sex. As the illustration's title continues, "A Craven Red Devil Weakens in the face of a resolute White heroine," who had "exciting adventures in an Indian village in Arizona." The illustration and its caption suggest that these Indians are really not so brave or threatening after all—at least not in the face of a determined Anglo-American. For his part, Mr. Stevenson stands still and aloof, almost like a statue dressed in explorer's attire. His silent presence here is a symbol for a broader colonial authority that empowers—backs up, as it were—the orders from Washington, DC.[45] One can only wonder what would have transpired had the Stevensons confronted Apache or Navajo Indians, rather than the more gentle and docile Hopis. The year of the illustration—1886— suggests considerable bluster as well as bravado, as the battles with Indians like Cochise and Geronimo were beginning to wind down at just this time.

It is here that we need to look more closely at how the native peoples responded. Although it is easy to think of them as victims of a pernicious process of cultural transference and denigration—and that is partly true—it is not the whole story. In fact, Indians were becoming expert at playing the game of seeming primitive while fitting into a broader capitalist economy at just the time that the Santa Fe Railroad penetrated this region in the early 1880s. Within ten years, even the Apaches were serving as goodwill ambassadors at the World's Fair in Chicago, at which simulated southwestern Indian villages were constructed. By 1904, Indians were depicted along with other examples of "primal" peoples from remote parts of the world at the Louisiana Purchase Exposition in Saint Louis. As anthropologist Don Fowler noted, "The expositions from 1889 through 1904 took place during the time when literary, artistic, and touristic attention began to be focused on the Southwest and the commodification of the Indian 'arts and crafts' market got underway."[46] Some Indians were ruined by the process, others tried to avoid it in one way or another, and some managed to benefit from it—taking on a new identity on one level, and increasing their fortunes as a consequence.

Because Anglo-Americans were ambivalent about the peoples of the East, reactions to the Indians here varied. Some Christians were especially critical of

Courtesy Palace of the Governor's Photo Archives (NMHM/DCA, negative no. 012422)

Fig. 4-6. Philip E. Harroun's cyanotype photograph of "A New Mexican Rebecca" (1896) helped endorse the popular view that New Mexico's indigenous peoples were similar to those described in the Bible.

the similarities between Indians and Arabs. Not especially positive about the Orient or the Orientals he encountered in the American Southwest, bombastic and pushy easterner George Wharton James described the Indians negatively. James called them "the Bedouins of the United States, who rival in picturesqueness if not in evil, their compeers of the deserts of the Nile."[47] It should be noted, however, that the southwestern Indians were highly attractive people to the more hedonistically inclined elite of America—Mabel Dodge Luhan being a case in point. She took (and later married) an Indian lover and otherwise went native, or rather Bohemian, in her new Southwestern setting.

Around the turn of the century, then, the Southwest took on the cachet of an exotic and desirable locale. This was a time of florid prose and artistic photography, as Philip E. Harroun's stunning picture of "A New Mexican Rebecca" (1896) reveals (fig. 4-6). To these travelers and photographers, the Pueblo Indians were remarkable survivors of ancient cultures; moreover, their days were numbered, or so travelers thought. This made the tendency to snatch trappings from their culture—rugs, pots, jewelry—all the more tempting. These appeared throughout the Midwest and Eastern Seaboard, as parlors and mantels sported artifacts from America's own ancient land. Native customs also provided a glimpse into what seemed an ancient, Asian world. For example, the Pueblo Indians' fascination with, and use of, the snake in various ceremonies (such as the Hopi Snake Dance) titillated Anglo-American

Protestants. The latter regarded snakes with terror and disdain and equated the Indians who handled them with the "snake charmers" of the East. That one element alone—veneration of snakes—helped cast Native American identity here in terms of the Orientals who felt no compunction about venerating the same serpents that had tempted Eve.

Well into the twentieth century, ethnographers and physical anthropologists alike Orientalized the American Indians of the Southwest as they searched for connections linking them to the peoples of antiquity. Consider, for example, Aleš Hrdlička, a Czech-Bohemian-born American medical anthropologist who believed in the oneness of the human race. Widely read and widely traveled, Hrdlička made an interesting observation while in Mongolia in 1912. Of the village of Urga, Hrdlička claimed that "people are swarming in the markets which is a harvest [that is, feast] for my eyes; and so many resemble the [American] Indian that I feel as if I were in a Mexican rather than an Asiatic town." Hrdlička was obsessed by the similarities between Asians and Native American Indians, for as he put it, "There can be no question about it that many of these [Mongolian] people have the same blood in them as the American natives."[48] This claim is, of course, partly true in the genetic sense, but its cultural implications are enormous. Rather than being racists, many observers like Hrdlička viewed race as a series of physical traits that could ultimately unify all of humankind. Also enormous was the realization that cultural similarities, like the crowding of a marketplace, united peoples on two continents. This kind of Orientalism, then, is paradoxically something that differentiates at the same time it unifies.

Orientalism can work both ways, or rather in both hemispheres. Therefore, we must also recall that Anglo-Americans who experienced the Southwest could travel to the "real" East and bring New Mexico with them. In traveling into the hills near Beyrout (Beirut), Lebanon, American writer Bayard Taylor was accompanied by two men: "Dervish, an erect, black-bearded, and most impassive Mussulman [i.e., Muslim], and Mustapha, who is the very picture of patience and good-nature." These men, Taylor claimed, "are both masters of their art, and can load a mule with a speed and skill which I would defy any Santa Fé trader to excel." The use of the name *Santa Fe* is noteworthy here, for Taylor was at least six thousand miles from that New Mexico community. Yet he could in effect Occidentalize the Muslims here in the Middle East by comparing them to their New World counterparts, who were ironically often compared to their Old World counterparts.[49]

Being interfaces between words and pictures, maps of the time can help us understand the subtle (and sometimes not so subtle) relationship between the

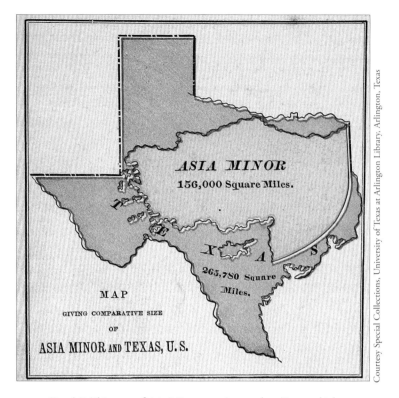

Fig. 4-7. This map of Asia Minor superimposed on Texas, which appeared in Jesse Lyman Hurlbut's *The Bible Atlas* (1884), provides a size comparison but also equates the two places in the popular mind.

American Southwest and the Orient. Consider a map of Texas on which Asia Minor is superimposed. This "Map Giving Comparative Size of Asia Minor and Texas" was first published by Rand McNally. It appeared in the *Bible Atlas: A Manual of Biblical Geography and History* by the Reverend Jesse Lyman Hurlbut (1884) and was published in numerous editions into the twentieth century (fig. 4-7). That name *Asia Minor* served to identify an area that was transitional between the real Asia and Europe and included Turkey. The juxtaposition of Asia Minor on Texas, purportedly to provide a size comparison, is doubly interesting, as Texas is likewise a transition from the eastern United States and the real West, which reportedly began in the vicinity of Fort Worth. Significantly, that city is about centered on the Asia Minor portion of the map.

By the early twentieth century, postcards perpetuated Orientalized images of both the landscapes and the peoples of the Southwest. In them, more or less anonymous Indian pueblos could double, or nearly double, for villages in the Middle East or southwestern Asia. Consider, for example, Laguna Pueblo

Fig. 4-8. In popular art and photographs, New Mexico's Indian pueblos were depicted as timeless places that could be in either the Near East or the American Southwest. Postcard titled "Plaza and Old Church, Laguna Indian Pueblo," distributed by the Southwest Post Card Co., Albuquerque, ca. 1930.

(fig. 4-8), which at first glance could be a colorized postcard from Turkey. Only by looking more closely do we make out the church, but the architecture and colorful apparel suggest the East as much as they do the American West. Then, too, consider the "formula" that such postcards' photographers employed. The photographer usually stands facing a row of stone or adobe buildings and includes the rugged setting behind the village as a background. This reveals the seemingly minimal impact that the population has had on the surrounding environment. A lone figure or two in costume usually stands in the scene, enabling the viewer to identify the person as indigenous and the village as occupied rather than abandoned.

When the human subject is central to the scene, as in "Pueblo Indian Woman at Spring" (fig. 4-9), the photographer emphasizes the indigenous person's role in a traditional activity—herding, spinning, or collecting water. In point of fact, many such postcards are enhanced; the costumes are made even more colorful and the artifacts' details more ornate than they were in real life. After all, these figures are supposed to look (and hence be) exotic. In a telling blurring of Indian and environment, the verso of the postcard points out "the Indian head which nature has sculpted into the rock." That stone face, presented side by side with the living person, implies that the Indian, like the

Fig. 4-9. Images and words frequently portrayed Native Americans in the Southwest as ancient or natural subjects. The verso of this postcard (ca. 1930) titled "Pueblo Indian Woman at Spring" adds: "Note the Indian Head which nature has sculptured into the rock above."

environment, is timeless. Unlike the Anglo-American, the Indian is portrayed as more a part of nature than modern civilization.

These landscapes-as-cultural-analogies are fascinating, and they often lead us back to images captured in the real Orient—images that appeared in the popular press of the time. Naturally, the tendency to "see" the Orient in Native American culture says more about Anglo-Americans than it does about Indians, or for that matter Asians, but that does not make the process any less real. The point here is that by around the turn of the twentieth century, a perceived taming of the Southwest, through the subduing of Native Americans and the arrival of sufficient civilizing, orderly elements, finally won out over those political and social interests who resisted giving statehood to this once seemingly lawless and barbaric region. The marketing of the images of peoples and landscapes here also helped lay the groundwork for a modern tourist industry based in part on enduring stereotypes of the Asian or Middle Eastern exotic in what now became home after New Mexico and Arizona were both finally permitted to become states just a century ago (1912).

5

The Far East in the Far West
Chinese and Japanese California

"The Pacific Coast has its natural front door toward the Orient."

Rollo Walter Brown, *I Travel by Train* (1939)

THE DISCOVERY OF GOLD IN THE WINTER OF 1848, followed by official confirmation of the gold strikes a few months later, bound California to Asia as surely as it bound it to the rest of the United States. In California, the real Orient, in the form of Chinese immigrants, was destined to meet the fantasized visions of the Orient carried westward by Anglo-Americans. Stories of mining wealth brought both the Asians and the Americans face-to-face for the first time. For their part, the Anglo-Americans were primed by literature to conceive of such fabulous wealth in Oriental terms.

Consider again the popularity of the *Arabian Nights* tale about Aladdin and the magic lamp as a case in point. As Felix Paul Wierzbicki wrote in *California As It Is, and As It May Be* (1849), "Heretofore we have heard nothing but Arabian Nights stories about the gold region, drawn, if possible, with more vivid colors than even the Asiatic fancy could conjure up." Wierzbicki went on to warn would-be gold seekers that although "the whole civilized world is electrified with these surprising stories and set in motion, and every day brings strangers to our shores from the most distant regions of the earth," people should be wary of such extravagant claims. As Wierzbicki put it, "Even our government at home had not received an official account from its subordinates here, that represent the truth in its simple garb," but nevertheless people "were content to seize upon a few remarkable cases" and act with near abandon. One wonders whether Wierzbicki was being overcautious or simply found the crush of newcomers from all "regions of the earth" disquieting to his sense of California as bucolic paradise.[1] For whatever reason, Wierzbicki was too

155

cautious in this case, for the historical record confirms that California's Gold Rush represents one of the truly remarkable mineral discoveries, and resulting migrations, in world history. Even though a substantial number of the argonauts returned home within a decade, the die had been cast. California soon became the Golden State. Small wonder, then, that references to Aladdin's magic lamp abounded here. As a popular 1850 history noted, "When miners had seen the hoards of gold, some of it in flakes, but greater part in coarse dust . . . it seemed as if the fabled treasures of the Arabian Nights had suddenly been realized before them."[2] Significantly, although Aladdin's story is Middle Eastern in origin, that young man discovers the hidden wealth underground as he travels to China. By using his newfound magic lamp, Aladdin not only becomes rich but also attains a social status that he once only dreamed of. The story of Aladdin involves traveling great distances and returning home able to transform one's life. Small wonder that it became one of the premier metaphors in describing the mining West over the next fifty years.[3] Aladdin became what Americans commonly called a nabob—a Hindi term for one who returns home from the East a rich man.

Word of the California Gold Rush spread so quickly that it reached the east coast of Asia at about the same time it reached the Eastern Seaboard of the United States. When news of the "Golden Mountain"—or *Gum Shan,*" as California was called in China—reached Guangdong Province in 1849, portions of China were in chaos. Extensive flooding in the Pearl River had displaced thousands, and food shortages now brought the country to the brink of catastrophe. Learning of opportunities to mine gold in California, thousands of Chinese men joined the Gold Rush, rapidly transforming the landscape and ethnicity of the American West shortly after their arrival. Although there were a hundred or so Chinese in California in 1849, the number soon swelled to thousands, as those who sought new opportunities in Gold Mountain boarded ships in Canton (Guangzhou). Most of these Chinese men who migrated to the West at this time were from the hard-hit Guangdong Province, and most of them left families behind for what they thought would be a relatively short time—only long enough to return home wealthy. Their journey seemed natural for several reasons, among them Guangdong Province's long history of gold mining.

By the early 1850s, Chinese miners and their works became an integral part of the western landscape. Driven away from many of the richest placer mining sites by Anglo-American miners, the industrious Chinese often picked over the dregs. Despite this, they had a knack for recovering a substantial amount of gold, though how much they found is unknown. As the Chinese became a fixture in the California goldfields, they transformed the landscape, leaving carefully piled stones in their wake. This methodical handiwork typified the discipline and organization with which the Chinese worked. They soon participated in other gold mining booms, including southern Oregon, but it all started in California.[4]

For their part, Anglo-Americans lured to the Gold Rush had a revealing expression about their experience. To them, it involved "Seeing the Elephant," a term of obscure origins but signifying the exotic or unusual. According to Gerald Conti, "Seeing the Elephant" may have originated as far back as the time of Alexander the Great, whose Macedonian warriors triumphed over King Porus's elephant-mounted troops in the Indus Valley. A thousand years later, the Frankish world got its first look at an elephant when an enterprising Arab merchant brought one from Baghdad to Aix for the Frankish emperor. But the use of the term *seeing the elephant* in America has, according to Conti, a "more ironic derivation." It may have originated in 1820s New England, when a farmer traveled to town to see a circus but never made it. Like all respectable circuses, this one had an elephant, and the farmer looked forward to seeing it. According to the tale, the farmer's horse-drawn wagon had entered an intersection obscured by trees, only to be smashed to smithereens by a circus wagon. The farmer's wagon was wrecked and his horse killed, but he consoled himself with the fact that he had "Seen the Elephant."[5]

The term was so intriguing that it was used to signify one's experience in searching for adventure a couple of decades later by soldiers in the US-Mexican War. However, the phrase became especially widespread during the California Gold Rush, when many Americans from the nation's East and Midwest dropped everything in order to strike it rich in the goldfields. Interestingly, even those who failed to find wealth in the Gold Rush could still claim to be enriched upon their return. They may not have become rich, but at least they had seen the elephant.

The elephant, of course, is native to both Africa and South Asia, and it became the perfect symbol for the exotic. In the vivid imaginations of mid-nineteenth century American gold seekers, seeing the elephant personified adventure. In *Great Platte River Road*, Merrill Mattes concludes that the elephant was "the popular symbol of great adventure, all the wonder and the glory and the shivering thrill of the plunge into the ocean of prairie and plains, and the brave assault on the mountains and deserts that were gigantic barriers to [finding] California gold."[6] Appropriately enough, one of the Far West's first locomotives was named "Elephant," and it operated on California's Sacramento Valley Railroad in the mid-1850s.[7]

In Gold Rush–era California, seeing the elephant might also mean getting an eyeful of the bawdy side of life that was forbidden in much of rural and small-town America. As San Francisco began to boom during the Gold Rush, one part of the city—the Barbary Coast—soon gained the reputation as the proverbial den of iniquity. Situated on the city's northern edge, the Barbary Coast was named after North Africa's famed shoreline of the same name, the lawless zone where slave traders plied their human wares, pirates and other miscreants congregated, and vice flourished. Similarly, in the San Francisco counterpart, social critics found much to abhor. Writers in the 1850s and 1860s tell of Asian women being purchased, opium being consumed, and violent crime running rampant. One nineteenth-century observer noted that one could go from a largely Caucasian area of the city and within ten steps enter "another world," where "the uncouth jargon of the Celestial Empire resounds on every side." In the Barbary Coast, he observed, "the stores are filled with strange looking packages of goods from the Orient; [and] over the doorways are great signs, with letters in gold and vermilion, cut into the brilliant blue or black groundwork, the purport whereof we know not." This writer also described the many pleasures available in this "barbaric" portion of San Francisco.[8] Note, however, that if the real Barbary Coast suggested a North African Muslim presence, the San Francisco equivalent found the Chinese filling the niche as prostitutes, drug dealers, thieves, and worse. In a way, this is similar to the general term *street Arabs* that one often heard in American cities. These were not real Arabs but rather impoverished people of any race, including poor whites. The term's origin, though, no doubt refers to what was then a common sight in portions of the Arab world, namely, the proliferation of beggars in public places.

Anglo-American residents in California continued to marvel at the handiwork of Chinese miners long after the Gold Rush subsided in the 1860s. So too did increasing numbers of tourists seeking a firsthand look at the Golden State. Chinese miners toiling in boulder-strewn riverbeds were popular subjects for late nineteenth-century photographers. In a striking stereopticon photograph, properly dressed Victorian-era European Americans observe Chinese miners at their craft in Northern California (fig 5-1). The miners have diverted water and have in effect turned the creek bed's rocks and gravel upside down in order to extract the gold. The contrast between the miners, in their traditional (and practical) ethnically rooted dress, and the more elegantly attired observers, is noteworthy—a reminder that sustaining Victorian culture took backbreaking work, much of it performed by lower-class laborers. This photograph also serves as a reminder that increased leisure time, a hallmark of Victorian culture, was not shared by all.

Fig. 5-1. In this pair of nineteenth-century stereopticon photographs juxtaposing work and leisure, tourists observe Chinese miners reworking a played out placer mine in Northern California.

China's special and peculiar relationship to the American West since the era of the California Gold Rush intensified with the building of the transcontinental railroad. As an astute observer and shrewd entrepreneur, Central Pacific Railroad's Charles Crocker realized that Chinese workers could perform miracles for the transcontinental railroad he and other members of the "Big Four" envisioned. Thus, in the mid-1860s, the Central Pacific Railroad induced even more Chinese to come to California. In 1866, aware of the industriousness of the Chinese in California who were now performing wonders constructing the Central Pacific Railroad as "Crockers's Coolies," Union Pacific's manager, Grenville Dodge, wrote that "I have for several years been anxious to visit China, with a view to endeavor to introduce and build Rail Roads, believing it would be one of the best and quickest agents to build up and bring into communication that Empire." By doing this, Dodge felt "I could so develop the facilities of Rail transportation in China as to make it there as it is here a national blessing."[9] Despite Dodge's enthusiasm, however, China was not as open to westernization at that time as he had hoped. Forty years later, an American entrepreneur offered a more sobering assessment: "It must always be kept in mind that the twentieth century development of China will be along lines Chinese and not European; that is, it will be in conformity with native characteristics, modified by modern ideas."[10]

Regardless of his enthusiasm in 1866, Dodge had his hands full competing with the Central Pacific. And besides, history has shown that more than a century would pass before China could blossom into the commercial giant it is today. Nevertheless, Dodge knew something about the character of the Chinese worker, which helped explain the intensity with which railroad construction proceeded. By summer of 1868, the Union Pacific was rapidly laying rail across the Great Plains, bound for a meeting with the Central Pacific Railroad somewhere—the location was yet to be determined—in the interior West. For its part, Central Pacific was performing herculean roadbed grading with its force of Chinese workers, who repeatedly proved their ability to get jobs done quickly and efficiently.

In popular culture, no single aspect of the western drama was more associated with the Chinese than the building of the transcontinental railroad in the mid to late 1860s, and no place more so than California. The relationship was symbiotic. Facing stiff competition from the Union Pacific, which was rapidly building west out of Omaha, the Central Pacific's Chinese laborers helped the California-owned railroad surmount the Sierra Nevada in 1865. By 1868, more than ten thousand Chinese workers were on the Central Pacific payroll grading the railroad line through Nevada. To document their efforts for the reading public, *Frank Leslie's Illustrated Newspaper* dispatched Joseph Becker to California. Becker's goal was to write a series of articles, but he had to move quickly because the newspaper's goal was to "scoop" other publications flocking to the West. Given the growing power of visual images at the time, the newspaper also dispatched two artists, Harry Ogden and Walter Yaeger, to help Becker record the railroad's construction. In California, especially, their drawings featured Chinese workers engaging in the drama of building the West. Cultural historian Deidre Murphy observes, however, that these scenes show the Chinese workers as deferential to the American technology: "Mesmerized and physically 'sidelined' by the train, they linger somewhere between the landscape all around them and the speeding railroad cars before them."[11]

Even when a train is not present, however, the Chinese are significant features in the California landscape. In this regard, Joseph Becker's *Wood-Shoots in the Sierra* is worth a closer look (fig. 5-2). Becker depicted the distinctive flumes or chutes that conveyed lumber (notably redwood railroad ties) down to the Chinese working on the railroad. These enter the scene at steep angles, emphasizing the canyon's depth. Situated in the deep canyon, the Chinese workers are elements in this composition, their forms unifying the "shoots" (i.e., chutes) with the railroad. That railroad line disappears around the bend, where a huge pine tree marks the juncture of mountain and railroad bed. The sheer size and steepness of those mountains render the scene exotic—rather like a Chinese painting where sky and landscape merge in a hazy, ethereal mix. It is above all, though, the presence of Chinese workers in the scene

Fig. 5-2. In *Wood Shoots in the Sierra*, Chinese workers supply wooden ties to the Central Pacific Railroad they helped build through the mountains. Source: *Frank Leslie's Illustrated Newspaper,* 1868.

that renders it exotic. As most observers and readers of the period knew, the railroad line would not have been built the way it was without Chinese labor.

On May 10, 1869, when the Pacific Railroad was completed, and the golden spike was driven home at Promontory Summit, Utah, many people commented on the nation's changing geographic position and geopolitical situation. When the two locomotives touched pilots (cowcatchers) to complete the transcontinental railroad in 1869, an illustration immortalizing the event noted "The East and The West" had met, with "The Orient and Occident Shaking Hands after Driving the Last Spike." Given the position of the trains, the illustration's caption considers the Central Pacific to be the Eastern (Oriental) road and the Union Pacific is the Western (Occidental). This at first seems counterintuitive, for after all, the Central Pacific came from the west, and the Union Pacific from the east. However, the caption also represented an ironic truth: the Central Pacific, with its large contingent of Chinese workers and its direct connection to a Pacific port (San Francisco) directly linked to ports of the Orient was, in fact, the truly "Eastern" (that is, Oriental) railroad in the drama. Similarly, the Union Pacific, building from east to west, would normally be considered the eastern road, but symbolizes the push to open the West—that is, it represented the driving spirit of a westward-moving nation.[12]

In reporting events of that day, the *Pacific Tourist* related "a curious incident" associated with "the laying of the last rails," which "has been little noticed hitherto." This incident took place when "two lengths of rails . . . had been omitted." To fill this gap, the Union Pacific had rails brought up and placed "by Europeans." The Central Pacific, however, brought up its rails with "the labor being performed by Mongolians." As might be expected, the foremen overseeing the work of both crews "were Americans." This the *Pacific Tourist* viewed as highly symbolic. As they put it: "Here, near the center of the Great American Continent, were representatives of Asia, Europe and America—America directing and controlling."[13] One of the many motives that Americans had to Orientalize the West was a belief that the United States was destined to rule peoples of diverse ethnicity there, and elsewhere.

In addition to their major role in transcontinental railroad construction, the Chinese also worked for other railroads. For example, they helped grade rights-of-way and bore tunnels for California's narrow gauge Santa Cruz & Felton Railway. In 1879, a blast in one of the tunnels killed two dozen Chinese workers, only one of whom was identified by name in a report published in the *Santa Cruz Sentinel*. That Chinese worker was named "Jim" and, as a telegraph agent named Cook noted, possessed a "heroic spirit that dwelt in the clay of the Mongolian slave." Given the virulent anti-Chinese sentiment at the time, however, many white laborers felt that the remaining Chinese workers should be sent into the most dangerous part of the tunnel, where they would either "wing their flowery way to the Celestial land or hunt the sources of the fires that keep the volcanoes in perpetual motion." This was a perfect Victorian-era metaphor for what the white workers felt about the Chinese, who would either find heaven or hell, but be gone in any event. In reality, things were not that simple. The conditions in the tunnel remained so dangerous that Chinese workers refused to enter, that is, until an exorcism of sorts was performed to rid the tunnel of its evil spirits. The *Sentinel* noted that ridding the site of "the devils they asserted were in the tunnel" was accomplished when the Chinese "proceeded . . . by burning incense and plastering Celestial hieroglyphics over the face of the first set of timbers."[14] Arcane rites like these fascinated Anglo-Americans and helped impart an exotic touch to California's engineering works.

As historian Daniel Liestman noted in a recent essay, the arrival of the Chinese in the American West was treated with ambivalence by Anglo-Americans.[15] Historian Laurie Maffly-Kipp also interprets this ambivalence by noting that despite the negative characterizations of the Chinese, "many Anglo Westerners, particularly those in California, also evinced great aesthetic delight in the distinctive substance of the 'mystical East,' seeing the presence of Chinese culture as a singular hallmark of their Pacific paradise." Maffly-Kipp also observes that the characterization of Chinese ceremonies in California, such as "Chinese Feeding the Dead," which appeared in popular publications like *Harper's Weekly*, "reminded Euro-American readers that religion was a physical and communal experience" shared by all peoples. However, "it also suggested the disquieting elements of such ceremony, gestures and actions hidden in the blur of bodies and shadowed places." Whereas the Anglo-American elite at the time sought to depict the Chinese as having a valid religion, popular culture knew (or believed) better: writings like Bret Harte's story "Wan Lee, the Pagan" offered an "array of physical and emotional responses—both positive and negative" that were intellectual and visceral. Anglo-Americans took a strong interest in Chinese burial customs, rites, and ancient spirits, which somehow seemed far more potent and far less benign than Christian saints. Maffly-Kipp astutely notes that Anglo-Americans inherently feared certain aspects of Chinese culture, especially those (like opium) that could insinuate themselves into one's body. And yet, "the encounter with religious difference"—like Orientalism itself—"could also lead to a new acquaintance with oneself." [16]

The Chinese presence expanded into other parts of California. In addition to gold mining, the Chinese were involved in other mineral production ventures. In describing the well-organized efforts by Chinese workers in late nineteenth-century Death Valley, historian Dean Lemon noted that borax ore "was scraped by Chinese laborers from the valley floor into piles so that it could drain, then shoveled into carts, transferred to horse drawn wagons and [then] brought to the plant." The ore that the Chinese workers excavated from the dry lake bed here was cottonball ulexite, one of nature's peculiar products in extremely arid lands such as interior California and Tibet. The description of the Chinese workers' handiwork here, though, is particularly interesting to those fascinated by how people make sense of cultural landscapes. As Lemon went on to observe, "Those who have been fortunate enough to fly over Death Valley have seen the extensive patterns of the [ulexite] harvesting areas, which look exactly like huge Chinese checkerboards still apparent after 115 years." [17] This, of course, is a partly accurate and partly fanciful description. The regularity of this ordered landscape is indisputable, but comparing it to an evocative aspect of Chinese material culture—a board game—imaginatively reinforces a sense of Chinese order on the otherwise chaotic landscape of California's Death Valley. By making such connections, Lemon ingeniously brands the landscape with a Chinese rectangularity that in turn mirrors their highly organized and highly effective work habits. Lemon's imaginative description is a reminder that perceptions of cultural landscapes reflect deeply held beliefs and values.[18]

Not far west of Death Valley as the crow flies, but almost three miles (5 km) higher in elevation, California's stupendous alpine scenery called for an explanation. Given the Orientalism of the times, some observers interpreted it in Asian terms. In describing the Sierra Nevada, for example, Orientalist writer William Speer noted that "the Creator has set, in royal majesty, the throne of the sovereigns of the vegetable world" here. Those sovereigns were, of course, the regal giant redwoods, which appeared "taller than the tallest columns or spires that man has built in the New World, towering in a pyramid of living green." These trees were so ancient that they invited high praise, and Speer was up to the task. As he put it, "There is an empire with which we associate naturally such an emblem, the oldest empire in the world." This, Speer noted, might suggest "Assyria, Persia, Egypt, Greece, [or] Rome, [which] have risen and gone," but he had something else in mind. It was, in fact, "the Chinese race," as he called it, which he noted "is still the same, scarcely tinged by the admixture of others." In Speer's mind, China was a venerable empire where "the primeval religion, customs and literature are still vigorous and fresh." Like the sentinels in the Sierra, China was magnificent: "We contemplate, amidst all the ruins [that] Time has wrought elsewhere, such an empire with constant amazement and curiosity." China, in other words, reflected a culture that was both ancient and essentially unchanged. Like the giant trees, it was magnificent. Pondering both the trees and China, one could stare down time, that is, witness it operating without creating ruin. In this manner, Speer juxtaposed features of what he called "The Oldest and Newest Empire."[19] The observers quoted here recognized that Chinese and other eastern Asian peoples had become a significant element in the West's cultural landscape since their arrival in the mid-nineteenth century. More to the point here, Asians had also now become a significant element in broader popular perceptions of the West. To Anglo-Americans, Asians stood out. Given the vast cultural differences between "the races," as people put it, Chinese people tended to be segregated from the white population. One writer went so far as to claim that "Whites and Chinese seem as incapable of mixing as oil and water."[20] In this regard, postcards can be especially informative of popular sensitivities, or rather insensitivities. In addition to mining and railroad scenes, images of the Asian West appear in two other distinctly different but related forms—the built urban landscape loosely called *Chinatown*, and the human-centered portraits best called *Asian subjects*.

The first, Chinatown, commemorates one of the West's more easily recognized repositories of Asians. Although other cities in the United States, including New York, might feature a Chinatown, it is a peculiarly western phenomenon, closely associated with mining and railroad development. California played a major role in the establishment of Chinese American culture, but it soon spread to other areas. Consider, for example, the Nevada mining and railroad towns of Virginia City, Elko, and Winnemucca. All have an identifiable section of town that earned the name *Chinatown*. Similarly, each of the West Coast's larger cities—Seattle, Portland, San Francisco, and Los Angeles, for example—has a substantial Chinatown. In Chinatown, an encounter with the Orient—sometimes sinister, sometimes inspirational—awaited.

Although the name suggests the negative factor of segregation, Chinatown was, and is, a place of considerable charm, intrigue, and mystery. On the negative side of its attractiveness, at least in the mainstream view, Chinatown was associated with vice, namely drugs (especially opium) and sex (prostitution). In prose and fiction, writers would explore and exploit Americans' fascination with Chinatown. Those writings involved racial and cultural stereotyping but above all promoted the idea of Chinatown as offering pleasures forbidden to the broader Anglo-American Christian culture.

The growing popularity of Chinatown in the 1880s suggests its close ties to evolving Victorian culture. As historian Kenneth Ames observed, the tendency for Victorians to surround themselves with an array of artifacts borrowed from many places, including the Near and Far East, suggests something deeper than simple aesthetics. As he put it, "People in Victorian America were deeply conflicted over most of the central issues that occupy human societies—issues of power and power relations, the distribution of wealth and resources, gender roles and expectations, definition and enforcement of appropriate beliefs and behaviors, and resolution of tensions between continuity and change."[21] Small wonder that their material culture was a hodgepodge of artifacts borrowed from around the world.

Not so coincidentally, perhaps, this era also gave rise to the museum. It too was a collection of material things—specimens, artifacts, and the like—that might reflect "bourgeois acquisitiveness" on the one hand but were also "invested with a meaning deeper than as signifiers of status." To Americans, as historian Steven Conn observed, these objects "were connected directly with ideas and with knowledge of the world." Conn also argues that the fifty-year period from about 1876 to 1926 witnessed a profound change in American intellectual life from an object-based epistemology to one in which the objects lost meaning.[22]

During the Victorian period, Oriental (and other) artifacts became so commonly used as to nearly overwhelm the typical dwelling and its occupants as well as the cultural landscape itself, as replicas of pagodas and ancient palaces sprang up full-blown and Chinatowns became centers of interest. This, according to historian Siegfried Giedion, represented a devaluation of symbols. It resulted from the mechanization of the culture, which could now produce a huge number of near replicas of things that were once associated with nobility.[23] As Ames succinctly put it, "We still do not really know why the culture chose to give its material culture exaggerated form," but as he concludes, "Victorian Americans' culture was . . . consciously and deliberately a culture of artificiality, of imitation, of pretending and pretention."[24] Art historian John MacKenzie observes that Orientalism represented "a reflection of Victorian doubt and apprehension, suffused with a yearning for transcultural inscription."[25] By this, MacKenzie meant that Orientalists were intrepid enough to adopt new designs from a foreign culture that could enrich their own, but this tendency revealed some very deep concerns about cultural solidarity and identity.

These statements may be true enough, but in the case of Chinatown there is another factor at play. Although Chinatown seems to be as much an Anglo-Orientalist invention as a real place, it is worth noting that it was as much the invention of Chinese American entrepreneurs who lived and worked there. Typically, an association of influential Chinese Americans worked closely to create the image of Chinatown, from stylized architectural elements (for example, pagodalike facades) to stylized urban design elements (such as impressive, Chinese-style arches) marking the entryway to this part of town. Colors were, and are, important to capturing the feel of China. Bright, saturated colors—Chinese or China red, for example—dominate here. This deliberate visual theming began about 1890 and continues to the present, for Chinatown has become as much a marketable commodity as an authentic cultural neighborhood. However, Chinatown also represents an early flowering of Chinese American cultural pride as well as a partnership between European American and Chinese American leaders.

In 1900, the *San Francisco Call* enthusiastically predicted that the city "will become the twentieth century art center of the world." Anticipating readers' questions, the paper rhetorically asked: "Why? Because nature has offered with a prodigal hand mountain and sea together; sand dunes, Chinatown, and the bay, and, most of all and above all, the true sentiment of this city's mysterious charm—the fog." This city's mysterious quality was portrayed in decidedly Orientalist terms by the *San Francisco Call*, which could only gain from the characterization. In describing "Theodore Wores [who] spent five years in the

Fig. 5-3. In this postcard mailed in 1905, Fish Alley in San Francisco's Chinatown offered a glimpse of the exotic in this part of the city.

Orient and returned to San Francisco to find a perfect garden of Oriental bloom right here in our Chinatown," the *Call* was pleased to offer a version of the "why-travel-abroad (when you can have it here)?" sentiment. As Wores put it: "If you wish to study the Orient [you should] locate in San Francisco." To further prove the point, the paper printed photos of several Asianlike scenes, including two Chinese children in authentic Chinese dress, a scantily clad and shapely young Asian girl, and a number of equally evocative landscapes such as the rocky wave-pounded seashore, small sailing vessels in the harbor, and forested hilly scenes.[26]

Turn-of-the-century postcards of Chinatown in San Francisco are especially evocative and deserve a closer look for the image(s) they convey of a people and place. A color postcard of Fish Alley in San Francisco's Chinatown (fig. 5-3) offers a glimpse of the ethnic character of this district, with its hanging lanternlike ornaments, ornate railings, and a sidewalk lined with tables and baskets. The dress of all the people in the postcard is authentic enough to suggest the real thing—at least in the mind of the postcard buyer/sender. Inscribed on December 31, 1904, this card was postmarked San Francisco, January 1, 1905, and sent to relatives in Los Angeles as a New Year's greeting.

Tellingly, many early twentieth-century postcards of Chinatown feature residential scenes, almost invariably with Chinese individuals or families. "A

A HAPPY FAMILY IN CHINATOWN

Fig. 5-4. As seen in this postcard of "A Happy Family in Chinatown," ca. 1906, this part of San Francisco reflected a mix of peoples living in humble surroundings.

Happy Family in Chinatown" (fig. 5-4) builds on that theme, but looking more closely, we see that the family members appear to represent several ethnic groups. On Chinese American menus, "Happy Family" refers to a meal featuring a mixture of chicken, beef, and shrimp as well as vegetables; thus this Happy Family terminology on the postcard suggests an ethnic smorgasbord of mixed races. Moreover, the condition of the home, with its ramshackle siding and jerry-built stovepipe, might have reminded postcard viewers that many of these "happy" families were not well-off. Here we are supposed to interpret the Oriental as both satisfied and acculturating. Throughout the West, however, such seemingly mundane scenes revealed the Chinese family as the "other," a counterpart to the ideal American family that was likely white, Christian, and upwardly mobile.

The California encounter with the Chinese was always ambivalent. Recalling her experiences in a central California Chinese mining camp, Helen Rocca Goss noted that "it was a childhood thrill to look into an open door and see a squatting man holding his bowl of rice and using chop sticks." However, she quickly added that it was "not such a thrill sometimes, to see and have to pass, cross old sows, wallowing in a dirty muddy ditch."[27] Then, too, sometimes the Chinese were cast in truly sinister roles. They had a reputation of being both deferential and vengeful. In this latter regard, which titillated Anglo-American cultural fantasies, they were associated with sensational crimes in numerous cities, such as San Francisco, Los Angeles, and Seattle.

Consider lastly a postcard featuring a lone male subject. Its main theme—a "Chinese Highbinder"—stands proudly, some might say defiantly, on a boardwalk in front of a building (fig. 5-5). This color image makes one wonder just where the picture was taken. Was it in San Francisco, where the postcard was published in about 1904? Or perhaps in China, taken by a traveler or missionary visiting that foreign land? It is probably a San Francisco scene, for *highbinder* was a common term in that city. As the term was used for someone who can be hired for criminal deeds, including assassinations, this highbinder seems ominous indeed. But then we must also wonder: Is this Chinese man really a highbinder at all, or just posing as one?

Postcards like this raise as many questions as they answer: Was the Chinese man (whether or not he was a real highbinder) paid for posing, or was he just standing there in a more or less natural state? Most revealing about this image is the simple, four-word message inscribed below the picture: "Don't he look fierce." We know that the card was sent to a woman, but was the sender male or female? The sender of this postcard obviously thought the subject seemed, or was supposed to seem, menacing. So we are here left with additional questions. Because there is no question mark at the end of that sentence, one wonders whether the sender meant it as a simple statement of fact—the Chinese Highbinder looks fierce—or as a mocking statement something along the lines of "he thinks he looks fierce, but I/we know better." If there was a gender difference between writer and sender, then that makes our speculation about the reaction of the addressee when she received the card all the more interesting. Was this some male on a visit to San Francisco trying to impress a woman he knew? Our question, however, is mooted by an interesting fact about this card: mailed from Watsonville, California, on October 1, 1906, and sent to a Miss Helen Wheeler in Santa Barbara, the verso of this card reveals that it

Fig. 5-5. Mailed in 1906, this postcard of "A Chinese Highbinder" contains the provocative inscription "Don't he look fierce."

was never actually received, or as the postal mark soberly indicates, "Failed of delivery for want of time."

The seamless equating of California with the Orient coincided in part with the visibility and effectiveness of Asian workers here. In 1870, George W. Pine discussed the Chinese and Japanese in considerable detail in his "Bird's-Eye View of California." As the large estates were being "divided up for the good of the many," Pine noted that "the Japanese have purchased large sections of land here, for the purpose of cultivating the mulberry and making silk." Pine added that "they are, no doubt, the most skillful silk growers in the world" but noted that the physical environment helped support their activity. Here in California, as Pine concluded, "the climate and soil is supposed to be admirably adapted to the business"—a subtle way of implying that climatic conditions are similar between Asia and California.[28] In point of fact, California's Mediterranean climate differed from that of humid East Asia, though both places could sustain mulberry trees whose bark could be converted into a silk-like linen, according to Louis Prevost's 1867 book titled *California Silk Grower's Manual.*

The efficiency of the Asians was disquieting to Anglo-Americans, who hoped California would be a land of plenty and ease. Upon arriving in California, Anglo-Americans assumed they could purchase a place in the sun where living would be easy and competition nonexistent. But, as J. Russell Smith reflected in 1925, "the Oriental, willing to work longer hours than we, willing to live on less, could pay more for the land which he bought or leased." The question, then, boiled down to this: "What race, what culture, shall own California? Shall it be the economically efficient Mongolian or the less economically efficient Caucasian?" The answer, Smith felt, was self-evident: Asians would wind up the winners. This realization, according to Smith, explains "the movement for the exclusion of the Chinese and Japanese, largely at the insistence of California and other Pacific states."[29] That, however, assumed a level playing field, which California and the West was anything but, especially for Asian workers. After thirty years of tensely coexisting with Asians, white Californians agitated for their exclusion. The 1880 Treaty Regulating Immigration from China was followed by California's homegrown Chinese Exclusion Act of 1882. The popular press of the time not only agitated for such legislation but also had a field day depicting its outcome. The cover of the August 18, 1887, issue of the *WASP*, published in San Francisco, proudly depicts "The Last Load" of Asians arriving on the west coast. Although the *WASP* could sting any ethnic group with impunity, it was especially hard on Asians. However, immigrants often find a way of circumventing restrictive policies banning them from entering countries, and the Asians were no exception. Despite official policies, many were able to arrive in California undetected. When the San Francisco earthquake and fire of 1906 destroyed most of the official immigration records, authorities had an even more difficult time determining who was, and who was not, in the Golden State legally. Despite efforts to prohibit their arrival, then, Asians were here to stay, albeit as second-class citizens.

Throughout much of the nineteenth century, the Asian population was either segregated into well-defined sections of cities or settled in scattered locales such as mining districts and railroad workers' camps. This separation, however, did not guarantee a safe haven for Asians who lived in California. In Los Angeles, for example, the Chinese Massacre of 1871 involved a mob of about five hundred whites storming the city's Chinatown, where about twenty Chinese were killed, and some of them mutilated and hanged. At this time, Los Angeles was still pretty much a sleepy Mexican town, though Anglo-Americans were beginning to arrive in larger numbers. The part of town most affected was a mixed-race area called "Calle de los Negros," which had been home to some of the community's most wealthy Anglo-Americans, but by the 1860s was called Chinatown by some. With the arrival of the railroad to San Pedro, though, the area had become downright rough and increasingly disorderly. The cause of this vicious mob action was the accidental shooting of an Anglo-American rancher who got into the cross fire of two Chinese men fighting over a woman. As historian Scott Zesch noted, the aftermath of the mob violence was chilling: "The dead Chinese in Los Angeles were hanging at three places near the heart of the downtown business section of the city; from the wooden awning over the sidewalk in front of a carriage shop; from the sides of two 'prairie schooners' parked on the street around the corner from the carriage shop; and from the cross-beam of a wide gate leading into a lumberyard a few blocks away from the other two locations." Adding to the savagery of the event, one of the victims had been hanged without his trousers, and a finger on his left hand had been removed.[30] Not all places in California were violent, but an air of racial oppression still hung in the air well into the twentieth century.

And yet Asians were becoming a vital part of the character of the West, and no amount of racial prejudice could stop that process. If, as we have seen, Americans were ambivalent about the Orient (and Orientals), no place better illustrates these feelings than San Francisco in the early twentieth century. Consider, for example, developments in Golden Gate Park, a huge tract of land that had been a forlorn area of sand dunes and marshes until visionary city leaders in the 1870s sought to cultivate it and make it part of city beautification. As part of the city's face-lift after the earthquake and fire of 1906, Golden Gate Park was revitalized to feature vignettes from varied cultures. Given the long-held fascination with Imperial Japan, the Tea Garden represented a magical area, complete with pavilions, statues, and lush plantings. As seen in a beautifully tinted postcard from the 1915 Panama Pacific International Exposition (fig. 5-6), the Japanese Tea Garden imported the beauty and mystery of the

Fig. 5-6. A beautifully colored postcard from the 1915 Panama Pacific International Exposition provides an ethereal view of the "Japanese Tea Garden, Golden Gate Park, San Francisco."

Orient into a heavily visited part of the city. It also confirmed that the city had consciously embraced Asia as part of its public identity.

At the same time that this was happening, however, Japanese and Chinese farmworkers in California were living in near poverty in agricultural areas nearby. To experience another China in the West, one might visit the numerous Chinese farm towns in California's Sacramento Valley. None of them is more poignant than the Delta town of Locke, whose "buildings stand empty" even though it "has been designated an historic landmark to keep North America's last rural town built by those Chinese from passing unnoticed into oblivion" (fig. 5-7).

Locke was one of several Chinese towns in the Delta where workers found menial employment. These laborers "often were isolated from the rest of the community," and "the Chinese viewed the ghettos as temporary residences until the time for 'bitter strength' was over and the laborer could return to his native village in China to live out the remainder of his life in comfort."[31] As Peter C. Y. Leung observed in a moving poem, for a dollar a day (or as he put it, "one day—one dollar") the Chinese built "a hundred miles of levee" and made the tule marsh fertile, and so by "our labor, now this land becomes grand." And yet, "here we are, these Chinese immigrants our story untold, our words scattered, like the fruits [*sic*] forgotten seed." As Leung concluded, "Only our pictures remain / tattered and yellowed, waiting to be seen."[32]

Photo courtesy Clarence Chu

Fig. 5-7. In the historic Chinese agricultural community of Locke, California, this former gambling house was closed down by the state in the 1950s and now serves as the Dai Loy Museum.

These rural "China towns," as Leung called them, were vanishing, but Chinese communities could pretty much disappear even from urban places such as San Jose. Here, in the section of town once called Hellendale, a Chinatown thrived in the 1870s but was destroyed by fire. Undaunted, members of the community built a new Chinese temple, or joss house. Described as "a two story brick structure, unmistakably Oriental in appearance," it was constructed under the direction of Yee Fook in the mid 1880s. As the site of a spectacular Chinese New Year celebration in 1887, the temple became a landmark. It was indeed unmistakably Chinese, as its "large pieces of elegant wood carving, superimposed on a background of mother of pearl, gave an air of magnificence to the place." But alas, although the temple was "one of California's few landmarks of this type," it was "regrettably . . . torn down"[33] in the 1940s before its historical value was realized; today, there is little awareness that a Chinatown ever existed in San Jose.

Fortunately, the beautiful Joss House in the Northern California town of Weaverville (fig. 5-8) escaped such a fate. Typical of many gold mining towns in the area, Weaverville had a thriving Chinese community in the nineteenth

Author's photograph, 2010

Fig. 5-8. Dating from 1874, the historic Joss House (Chinese Temple) in the Northern California mining town of Weaverville is now a State Historical Park.

century. Weaverville attracted Chinese miners from several different parts of China and was the site of the infamous 1854 "Chinese War," or Tong War—a bloody internecine melee that involved four separate Chinese companies (the Yong-Wa, Se-Yep, Neng-Yong, and Sam-Yep) and left eight men dead and twenty wounded. Constructed in 1874, Weaverville's Joss House became the crown jewel of the Chinese community. The building's exterior startled travelers with its unique zigzag-style gable ends simulating waves of water that could extinguish a fire—yet another example of what some Anglo-American observers called "Chinese superstition." The building's equally remarkable interior was imported from China and includes statues of emperors and ancestors, as well as a profusion of stylized animal statues and other icons, each of which had symbolic meaning. Called the "Temple of the Forest Beneath the Clouds," this Joss House is one of Northern California's most distinctive buildings. Unlike San Jose's ill-fated Joss House, Weaverville's became a state park in 1954, a result of the vision of Moon Lim Lee, who was one of Weaverville's last Chinese residents, and the farsightedness of a state that was just beginning to recognize the importance of its diverse cultural history to future generations.

6

Syria on the Pacific
California as the Near/Middle East

"The same power which changed the map of the Orient . . . is laying the foundation for civilization in what is to be a modern and glorified Syria of the Southwest."

William Smythe, "San Diego Owns the Future" (1905)

In addition to developing an Asian identity in the nineteenth century, California also became closely associated with the Near East in the popular mind. To Anglo-Americans who first encountered Mexican California in the 1830s and 1840s, the place seemed to be paradise, especially when they looked at their calendars and realized that balmy days could occur year-round. If part of the spell California cast came from its climate, which seemed to have banished winter, especially along the coast and in the low-lying areas, part of the spell also related to a beautiful, idyllic landscape populated by traditional peoples who seemed to have few of the cares that plagued modern civilization.

Although searching for Eden was part of the westward move, there is evidence that Spaniards in the New World had similar ideas long before Anglo-Americans ever reached California. A painting that hung in a church in Tepemazalco, Mexico, for more than two centuries demonstrates how an artist could render an Eastern theme in the landscape of the Mexican highlands. Titled *The Expulsion from the Garden,* this painting features Adam and Eve being driven out of Eden, along with the serpent, in a landscape that is not Middle Eastern but rather central Mexican. In this painting dated to 1728, the expelled humans and serpent move across the foreground while in the middle ground, horses, lions, and other creatures—some fanciful—peacefully coexist along the shores of a huge lake which appears to be Lake Texcoco; in the distance, volcanic peaks loom, and these too are right out of the Mexican landscape. In a scene that effortlessly interchanges Old World and New World icons, the archangel Michael looms overhead with his fiery sword, as does the dove of the Holy Spirit. This stunning painting was recently returned to Mexico by the San Diego Museum of Art, which had acquired the painting unaware that it had been stolen several years earlier. The website Exploring Colonial Mexico describes the return of the painting under the title "Tepemazalco: Paradise Regained." As the website concludes, "Although clearly stylized, the earthly landscape is surely intended to represent the Valley of Mexico and Lake Texcoco as they might have appeared in the early 1700s—a theme echoed in the recently discovered early 16th century mural at Tlatelolco, in which the lakeside environment is also nostalgically pictured as an idyllic Garden of Eden."[1]

The Spaniards settled California rather late (1769), and only gained a foothold fairly close to the coast. By the 1830s as part of Mexico, the California mission system was pretty much in ruins. By the late 1840s California became part of the United States and Anglo-Americans began to arrive in great numbers, bringing a long legacy of looking westward for opportunity but looking eastward, often as far east as the Orient, for inspiration. These westward-moving Anglo-Americans found that reaching California in the 1840s and 1850s was both costly and dangerous, and a look at a map revealed why. Getting there required either a long sea voyage or an overland trip across vast deserts and over towering mountain passes. California thus became part of the North American consciousness as a paradise that required going through hell to reach. After the mid-1840s, that made California all the more irresistible—provided one was up to the challenge.

The "extreme West," as D. G. W. Leavitt called it in an 1845 issue of the *Arkansas Gazette*, was reached at a time when the Bible was the most common book people owned, and when stories of the Middle East were frequently used as metaphors. In describing the ill-fated Donner Party under the heading "THE FATE OF THE LAST EMIGRANTS," for example, the *Californian* of Monterey observed that "it is a most horrid picture of human misery: such as has not been witnessed since the siege of Jerusalem." Given the awful facts of cannibalism that emerged as the remainder of the snowbound Donner Party was rescued, the *Californian* added that "it is said by Jewish historians, that parents subsisted upon the bodies of their children, in time of siege by Titus." Educated readers would here also recognize Shakespeare's *Titus Andronicus*, wherein Tamora (like a legendary Tyestes) consumes the flesh of her sons at a banquet. The *Californian* went on to report the macabre details of the California version of this nightmarish experience—namely, that "in the Mountains, mothers possessing portions of their dead companions, refused to divide it [*sic*] with their own children, while *alive*, and when the children died, actually devoured the bodies of their own offspring!" If, as cultural historian Lawrence Levine noted, "by mid-century, Shakespeare was taken across the Great Plains and over the Rocky Mountains and soon became a staple of theatres in the Far West," then we should also add newspapers like the *Californian* to the list of those who freely used the words of the great bard(s) here.[2]

There was, however, another source of such vivid, judgmental language. Moralizing further about the reprehensible behavior exhibited by the Donner Party, the *Californian* added, "Truly the 'mother may forget her sucking child.'"[3] Readers of that era recognized this as another quote right out of the Bible, namely Isaiah 49:15, "Can a woman forget her sucking child, that she should have no compassion on the son of her womb?" That reference to the Old Testament provided a sense of stern Hebraic morality compromised by human failings. It is easy to think of this as only so much biblical or Hebraic literature until we realize that Jews were part of the equation of Orientalism: their ancient literature and arcane, tortured history placed them as the "other" in Orientalist discourse.[4]

For travelers, the interior western deserts of North America, including California, represented a significant perceptual challenge. When they encountered arid land here, especially in the vicinity of salt flats and salt lakes, they were self-consciously aware of its austerity and its resonance as spiritual testing ground. Both depressed and depressing, the valley bottoms were especially mood altering. When the Jayhawkers in 1849 toiled across the Basin and Range country, these naive Gold Rush–bound Kansans thought their prospects would improve with each successive crossing of mountain ranges. And why not? They were, after all, a pretty hardy breed of people who had experienced the prairies of the Great Plains firsthand. Alas, however, in the western Great Basin, they encountered more, or less, than they bargained for. As they trudged westward, they became more and more concerned with each descent into bone-dry valleys. The Jayhawkers finally met more than their match in a valley that broke their spirit and shattered their cohesion. That valley in California turned out to be the lowest (and consequently the hottest and driest) place in North America—282 feet below sea level. The name that they gave it—Death Valley—was not only romantically dramatic; it also resonated in their spiritual lexicon, which was rich in valleys of death, or at least the "shadow of death," as evident in the twenty-third Psalm. Such passages furthered the comparison of the American desert with its counterpart in the Levant.[5]

Things were far brighter for other travelers, though. With its delightful climate and fascinating scenery, California readily served as a source of spiritual renewal. In addition to its Spanish, or seemingly Spanish, heritage, California has long been portrayed as the "Promised Land." In 1849, Sarah Royce arrived sick and exhausted from the overland journey across desert and mountains. Upon reaching the Sacramento Valley, and sensing her pending rejuvenation, Royce stated that she had found "our promised land." Interestingly, this metaphor persisted well into the twentieth century, though "Holy Land" is sometimes substituted—perhaps to give this land an even more sacred or blessed quality.

Then, too, one could live a very different lifestyle in California, one as Arab as American. In 1850, British writer Sidney Smith offered a fascinating, Orientalist explanation of California's almost magical powers. "California," as he put it, "is notoriously the region of gold, and also of that most desperate of all classes of men, gold finders." Having set up that tension, Smith went on to wax poetic about what awaits the traveler here using a characteristically long Victorian sentence: "To the bold and intrepid, to all who are imbued with the spirit of adventure, to that frame of mind which is essentially gipsy, Kalmuck, and Arabian in its desire for a wandering and restless life, these regions offer the inducement of a climate which admits of constantly living in the open air, of productiveness which renders rough substance easy with little labour, and of the chances of getting rapidly rich by the lucky acquisition of the precious metals." Smith was convinced that California offered "a life that may become easy to Americans on the borders of civilization, [but which] would be full of anxiety and difficulty to a European and ought not to be encountered under any circumstances whatever."[6] Note here, though, that Smith casts Americans who seek freedom through unfettered mobility as, among others, Arabians. More importantly, that tendency to be Arabian is not, in his subversive reasoning, all bad; it was in fact rather liberating.

As California was settled in the 1850s and 1860s, the herculean task of connecting the state to the rest of the nation called for some powerful metaphors. In the spirit of Orientalism that prevailed in the Victorian West, the completion of the transcontinental railroad was also given an Arabian twist. In its flyer titled "What the Religious Press of New York Says of the Pacific Railroad," the *New York Independent* noted, "What we demanded has been given. All the resources of the Sultan's jewel-chests failed to complete the 'unfinished windows in Aladdin's tower.' But, . . ." the *Independent* quickly added, "Aladdin had only to order it, and the work would be done, because Aladdin had unlimited resources behind him." The writer's literary hyperbole continued with the following: "Perhaps the projectors of the Pacific Railway were, metaphorically, at least, placed in a position a little like that of Aladdin.

So they have got the work done; and, for the present, that one fact naturally obscures, or event occults, every other in the history of the enterprise."
Hinting at the fantastic character of a project as ambitious as connecting
America to the Orient using a railway link, the *Independent* reminded readers
that "ten years ago it was regarded as a dream, a chimera, a craze."[7]

As several factors—Manifest Destiny, the US-Mexican War, and the Gold
Rush—joined forces to transform the West's landscapes and peoples, California
proved irresistible. To many nineteenth-century travel writers, California resonated as the exotic Near and Far East. Under the passages titled "The Mirage"
in his popular book *Crusoe's Island* (1864), J. Ross Browne described the landscape of the Salinas Valley: "The scene that lay outspread before me . . ." he
wrote, "resembled rather some wild region of enchantment than any thing that
could be supposed to exist in a material world—so light and hazy were the distant mountains, so vaguely mingled the earth and sky, so rich and fanciful the
atmospheric tints, and so visionary the groves that decorated the plain." Even
though the word *mirage* could suggest the chimerical, it also referred, especially
at that time, to something evanescent. In an age when subjectivity was valued
as a hallmark of romanticism, the mirage was something special: the person
who experienced a real mirage was not deluded, but actually privileged.

Then, too, a mirage could literally transform one place into another. This
surreal scene Browne experienced in California called for comparisons with
another part of the world where the mind also played tricks on the traveler,
namely, the Near East. Browne noted that "mounds of yellow sand, rising
a little above the level of the plain, had all the effect of rich Oriental cities,
with gorgeous palaces of gold, mosques, and minarets, and wondrous temples
glittering with jewels and precious stones." Seeking a rational explanation as
to why a herd of antelope "seemed rather to sail through the air than touch
the earth," Browne stated that "by the illusory process of the refraction, they
appeared to sweep into the lakes and assume the forms of aerial boats, more
fanciful and richly colored than the caciques of Constantinople." As Browne
traveled, the scene continued to change as if by magic; a vulture appeared to be
"a fabulous monster of olden times . . . lakes disappeared with the islands and
fleets, and new lakes, with still stranger and more fantastic illusions, merged
into existence out of the rarified atmosphere."[8] This refraction was both visible
and metaphorical, for Browne's imagination was reflecting upon the adventures of earlier travel writers and novelists.

The human population of California was also easy for Browne to
Orientalize. Part of this trip was, as he put it, a "dangerous journey." In describing an intriguing "dark eyed, fierce-looking woman of about six-and-twenty,

a half-breed from Santa Barbara," Browne noted she seemed part animal and that "every glance of her fierce, flashing eyes was instinct with untamable passion." Strangely attracted to this dangerous woman, Browne observed that "she was a mustang in human shape—one that I thought would kick or bite upon very slight provocation." Like many commentators who described such tempestuous *mestizas*, Browne observed that "in the matter of dress she was almost Oriental." Her dress was of "the richest and most striking colors," and it "made a rare accord with her wild and singular physique." Her ornate gold-cased breast pin featured glittering diamonds, her ears were "loaded down with sparkling ear-rings," and her long hair was "gathered up in a knot behind, and pinned with a gold dagger"—all of which made her seem like "a dangerous but royal game-bird."

Although Browne's fantasy-filled description is fraught wth sexist and racist overtones, it drew on the tradition of the Eastern temptress so common in literature, song, and even the Bible. This woman was trouble, and Browne sensed it. He imagined that she cast a "spell" on men who quickly fell for her, and this gave Browne "a foreboding of evil" that soon played out. As he relates the story, this "belle" was remarkably flirtatious, and one can imagine what was about to happen. Later that evening, two men—a local Mexican and a tall white man dressed in the "picturesque style" of a Texas Ranger—fought over her with fatal results. The Texan, whom she had earlier rebuffed but apparently loved, was stabbed to death. Although this tragic story appears to be overwrought and melodramatic—the type of event that Marty Robbins' classic "western" song "El Paso" immortalized about a century later (1958)—the point here is that such passionate, irresistible Jezebels are one of the many Orientalist tropes by which Anglo-Americans characterized the American West as man's country filled with mind-altering mirages and dangerous temptations. As Browne candidly put it, "The rarest charms of scenery and climate" here in California were desecrated by "the worst passions of human nature." [9]

Despite its idyllic qualities, then, California could still humble travelers and even motivate a scientist to wax poetic about the perils here. In the early 1860s, when geologist Raphael Pumpelly was nearing the end of the first part of his trip that would ultimately take him to the Orient, he ascended the mountains to leave California's Colorado Desert country, which features one of North America's largest expanses of sand dunes. This area is comparable to the Sahara in temperatures and aridity, and Pumpelly described it in harrowing terms as he felt his energy sapped and his imagination racing: "All night long," Pumpelly wrote, "we forced our way through the deep sand of the gorge, winding among countless skeletons, glittering in the moonlight, scorched by hot blasts ever rushing up from the deserts behind us." Concluding this memorable passage, Pumpelly stated that the experience was like "wandering through the valley of the shadow of death, and flying from the very gates of hell."[10] This too was wording very loosely taken from the Bible, and it brought to mind trials and tribulations in the deserts of the Old World. The reference to skeletons and bones along the way, so common in descriptions of both the Sahara/Arabian and the American desert, only added to the dramatic effect. Pumpelly had plenty of company among other scientists as he equated the interior desert West with its Old World counterparts.[11]

Given the Victorian imagination, California's abandoned mining towns evoked far-off places. For example, when Robert Louis Stevenson traveled through the northern part of the state in the late 1870s, he wrote down his observations in *Silverado Squatters*. As Stevenson put it, "One thing in this new country very particularly strikes a stranger, and that is the number of antiquities." Noting that "already there have been many cycles of population succeeding each other, and passing away and leaving behind relics," these abandoned mining towns were evocative. As Stevenson put it, "These, standing on into changed times, strike the imagination as forcibly as any pyramid or feudal tower." Stevenson concluded that "when the lode comes to an end, and the miners move elsewhere, the town remains behind them, like Palmyra in the desert." It is significant that even though Stevenson was in a partially forested area of scrub oaks and madrone trees, the use of a fabled desert town in far-away Syria served his purposes perfectly.[12]

If travelers were prone to see the Near East in California, they also carried images of California with them to the Orient. Traveling through Palestine, American writer Bayard Taylor encountered the beautiful landscapes on the Plain of Esdraelon, which looked like a "green sea, covered with fields of wheat and barley, or great grazing tracts, on which multitudes of sheep and goats are wandering." Taylor was struck by the landscape here, which seemed familiar. Pondering the similarities, he realized that it reminded him of what he had explained in the Golden State. As he put it, "In some respects, it reminded me of the Valley of San José and if I were to liken Palestine to any country I have seen, it would be California." The climate of both places, he declared, is "the same, the soil is very similar in quality, and the landscapes present the same general features." Taylor found in Palestine "the same rank fields of wild oats clothing the mountain-sides, the same aromatic herbs impregnating the air with balm, and above all, the same blue, cloudless days and dewless nights." Taylor concluded, "Traveling here, I am constantly reminded of our new Syria on the Pacific."[13]

No small part of the Orientalization of California and the entire American West relates to the way in which irrigation transformed the area into a garden—at least in spots. This was not a feature of the original landscape, though Paiute Indians in California's Owens Valley practiced irrigation. The new irrigation, though, was an aggressive, technologically oriented application of water to land and city that was unparalleled in world history. The diversion of water, in fact, not only gave life to much of California but also helped create water-dependent civilization here not unlike that of the Near East.

Environmental historian Donald Worster observes: "In California and the West has emerged the most elaborate hydraulic system in world history, overshadowing even the grandiose works of the Sassanians and the Pharaohs."[14] Worster's smooth integration of new West and ancient East in this one sentence is noteworthy because it reminds one how even seemingly "modern" works, such as pipelines and mechanical sprinklers, can convey a sense of the Byzantine drama of those mysteriously named "hydraulic civilizations." The American West owes a debt, if we can call it that, to these civilizations along "the Tigris, the Euphrates, and the Nile [which] were then, according to the theory of hydraulic society, the environmental basis for the first authoritarian, complexly hierarchical civilizations."[15]

There is something perversely fascinating to Americans about the accumulation of such political and technological power and the seemingly despotic ability to use it at will. True, as Americans who salute the underdog, we can side with the Owens Valley farmers and ranchers whose lands were turned to dust by a water-hungry Los Angeles as the beautiful Owens Lake turned into a dry, salt-filled bowl. But Owens Valley is still dry, while Los Angeles continues to grow—a testimony not only to the city's power but also to our fascination with, and complicity in, a grand scheme that might even put the despots of the ancient Near East to shame.

In western American history, such water engineering schemes were clearly male-inspired, but Worster gives us reason to pause. He correctly noted that the roots of such water piracy can be traced back to "the fabled Assyrian ruler, Queen Semiramis, [who] was reputed to have inscribed on her tomb what may stand as the ecological creed, and the hubris, of the advanced hydraulic civilizations: 'I constrained the mighty river to flow according to my will and let its water to fertilize lands that had before been barren and without inhabitants.'"[16] Worster's suggestion here, of course, is that the aggressive diversion of water in the West is not really Western at all but rather Middle Eastern in origin and spirit. We know much, perhaps too much, today about the downside of such actions, but without them the arid and semiarid West would be a very different place, devoid of the intoxicating fragrance of orange blossoms in spring and cut alfalfa in summer, not to mention huge reservoirs luring swimmers and boaters and the impressive sight of water coursing through the desert in canals.

California is one of many places that historian David M. Wrobel calls "Promised Lands" that were created in the promotion and selling of the American West. Mixing metaphors a bit in 1885, Frank Pixley, the editor of the *San Francisco Argonaut*, printed a letter that described how "God" would have characterized the area near Riverside, California: "This is the happy Canaan—the holy land; that God, when He made the world, and had gathered the experience of all His efforts, said to himself: 'I will now illustrate the crowning glory of My Labors with the production of the perfect spot.'" According to Pixley, that spot was both Edenic and productive. It had "wealth of soils and wealth of precious metals," and "splendid mountains, rich and gorgeous valleys, grand and stately forests." Adopting the persona of God again, Pixley concluded that in this perfect place "shall be found the highest social condition of which the creation of My image is capable."[17] This description reminds one a bit more of "the good land" in Deuteronomy than the real, and rather more difficult, Canaan. But then again, *any* biblical reference would suffice to get the point across: God himself endorsed the settlement and the promotion of not only Riverside but also much of the Golden State.

California's Spanish or Mexican heritage was nominally Christian but was given an Oriental identity by promoters such as Charles Lummis. As an easterner, Lummis had grown up looking westward but romanticizing both the Near and Far East. Never particularly healthy, Lummis sought revitalization in the West by taking a position as a newspaper editor in California. Along the way he fell in love with the Greater Southwest, which was united to California in part by Spanish heritage. In Lummis's view, however, it was the exotic Moorish heritage of Spain that made that country so different from the rest of Europe—and that Moorish heritage was part of the Spanish heritage in California and the Southwest. As noted earlier, the Moors, though North African, were easy to Orientalize because they were Muslims whose cultural roots linked them to Berbers and Arabs of the Near East. It was thus a Near Eastern rather than purely Spanish heritage that made Lummis's beloved Southwest and California so different from anything else the United States had to offer.

Lummis was not alone. In fact, some observers claimed that the Moorish heritage of Spain was that country's only saving grace. Bayard Taylor put it rather undiplomatically in 1904 when he noted, "In Granada, as in Seville and

Cordova, one's sympathies are wholly with the Moors." Even today, as Taylor observed, "The few mutilated traces which still remain of their power, taste, and refinement, surpass any of the monuments erected by the race which conquered them." Using a sentiment that Washington Irving had popularized about half a century earlier, Taylor concluded that "the Moorish Dynasty in Spain was truly . . . a splendid exotic [flower], doomed never to take a lasting root in the soil" of Spain. As a person who romanticized the spread of civilized Islam into Spain from the Near East, Taylor used another, less flattering, biological metaphor of his own for Spain. Moorish culture, he observed "was choked to death by the native weeds; and, in place of lands richly cultivated and teeming with plenty, we now have barren and almost depopulated wastes—in place of education, industry, and the cultivation of the arts and sciences, an enslaved, ignorant and degenerate race."[18] Such sentiments were common, especially among both freethinkers and Protestant anti-Catholics who felt the church and pope in Rome were the oppressors; such sentiments fueled the "Black Legend," which portrayed Spain as the New World tyrant.

As Lummis and others were well aware, that hint of the Moorish in Spain's presence in California was intriguing, and potentially marketable. Although the missions were Spanish (and later Mexican, which was far less mentioned), their architecture included Islamic or Moorish elements. After all, the lands encircling the Mediterranean had a long connection with Islam. And yet many people doubted the Moor's superiority. In some quarters, the racially white qualities of Spain were contrasted with the darkness of the Moors (and by conflation, the American Indians). This whiteness became an important issue in romanticizing and purifying California's Spanish heritage, as opposed to Mexican (which suggests Indian or *mestizo* identity). Much the same occurs in present-day northern New Mexico, where Hispanic residents of small towns north of Santa Fe often emphasize their Spanish heritage and vehemently deny that any "Indian blood" has ever entered their family line. Further complicating this, however, is the presence of an underlying Jewish converso heritage even among some of the purest of Hispanic Catholic families; this, of course, is an Oriental intrusion often left unexamined and unspoken.

In California, though, Lummis's friend and fellow writer Helen Hunt Jackson (1830–1885) subversively undermined whiteness by introducing a novel character as a novel's main character—the fictional Ramona—whose love for a Native American man ultimately helped increase the visibility of California's indigenous peoples. When published in 1884, *Ramona* created a sensation. Although not written as an Orientalist story per se, *Ramona* reminds us of the power of fiction to affect reality by reshaping attitudes toward race—and helping to create regional identity based in part on Orientalization of the subject matter.[19]

References to the Orient run like a subliminal undercurrent in *Ramona*. When Jackson describes the coastal hills of Southern California as "like nothing in nature except the glitter of a brilliant lizard in the sun or the iridescent sheen of a peacock's neck," she plays with the same exotic imagery that authors used to describe the East. Similarly, when she observes that "the wild mustard in Southern California is like that spoken of in the New Testament, in the branches of which the birds of the air may rest," Jackson gives the Golden State's natural history the stature of its biblical counterpart. The many shepherds in *Ramona* appear ageless, actually biblical, in their ancient occupations; even Ramona herself is described as having "just enough of an olive tint in her complexion to underlie and enrich her skin without making it swarthy." Her Indian lover, Alessandro, is darker—an Indian cast in the role of the Moor wooing a Spanish beauty.[20] But what makes *Ramona* especially interesting is Jackson's ability to render California, and Californios as they were then called, into America's own version of the Orient, with its timeless villages, tribal distinctions, petty squabbles, rigid religious authority, Byzantine intrigue, and the timeless oppression of fatalism. Despite this, or perhaps because of it, Jackson romanticized the state's history. In 1883, she claimed that the character of Californios embodied a kind of alchemy. As she put it, "Simply out of sunshine, there had distilled in them an Orientalism as fine in its way as that made in the East by generations of prophets, crusaders, and poets."[21]

One more example will suffice to show how California becomes East and how Westerner becomes Easterner. In her classic book *The Land of Little Rain* (1903), Mary Austin was prone to see the East in the West's sheepherders and its Indians. Of the former, she notes that "it appears that shepherds have not changed more than sheep in the process of time." Austin quickly adds that "the shy hairy men who herd the tactile flocks might be, except for some added clothing, the very brethren of David." Note here that one character from the Bible is strongly defined enough to serve as a surrogate for all herders past and present. Moreover, the shepherds need a place, that is, landscape, to help define them as biblical in age. Place and time conspire to reset, as it were, the western American drama in the East—or rather, transform the American West into the East. As Austin puts it, "When the fire kindles and savory meat seethes in the pot, when there is drowsy blether from the flock, and far down the mesa the twilight twinkle of shepherd fires, when there is a hint of blossom underfoot and a heavenly whiteness on the hills, one harks back without effort to Judea and the Nativity."[22]

To complete this allusion to American West as Holy Land, Austin needed one more ingredient—woman. In describing a basket-making Paiute woman in California, Austin notes: "In her best days, Seyavi was most like Deborah, deep bosomed, broad in the hips, quick in counsel, slow of speech, esteemed of her people."[23] This is Orientalism at its most flattering, or rather self-flattering, for Austin is here confessing that the noble shepherds and Indian women are in effect her own ancestors. By placing them—and us—in this new Western setting, Austin transforms the American desert into the Holy Land. She also mythologizes the New World desert by weaving it into an Old World narrative whose roots sustain the tree of Western culture. Popular beliefs about California's Middle Eastern Old World countenance also appeared in other guises. The culture of Anglo-American California was well primed to see Oriental messages in the marketing of this new yet very old paradise. Consider, for example, the exuberant labels on fruit crates for a wide variety of semi-tropical products—dates, oranges, grapefruits, figs—which reveal something of California's fascination with the Orient. One in particular, Bradford Bros. Miracle Brand (fig. 6-1), features what appears to be a genie—or perhaps it is Aladdin himself—holding a tray of large, luscious oranges. The man is clearly Middle Eastern: dark, handsome, with a downward gaze that conveys a sense of "Eastern" contentment and mystery.[24] His face, while undeniably male, also has an androgynous quality, in that his features are fine and his countenance serene. This sexual mysteriousness is a hallmark of Orientalism. The magic lantern present in the lower left-hand portion of the label is also noteworthy, a literary reference that serves as a subtle reminder that magic was required to make the scene a reality. For Southern Californians who could remember when these semiarid lands were barren in 1900, the labels from the 1920s and 1930s confirmed that the genie had granted their wishes.

In *California Orange Box Labels* (1985), Gordon McClelland and Jay Last demonstrate how art and advertising work hand in hand to give places and products new identities. The California citrus industry used a wide range of images to advertise its citrus products: "Their purpose—to rapidly catch the attention and interest of prospective purchasers—was the same as for advertising posters developed in the 1880s and 1890s." The labels were intended to reach the wholesaler, who would in turn sell the product to the public. Over eight thousand distinct designs were introduced, many of them emphasizing the exotic, even sensual, quality of citrus fruit. According to McClelland and Last, "naturalism" dominated from 1885 to 1920. These labels often featured local scenes, such as palm-treed landscapes, bridges, and orange groves, but the area's romantic Spanish history (missions and vaqueros) and images of

Fig. 6-1. Citrus labels such as those on Bradford Bros. Miracle Brand Oranges featured exotic imagery that helped Orientalize California—in this case referencing the popular Arabian Nights story "Aladdin and the Magic Lamp."

Indians were also popular. At this time, too, images of attractive women were in vogue and remained so "throughout the years." It is here that one glimpses not only beautiful Anglo or other European or other women but also more exotic women, as exemplified by the Gypsy Queen, Chinese Girl, and Geisha Brand labels. By the early 1900s, commercial growers were using the pyramid (complete with sphinx, date palms, and camels), and by the 1920s, the labels were full-blown commercial art appealing to national tastes. It is no surprise that they mirror some of the popular interest in "Oriental" subject matter, hence a proliferation of Egyptian, Cleopatra, and Sheik brand images; in the 1930s, the Endurance brand featured a caravan of camels, and a queen series that included Esther (complete with Egyptian-style servants) and Rebecca.[25] Orientalism was clearly an influence here. Through these labels, we see that California citrus producers at first manufactured a California image or identity. That identity, however, was soon supplemented, if not supplanted, by more foreign—usually Oriental—motifs. In this sense, we see Orientalism as intersecting, and sometimes vying, with attempts at creating nativistic identity.

In 1920, when California orange crate labels celebrated mythical characters from well-known stories such as the Arabian Nights, the spectacular Samarkand, Persian Hotel and spa in Santa Barbara opened its doors to a public long enchanted with the Orient. Located in the rugged, chaparral-covered Samarkind Hills behind the city, the facility transformed a struggling boys' school into a posh Oriental wonder. The setting—which was formerly grazed but now becoming part of Santa Barbara's tony tourist scene, was evocative. The name Samarkand was legendary, said to be Persian for "Land of Heart's Desire." Moreover, that fabled city's name was a household word as it was the locale in which the ingenious Scheherazade had told her fabulous 1001 Arabian Nights stories. At its grand opening, the Samarkand Persian featured a troupe of "Hindi dancers." It was said that they "captivated the audience, but the Samarkand captivated the dancers." This was no surprise, given the hotel's setting and beautiful Persian gardens and fountains. To further perpetuate the exotic southwestern Asian ambiance of the place, the hotel's administrator Charles B. Hervey was known as "the Caliph of the Samarkand."[26] That title was perfect as it suggested a mysterious and powerful Oriental potentate—in this case a Muslim potentate—who could orchestrate the magic, and provide a sensual, out of the ordinary experience.

California's search for a regional identity explored numerous Old World alternatives. One that proved irresistible attempted to recapture a nearly lost and allegedly noble Spanish heritage. This, in a sense, was distinct from a "Mexican" heritage, which had also characterized California, but at a later period (1821–1848). However, whereas *Mexican* suggested a mixing of Spanish with Native American, the concept of *Spanish* seemed purer, that is to say, purely European. That, as suggested above, was problematic for at least two reasons. First, *Spanish* itself suggested a Catholic tradition that was, to many Protestant Anglo-Americans, not pure at all but rather sullied by papal corruption and idolatry. California could overcome this anti-Catholic bias only with the increasing liberalization that occurred in the later nineteenth century as Irish Catholics and others began to assimilate. As part of those liberalizing attitudes, as well as a growing fantasizing about the romance of old California, the Spanish heritage was embraced by Anglo-Californians. And yet that California Spanish identity always had as one of its ingredients an underlying Moorish/Islamic heritage that was both fascinating and troubling.

This ambivalence requires greater clarification. Half a century before Lummis, Anglo-Americans during the mid-nineteenth century were well

aware that Spanish architecture was not purely European. In 1849, when
US-Mexican War veteran Mayne Reid wrote about his experiences in the
Saturday Evening Post, he described the city of Puebla, Mexico, as "indeed a
glorious picture . . . The eye is struck with the heavy half Moorish style of its
architecture—the dusky color of its terraced roofs—the quaint old cupolas of
the churches."[27] A similar situation prevailed north of the border, where ordinary Anglo-Americans were fascinated by the Moorish look of architecture.

Lummis, though, became the most persuasive promoter of California's
exotic heritage. He had a major role in the rise of mission-style architecture
in California in the early to mid 1890s. This represented a significant trend
in American architecture, for it spread eastward quickly. Moreover, it involved
the diffusion of faux Spanish design to areas never visited, much less settled,
by the Spaniards. [28]

As Lummis was well aware, Moorish-style architecture was both evocative
and seductive. Some of Spain's most exquisite buildings, such as the Alhambra
in Granada and the Alcázar in Seville, were built during Muslim occupation and are in fact largely Middle Eastern rather than European in design.
Although the public had little difficulty conceiving the mission style to be
Spanish, and hence Catholic (Christian), in origin, these buildings resonated
on two levels. On the surface, they were Spanish and hence European, but
just below the surface, they were Moorish and thus connected to a widely
held fascination with Orientalism. For example, revival-style buildings like
Scotty's Castle in Death Valley, built by Albert Johnson and named in honor
of that eccentric desert dweller in 1925–26, were often called Spanish but
were clearly also Moorish. That made them interesting as well as somewhat
threatening. The Moors—as all educated people from sixteenth-century
Spaniard Álvar Núñez Cabeza de Vaca to the Protestant Anglo-American
Spanish revival architects of early twentieth-century California knew—were
the North African Muslims who had lived in Spain for about seven centuries
before being driven from Iberia in 1492. Their roots are Middle Eastern and
their religion is Islam. The missions represent not only Spaniards per se but
Easterners who conquered Spain. To further complicate any interpretation of
Spanish revival, then, it should be noted that Spain's heritage attracted (and
sometimes repelled) Protestant mainstream America not simply because it
embodied an esoteric Catholic quality (which was, in their eyes, bad enough)
but precisely because it also resonated with an exotic Islamic, Middle Eastern
character. This made Spanish revival architecture doubly intriguing. It was
loved by some and despised by others precisely because of its connection to
the more mysterious and exotic Arab world and Islam.

By the late nineteenth and early twentieth centuries, sophisticated Californians were well aware of the Orientalist component in their otherwise "Spanish" idyll. Author Helen Hunt Jackson herself said it best when she observed that California peculiarly combined "an almost dreamy, otherworldly Orientalism with a frenetic Anglo American Bustle." As suggested above, Jackson was an appreciative Orientalist. However, she was also as conflicted as she was idealistic—beholden to the technological prowess of modern society to share her increasingly subversive beliefs about that society's impacts on indigenous people. Her epic *Ramona* helped gain support for Native Americans whose culture and heritage had been savaged by aggressive "Yankee" development.[29] As a former Yankee herself, Jackson had fallen under the spell of a California that was at once West and East,[30] and used that Orientalism to support social reform.

On the Pacific coast, San Diego was widely touted for its similarities to southern Europe. But even though writers often compared it to Naples, Italy; Rio de Janeiro, Brazil; and Nice, France; that was not exotic enough. Rather, in developing the grounds for the Panama-California Exposition of 1915–16, a large urban park (Balboa) would be transformed into a fantasylike landscape based on the Spanish cities of Salamanca, Seville, and Toledo—all of which exhibit Moorish influences—as well as the Mexican cities of Guadalajara, Mexico City, and Taxco. The exposition's more imaginative proponents, especially that now-famous regional magpie Charles Lummis, were more likely to draw parallels with the Middle East. The Southwest, as Lummis portrayed it, was no Spanish imitation. It was, as he put it, the real thing—"an exotic land equal to the Orient of the Nile River Valley in Egypt." In ensuring that the cultural exhibits in the exposition would be authentic, Lummis threw his support behind ethnographer Edgar Hewett, who believed that "Native Americans retained a culture and way of life as significant and unique as the classical antiquity of Europe, the Middle East, and Asia." To Hewett, "the Southwest beckoned as the Greece, Mesopotamia, and Orient of North America." But the similarities did not stop there. As Hewett claimed in 1915, archaeological study of ancient Central and South America revealed the presence of a once-grand classical world. In America, Hewett stated, "the brilliancy of the new race suggested another Orient," and, more to the point, "the ruins of Central American cities seemed to entomb another Egypt."[31]

So much has been written about the seemingly Spanish (but, in reality, simultaneously European and Oriental) California mission style that full-blown Oriental revival architecture in the Golden State has been neglected. Here, as in many other locales, developers built huge assemblages of buildings

Author's collection

Fig. 6-2. In an evocative night scene that hints at pleasure palaces in the Near East, a postcard mailed in 1910 shows the ornate Bath House in Redondo Beach, California.

that played on an unabashedly Eastern theme. Consider, for example, the seaside resort of Redondo Beach, which featured a stunning 225-room hotel. Built in 1890, that huge hostelry was topped by turrets and towers right out of an *Arabian Nights* tale. Then, too, the incredible Auditorium and the Plunge Bath House in Redondo Beach featured "the largest indoor salt-water-heated pool in the world." Built in 1909 and served by the ubiquitous "red cars" of Henry Huntington's Pacific Electric Railway, this was one of Southern California's landmarks (fig. 6-2). California's Ocean Park (Santa Monica) and Casino/Natatorium (Santa Cruz) also featured Oriental-style buildings, which, like Utah's Saltair, provided carfree pleasure in an exotic setting.

At the height of the popularity of Oriental architectural splendor, California blossomed with public buildings that provided a touch of the Near and Middle East. The Santa Fe Railway, in particular, built several large stations in this style over about a thirty-year period, including the La Grande Station on Second Street in Los Angeles (1893) and the fabulous San Bernardino Station (1918). In an attempt to capture the flavor of the Orient, these impressive buildings featured large domes, ornate turrets, and spectacular arches. Just northeast of Los Angeles, the ornate Pasadena Grand Opera House on South Raymond Avenue (built in 1888–89) featured several Orientalist flourishes—including Islamic pointed arches, ornate "Arabian" window trim, and spectacular towers capped by multicolored domes—all of which gave a Middle Eastern character to an otherwise Victorian building.

Yet the very thing that made structures like this so exciting—namely, their fantastically ornate "Arabesque" or "Oriental" architecture—proved terribly expensive to maintain. Alas, in Redondo Beach, the seaside resort buildings were mostly gone by the 1930s—torn down to avoid costly taxes and potential liabilities as people found other, new diversions. Only a few such ornate buildings—for example, the Santa Fe Railway's huge, Turkish-style San Bernardino Station—remain in the twenty-first century, but those that do are now appreciated for their elaborate, eclectic Oriental style.

These Oriental-style buildings were part of a broader trend. It is telling that they coincided with lavish Victorian-era architecture. It should be noted that rather than being the sole style of architecture, these Oriental gems represented one of numerous styles—for example, Italianate, Romanesque, Venetian, Mission—that flourished during a time when Californians tirelessly experimented with their identity. This was a time when entrepreneurs were liable to try anything novel, anything interesting, anything exotic, in order to attract patrons or customers to their business enterprises. Residential developers too created exotic styles of homes for enthusiastic homebuyers. Thus it is that even the bungalow style, which proved very popular in California and spread elsewhere, also plumbed an Oriental motif, namely, the architecture of colonial India. With its rustic look and ornate veranda-style porch, the bungalow suggested a tropical climate and exotic surroundings. It also introduced yet another Oriental element into the English language: the word *bungalow* is of Hindi origin and may be derived from Bengal.

Although it is likely that few people really thought these Orient-inspired commercial and residential buildings were authentic, they certainly helped create, and then sustain, the impression that California was both exotic and innovative. The most ornate of the faux Oriental buildings are what environmental design professor Dean MacCannell calls "ideological castles." These huge, elaborate edifices are part of the mythology that sustains Western culture, though some critics like Roland Barthes consider the myth an inherently parasitic aspect of culture that "'nourishes itself' on history, and distorts language for its own ends."[32] That interpretation suggests something sinister—a common response by cultural critics. However, one might take the opposite stance—namely, that business culture is based on borrowing and trading, whether it be capital, products, services, or advertising. Moreover, even culture itself represents a synergy of different forces and influences in constant flux.

Architects found the ornate skylines of Islamic cities, with their graceful domes and tall spires, irresistible in the Victorian period. Those ornate Oriental-style buildings were visually exciting, as they suggested the fairy tales of the *Arabian Nights*. Small wonder they became so popular for amusement parks and waterfronts like Redondo Beach, Santa Cruz, and even Utah's Saltair, for all these places further associated the Orient with amusement and pleasure. Of course, the real structures in the Orient are as likely to be associated with religious or civic life, but when translated into American popular culture, they serve very different purposes more in line with the needs of the Orientalist imitators.

In the United States and other Western countries, these ornate buildings filled an important niche in the collective psyche that viewed foreign countries as sources of products and pleasures unavailable in industrialized and otherwise civilized nations. To this end, the Columbian Exposition in Chicago (1893) featured a midway lined with fanciful Oriental-style buildings. In 1894, J. W. Buel published *The Magic City*. Buel began this booklet by noting that "there are magicians still who rival the proudest conceptions of imaginary demons with realities as splendid as ever Oriental fancy painted." He then added an even more immodest but revealing idea—namely, that "this is not an age of miracles, but is one of works, in which the powers of human genius transcend the beauty and opulence of Arabic dreams, when the airy unsubstantials of intoxicated reveries seem to be fabricated into living ideals of grandeur more magnificent than any that every Rajah or Caliph beheld in vision or fact."[33]

This was a presumptuous but honest sentiment: it was Buel's way of positioning the imagineering of popular culture icons above their prototypes—a clearly arrogant but necessary philosophical stance in the Gilded Age, when image trumped substance. Buel's surprisingly candid statement is central to the concerns of postmodernism. With little modification, one could replace Buel's "Magic City" with Disney's "Magic Kingdom" (1955) or—for that matter, today's magical city, Las Vegas—without missing a beat. That is what makes Orientalism, which was a nationwide phenomenon, so perfectly suited to the American West. As historian John Findlay observed, the West could reinvent itself on occasion, encouraging and then sustaining extreme innovation.[34] Although Orientalism was one ingredient in that creative process, it was among the most important and persuasive for developers.

California emerged early on as a land that imported and embraced the best of the exotic. As opposed to New York or Illinois, though, California's physical environment could in part justify the tradition. Its incredible climate, or rather climates, helped sustain the feeling that people were experiencing something akin to the original, and with good reason. The state possesses the widest variety of landscapes and climates of any US state. Somewhere in the state, one could probably find climate types that represented most of the Orient, except the sultry coastal climates of Southeast Asia. It is one thing to experience an Oriental-style building in the eastern or midwestern United States, but quite another to experience it in California. The point here is that Oriental-style amusement parks in the East and Midwest went only so far in pulling off the total effect. However, on a balmy March evening in Los Angeles, with snow-covered mountains looming in the distance and the incredibly potent fragrance of orange blossoms scenting the air, it was far easier for crowds to imagine that they had been transported either to Babylon or Eden.

The search for the Garden of Eden in Spain's (and Mexico's) far north-west—which is to say California—intensified well into the twentieth century. In *Orange Empire: California and the Fruits of Eden*, Douglas Cazaux Sackman makes it quite clear that California presented a new kind of Eden in the nineteenth century. As Sackman put it, this was a "second edition of Eden," which "was not meant to be a sacred place, walled off from the world of commerce." This Eden would, as Sackman states, or rather understates, "have economic functions." It would become part of an economy linked to "material dreams"—a garden featuring "the most worldly delights." This California Garden of Eden, Sackman concluded, "contained the seeds of empire."[35] And yet the seduction of citrus also depended on the appeal of an Eden that was particularly primal—much like the original Garden of Eden. Sackman astutely observes that orange crate labels frequently used sex to sell the product, as in the Tesoro brand, whose label used a provocatively dressed woman who reached "into the treasure chest between her legs and pulled out a golden fruit, seductively displaying it as an object of desire." As Sackman observes, "To have an orange is also to 'have' a woman."[36] This woman is Eve, who continues to tempt long after her, and our, expulsion from the garden.

Sackman's observation that Eden is a troubled place regardless of who is to blame is insightful. As he puts it, "The Fall—whether we blame the snake, the woman, the man, or the god—splits the harmony between humans and the rest of creation." This act ejects people from that garden. However, "the dream of a return has persisted," despite the fact that "such a garden has always been a fabrication." Sackman concludes that "there is no Eden,"[37] but that negative sentiment is as easy for an academician to claim as it is difficult for a culture to comprehend. The Garden of Eden, the garden of earthly delights, is a Middle Eastern concept deeply embedded in three major faiths (Judaism, Christianity, and Islam). It is synonymous with *paradise*, an originally Iranian concept that is both a place and a state of mind, even a state of grace. In one sense, it is a time of innocence before the responsibilities of adulthood—personal, cultural, or national—confound us with choices that are ultimately moral or ethical. For our culture to disavow such a garden, it would have to both discard its soul and abandon its hope. That realization makes it easier to understand the West's fundamental and perennial connection to the East. Paradoxically, although the Orient is a foreign place, it is also the source of many of our deepest beliefs and most enduring myths.

Paradise, whether here or there, deserves one more comment that sets it in a broader cultural context. The fundamental difference between the West (by which I mean the Western world) and the East (the Eastern world) is not the belief in paradise, which both espouse, but rather whether or not that Eden is attainable in this life. As historians Ian Buruma and Avishai Margalit note in their seminal book *Occidentalism: The West in the Eyes of its Enemies*, the West is committed to finding, or even creating, that Eden in the here and now. By contrast, the East knows that paradise is only attainable either by separating oneself from the material world entirely (Hinduism and Buddhism) or, in the case of Islam, by dying. Buruma and Margalit contend that the hatred of the West by the East, which is fairly recent, involves considerable essentializing of the Occident. A core belief of Occidentalism is that Westerners are soft and weak. They seek comfort in this life—and hold on to life tenaciously, even desperately. By contrast, Easterners (as exemplified in the extreme actions by Islamist terrorist suicide/homicide bombers) gladly embrace death as offering the real paradise.[38]

If some people believe that only detachment or death brings entry into heaven, Californians set out to prove the opposite, namely, that earthly paradise could exist in the here and now. When the second International Irrigation Congress met in Los Angeles in 1883, it chose as its motto a line from Genesis: "A river went out of Eden to water the Garden." Historian Donald Worster noted that the congress combined secular and religious zeal in its mission to irrigate the West. As Worster put it, the delegates met "for five days of speeches, soaring hymns, and fervid, sustained applause." Their mission was both bold and biblically inspired: "They too wanted to capture a river flowing out of Eden and create a garden where the American Adam and Eve could live in perfect harmony." To leave little doubt about what the congress hoped to create, Worster notes that they envisioned not only a land "where there would be no work" but also a land of secular bliss where there would be "no sin," and "no one saying no." But not everyone at the congress agreed, especially the key speaker. That dissenting voice was provided by John Wesley Powell, the former New Englander turned western guru, who undiplomatically warned them that they were piling up a "heritage of conflict of all waters." In this, his last public appearance in the West, Powell threw diplomacy to the wind. Stating that it did not matter to him whether his message would make him "popular or unpopular," Powell repeated his hard-learned mantra that "there is not sufficient water to supply those lands." As Powell evidently predicted, the message stunned and angered the congress. As a consequence of his straight talk, Powell's popularity in the West fell—at least for the time. As Worster notes, however, Powell is a hero vindicated by time.[39] But for every Powell, there were a million westerners who thought the waters limitless and sin wageless. The myth of Eden and its rivers was an irresistible legacy of the West's Eastern roots.

Among irrigation's many proponents, few were as ardent as William E. Smythe (1861–1922), a transplanted New Englander who traveled extensively in search of stories that demonstrated how progress could enhance both the individual and the nation. As a prolific writer, Smythe traveled westward for examples, and his experiences in Nebraska and New Mexico brought him face to face with the challenges agriculture faced in semi-arid and arid lands. Smythe was impressed with how water could transform arid lands— so impressed, in fact, that he founded the magazine *Irrigation Age* in 1881. Gaining a comprehensive understanding of how irrigation had transformed the Near East, Smythe envisioned transforming the American West. His book titled *The Conquest of Arid America* (1899) became so popular that several editions were printed. In researching his book, Smythe came to know much of the Southwest. In the process, he was lured by the charm of San Diego, and, as might be predicted, soon became one of the city's foremost boosters. But it was what lay on the other side of the mountains from San Diego, namely the Colorado Desert, that naturally intrigued Smythe. In addition to promoting San Diego as a new version of Syria, therefore, Smythe also envisioned his adopted city serving a new hinterland—California's Sahara-like Colorado Desert, the very wasteland that had been cursed by so many travelers, including Raphael Pumpelly. In Smythe's vision, this infernal desert would succumb to irrigation. Smythe, of course, was not the first to envision such a transformation, but he could articulate it better than most. As he observed, or rather predicted, in a 1901 article titled "The Blooming of a Sahara" in *World's Work* magazine: "Under the magic influence of national prosperity and Oriental expansion a new impulse of development is sweeping over our Farthest Southwest." [40]

In this context, Southern California's most truly Middle Eastern environment, namely the Coachella and Imperial Valleys, was easy to Orientalize.

The climate here is, as Smythe and others claimed, fairly similar to portions of the Arabian Peninsula and adjacent North Africa. Moreover, the presence of the Colorado River helped further equate this area with Egypt. As geographer Robert Sauder observed, "With its delta in the desert, the Colorado [River] has no parallel in the Western Hemisphere, but in the Old World the lower Nile Valley is a fitting correlative." Both rivers rise in distant mountains in summer, deposit "fertile soil in the midst of barren deserts through which they flow," and are extensively used for irrigation. "It is because of these similarities . . ." Sauder concludes, "that the Colorado River is often referred to as the American Nile."[41]

This American Nile would help transform the Coachella and Imperial Valleys just after 1900, when careless construction work sent waters from the Colorado River sweeping into the formerly dry Imperial Valley sink.[42] What followed was a modern miracle, or at least an example of people miraculously turning disaster into economic and touristic opportunity. After the leak was plugged by the railroad workers dumping everything they could find into the opening, the resulting scene was very evocative. Like the Nile, the Colorado River had given life to this area, as those branding it with an "Oriental" identity were well aware. In 1916, the Imperial Farm Land Association recognized the appeal of the exotic, changing the name of a stop on the railroad from Imperial Junction (formerly Old Beach) to Niland—a combination of Nile and Land.[43] But the area that the river had inundated also reminded observers of a similar environment in the Near East. By the early twentieth century, with the waters of the Colorado River lying like a blue mirror on the Imperial Valley's floor, this huge depressed desert trough took on a new identity based on an Old World counterpart. At the northwestern edge of the Salton Sea, the otherwise businesslike Southern Pacific railroad imaginatively named a train-order station Mortmere, a slightly corrupted rendition of "Dead Sea" in French. Through the years, the dramatically named place was given a different spelling, Mortmar,[44] which means much the same thing in Spanish. Within a few years, the resulting inland sea became a tourist haven, and the enterprising agricultural industry took advantage of the subtropical climate to produce a garden spot filled with Middle Eastern and Mediterranean crops, including date palms and citrus.

The feeling of a Middle East imported into this area may be fanciful, but it is not without merit. In terms of environmental surrogates, the Salton Sea is about as close to the real Dead Sea as one can get in North America. The fact that the Salton Sea now fills the bottom of the valley, its surface well below sea level, helps people equate it and its surroundings with the area near the

Dead Sea. Even the name "Salton" Sea, however, must be considered carefully, for this fabricated name has more than a little subliminal resonance as the word *sultan*. Following the creation of the Salton Sea, the valley responded to a themed boosterism that emphasized its exotic landscapes, desert vegetation (including native palm trees), and subtropical climate. Given the propensity for westerners to create surrogate landscapes, it seemed inevitable that portions of Southern California would take on an "Arabian" identity almost overnight—no surprise in that all of the "Southland" sought exotic identities associated for the most part with the Mediterranean and the Near East.

The date palm (*Phoenix dactylifera*) played a role in helping to transform the California (and Arizona) desert into a Middle Eastern oasis. Native to Egypt and much of the Middle East, it is an enduring symbol of the West's connection to the Orient. The first date palms were brought to California by the Spaniards, but it was the Anglo-Americans who would help make them a premier symbol of the new Near East in Southern California. These palms were, in a word, exotic. Although the American Southwest does have native palm trees, namely, the California or Washington palms (*Washingtonia filifera*), which thrive in the tropical and subtropical lower desert of the United States (notably the palm oases of Southern California's Colorado Desert as far north as Twentynine Palms, and in southwestern Arizona's Kofa Mountains), these do not yield edible fruit nor do they have the exotic aura of the date palm.

The low deserts of the American West, in Southern California and adjacent Arizona especially, seemed perfect places for the dromedary date of the Middle East to thrive, and it did just that. Within a decade or two, the early twentieth-century landscape of the Coachella and Imperial Valleys was awash with orderly groves of date palms. Like all palms, which the Arabs astutely claim "stand with their heads in sun and their feet in the water," these palms contrasted beautifully with the arid landscapes of the hottest of deserts. Whereas the region's native palms were (and are) found in well-watered locations where fault lines permit the plants' roots to be constantly moistened by groundwater, the newly planted date palms depended on a network of man-made irrigation canals and ditches—much like their counterparts in Middle Eastern locations like Israel, Jordan, Arabia, and Egypt. The Muslim Arabs placed date palm trees high on the list of meaningful creations, claiming that they represented the material that was left over immediately after God created humankind. To Californians, however, date palms meant big business both for the agricultural products they yielded and the exotic, Near Eastern locales they suggested.

Fig. 6-3. Introduced to California in 1890, commercial date growing had become well established by the early 1930s, when the verso of this postcard claimed that "the dates grown in California are found to be superior to that of Arabia, Egypt, and Palestine."

Most of the dates produced in the Middle East are important foodstuffs locally, though some of the finest are imported. Most of the dates grown in California and Arizona, however, are shipped far and wide, and their marketing played on an exotic Middle Eastern theme while promising a home-grown product. By the 1920s and 1930s, the date producers in the Southern California desert were using Middle Eastern iconography to promote their "succulent" and "nutritious" dates. Stylized lettering that appeared Arabic, silhouettes of camels, and mosquelike towers were favorite themes, lending an exotic *Arabian Nights* quality to the product. As travelers encountered the Imperial Valley, they were treated not only to the delicious dates themselves (an energy-packed food containing some protein but very high in sugar) but to exotic innovations like "date shakes"—that is, milkshakes containing dates blended with milk and ice cream—which also drew tourists. A color post-card of "Date Palms" contains the message on the verso that "hundreds of thousands of pounds of dates are shipped every year from the gardens of the Southwest, where the climate, like that of Egypt and Arabia, is most conducive to the raising of this delicious fruit."[45] The verso of another equally color-ful postcard, circa 1920 (fig. 6-3), goes even further, claiming that "the dates grown in California are found to be superior to that [*sic*] of Arabia, Egypt, and Palestine where for centuries it has been a highly prized food for King and

Peasant alike." Note that Californians are here appropriating and attempting to surpass the real Middle East. This may be hyperbole, but it was part of a seamless process in which agriculture and regional image building worked hand in hand to transform this part of the desert West into a Middle Eastern oasis—at least in the popular imagination.

7

To Ancient East by Ocean United
The Pacific Northwest as Asia

"If the Chinamen in our midst are an evil, who is to blame for it?"

Choir's History, Business Directory and Immigrant's Guide Book to and Throughout
Washington Territory and Vicinity (1878)

B<small>Y THE LATE</small> 1870<small>S, WHEN</small> *Choir's Guide Book* <small>TO THE</small> P<small>ACIFIC</small> N<small>ORTHWEST</small> was published, the Chinese presence was palpable throughout this large region lying north of California and south of Canada. Choir's took the opinion that Chinese people per se were not to blame. They were, after all, victims of age-old oppression. As the writer of the guidebook asked rhetorically: "Did not the emperor of China wall in his kingdom and declare it locked up against all foreign association? And did not the latter break down these barriers and invite and encourage immigration?" By this the writer meant the Treaty of Tien-tsin (1860), which had essentially opened China to outside influences, including the establishment of Western embassies and Christian missionaries, and the legalized importation of opium.

To many xenophobic Americans, this was bad enough, but the real question, as *Choir's Guide Book* saw it, was tied to more recent legislation. As this popular source of information about the Pacific Northwest pointedly asked: "Is not that feather of aristocracy, the Burlingame Treaty, to blame for the hordes of Chinamen here to-day?" That 1868 amendment to the earlier treaty recognized what it called "the inherent and inalienable right of man to change his home and allegiance, and also the mutual advantage of the free migration and emigration of their citizens and subjects, respectively for purposes of curiosity, of trade, or as permanent residents." Although the Burlingame Treaty shied away from actual naturalization of newly arrived peoples from China, it had the effect of liberalizing immigration and stirring considerable debate among nativists. The discussions were particularly virulent in areas of the United States with large populations of Chinese, namely California and the Pacific Northwest.[1]

These concerns had grown since about 1850, but the subject of Asia's relationship to the Pacific Northwest goes back much further in time, for it had fueled unsuccessful searches for a fabled Northwest Passage for several centuries. As late as 1800, such a passage was still on Thomas Jefferson's mind. By 1805 Jefferson had dispatched Lewis and Clark to find an easy water passage through North America that would bring the new United States closer to Asia. Instead, they discovered a poor substitute—the Columbia River—and encountered near its mouth a forested land where rainfall seemed incessant and a carpet of moss appeared determined to cover everything, especially during the long winter months. These explorers were not impressed with their stay, and for that matter, acknowledged that they had failed in finding the passageway they sought on behalf of the president. Nevertheless, they were the first Americans to reach the Pacific on a venture that had clear implications for future US-Asian relations.

Although this challenging corner of North America partly overwhelmed Lewis and Clark, the material contained in their report suggested that the region held real promise for the United States. By the 1840s, with the question of British control here nearing peaceful resolution, Anglo-American settlers began moving to the Pacific Northwest. In western Oregon, they found a climate that had dry summers and mild, wet winters. Within a short time, they too began to think of this area as the new Eden. Although their goal was to create a new and vibrant part of the United States, the more enterprising among them were intrigued—as had been earlier generations of mapmakers and explorers—by this region's proximity to Asia. However, while these nineteenth-century visionaries in the Pacific Northwest sensed a great commercial future with the Orient, that future would take a couple of generations to materialize.

In the meantime, the more fertile parts of the Northwest were settled by land via the Oregon Trail, while Chinese immigrants began to arrive via California by the early 1850s, when gold mining boomed along the Rogue River in southern Oregon. Most of these Chinese miners had arrived from California, but soon Chinese immigrants debarked in Astoria and Portland. By the 1860s, the Chinese were mining gold in central and eastern Oregon (and Idaho), but many also found work as cowboys and farmers. Of the miners, most selected spots some distance away from European Americans, and they often seemed to have a special knack for finding gold where others failed. Mostly, though, the techniques used by Chinese miners were especially

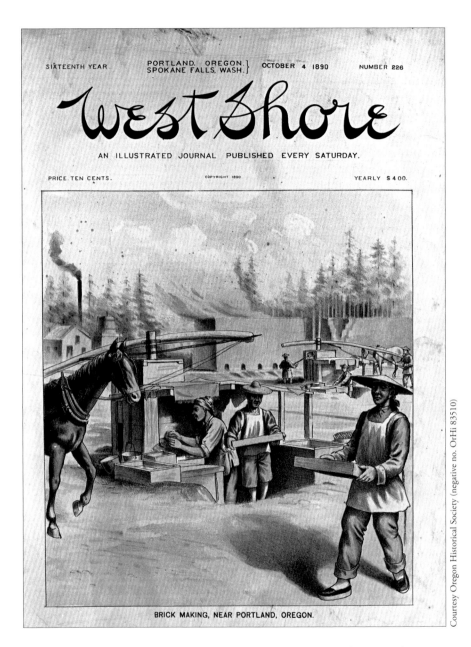

Fig. 7-1. The presence of Chinese workers in this cover illustration from *West Shore Magazine,* 1890, gives an Asian feel to a brickyard near Portland, Oregon.

effective. Their relative isolation, however, did not guarantee safety. In 1887, at least thirty Chinese miners were killed in one of the West's bloodiest events, the massacre at Hells Canyon, Idaho. If, as historian R. Gregory Nokes claims, thirty-four Chinese miners were killed in this event, it ranks as *the* bloodiest episode in Chinese American history.[2]

Although tragic events like this left the landscape stained and the Pacific Northwest's history tarnished, there were some bright points in the relationship between the Chinese and the European Americans. As a writer for *West Shore* magazine observed in 1889, the Chinese were hard workers; one of them could accomplish "daily as much as two Caucasians would." Their handiwork was everywhere evident in the landscape: "By utilizing every inch [of land], by cropping the same ground several times a year, and by constant use of the irrigation ditch and watering can, he secures a marvelous quantity of vegetables from a very small patch of ground."[3] If *industrious* is a word often associated with the Chinese, it included more than mining and agriculture. Chinese workers were also prominent in the canning and brick industries: an 1890 lithograph of a brickyard near Portland transforms the Pacific Northwest into a nominally Asian scene as Chinese brick makers and hod carriers—recognizable by the characteristic dress, including broad-rimmed hats and cloglike shoes—produce and trundle bricks (fig. 7-1).[4]

The clothing worn by Chinese workers frequently caught the attention of Anglo-Americans. In particular, their conical, broad-rimmed hats were so distinctive that topographic features were often named after them. In Oregon alone, there are several evocatively shaped buttes bearing the name "China" or "Chinese" in reference to such distinctive headwear. These include China Cap in Union County, which "bears a close similarity to the hats worn by Chinese laborers throughout the Pacific Northwest in the early days of development," and therefore "it must have been named on that account," and China Hat, a butte in Deschutes County that "received its name because, when viewed from Fort Rock, it resembled the style of hat worn by Chinese during early days of the Pacific Northwest" (fig. 7-2). Toponyms like China Creek, China Flat, and China Bar commemorate the Chinese gold miners in parts of Oregon, and China Ditch recognizes their work in digging a drainage ditch alongside a branch line of the Union Pacific in Gilliam County.[5]

The Chinese were now part of the scene, and their colorful customs were often commented upon, but many found their presence disturbing. Nowhere is this ambivalence more apparent than among Anglo-American religious leaders on the West Coast, and the Pacific Northwest was no exception. In 1882, a Baptist minister in the Northwest made a generous claim pretty much

Author's photograph

Fig. 7-2. Nick Yehnert wears a "coolie hat" as he gazes at the aptly named China Hat in Deschutes County, Oregon, in September, 2010.

in sympathy with liberal legislation: "We believe that the gospel is for the Chinese; and we believe that we ought to meet the incoming tide of immigration with the open Bible." To this, he added that "the Lord our God has had a hand, at least, in sending the Chinese to the Pacific Coast."[6] Another minister stated that "the coming of the Chinese to America is excelled in importance by no other event since the discovery of the New World. It is," as he put it, "one of the impulses, beyond all human conception or management, by which God is moving the history of mankind onward to its great consummation."[7]

That is one side of the coin, but not everyone was quite so sanguine or generous. In 1909, the Portland *Oregonian* concluded that the Chinese "have not a dollar's worth of real property or any kind of foundation to show as a result, but only a small group of 'boys,' as they are called, meeting in or moving from one little batty room to another, with the pretty white girl always the chief attraction." Note the overtones of sexual jealousy here, with the Asian men seeming to prefer white women and thus threatening the manhood of Anglo-Americans by stealing their women. Leaving no doubt where it stood, the paper categorically stated that "Oriental persons cannot be 'converted' to Christianity."[8]

As in California, Chinatown was a fixture of urban life in the Pacific

Northwest. In 1890, writer Harvey Whitefield Scott described Portland's Chinatown as a fascinating mélange of American and Chinese architecture. The buildings that composed Chinatown were brick and had been "put up in the first place largely by Americans." That, however, did not prohibit the Chinese here from tailoring the environment to their own needs—or as Scott put it, modifying it "according to their convenience and ideas of beauty." These buildings, Scott continued, "are intensely oriental in their general air, with piazzas of curved roofs, highly ornamented with yellow, white, and vermilion paint, and paper globes and gegaws." Along the streets, "red paper inscribed with characters in black serve as signs, and are pasted numerously over doors and windows." The impression created was both exotic and festive. Scott further noted that certain events could make Chinatown even more enchanting: "On gala days, the entire area is lit up by lanterns, or gaily ornamented with paper." Moreover, the sounds in Chinatown were different, too. Here, "the tones of their flutes and fiddles, and . . . gongs" filled the air.[9]

A map showing the distribution of western American communities with a significant Asian population, usually in the form of Chinatowns, is noteworthy (fig. 7-3). It reveals how intimately the Chinese were associated with mining and railroads and also how connected they remained to the Pacific Coast cities that served as their initial points of arrival to the United States. The remnants of the Chinese presence are etched into the rural landscape of the entire West from Arizona into Idaho, but their presence is most palpable near the Pacific Coast itself. As the map confirms, the Pacific Northwest was a major center for the Chinese; however, the Japanese also had a significant presence here, although many arrived somewhat later than the Chinese.

The acceptance of Asians into the fabric of the Pacific Northwest had taken considerable time as part of an elaborate image-building process. In fact, at the same time that an Asian presence was being established in the 1850s and 1860s, Anglo-Americans began to become aware that this new region had its own unique character—if only they could identify it. For the general public as well as writers, the Pacific Northwest's landscapes conspired to link it with someplace more exotic. To some, it was the mountainous area bordering the northern Mediterranean Sea, notably Greece. In the 1860s, writer Joaquin Miller observed that even the Indian and Anglo-American names in Oregon wouldn't suffice. As Miller put it: "Ah, you look incredulous and think of the practical names of the Luckimute [sic] and Long Tom and Soap Creek, but never mind them, look at Mt. Hood. It is itself a Parnassus." By equating Mount Hood with one of the most sacred places in ancient Greece, Miller simultaneously elevated it above mundane places and gave it an air

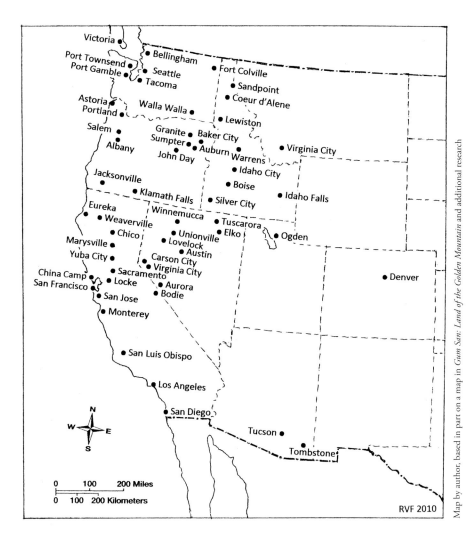

Map by author, based in part on a map in *Gum San: Land of the Golden Mountain* and additional research

Fig. 7-3. A map of the American West showing communities with significant Chinese populations, ca. 1900, reveals their presence in ports (fishing, commerce), along railroads, and in mining areas.

of the exotic. This meshed perfectly with Miller's romantic interpretation of Oregon's landscapes, which, he repeatedly reminded readers, were exceptional. While serving as editor of the *Eugene City Review* in the 1870s, Miller admonished his readers to "look at the Cascades. . . . Look at the little knolls and buttes that lay stretched up and down the [Willamette] valley, covered with white flocks and fat herds, and listen to the foaming sea afar off that beats with eternal roar over rock bound shores, and tell me if this, our sunset land, is not a land of song and poetry."[10] As Miller hinted, song and poetry would later play a role in regional identity, but travelers' experiences elsewhere helped in the meantime.

But it was a new breed of educated person, notably the geologist, who would ultimately play a role in finding a more suitable counterpart to the Pacific Northwest's landscapes in the nineteenth century. As geologists traveled to Asia in the 1860s and 1870s, they found a landscape analogue for the region in Japan. Like that island empire, the Pacific Northwest is shaped by volcanism. In contrast to much of the West, the Pacific Northwest is a land where tall volcanic peaks form the horizon not far from the coast. West of the towering Cascade Range, the region's thick, fragrant forests of fir and cedar are reminiscent of what travelers encountered in Japan. Here and there, from the Canadian border south to extreme Northern California, snowcapped volcanic peaks crown the skyline. As with other landscapes around the Pacific Ring of Fire, volcanoes slumber but may awaken from time to time. The serene sapphire countenance of Oregon's Crater Lake disguises a volatile landscape capable of sending volcanic ash and destruction over thousands of square miles, which it did about seven thousand years ago. There is something exotic about these mountains. Even the name of the former mountain that occupied the site of Crater Lake—Mount Mazama—sounds strangely Japanese. These and other aspects of the landscapes in the Pacific Northwest suggest a familiarity with, and similarity to, Asia.

The historical process by which the Pacific Northwest began to be Orientalized in the nineteenth century reveals much about the role of sophisticated travelers in securing information in Asia and bringing it back to America. Some of these travelers were scientists and some were writers. A few, like geologist Raphael Pumpelly, were both. We have already seen how Pumpelly characterized portions of the American Southwest and California, but he was traveling through the area with a more exotic goal in mind, namely, reaching the Orient and comparing its geology to that of the western US.

Upon reaching San Francisco on his epic westward journey in the early 1860s, Pumpelly observed that "the Japanese Government had instructed Mr. C. W. Brooks, their commercial agent, to engage two geologists and mining engineers, for the purpose of exploring part of the Japanese Empire." However, Pumpelly added that he came by this job serendipitously. Because of a misunderstanding, a copy of the Japanese officials' correspondence had been sent to the US government in Washington, DC, but "by a pure coincidence, I was chosen as one of the two men."[11] "Coincidence" seems a strange word for a scientist like Pumpelly to use, but it was accurate. Actually, Pumpelly's confession reveals several aspects of Orientalism that are not often recognized. First, American and other Western explorers often came to Asia at the behest of governments in the Orient. Second, scientific explorers, not just political officials, were often at the cutting edge of observing the Orient firsthand and conveying images of its culture and landscape to the United States. Lastly, sometimes serendipity plays a role in the process of Orientalization. Pumpelly was not only one of America's scientific luminaries at the time but was also a gifted writer. His popular *Across America and Asia*, published in 1870, provided an evocative look at the Orient from Japan and China across the steppes of Russia. It did for Asia what John Lloyd Stephens' *Incidents of Travel in Egypt* had done for the Near East about a generation earlier. Pumpelly's book was widely read and played a role in shaping attitudes about Asia by simultaneously demystifying, and yet romanticizing, Asian culture and landscape.

Even though Pumpelly was an earth scientist, he was also an astute observer of culture and history. That is what makes his writings so rich in content about the character of Japan. In a telling section, Pumpelly discusses the "executive power centered in the Mikado," adding that such a person was "too holy to be seen by other than the very highest of his attendants, the Sun, although himself a deity, not worthy of shining on his head, the Mikado may not touch the ground with his feet, nor even cut his [own] nails and hair, so sacred is his body."[12] That type of description fascinated and sometimes disgusted otherwise democratic Americans who insisted their leaders be both approachable and accountable. Similarly, those Americans like Stephens, who had had an audience with the Pasha in the Middle East, often noted the incredible social distance between a potentate and his people. This distance was both social and metaphorical, for it represented distant exotic places that seemed stuck in time—that is, had not, and perhaps could not, "progress" as did the Western world. It is telling, though, that Americans were impressed enough with Asian leaders like these to name two types of locomotives after them, the Mogul type (2-6-0) and the Mikado (2-8-2) being examples from the nineteenth and twentieth centuries, respectively.

For his part, Pumpelly philosophically mused that every culture that tried to subdue Japan had failed. Even the great and terrible Kublai Khan, who hoped "to see all mankind united in one family," and would take Japan by force if necessary—"failed ingloriously." Idealistically, perhaps, Pumpelly believed that the "peaceful diplomacy" he was experiencing in the 1860s had actually "paved the way for bringing that empire into the circle of nations."[13] That notion of the circle of nations was, of course, a Western concept that included the United States center stage—though Pumpelly would have been chagrined to learn that Japan's membership in this circle of nations would only follow the world's most destructive war almost a century later. Interestingly, it would be Japan, rather than China, that would ultimately have the closest connection to the Pacific Northwest.

Asian culture in the Far West was marginalized for a long time, but some Anglo-Americans—especially those in education, commerce, and religion—strongly resented that marginalization. Repudiating such discrimination, many educated and worldly Americans tried to promote a better understanding about Asians, as did Pumpelly. In his extensive section on Japan, for example, he observed that "the thoughtful traveller learns in the first stages of his wanderings, that the more distant the relationship between the two races, the more difficult it is to measure them by the same standard."[14] Those two races, of course, were Americans and Asians. Many more Anglo-Americans, however, were in no mood for such generous cultural relativism, that is, making "us" better understand "them" through reasoning. Despite the inherent conflation of East and West that occurred in many parts of the West, the differences between the two cultures were difficult to reconcile. And so, Orientalism played out with considerable ambivalence: On the one hand, it could portray positive connections between East and West. On the other hand, it could emphasize differences that often led to tension, and even violence.

Pumpelly also revealed something significant about the character of Japanese landscapes, and his descriptions shed light on how Americans came to appreciate those exotic landscapes. In an insightful passage about his excursions in the Japanese countryside that would influence the creation of Asian gardens in America, especially the Pacific Northwest, Pumpelly noted that "a view presented itself in which I immediately recognized a scene familiar to all who have seen much of the Japanese lacquered ware." In addition to the beautiful smooth waters of Wodowara Bay and the neck of sand that joined the beach to rocky Enoshima Island, this view contained an icon: "Far away over this neck, and the bay beyond," Pumpelly noted, "rose the lofty and graceful cone of Fuziyama." We call this mountain Fujiyama or Mount Fuji today, but it remains the premier topographic icon of Japan. How did it become so? Writing in 1870, Pumpelly observed that "this view of the mountain is a favorite subject of Japanese artists." He underscored the significance of this "most perfect of volcanic cones," which had become "an object of national [Japanese] pride, and the subject of innumerable sketches and verses." To be sure that readers comprehended the significance of Fuji, Pumpelly included an illustration of this scene, which was based on a Japanese sketch, in his book (fig. 7-4). The iconic image of Fujiyama looming above Enoshima Island at

Author's collection

Fig. 7-4. In his popular book *Across America and Asia* (1870), geologist Raphael Pumpelly illustrated "Inosima and Mount Fusiyama from a Japanese sketch."

the mouth of Sagami Bay is enduring indeed. From Pumpelly's time onward, Americans also recognized it as a symbol for Japan, especially in postcards after about 1900, some of which were comercially printed and others of which were actually hand painted by Japanese artists (fig. 7-5).

In the Pacific Northwest, Mount Fuji had several counterparts—impressive, snow-covered volcanic mountains that ruled the skyline. The towering Mount Hood to the east of Portland is that city's signature landmark. It appears in countless photographs, paintings, commercial advertisements, and logos such as the University of Oregon's seal, which was adopted in 1877. Portland actually had two such signature topographic landmarks at the turn of the century, though one of them was located north of the Columbia River in the state of Washington: Mount Saint Helens also appeared in many postcards and paintings (fig. 7-6) and was considered to be "one of the world's most symmetrically beautiful mountains, in a league with Japan's Mt. Fuji."[15] However, Portland lost this iconic landmark in 1980 when a thunderous volcanic eruption blasted the top off of the mountain. In the wake of that catastrophic volcanic eruption, Mount Saint Helens is still visible from the city but reduced in stature and more a natural curiosity than an imposing, Fujilike landmark. Farther north, the urbanizing Seattle-Tacoma area also featured stunning, Fujilike volcanic mountains. In postcard views of the time, it was easy for artists to slightly retouch the peaks of Mount Baker and Mount

Fig. 7-6. Postcard view of Mount Saint Helens, Washington, rising above Spirit Lake (ca. 1920).

Fig. 7-5. In this beautiful, hand-painted postcard (ca. 1915), Fujiyama looms above the surrounding forested landscape near the coast.

510 – MOUNT RAINIER AND CITY OF OLYMPIA, WASHINGTON.

Author's collection

Fig. 7-7. Postcard view of Mount Rainier as seen from Olympia, Washington (ca. 1915).

Rainier to give them their perfect, which is to say Fujilike, form. In a postcard view of Mount Rainier and the city of Olympia, Washington, the mountain interrupts the horizon in a manner very reminiscent of the Japanese paintings of Fujiyama (fig. 7-7). These snowcapped volcanic mountains were incorporated into the developing boosterism of the Pacific Northwest. More to the point, however, they subliminally equated the Pacific Northwest with the Far East. The verso of one revealing 1912 postcard notes that Mount Saint Helens is "our Fujiama," though Mount Hood was also equated with that venerable Japanese mountain on occasion.[16]

These Northwest-as-Japan topographic comparisons were more than simply Anglo-American fantasies. The historical record confirms that immigrants from Asia could also feel the Pacific Northwest's similarity to their native lands. After visiting several parts of the United States when he arrived from Japan in 1905, for example, Masuo Yasui ultimately settled in Hood River, Oregon, a small community situated in the shadow of Mount Hood. According to Yasui's biographer, he became "transfixed by the beauty of the passing scenery" on a train ride through the Columbia River Gorge: "The dense, green valley sloping back to touch the base of a snowcapped peak that resembled the beloved Mount Fuji reminded him so much of Japan that he got off the train then and there, declaring Hood River his home."[17]

Elsewhere in his discussions of the Japanese landscape, Pumpelly describes

the temple in Yeddo, the grounds of which "contained some beautiful specimens of Japanese gardening, consisting of dwarfed trees and rock work, with
ponds containing gold fish and silver fish." While discussing the Yeddo temple
grounds, Pumpelly noted, "One feature that struck me was the abundance of
large trees, many of them primeval forest pines, which met the eye at every
turn, crowning the low hills or rising from the grounds of a daimio's yaski."[18]
Pumpelly's descriptions here emphasize several aspects of the Japanese landscape, namely, (1) the texture of varied objects such as rocks, trees, fish, and
even mountains, (2) the placement of these objects in varied planes—foreground, middle ground, and background, (3) the concept of a primeval or
pristine nature that is (4) altered, with positive results, by the artistic hand of
man. *Artistic* is the operative concept in Pumpelly's descriptions, and it appears
at three levels. First, in the very aesthetic quality of the landscapes he describes;
second, in the fact that Japanese artists are recording and interpreting the
scenes with considerable emotion; and third, in the actual artistic manner
in which the Japanese were shaping the landscape itself—cultivating stunted
trees, placing rocks, and so forth. These three levels of appreciation all have
a spiritual quality to some degree—after all, Fujiyama is a spiritual locale—
but they remind us how closely aesthetics and spirituality are connected in
Japan. This artistic impulse and the spiritualization of the landscape in Japan,
of course, combine to create something we recognize as the "character" of
Oriental landscaping today. However, Pumpelly's book revealed it at just the
time that the Pacific Northwest—with its lofty, snow-covered, volcanic mountain cones looming, Fujilike, above primeval green forests, stunning seascapes,
and thriving cityscapes—was being articulated for public consumption.

Although the developing regional identity of the Pacific Northwest was
influenced by Asia, there was also strong competition from other places. In
fact, the Pacific Northwest is heir to two very different influences. On the one
hand, it has a strong connection with Asia, but it has perhaps an equally strong
affinity to the British Isles and New England. In 1925, J. Russell Smith noted
that the "Puget Sound Valley" was "the climatic duplicate of England." In this,
Smith was somewhat more enthusiastic than perfectly accurate, but the coastal
Pacific Northwest is indeed cool and cloudy enough to seem like England,
Scotland, and Ireland. And yet the far northwestern corner of the continental
United States also has strong connections across the Pacific Ocean. As evidence of this dichotomy, consider two invasive plants in the Pacific Northwest
that have become weeds but otherwise give the landscape a distinctive look—
the flashy yellow Scotch broom (*Cytisus scoparius*) that decorates hillsides
and reminds one of the British Isles, and the Himalayan blackberry (*Rubus*

armeniacus), which forms thick stands of tangled vines that yield delicious fruit in late summer. Both symbolize the region's dual personality, or at least dual sources of inspiration.

Even though the Pacific Northwest has long recognized and touted its British Isles and its New England Atlantic heritage, its connections to Asia were especially appealing to business and commercial interests from a fairly early date. In fact, Seattle's position on the most direct route between New England and Asian ports made it the perfect jumping-off place for anyone traveling from the Northeast to the Orient. As Smith continued, in Seattle "there is also much Oriental talk and trade, for this harbor, [situated] from one to three days nearer to the Orient than San Francisco, has several important steamship-lines in the Asia trade." To clarify this, Smith explained that "the route is shorter than more southerly routes because the spherical shape of the earth makes the north great-circle routes shorter than the southern routes." If Asian silk were shipped through Seattle, Smith observed, it could go from Yokohama, Japan, to New York in just two weeks. As Smith concluded, "In Seattle, more than any Pacific city, one can feel commerce."[19] One manifestation of this expedited trade was the high-speed "silk trains," which rushed their precious cargo east from Seattle on passenger train schedules.

Smith was here building on a theme Seattle had begun capitalizing on at least a generation earlier. This was some time in the making. As early as 1878, a poem titled "SEATTLE" began with the words "Enthroned Upon thy emerald hills / Queen City of the Sound" but praised the fact that the city was "To Ancient East by ocean united."[20] Like San Francisco, Seattle looks both eastward and westward. Unlike that California city, however, Seattle had no nearby goldfields. Rather, the city found itself perched in the far northwest corner of the continental United States in a location that was peripheral to the rest of the nation, but—as Seattle's elite often pointed out—actually much closer to the Orient than was San Francisco. Despite its relative isolation, though, Seattle's dream was a step closer to reality in the early 1880s, as two northern transcontinental railroads—the Northern Pacific and Great Northern—now linked it to the eastern and midwestern United States. Those railroads further helped Seattle (and Portland) tap their vast interior hinterlands yielding wheat, lumber, and mineral wealth. That, and the Alaska and Yukon mining booms of the late nineteenth century, finally put Seattle on the map; Seattle was often placed in the middle of a map that included both the United States and Asia. Seattle's connections to Asia were, in fact, a key element of its success. Its port had come of age in 1896, as a huge crowd gathered there to celebrate the arrival of the Nippon Yusen Kaisha's steamship *Miike*

Maru from Japan. According to the local newspapers, the enthusiastic crowd went wild as "the yells of thousands of people on the docks and the blowing of every steam whistle for five miles along the waterfront . . . celebrated the glad event and welcomed the Oriental visitor of the East to the Occident."[21]

The Seattle business community was a major factor in the city's westward-looking philosophy, which is to say fascination with Far Eastern Orientalism. In early twentieth-century Seattle, Japan became a major focus of efforts when two major events—the Yukon-Pacific Exposition (1909) and the International Potlatch Festival (1934)—were held as part of the white, elite, commercial agenda. This top-down flow of ideas helped Seattle become more "cosmopolitan," and the positive side of Orientalism was no small part of the equation. By "bridging the Orient and Occident" and including Japanese residents, Seattle was rather unusual. As historian Shelley Lee observes, conditions in Seattle "allowed cosmopolitan ideology to take root" and encouraged "internationalist and pluralist trends in American politics and intellectual life that paralleled, but did not displace, racism and nativism." Although Lee states that the latter "reaffirmed [that] Orientalism" was alive and well, the cosmopolitanism countered it. Lee here uses the term "Orientalism" in the most negative (i.e., Saidian) sense. Arguably, though, both the positive welcoming of the Japanese and the negative resistance to them operated simultaneously as two sides of the same Orientalist coin. One side, as we have seen, was dark indeed in that it plumbed deep fears, while the other brighter side embraced the richness of the Orient, bringing it home, so to speak. Seattle's general reception to the Japanese led a local commentator to claim they "had become an integral part of Seattle and [*sic*] a center combining both Oriental and Occidental features."[22]

As in the American Southwest, the railroads in the Pacific Northwest played an important role in Orientalizing their region. This began in the late nineteenth century and continued well into the twentieth. The goal was nominally commercial—that is, increasing revenues by increasing traffic—but it involved considerable aesthetic skill on the part of railroad management. The Northern Pacific Railway's advertising department, for example, employed the monad, a yin and yang symbol closely associated with the Far East. E. H. McHenry, the railroad's chief engineer, had seen the monad on a Korean flag in an exhibit at the 1893 Chicago World's Fair and realized it would make a perfect trademark for the Northern Pacific. McHenry learned that the monad was Chinese in origin, and his railroad soon adopted it. The railway's promotional literature pointed out the symbol's enlightening cultural history. As a symbol, the monad perfectly captured the belief that two complementary opposites (light and dark, male and female, East and West) were meant to be naturally (re)united. In this case, it was the Northern Pacific Railway that would fill that natural role of bringing together the western United States and the Orient. The Northern Pacific Railway's art, too, often provided an Oriental touch to posters and other railway advertisements. In a poster for the North Coast Limited in the 1920s, the Northern Pacific Railway artists featured not only that train speeding through a Montana landscape but also another suggestive icon—a pine tree rendered with characteristic "Oriental" sketchiness —is evidently well rooted on the hillside but seems to stand almost in thin air (fig. 7-8). This poster confirms that commercial artists were looking "toward Asia to forge an independent artistic identity."[23] The integration of the monad and the rugged, forested landscape suggests an Asian affinity and serves as a reminder that the Northwest's physical setting and Asian connections would continue to play a role in the region's Orientalization.

Both the Northern Pacific Railway and the Great Northern Railway were influential in creating this Asianized regional identity that linked people and place. The Great Northern named its premier Minneapolis-Seattle train the "Oriental Limited." Given the strong interest in the Orient in early twentieth-century America, that train was aptly named to embody both the American penchant for speed and the enduring allure of the Far East. The Oriental Limited was one of several transcontinental trains created to get people not only to the West Coast but also across the Pacific. Both the Northern Pacific Railway and Great Northern Railway had fleets of steamships that did exactly that, serving the ports of China and Japan. The Oriental Limited operated under that name between 1905 and 1929. It was the railway's premier "name train," so important that its name was painted on the letterboards of the passenger cars, which were two-toned green. The name Oriental Limited was inspired by Great Northern president James J. Hill, a turn-of-the-century transportation magnate who envisioned his trains and ships playing a major role in Asiatic commerce. Originally the Oriental Limited's drumhead (the sign placed on the back railing on the observation car) featured a logo dominated by an orange circle—suggesting a rising (or setting) sun. That venerable symbol for Imperial Japan served as the train's logo for years but was later replaced by one featuring a mountain goat in an open circle. That change was symbolic indeed, for it revealed the railway's desire to supersede the previous Asian identity with a symbol associated more with the region itself. Affectionately called "Rocky," that Rocky Mountain goat became Great Northern's premier symbol, and he decorated the drumhead of the Oriental

Fig. 7-8. Poster of the North Coast Limited in the Montana Rockies by Gustav Wilhelm Krollman (ca. 1930), features the Northern Pacific Railway's monad (yin/yang) logo.

Limited until service ended in 1929.[24]

Although Rocky helped to de-Orientalize the Oriental Limited to some extent—perhaps simply as an admission that more people traveled to and from the Pacific Northwest on this train than would ever go to East Asia—the railway and the National Park Service had laid the foundation for Orientalizing the parks along its route. In her book *See America First*, historian Marguerite S. Shaffer notes that Glacier National Park, which was served by the Oriental Limited, enthusiastically embraced the Asian theme. Within the Glacier Park Hotel itself, "Japanese references further added to the eclectic mosaic presented in the park." As Shaffer noted, "The Japanese lanterns, the couple serving tea, and the cherry blossoms decorating the hotel dining areas embellished the Oriental theme already exploited in the Great Northern's first-class transcontinental train, the Oriental Limited." Like the train itself, the Glacier Park Hotel was themed for a good reason. As Shaffer put it, "The Japanese accents in the rustic décor of the Glacier Park Hotel added to this imagery, positioning the park, Great Northern, and by extension America in a global framework and suggesting that the strenuous life of the American frontier and domination of world trade were two sides of the same success story—Manifest Destiny." Shaffer concludes that "these eclectic references brought together to define the Glacier Park landscape embodied the vision of an American nation that borrowed from and built on an eclectic mix of cultures to create an ideal republican empire."[25] This is a reminder that Orientalism serves two sometimes opposing purposes. It can impart a venerable and noble Eastern quality to the nation, thus increasing national pride through appropriation. Conversely, it can become an obsolete element in the system of image building when the goal is emphasizing American roots, rather than Oriental connections. Paradoxically, though, Orientalism can be employed to empower the United States to envision its horizons beyond its own borders. That premise, in fact, is a key factor in the Orientalization of the American West in the modern era.

II

The Modern West as the Orient

Fig. II-1. Cleopatra's Needle and Planetarium in Rosicrucian Park, San Jose, California.

8

Lands of Enchantment
The Modern West as the Near/Middle East

"No I am not in Egypt and no the Sphinx has not gotten a recent facelift. Instead I am in Las Vegas."

Posted by a traveler on the *Amateur Traveler* website

IN THE PREVIOUS CHAPTERS, I DEMONSTRATED THAT PORTIONS of the American West were Orientalized in various ways and for various reasons during the nineteenth and early twentieth centuries. Most of this Orientalization was a result of travelers and would-be settlers coming to grips with the overwhelming geography here, a process that called for analogies to be drawn between new and old, and East and West. By the 1870s and 1880s, however, the West began to take on a different demeanor as people began to conceptualize it as uniquely American. Nevertheless, Orientalism had become such an important part of the image of the American West that it would be involved with the region's identity throughout the twentieth century, taking on a new life in modern literature, film, and tourism. Even western cities themselves would embrace elements of Orientalism in their design. In part, the impetus for a new Orientalized identity was a result of the United States becoming a major world power after the Spanish-American War (1898). However, it is also related to the United States' rise as a giant in entertainment technology, such as film, that facilitated and yet complicated the transmission of cultural image building.

One of the vehicles that enabled this to happen was the modern American Western—both as literature and as film. It has roots in the nineteenth century as the dime novel but took concrete form as a major literary and cinematic art form at a pivotal time, namely about 1900, as both the novel *The Virginian* and the film *The Great Train Robbery* were released in 1902 and 1903, respectively. Looked at more closely, though, characteristically American Westerns are more dependent on two sources of Orientalism (the Bible and fantastic folktakes like the *Arabian Nights*) than is commonly recognized. In Owen Wister's classic Western, for example, the rugged Virginian himself characterizes Wyoming as "a world of crystal light, a land without end, a space across which Noah and Adam might come straight from Genesis."[1] In one fell swoop, Wister not only taps the Bible but also depicts Wyoming as a characteristically western American locale—desolate, even forlorn, and brimming with conflicts, including man vs. nature and man vs. man. I will explore the Oriental nature of the American Western shortly but first want to demonstrate that the Orient-in-the-West could also play out in other genres, especially fantasy. As the remainder of this book will show, fantasy literature and film must be recognized as sources that both contributed to, and reflected, the Orientalization of the American West. In other words, fantasy worked not only side by side with the Western but sometimes hand in hand with it— which is to say that western and fantasy literature and film converged to help Orientalize the American West.

This convergence emerged full-blown in 1900, using the western landscape of Kansas as the setting for what would become one of the most enduring American parables about the search for the exotic, namely, *The Wonderful Wizard of Oz*. In the mind of novelist Lyman Frank Baum, the flatness and drabness of the Kansas prairie demanded a counterpoint—a magical tower, an ancient spire, or a similarly fantastic form—to break the monotony. In this regard, Baum had something in common with earlier travel writers. However, as a modern American educator and newspaper editor, Baum wanted to supersede the "old-time fairy tale" by writing a book in which, as he put it, "stereotyped genie, dwarf and fairy are eliminated, together with all the horrible and blood-curdling incidents devised by their authors to point a fearsome moral to each tale."[2]

At first blush, *The Wizard of Oz* appears to be a fantasy residing in the mind of a child, but it is also a geographical travelogue. It above all contrasts the bleakness of the Kansas prairie—where "not a tree nor a house broke the broad sweep of flat country that reached the sky in all directions"—with the mystical city of Oz. By so doing, it not only builds on an age-old tension between experience and imagination but also uses the western American plains as the jumping-off point for that adventure.

Baum employs the most fearsome phenomenon the plains has to offer—a tornado—as the device that transports Dorothy from consciousness to unconsciousness. The tornado carries Dorothy, Toto, and the entire house from

Fig. 8-1. As illustrated by W. W. Denslow, original editions of J. Frank Baum's *Wizard of Oz* transform the Emerald City into a decidedly Middle Eastern locale, complete with domes and minarets.

Kansas to the magical land of the Munchkins, setting in motion a tale as captivating as one from the *Arabian Nights*. From the land of the Munchkins, Dorothy is urged to travel to the Emerald City of Oz, where her wish to return home will be granted. Like a city in an Arabian tale, Oz is surrounded by deserts and requires considerable effort to reach. That city, though, enchants those who seek it. As they walked in the direction of the Emerald City in the morning, Dorothy and her companions "saw a beautiful green glow in the sky just before them." Nearing the city, its "green glow became brighter and brighter." By afternoon, they "came to the great wall that surrounded the city." Like an ancient city in an Oriental fable, Oz had to be entered through "a big gate, all studded with emeralds that glittered so in the sun that even the painted eyes of the scarecrow were dazzled by the brilliancy." Upon entering the city, they found themselves in a "high arched room, the walls of which glistened with countless emeralds." It was this magic world that enabled Dorothy to tell Toto, "We're not in Kansas anymore"—an understatement, of course, but one that overlooks an important point: it was precisely *because* they were in Kansas that this magic land was possible. In other words, Dorothy's bleak setting in Kansas was the springboard that vaulted her into the imaginary and the exotic.

Although the phrase "We're not in Kansas anymore" has become synonymous, in American culture at least, with finding oneself in a new and unusual setting, yet another term from Baum's masterpiece has also been immortalized. The term *Oz* itself has come to signify something far beyond one's normal expectations. So how, then, did Oz appear to Dorothy? The early versions of *The Wizard of Oz* (1899, 1903) illustrate the cityscape of Oz as Middle Eastern, its skyline bristling with at least nine minarets and several domes (fig. 8-1). The river in the foreground meanders toward the fabulous city, whose site is reminiscent of the Near East's magical cities, for example Baghdad or Cairo. Whereas Baum endeavored to write a new story shorn of antecedents, the illustrations by W. W. Denslow give Oz a decidedly Mesopotamian or Egyptian character.[3]

Although Baum wrote many *Oz* sequels, none became the enduring classic that the original has. Much the same can be said of the 1939 movie version of *The Wizard of Oz*. When Vincent Minnelli and his crew tackled the project, they had no idea that it too would become a classic—nor did they likely comprehend its Orientalist implications.[4] *The Wizard of Oz* film translates the Emerald City into a cluster of "modern"—given its date of production (1939) toward the end of the Great Depression—art deco–style buildings. Still, the place possesses a magical quality right out of Orientalist tales. That the Emerald City endures as Middle Eastern cityscape is evident in David Russell's recent renditions of it. Russell, a noted film illustrator (*Batman, Chronicles of Narnia: The Lion, the Witch and the Wardrobe*) elected to use a magnificent Oriental cityscape with domes, minarets, and other features. As seen on Russell's website, the new Oz is a dazzling landscape much more in harmony with Baum's earlier version, and vision, of Oz.[5]

Both the original book and the film utilize a remarkably effective three-part structure based on origin, search, and return (leaving Kansas, traveling to mysterious and wonderful places, coming back to Kansas) that contrasts the everyday landscape of the American prairie with the landscapes of magical lands (Deadly Poppy Fields, Fighting Trees, Dainty China Country, Jeweled City). Like the *Arabian Nights*, Baum's *The Wizard of Oz* is as much an adult story as a kid's tale. Like its Oriental predecessor, it employs enduring Oriental-style storytelling elements, including epic travel and magical characters and locales (the faux potentate and the intoxicating poppy fields being but two examples).

Oz was born in the American Midwest, yet builds on a sense of the exotic and fantastic that the Orient readily provided. Over time, if the term *Oz* came to signify any fantastic city, it took on special meaning in the oil-rich Middle East in modern times. Dubai, with its spectacular high-rise buildings, offers perhaps the ultimate example, though Saudi Arabia also has its share of spectacular, almost surreal, urban skylines. A *Los Angeles Times* report by Jeffrey Fleishman discussed "life in this exotic, repressive and often beguiling [Saudi] society where tribal customs and religious fervor rub against oil wealth and the tinted-glass skyscrapers that rise Oz-like in the blurry desert heat."[6] Fleishman's use of the term "Oz-like" is revealing indeed, for it shows how easily, perhaps even inevitably, Baum's American characterization of Oriental-like fantasies could be reapplied to the original source area of such poetic prose—the real Middle East.[7]

We can find examples closer to home. In the modern West, the process of creating the Emerald City played out in southern Nevada. The location is the once-sleepy Mormon agricultural village of Las Vegas, which in the last two generations has experienced a transformation that might make Baum blush and his city of Oz pale in comparison. The creation of modern Las Vegas, in fact, used some powerful Orientalizing themes to help make a dream reality. Although Las Vegas took on new life when the San Pedro, Los Angeles and Salt Lake Railroad arrived in 1905, it gained greater appeal in 1931 with the legalization of gambling in Nevada. By the late 1940s and early 1950s, the mob recognized the community's potential as Sin City. Given improvements in transportation, including the establishment of convenient train and air service, not to mention the miracle of air conditioning, Las Vegas's desert setting represented no problem. In fact, the surrounding stark landscape, heat, and aridity simply added to the city's allure as an exotic locale where forbidden pleasures awaited. Las Vegas in the 1950s and 1960s creatively used Middle Eastern desert themes, such as the Sahara and Aladdin, to create part of the allure and the magic. Like John Charles Frémont a little more than a century earlier, the developers here in Nevada recognized the enduring power of Oriental icons. One of the city's recent crowning achievements offers a stunning counterpart to Frémont's stone pyramid, albeit about 150 years after the fact, and about 350 miles southeast of Pyramid Lake.

In the late twentieth century, when developers sought a design for the luxurious Luxor Hotel, they too used the ultimate symbol for the mysterious and exotic—the Egyptian pyramid. As opposed to Frémont's natural topographic feature, though, this man-made one is a dark glass incarnation that adds a stunning element to the eclectic skyline of an eccentric desert oasis (fig. 8-2). Its sides, like those of its prototype in Egypt (and more imperfectly, Frémont's rock), slope at thirty-two degrees. The Luxor's striking black glass pyramid—so evocative as an abstract form, especially given the presence of black diorite in real Egyptian artifacts—harmonizes with, and yet also stands in contrast to, Frémont's light-colored pyramid. American culture has changed remarkably since Frémont's time, and today Orientalism is far more associated with sensual pleasure than it is with concerns about ancient wisdom and biblical events. By the 1990s, the connection between Jews and Egypt had pretty

Author's photograph, 2010

Fig. 8-2. In Las Vegas, the Luxor Hotel uses venerable Egyptian icons, such as the pyramid and sphinx, rendered as King Tut, to convey a sense of the exotic.

much vanished from popular culture. Today, the Egyptian idiom is more likely to evoke mystery and sensuality than Judeo-Christian religion. Although the secular nature of the pyramid today represents a gulf in perception between the mid-nineteenth century and the early twenty-first century, one underlying element remains: the Luxor pyramid, like Frémont's rock in Pyramid Lake, plays upon the power of Egypt as both exotic and Oriental. The Luxor proves that pyramid as motif still works despite the fact that a great deal of social change occurred between Frémont's time and the 1990s.

The pyramids are the premier, but not the only, landmarks associated with ancient Egypt. Like its original standing guard near Egypt's pyramids, the sphinx next to the Luxor pyramid is also intriguing and arresting. The seemingly restored replica recalls the stunning original, but is miraculous in that while the passage of time has weathered the original, the sphinx in Las Vegas is simultaneously new-old. In Las Vegas, both the Tut-like sphinx and the glass pyramid are perfect—better, in a perverse sense, than their originals in Egypt, which, as Frémont implied, were compromised by the passage of centuries filled with blowing sand, spalling stone, and profiteering artifact hunters. Nevertheless, the durability of these monuments as symbols is noteworthy. Their ability to evoke strong feelings about place and time makes the Luxor pyramid highly successful as both premodern and postmodern architecture.

In *The Necessity for Ruins* (1980), J. B. Jackson speculated that the redis-covery of the past is tied to a culturally shared belief that there is first a "golden age, the time of harmonious beginnings," after which the culture experiences "a period when the old days are forgotten and the golden age falls into neglect." These two stages are then followed by "a time when we rediscover and seek to restore the world around us to something like its former beauty." But in doing this, Jackson asks, "Are we perhaps trying to re-enact some ancient myth of birth, death, and redemption?"[8] Another question we might also ask is why, in selecting items from the past, do we resurrect objects, buildings, and structures that were not originally ours at all, but belonged to others? When we reproduce their ruins instead of ours, are we in effect vicariously reliving the lives of others? We may try to appropriate their past by imitation, but of course it is our own culture rather than theirs that we reproduce. Depending on one's personal or political philosophy, this appropriation can represent the basest form of thievery or the highest form of flattery. Regardless, few can deny that counterfeiting the great pyramids allows their classic form to endure in yet another desert setting, this one in the New World.

However, the Luxor pyramid is not a ruin but rather a vibrant structure that builds upon modern Oriental fantasies. Similar in shape and size to the pyramid that so overwhelmed John Lloyd Stephens on his trip to Egypt in 1835–36, the Luxor has become one of the city's most recognizable land-marks. This ersatz pyramid in Las Vegas is a structure of superlatives in a city that constantly strives to outdo itself. At 350 feet (107 meters) in height, the Luxor Hotel houses thirty floors of plush guest rooms and recreation space. The sloping angle of the pyramid's exterior is carried to the interior, where guests must use an "inclinator," a clever term for an ingenious elevator that runs at a thirty-nine-degree angle. The black glass pyramid is striking enough by day, but it becomes even more so at night, when a bright beam said to be "the most powerful light in the world" thrusts skyward from the pyramid's uppermost point. This sky beam is so bright that it can be seen 250 miles away by people flying in airplanes. Apparently there is no better way to build on the Las Vegas urge for attention than to plumb an Oriental motif. The Luxor is both radically new and highly imitative in that it calls upon one of the world's original seven wonders for inspiration. Of those seven original wonders, only the pyramids of Egypt remain.

Cultural anthropologist Margaret Malamud astutely noted that "the Luxor capitalizes on a positive set of images Americans have of ancient Egypt, and it caters to the New Age interest in Egypt as a source of occult wisdom." Given the Luxor's enthusiasm for conveying and selling artifacts from Egypt in its gift shop, Malamud concludes that "a trip to Las Vegas substitutes for a trip to Egypt."[9] But it may also take us even further back in time. Architectural historian Jerilynn D. Dodds considers the shape of a pyramid to be elemental, "the prime image of New Age pan-spiritualism, its universality confirmed by its appearance in multiple pre-Industrial cultures."[10]

Pyramids constitute a tangible landscape element on the one hand, and the stuff of deeper imagination on the other. On the Luxor website, striking visuals are accompanied by music that begins as majestic and soon turns Oriental, the rhythm becoming more measured and sensual. As the viewer clicks onto "The Power of the Pyramid" section of the Luxor's interactive website, a question appears: "How will the Pyramid affect you?" The viewer is given three choices—"Read minds," "Attract," and "Spark Anything." Interestingly, all three options emphasize the power to connect with attractive people. This, of course, is the sensual and sexual side of Orientalism, where exotic suggests erotic.

This is a reminder that Nevada's two pyramids are considerably different in their context. The nineteenth-century version created, if you will, by John Charles Frémont, signifies something very different than does its late twentieth-century counterpart in Las Vegas. The difference reflects a transition of Egypt as spiritual to Egypt as sensual and erotic that took place over several decades. To find the pivotal point in time, we need only recall the Columbian Exposition in Chicago (1893), which featured glimpses forward and back. While presenting the grand works of the ancients, it also played with Orientalism's erotic side, as evident in its "taffy-colored nudes" and "Sargent's Egyptian Girl, with her great dark eyes and inviting nakedness."[11] This was somewhat scandalous at the time, but it was a harbinger of much racier things to come in the twentieth century.

The Luxor hotel continues this tradition of perceiving ancient Egypt as hedonistic territory. When inside this nouveau pyramid, one can also satisfy many appetites, for example by partaking of the cleverly named "Pharaoh's Pheast Buffet"—which is billed as "a true delight for Kings and Queens of all ages," or visiting the "Sacred Sea Room," where fresh seafood from "oceans around the world" is available. Once again, the draw here is pleasure, in this case food that is guaranteed to "please even the most discriminating epicurean." Not satisfied yet? The Oasis Spa treats the outside of one's body with a full range of services, from the irresistible-sounding "Peppermint Head to Toe" massage bath to clay masques, loofah scrubs, and scalp treatments.[12] Again, the theme here is physical pleasure. Significantly, in this type of pop Orientalism, the ordinary person becomes a king or queen, living a fantasy experience of the type that would have been reserved for royalty in ancient Egypt. This is what makes the sensual side of Orientalism so irresistible: even when experienced by common folk, it can be unabashedly lavish and elitist.

Popular fantasy films also employ themes of the Orient as exotic and erotic. As Ella Shohat astutely observes, the 1965 Elvis Presley film *Harum Scarum* features "a carnival-like Orient reminiscent of Las Vegas, itself placed in the burning sands of the American desert of Nevada, and offering harem-like nightclubs." The film's title *Harum Scarum* is a takeoff on a term like *hocus pocus*—witty and more than a little suggestive of mysteries and magicians. By the time Elvis Presley starred in this "reflexive film," as Shohat calls it, Las Vegas had become America's most eroticized city—a city that Elvis took by storm around this time. Like most of Elvis's movies, *Harum Scarum* is short on plot but filled with songs. In it, Elvis frees a woman from two sinister Arabs, enters a normally off-limits *harem* (the very word which refers to something "forbidden" in Arabic), and sings his way through a series of mindless adventures. In one particularly memorable song that may serve as a metaphor for the lure of Las Vegas, Elvis proclaims, "I'm gonna go where the desert sun is; where the fun is . . . where there's love and romance—out on the burning sands." Here, Elvis observes, "You'll feel like the Sheik, so rich and grand, with dancing girls at your command." More to the point about the power of the Orient, and the seduction of places like Las Vegas, Elvis concludes, "I'll make love the way I plan. Go east—and drink and feast—go east, young man."[13] This, of course, is a delightfully subversive—and highly Orientalist—inversion of Horace Greeley's, or rather John Soule's, famous nineteenth-century credo, "Go west, young man." Now, however, in the mid to late twentieth century, that West is the East of cinematic fantasy—yet another new frontier, as it were, in a nation's changing popular Orientalist imagination.

In the 1970s, Maria Muldaur's popular novelty song "Midnight at the Oasis" was blatantly sensual and employed highly Orientalized imagery.[14] In it, Muldaur sings "I'll be your belly dancer, prancer, and you can be my sheik." Quite aside from a possible association of "sheik" with a brand of condoms, she also means Middle Eastern seducer. "I know your daddy's a sultan" who has "fifty girls to attend him," she knowingly states, adding a promise of sexual variety aplenty by telling her lover that "you won't need no harem, honey, when I'm by your side." More to the point, she promises a blissful night of energetic sex, claiming, "You won't need no camel, no no, when I take you for a ride."[15] Covered by The Brand New Heavies on the album *Brother Sister* (1994), this song endures, a reminder of the perennial appeal of the desert oasis as a place of uninhabited pleasure. The Oasis, though, is also a transported place, as it served as the name of hotels and motels in Las Vegas. In this it joined others, such as the Aladdin, Sahara, and the Dunes, in suggesting the Middle East.

Las Vegas fills an important niche in the contemporary American psyche. Here the spirit and libido are in a nearly constant state of war, or perhaps tug-of-war might be a better term, as even the tension between them seems to be a source of amusement. Las Vegas is expected to be decadent, but not too decadent, because it has now become a family entertainment city, too. A December 5, 2005, episode of the television show *Las Vegas* began with attractive women stripping off their clothing in several locations in the Montecito—at the casino/hotel's pool, in the elevator, and even on the casino floor. When the hotel security chief sees this, he asks his staff, "What the hell is going on? Is this Sodom and Gomorrah?" He is told that these are not regular guests but are here for an adult entertainment conference. In other words, the ribald men and women are pornographic movie stars and are engaging in wild behavior that would normally be considered X-rated. Offended by the goings-on in the hotel, an older woman observes that all these young people are doing is having "Sex! Sex! Sex! They never even come up for air." When she complains that the people in the room next to hers are making "animal noises," the security chief decides to move that raunchy group to another wing of the hotel where "decent families" won't be offended. That separation suggests that Las Vegas has two sides, one catering to decadence and the other to wholesome entertainment. An ambiguity between the good and pure and the risqué and dirty is embedded in Orientalism. But it is the decadent or naughty side that is frequently emphasized, as Las Vegas has earned that reputation as Sodom and Gomorrah since the 1940s. A town where "anything goes" somehow seems more natural in the desert—at least the very first book of the Bible set the standard for this type of drama about 2,500 years ago.

Las Vegas's reputation as Sodom and Gomorrah was given a nod in the 2009 spoof film *Year One*, in which Cain tells a young man who is engaged to be married and refuses to partake of the pleasures of Sodom not to worry because "what transpires in the confines of the walls of Sodom stays within the confines of the walls of Sodom." This, of course, is a reference to the popular advertising slogan "What happens in Las Vegas stays in Las Vegas."[16] Central to Las Vegas's edgy image of debauchery and materialism is its clientele hailing from all corners of the globe. The prospect of anonymity here is an age-old hope that one's actions will not be observed by the prying eyes of those in the home village. As Las Vegas hotel room service deliveryman Mark Zartarian colorfully put it, "The interesting thing about this job is when you knock on

Fig. 8-3. A 1950s-era postcard of Pyramid Lake, Nevada, shows both the pyramid-shaped rock and a light-colored tufa formation some call "the Sphinx."

the door, you never know whether the person on the other side has got a gun, it's a naked woman, or both."[17]

Those two pyramids in the Nevada desert—the rough, earth-colored natural pyramid in Pyramid Lake and the razor-sharp, black glass Luxor pyramid in Las Vegas—perfectly symbolize how landscapes reflect deeper thoughts about places and the broader worlds those places represent. If John Charles Frémont was part of the initial process of immortalizing the Old World, in this case the Orient, he had a good landscape to build upon in Nevada. The desert setting of Pyramid Lake was, and remains, quite evocative, and the similarities between Old World and New World deserts endure. A 1950s-era postcard of Pyramid Lake (fig. 8-3) perpetuates the island's iconic form and also offers another element: the white, oddly shaped rock to the right which has been construed as the sphinx, at least by some imaginative minds.[18] A postcard of "Exotic Pyramid Lake" from about the same time declared that the signature triangular rock was "older and larger than the ancient pyramids of Egypt." This sentiment had the effect of downplaying ancient Egypt and using the American West as the superlative. Fifty years earlier, Henry M. Field had helped begin this process when he compared the pyramids of Egypt to a geological feature in the American West. As Field put it, "Except the Kings' and Queens' chambers . . . the whole pyramid is one mass of stone, as solid as the cliff of El Capitan in the Yo Semite valley."[19]

Nevada's two pyramids also reveal stunning differences in the way perceptions of the American interior changed from the 1830s to the present. Although both perceptions involved translating the Orient into the West, the transition was not simply a swapping of one identity for another. Rather, the transition involved a fluctuation toward two poles of an Orient associated with religion and spirituality on the one hand, and sensuality and hedonism on the other. The path by which this change occurred was complex but usually plumbed the two very different faces of Orientalism—something much like two sides of the same coin—the contrast of the spirit with the flesh.

Lest we think that only the sensual side of Oriental history played out in the twentieth-century West, we might recall that the Garden of Eden was still on the public's mind. In 1924, amateur American archaeologist Alan Le Baron wrote a series of attention-grabbing articles for the *San Francisco Examiner*, wherein he claimed that he had discovered the Garden of Eden. Its location? Not in southwest Asia Minor, nor even in Missouri as the Mormons claimed, but rather on a hilltop overlooking the East Walker River about twenty miles south of Yerington, Nevada. At what Le Baron called the "Hill of a Thousand Tombs," he reportedly found indisputable evidence—such as the bones of camels, elephants, and lions and the remains of lush forests—that proved the site's antiquity to mankind. Le Baron further claimed that the petroglyphs depicting animals and abstract designs were related to, and probably even predated, Egyptian hieroglyphics.[20] We should place Le Baron's seemingly illogical claim in a broader cultural context, not as professional archaeology, but rather as a logical outcome of the hyper-Orientalization of the American West in particular.

But for all its heavenly qualities, the Garden of Eden is always subliminally associated with sex. After all, succumbing to temptation is what caused Adam and Eve to be expelled from it and their descendants to perish at Sodom and Gomorrah when they forgot the lesson of obedience. This again leads us back to the subliminal connection between the deserts of the East and lust, which runs deep, and helps conflate western American landscapes, especially the cinematic variety portrayed by Hollywood, with their exotic and sexually charged Middle Eastern prototypes. That sexuality, of course, is based more on fantasy than reality. Among the standard tropes of the East are the mysterious, sensual, seductive, worldly woman, and the mysterious, strong, potent, barbaric Arabian man. Both can ravage and liberate their presumably tamer Western lovers, a concept that is at once fearsome and delightful. This is related to what Edward Said called Orientalism's "imaginative geography," whose major sexual tropes are "the sensual woman, the harem, and the despotic—but curiously attractive—ruler."[21]

For their part, Arab rulers are often stereotyped as sexually potent, perhaps even predatory: in a wonderfully geographic metaphor in the 1954 film *King Richard and the Crusaders*, Richard later says of Saladin's interest in Edith—"he knows the geography of the female like the palm of his hand." A much earlier press release described actress Mary Conway (who played Lot's wife and the Queen of Syria in early films) as "a girl who evokes one's wildest desires and craves sacrifice, so that an honest man, robbed of his wits, is driven to commit deeds beyond his better judgment."[22] That European Americans might do things beyond their better judgment is exactly the point, and a factor in the lure of the Orient. The East's seduction here operates to break down the norms of Anglo-American Protestantism.

The desert East is the source of conflicting attitudes toward sex. After all, the Christian ethic that urges restricting nonprocreative sex (both in thought and act) is as Eastern as Saul (the Jew) turned Paul (the Christian); yet that same East abounds in tales of lust and sin that are legendary enough to bring an end to sinful cities in the desert. It is the difference between today's proper Mormon communities in Utah where lust is kept under control and those wild Nevada towns and counties where gambling and prostitution are legal. It is this tension and this ambivalence that make the desert anywhere so interesting. It is on the one hand seemingly sterile and yet so stimulating to the imagination.

By the 1950s, a century of irrigated agriculture had made the Wasatch Front into an oasis, and Mormon dairy farmers along Utah's Jordan River were involved in introducing farming techniques from Utah into the real Holy Land with the goal of helping improve the latter's productivity. This reinforced the perception of parallels between both New World and Old World lands. In his 1958 *National Geographic* article titled "Geographical Twins a World Apart," David S. Boyer described and photographed scenes in the Holy Land and Utah to show how similar both places appeared. Of two scenes taken along the River Jordan and Utah's Jordan River, for example, Boyer enthusiastically noted that both featured the "same scenery, same trees, Even the same name—Jordan—for the Rivers, yet one is in Utah, the other in the Holy Land." Primed to see parallels, Boyer erroneously cited the Australian eucalyptus trees in both places when, in fact, Utah's climate is too cold. In his search for similarities, Boyer lumped Utah's cold-desert climate and the Holy Land's hot desert, stating that the "climates of the Two Jordan Valleys across the globe have changed little in 5,000 years. Dry Years and Wet [years] come and go." Evidently unaware of the Striking Comparison Map from the 1890s, Boyer also placed maps of the Holy Land and Utah side by side—inverting the

Utah map—to show what he called "an intriguing parallel between lands on opposite sides of the world." Boyer's enthusiasm in finding perfect geographic analogies reminds us that oversimplification and faith are part of the process.[23]

In modern-day Utah, the Mormons themselves still resonate as somewhat exotic. Given their emphasis on mysterious temple rites and their continued use of seemingly arcane symbols, some observers still associate the Mormons with the Orient, albeit less frequently than in the nineteenth century when polygamy was condoned by the church and travelers viewed its leaders as Oriental potentates. Those seeking a symbolic connection between Mormons and the Middle East in modern times need look no further than Salt Lake City's Gilgal Garden, which plumbs numerous artistic traditions, including Orientalism, for inspiration. This sculpture-filled park, constructed by Mormon businessman Thomas Child from the 1940s into the 1960s, renders in physical form deep beliefs about the "unsolved mysteries" of life. As a masonry contractor, Child recognized the power of stone to symbolize permanency. He creatively used an oxyacetylene torch to sculpt the stone, giving it a unique burnished quality. The centerpiece of this sequestered urban garden, which underwent restoration beginning in 2000, is a remarkable statue depicting Joseph Smith as a sphinx (fig. 8-4). This selection might at first seem irreverent, but the sphinx was the perfect metaphor for a timeless dilemma. As a devout Mormon, Child sought to pose questions that inevitably arise about Joseph Smith—namely, who was this prophet and how can his beliefs, which were unveiled in the early nineteenth century, continue to inspire new generations of followers? It is not surprising that Childs chose both the sphinx and an oddly shaped stone, upon which words are inscribed, to ask such eternal questions. By doing so, he equated the mysteries of Mormonism with the mysteries of antiquity. Both of these Oriental-inspired symbols convey a sense of the enormity of time, a perennial theme in American Egyptomania. As if that were not enough to cast Smith in the role of Egyptian icon, Child added that large slab of rock inscribed with writing, which to some evokes the Rosetta Stone. Discovered by Europeans in the Egyptian desert more than two centuries ago, this stone containing the writings of three cultures helped scholars decipher Egyptian hieroglyphics—much like Smith helped to decipher deeper meanings of faith.

Utah has other twentieth century works that drew upon Egypt for inspiration. In Ogden, Peery's Egyptian Theater offers a remarkable example of 1920s-era Egyptomania but owes its existence to theatrical events that occurred in California. Although Egyptomania swept the entire United States and was evident in architecture, dress, and entertainment nationwide,

Author's photograph, 2010

Fig. 8-4. In Salt Lake City's Gilgal Garden, Mormon prophet Joseph Smith appears as the sphinx, situated in front of a Rosetta-like stone.

California embraced it with a special zeal. The timing was perfect, as California became the center of a nationwide and international entertainment industry. In regard to the latter, the new medium of film enabled "a magnetism between conceptual accounts of the nature of entertainment by projected light and Egypt—an imaginative association pulling together the ancient culture [of Egypt] and modern spectacular innovation."[24]

The California film industry also helped perpetuate Orientalism. In the early to mid-twentieth century, Hollywood filmmakers from D. W. Griffith to Cecil B. DeMille made movies featuring supposedly Oriental locales. What better way to premiere such exotic films than in an Egyptian-style theater? Hollywood's Grauman's Egyptian Theatre offers a remarkable case of good timing: the theater opened in 1922 just five weeks before King Tutankhamen's tomb was discovered in Egypt. Grauman's Egyptian was the "prototypical Egyptian movie palace" (fig. 8-5) and thus served as the inspiration for numerous theaters that opened elsewhere in the country, including Peery's Egyptian, which opened just a year later.[25] An Egyptian theater might be built anywhere in the United States, for its interior sets the theme for the exotic experience. In the West, however, the landscape and climate outside the theaters helped contribute to the region's Orientalization.[26]

Author's collection

Fig. 8-5. A 1922 postcard shows the newly completed Grauman's Egyptian Theatre in Hollywood.

The public also had an insatiable interest in the mysticism embodied in ancient Egypt, and the Rosicrucians helped fuel that interest and respond to it as well. In the early to mid-twentieth century, their ultimate contribution was the informative and spectacular Egyptian Museum in San Jose, California (figs. 8-6 and II-1). The Rosicrucian Egyptian Museum's website describes it beginning, "After the Ancient Mystical Order Rosae Crucis's (AMORC) headquarters settled in its present San Jose location, Dr. Harvey Spencer Lewis (First Imperator of the Rosicrucian Order, 1914–1939) conceived of a public collection, The Rosicrucian Egyptian Oriental Museum in 1928." The website further notes that the 1920s were a time of considerable enthusiasm, and by the early 1930s, "the collection had outgrown its second floor home, and additional construction was added as an annex to the Administration Building." Many of the artifacts in the collection were real Egyptian antiquities, but educational replicas were also made. In 1935, a replica of the Rock Tomb, "modeled on several originals in the Beni Hasan desert," was unveiled. Another replica, a model of the Djoser Step Pyramid complex, was made by museum staff and volunteers. The outside of the building was also carefully developed: "The familiar Byzantine design and Moorish arches of the Museum greeted visitors for over thirty years [but] as the collection grew and deepened, it became obvious to Ralph M. Lewis, AMORC's second Imperator, that a fully modern museum facility was needed for the more than 2000 artifacts." Accordingly, a

Author's collection

Fig. 8-6. A 1950s-era postcard showing the gardens at the Rosicrucian Egyptian Museum in San Jose, California.

new museum building opened in 1966, and it contained "the largest display of Egyptian artifacts in the Western U.S." The website further claims that the Rosicrucian Museum is "the only such Museum on the planet designed in the Egyptian style, and situated in an Egyptian revival park."[27]

This may be true, but we should recall that a forerunner of this impressive Egyptian-style structure could be found in San Francisco's Golden Gate Park in the first decade of the twentieth century. As already noted, this park offered a glimpse of the Far East, but its Near East–influenced Museum of Antiquities featured a beautifully stylized portico and facade crowned by an Egyptian pyramid. This distinctive building was a repository of ancient treasures, and the use of the Egyptian motif and style perfectly symbolized the appreciation of ancient Egypt as part of the "Cradle of Civilization." The fact that it was located in San Francisco was not surprising, for that city had a voracious appetite for all things Oriental.

Like San Francisco's Museum of Antiquities, San Jose's Egyptian Museum remains a treasure trove. The lengthy description provided by the Rosicrucians of their museum reveals the impact of active collecting in Egypt in the 1920s, when the United States was gripped by a fascination with ancient Egypt. It is easy to think that this is the same interest in Egypt shared by Frémont and Stephens, and it is certainly related to it. However, almost a century had transpired, and the Egyptian revival of the early twentieth century built on themes of increasingly personalized spirituality and incorporated Egyptian themes in popular entertainment (including dance) and popular fashion (Egyptian dress and jewelry). Note, too, that the museum was originally called the Egyptian Oriental Museum, a reminder that Egypt was popularly linked to a broader "East" at that time.

The impressive Rosicrucian Egyptian Museum does more than simply exhibit the many interesting artifacts from numerous expeditions to Egypt. It also subtly conveys what Rosicrucians view as the meaningful mysticism of ancient Egypt. The Egyptian Museum is a totally "themed" experience. By entering it, one not only experiences various aspects of Egypt but is transported in time and space to create, or rather re-create, place. That it works so effectively is a tribute to not only Egypt and the Rosicrucians but to Orientalism itself. This makes the Egyptian Museum, with its striking but restrained Egyptian exterior, part of the popular intellectual frontier of the twentieth century. Given Northern California's pivotal place in alternative spirituality, it is no surprise to find this museum in the San Francisco Bay Area.[28]

The Egyptian Museum appeals to even the accidental tourist, so to speak. In 2005, American Airlines included it on its list of the twenty-one places worth visiting during long airport layovers. An article by Tracy Staton in the flight magazine *American Way* reveals the museum's many treasures to people who can steal a few hours between planes. "Amateur Egyptologists," Staton began, "take note: The best collection of [Egyptian] artifacts in the western United States is within reach." To entice air travelers laying over in San Jose, Staton mentions that the museum is "modeled after the Temple of Amon at Karnak . . ." and that it "has a full-scale replica of a noble's tomb, human and animal mummies, tools and objets d'art, and a garden filled with statues of the gods."[29] Although an hour or two of free time might provide the visitor with a taste of these sights, they, like ancient Egypt, are worth considerably more reflection. And yet even when sandwiched into a hectic schedule in the American West, "Egypt" still has its allure.

Modern California's Oriental mystique is also dependent on people such as singer-actress Cher. Originally part of the Sonny and Cher duet, this dark-eyed Armenian American beauty from the Fresno area of the fertile San Joaquin Valley has enchanted the public since her debut in the mid-1960s. Born Cherilyn Sarkisian in 1946, Cher originally wore Egyptian-style eye makeup reminiscent of Cleopatra and traded on a mysterious Eastern ethnic identity. In doing this in the 1960s, Cher built on the popularity of Elizabeth Taylor's depiction of Cleopatra in the 1963 movie of the same name. But in songs like "Gypsies, Tramps and Thieves" and "Half-Breed," Cher critically addressed the theme of ethnic identity in an assimilating United States. The former song, clearly Oriental, is about a roving band of gypsies who are regarded with suspicion. More properly called Roma today, Gypsies themselves are Oriental in that they originated in India, and they are still regarded with suspicion in Europe as exotic outsiders. Then, too, Cher's song about half-breeds portrays the problems facing people who do not fit into clear racial categories. The "half-breed" she sings about is of Native American heritage but could be as easily conflated with anyone of mixed ancestry, as it is ultimately about bigotry. The point to be remembered about the multi-talented Cher, though, is that she is in part a product of Orientalism, particularly California's energetic type of Orientalism, which creates new identities from very old imagery.[30] Like the pyramids themselves, Cher has undergone an occasional facelift, but her underlying natural beauty and mystery help explain her enduring popularity for nearly five decades.

The California-as-Middle East fantasy still insinuates itself into the popular imagination in the early twenty-first century. In the Sci-Fi Channel original movie *Sands of Oblivion* (2007), a young man named Jesse returns home to California from service in the Iraq War to help his grandfather find a time capsule box that he buried as a child in 1923. Now about ninety, the grandfather was on the set when Cecil B. DeMille filmed the original *Ten Commandments*. This science fiction film builds on a real cinematic event—DeMille's construction of the movie set in the sand dunes on the central California coast. In *Sands of Oblivion*, archaeologists plan to conduct a dig to find artifacts from DeMille's early 1920s filming event. However, the movie set is haunted by a curse from ancient Egypt, and mayhem ensues as the grandfather is killed by Ra, the left hand of Seth—an ancient Egyptian avenging spirit. Led by head archaeologist Alice, the team also experiences tragedies, which the Iraq veteran investigates using what he learned in the Middle East. The archaeologists determine that one of the sets is indeed ancient Egyptian, brought in by DeMille for authenticity, and it houses the god of chaos and infertility. The archaeologist learns that the chamber was assembled in California by the only people who know how to build such things—the Freemasons. It even features the supposedly ancient square-and-compass Freemason symbol along with the other Egyptian hieroglyphic symbols. With the help of another veteran, who provides a veritable arsenal (including phosphorous grenades), Jesse ultimately fells the rampaging Ra and wins Alice in the process. The plot is timeless and timeworn, but the point here is that the East and West morph into each other through faux film history and pseudoarchaeology.[31]

Quite aside from these more or less fantastic, if not deceptive, aspects of identity, though, is California's real climatic similarity to the area around the Mediterranean Sea. Coastal California is the only portion of the United States that experiences the type of hot, dry summers and relatively mild, but wetter, winters found in a broad area from Spain to Lebanon. Just across the mountains, in eastern California, lie two deserts—the Mojave and Colorado—that possess climates similar to places such as North Africa, Arabia, and Egypt. For that reason, it was relatively easy for observers to note California's similarity to both Spain and the Middle East (or at least the coastal Mediterranean margins of the latter). In this regard, California certainly offers a climate (or rather climates) evoking the feel of the real Promised Land west of the Jordan and east of the Rock of Gibraltar, to paraphrase a song by Bob Dylan—the master of morphing identities.[32]

Before leaving the subject of how Hollywood Orientalized the desert American West, I should note that it creatively used American western locales to simulate Old World deserts. Cinematically speaking, the conflation of interior Asia and interior American West has occurred for almost a century, and thousands of films have substituted the West for Asia. Consider, for example, the John Wayne film *The Conqueror* (1956), which is often considered the worst in the Duke's long career. Directed by Dick Powell, *The Conqueror* features some bizarre casting, or rather miscasting, including Wayne as Genghis Khan and Susan Hayward as the Tartar princess Bortai. The landscape is also somewhat miscast, as the canyons and deserts of southern Utah become the Gobi Desert. Given the logistical and political difficulties of filming in Communist China during the height of the Cold War, however, Powell's selection of Utah was understandable enough. The sight of Wayne as Khan riding hell-bent-for-leather in this western landscape, complete with sagebrush, makes *The Conqueror* as much a Western as an Eastern. This mixing of landscapes serves as a reminder of the flexibility of the West in popular film and television, where the Mojave Desert may double for Iraq, and portions of Nevada become Turkestan.

What can we conclude about the varied and sometimes bizarre cultural examples from California and its stepchild, Las Vegas? First, California became the undisputed center of western American Egyptomania, and its influence spread to other parts of the region. Despite its self-conscious exceptionalism and much-touted innovativeness, however, California was (like China and Japan) also highly imitative. This is not a new finding, but the strong presence of Middle Eastern elements suggests that this aspect of Orientalism had a strong influence in shaping California's overall identity. Moreover, it reveals that Orientalism is both covert (as in the despotlike behavior of water barons) and overt (as in the East-enthralled Cecil B. DeMille). The enduring tropes of paradise and Promised Land—both closely connected to biblical literature—are noteworthy. Above all, though, in its elaborate creation of lifestyle and landscapes, California (and Californians) becomes part of a fabricated drama that is at once real and mythic. In other words, the identity of both people and place here is remarkably malleable. Small wonder, then, that subliminal perceptions of the Orient, with its excesses of power, beauty, sensuality, and even spirituality, resonate so strongly and self-consciously in the Golden State.

But California is by no means the only place to be so thoroughly caught up in this kind of magic. Orientalism thrives in the American Southwest today. Since about 1900, when Indian raids were a thing of the past, the region's "magical" quality has been stressed. For more than a century, in fact, the American Southwest has had a distinct regional identity based on its landscape, climate, and native peoples. Many travelers "feel" that there is something nearly magical about this region. Capitalizing on this appeal, New Mexico brands itself the "Land of Enchantment." The very idea of enchant-ment—the ability to charm or be charmed—is a hint that romanticism is at work here. New Mexico's slogan is a testimony to the power of modern tour-ism to give places special charm, but we need to ask how that charm develops and what its consequences are for the indigenous peoples swept along with it: first, unless the landscape or some other geographic quality is involved, the magic is not likely to happen. Consider the case of Santa Fe. Located in the scenically beautiful and archaeologically rich upper Rio Grande Valley, that city has a character that lures the wealthy sojourners and less well-off tourists who want to glimpse the exotic within the borders of the continental United States. If, as cultural historian Barbara Babcock claims, the Southwest serves as America's Orient, then Santa Fe is one of the places within that region that enables this magic to happen.

In his fascinating book titled *Explorers in Eden*, Middle Eastern historian Jerold Auerbach revealed that even people with considerable experience in the Holy Land can equate Santa Fe with Jerusalem. As Auerbach noted, when he and his wife, Susan, traveled to New Mexico, Santa Fe seemed enough like Jerusalem to them to evoke the sense of déjà vu. Auerbach recalled that "just moments into our first morning in Santa Fe, as we wandered through a maze of adobe buildings under a blazing summer sun, Susan turned to me and asked, 'Doesn't this remind you of Jerusalem?'" As Auerbach put it, Susan's "observation precisely expressed my own inchoate feeling that we had stepped outside the boundaries of the United States, beyond 'American' culture as we knew it, into a strangely familiar foreign land, with deep historical and personal resonance." The "maze of adobe buildings" that Auerbach mentions are a factor in the Orientalization of Santa Fe.[33] The prevailing design here is indeed reminiscent of portions of the Middle East and North Africa, where a series of cubic, earth-colored buildings lose their individual identities and become a *tout ensemble*. Collectively, the typical streetscape of the desert Old World and Santa Fe—with their adobe buildings in clay tones—suggests an intimacy between architecture and the earth. Santa Fe's setting in a valley flanked by mountains adds to the impression, but it is also enhanced by the omnipresence of the sky—often crystal clear—that appears to be a cobalt-blue dome suspended over the community.

The Auerbachs had a common experience, for we recall that Santa Fe impressed many early Anglo-American traders as both exotic and Near Eastern. Today, despite about 150 years of Anglo occupation, the community retains a similar feel. To modern travelers, Santa Fe seems to be a place that time forgot, but in fact it is precisely because time is *remembered* here that the charm is so palpable. Through the aggressive use of design controls that keep buildings to a certain style and color, Santa Fe deliberately conspires to appear ancient.[34] The ruse is so effective that few people even know it is operating; appropriately, architectural historian Chris Wilson refers to the city's ability to evoke magic through history as *The Myth of Santa Fe*. Although the city's goal is to remain Spanish and Indian, the buildings' design and colors help create and sustain an Old World look that is as much Oriental as it is Native American or Spanish.

The Southwest is one of America's most powerfully constructed regions in part because it builds on emotional response to earth, sky, and history. To visitors, the architecture and the physical landscape of Arizona, and especially New Mexico, seem to complement each other. As architectural critic Michael Sorkin observed of Albuquerque and vicinity: "The beauty of the Southwestern landscape is deeply architectonic; those buttes and mesas and striated cliffs are already so incredibly like architecture that there is a powerful incitement to literally inhabit them (as cliff-dwelling Native Americans did for thousands of years), to imitate their forms (take a look at the mountainous massing of an art deco skyscraper), or to create an architecture that participates in the same processes—sun, wind, rain, erosion—that sculpt the cliffs."[35] This helps to further equate the Southwest's indigenous peoples with "nature." No place better exemplifies this than the pueblos of the Southwest, where the architecture seems to rise out of the very earth itself, and where it is tempting to think that the people are as ancient as that landscape. Understandably, then, those peoples seemed to belong to the ancient world.

In the twentieth century, western American Orientalism was perpetuated by descriptive writers such as Mary Austin, who imagined that Hadji Ali (Hi Jolly) and his camels would be at home here. As Austin put it in her popular 1924 book *The Land of Journeys' Ending*: "I suppose that a Syrian lost in the country between the Rio Grande and Colorado [River] must have found many a touch of home there." To Austin, the star-filled night sky, topography, and the scents of vegetation were similar in both places.[36]

Southwestern Orientalism, some of it very imaginative, was also per-petuated by writers of romantic fiction. Ancient history and modern history were conflated when a young Texas writer, Robert E. Howard, penned one of the great Orientalist fantasies of the early twentieth century—*Conan the Barbarian*. Howard, who was born in 1906 and spent his youth in the oil boomtowns of West Texas, patterned his characters from some of the "rough-necks, gamblers, and opportunists" he experienced there. Texas fantasy writer Joe Lansdale recently suggested that the prototype for *Conan the Barbarian* was, in fact, "a combination of oil-field worker, rambling cowboy and card sharp." Although *Conan the Barbarian* put Howard on the literary map, so to speak, he wrote in what Judy Alter calls "an amazing variety of genres—hor-ror, sword and sorcery, fantasy, Western—while also creating popular charac-ters of lasting interest." Orientalism was an important element of Howard's fantasy genre. Like most Orientalists, Howard had an expansive imagination. His tendency to draw from the exotic, the ancient, and the frontier infuses his writings with a surreal quality. Howard's heroes included swashbuckler Solomon Kane; adventurer King Kane; a westerner called the Texan; and of course Conan, who manages to combine traits from each and position them in a mysteriously Eastern locale.[37]

In *Conan the Barbarian*, which began its literary life as a series of short stories published in 1933, Howard describes the desert of the ancient Middle East as a "mysterious expanse lying southeast of the lands of Shem," where "the great river Styx" marked "the land of Stygia, the dark-bosomed mistress of the south, whose domains, watered by the great river, rose sheer out of the surrounding desert."[38] Howard here seems to be referring to one of the Middle Eastern rivers, but the description could as easily match the Rio Grande, whose bends define a border between Texas and "dark-bosomed" Mexico to the south. But the land south of the Rio Grande offers more than a metaphor for feminine conquest. Like the Orient itself, its premise was that indigenous cultural elements could be—as historian Richard Slotkin observed—"by turns comic and cruel, sensual and indolent."[39] When finally published as a book in 1954, *Conan the Barbarian* had it all—desert vs. oasis, sensuality and sexuality, despotism vs. independence, and enough monsters and mirages to challenge the *Arabian Nights*. Howard built on a long tradition of casting indigenous peoples of exotic lands as wild creatures. So too did the numerous Marvel comic books, including *Conan*, that presented a lurid and exciting Orient to a generation of young readers.

If the popular novel *Conan the Barbarian* subliminally plumbs both American southwestern and Near Eastern landscapes for inspiration, it took Hollywood to make it blossom on the silver screen. The film's densely packed action and vivid imagery represent Orientalism on steroids. In the hands of screenplay writers John Milius and Oliver Stone, *Conan the Barbarian* (1982) became one of the more popular Orientalist fantasy films of the period, catapulting a nearly steroid-perfect but seemingly subliterate movie character (played by Arnold Schwarzenegger) to fame. However, consider the fate of Texas writer Howard, who penned the original story but found himself unable to cope with his demons. Howard's tormented life ended in suicide when his Orientalist fantasies could no longer sustain him. Schwarzenegger, by contrast, became rich, famous, and powerful—the quintessential perpetuator of California's golden dream, sexual scandals notwithstanding.

The physical landscape of the modern Southwest still possesses an Oriental identity through place naming. Consider, for example, the aptly named Rock Camel (interchangeably named Camel Rock) near Santa Fe, New Mexico (fig. 8-7). Confronted with an oddly shaped hill strewn with huge boulders of fractured stratified rock, the human mind searches for meaning—and similarities. The hill's humpbacked form is suggested by two particularly resistant rock units that escaped being broken off by the elements. At one side, a capped tower of rock suggests a camel's head, while the rock unit that tops the center of the hill appears to be the single hump of a dromedary camel. With the sun at the correct angle, and the hill's reddish-brown color so visible due to the scarcity of vegetation, Camel Rock appears aptly named, indeed. Then, too, the arid landscape hereabouts seems like a natural enough habitat for such a desert creature. Since the early twentieth century, Camel Rock has fascinated motorists and adorned postcards. As the verso of one postcard suggests, the camel has a purpose: "Perched on a rock where he can overlook curious visitors, is this stone figure along U.S. 285 north of Santa Fe."[40] Whimsical? Yes, but then again, the tendency for people to read such Old World symbols into a landscape of the New World (where, ironically, camels once thrived but vanished millennia before humans arrived) is given some credibility by stories of Hi Jolly and his camels in the nineteenth-century desert West.

Fig. 8-7. Postcard of New Mexico's Camel Rock (ca. 1930) uses an ox cart and a unique geological feature to suggest another (earlier) time and another (distant) place.

A somewhat more abstract but more readily visible feature near Phoenix also honors the camel. Rising about 1,500 feet above the city's skyline, the peculiar "Camelback Mountain" has become a regional landmark (fig. 8-8). Whether seen from the south (Phoenix and Scottsdale) or from the north (Paradise Valley), Camelback Mountain qualifies as this area's most prominent topographic landmark. As opposed to the Camel Rock, however, Camelback Mountain requires a bit more imagination to recognize. On a recent flight into Phoenix, two women seated next to me were discussing just what they comprehended when they saw Camelback Mountain out the window of the plane as it approached Sky Harbor Airport. Was it a one-humped dromedary camel, or a two-humped Asian Bactrian camel? Given the variation in elevation of Camelback Mountain's two protuberances, one might suggest either scenario. Is the camel, regardless of type, standing? Reclining? Sleeping? Most people probably visualize it as a camel lying down to rest, its head and hump defining the pose, or rather repose.

Camelback Mountain, or simply "Camelback," as it is usually called, is regarded with considerable affection. Even on hazy days, its uniquely shaped silhouette seems somehow reassuring. Architectural critic Michael Sorkin describes downtown Phoenix as having "a certain presence as a navigational icon (like its natural analog Camelback Mountain)."[41] Camelback also gives its name to a major east—west street as well as several businesses and housing

Fig. 8-8. As seen in this 1920s-era postcard, Camel Back (also called Camelback) Mountain near Phoenix has long been a regional landmark.

tracts; moreover, the fact that it is named after an exotic desert animal makes the peculiar feature seem perfectly named in the shimmering Sonoran Desert environment here. About thirty-five miles southeast of Camelback Mountain, another evocative feature—Dromedary Peak—forms yet another Orientalized Arizona landmark. It rises about a thousand feet above the hilly, cactus-studded landscape of Pinal County. Much farther to the north, in the Wasatch Range outside of Salt Lake City, rises another, much higher Dromedary Peak. It too reminds us of the power of romanticized icons to influence the popular naming of places.

Camels have not vanished from consciousness in the modern American West. A newspaper article titled "Camels on the Range" recently asked, and quickly answered, an Orient-inspired question: "Rocks and Sand. West Texas has 'em. So does the Sahara. What else do they have in common? Camels, thanks to Doug Baum." The story described the enterprising activities of Baum, a professional musician who also leads camel tours through several desert areas, including the sand dunes of West Texas, the Sinai Desert, and the Sahara. As Baum put it, "Many spiritual people come away with a renewed sense of this ancient land, [and] its people. And the religious significance for them is awesome."[42]

Further commemorating the camel is the pyramid-shaped, camel-topped monument to Hi Jolly located in Quartzite, Arizona, which makes a serious

Fig. 8-9. The album cover of Kinky Friedman's *Lasso from El Paso* (Epic
Records, 1976) humorously used stylized Middle Eastern imagery based on
the Camel brand cigarette label to Orientalize the American West.

and very positive statement about Hadji Ali and his camels (see fig. I-2). In the
West, though, Middle Eastern icons can be treated with considerable irrever-
ence and humor, too. The cover art of Texas musician (and erstwhile politi-
cian) Kinky Friedman's 1976 record album *Lasso from El Paso* (fig. 8-9) is a
case in point. Using the venerable Camel cigarette logo as a starting point,
Friedman westernizes this commercial icon it by positioning himself astride
the camel while wearing his signature western garb and swinging a lasso. In
an equally interesting and subversive use of the Camel logo, a recent (2008)
public service antismoking ad features an American-style cowboy seated on a
camel. As if by magic he morphs into the Marlboro Man as he rises from the
camel, ultimately succumbing to lung cancer.

   Modern literature continues this tradition of finding the Middle East
in the American West. In the novel *West of Babylon* (2002), Spanish writer
Eduardo Garrigues ingeniously recast the ancient Babylonian Gilgamesh epic
in New Mexico. Long before he visited North America, Garrigues observed

that Gilgamesh—"probably the first yarn in universal literature where men and not gods are the main characters in the story"—could easily be set in the Hispanic Southwest. Garrigues had long been fascinated by American Westerns and had succumbed to the Southwest's charms well before he ever visited it. In fact, two worlds were about to converge here, for even as a child in Spain, Garrigues sensed the traditions of the "eight centuries of Arab domination" that resonate to the present in the Iberian Peninsula.

Garrigues also had another source of inspiration: as he noted, "Inspired by the successful adventures of the British pioneers of Assyriology, I decided to travel from London to New Mexico, looking for the scenery and the cultural background of the story I wanted to tell." In other words, Garrigues was influenced by Orientalists and was about to become an Orientalist himself. He continues: "From the moment I set foot on Southwestern soil, I was convinced that my project of adapting the ancient Babylonian myth to the American West could succeed." In the process of setting (or rather resetting) the epic novel here, Garrigues discovered "some parallels between the Middle East and the American Southwest that I could hardly have imagined when I started this literary adventure"—namely, that travelers from Francisco Vázquez de Coronado to Charles Lummis had also found the Near East in the Far West.[43]

West of Babylon breaks new (and old) ground by setting an epic Mesopotamian story in the American Southwest, and transforming both landscape and people in the process. The Native Americans assume characteristics of Mesopotamians and Mesopotamians become southwesterners. In Garrigues's imagination, the protagonist Gilgamesh becomes Gil Gomez with the stroke of a pen, or the keystroke on a computer keyboard. Garrigues does this by merging Old World and New World identities. For example, while caught in a ferocious rainstorm, the book's narrator relates that "I began to offer prayers not only to the God of Israel, who saved Noah from the flood, but [also] to the pagan gods who seemed to reign in those mountains and to the Water Monster who had saved the Navajos from a deluge."[44] In Garrigues's *West of Babylon*, both people and landscapes resonate with the magic of the Gilgamesh epic; the landscape analogues here, including the fabled cedar forest and flood-scoured arroyos, are replicas of the cedar grove and wadis in the Old World, but ingeniously set in New Mexico.[45]

Not coincidentally, there is a dreamlike quality to Garriques's southwestern/Babylonian drama. At the beginning, the character Baltasar recalls an "old nursery rhyme" that "my mother used to sing us to sleep." As he plods through the Southwest, he now sings it:

How many miles to Babylon?
Three score and ten.
Can I get there by candlelight?
Yes, and back again.
If your heels are nimble and light,
You may get there by candlelight.

To the narrator, however, "the words to that ballad turned out to be prophetic, for we rode far into the night, taking advantage of a full moon that covered the landscape with its shiny shroud, and we only stopped to camp when the officer in command noticed that some of the animals were about to drop in their tracks."[46] This nursery rhyme allegory is a reminder that Orientalism is often first communicated through stories told to impressionable children, who, in that nether state between subconsciousness and sleep, are particularly susceptible to fantasies. In the passages above, Garrigues reveals how a childhood memory can sustain him through a grueling march in a "real" but magical world that is itself pure literary fantasy.

In transforming the American Southwest into the Orient, writers like Garrigues build on a long Spanish (and European) literary tradition. In their hands, the Orient is yet another metaphor for a world of eternal sunshine punctuated by jet-black, star-filled nights. Orientalism, in other words, was and is an antidote to the constrictions imposed upon the West by its own drive toward the regimentation of an increasingly industrial (factory) and bureaucratic (office) life. Consider the Catalonian writer Francesc Estival, who describes himself as an "author" who "day by day . . . fritters away his vital juices as a government bureaucrat, which brings little light to his life." However, Estival knows full well that "for a Spaniard raised on the Mediterranean, lack of light is slow death." To compensate for this deprivation, "the author escapes this dire reality by writing fiction," building "his stories around the Mediterranean Sea, its civilizations, its lights and its lies."[47] Lying along the Mediterranean Sea's southern and eastern shores, the Near East provided a ready source of inspiration for those who shaped popular images of the American Southwest.

The modern political implications of such regional Orientalism continue to concern scholars. As historian Jerold Auerbach further noted in his *Explorers in Eden*, "For postmodern academic critics, no term of opprobrium cuts deeper than 'Orientalism,' defined as an insidious strategy 'for dominating, restructuring, and having authority' over non-Western peoples." As Auerbach notes, Edward Said claimed that Orientalists always racialize and denigrate people of the East because "the one thing that the Orient could not do was represent itself" and therefore that "every European in what he could say about the Orient, was consequently a racist, and imperialist, and almost totally ethnocentric."[48] As Auerbach counters, though, "Said's scathing critique of Orientalist essentialism can easily be redirected to Said himself—and to his academic disciples." Auerbach here includes feminist scholars such as Barbara Babcock and Margaret Jacobs, who suggest that Orientalism essentially trivializes the Southwest's indigenous women, as it "exoticizes and appropriates Pueblo culture for purposes of Western entertainment and pleasure." According to Auerbach, however, such critiques are problematic because they assume that southwestern Indian women were helpless victims, when in fact, Native women in this increasingly tourist-oriented region had many ways of dealing with Anglos on their own terms.[49]

The conflation of southwestern Native American and Asian continues into the present and reveals that it offers the potential for reconciliation as well as conflict. In the 2003 Tony Hillerman PBS Navajo mystery film *Coyote Waits*, a Navajo policeman and a young man are discussing fate. The young man says his Navajo father learned about fate in Vietnam, adding sarcastically that fate's relationship to mankind is like the mongoose's relationship to a mouse (which is to say that fate specializes in consuming man). Upon hearing this Vietnamese proverb, the Navajo policeman says, "We have the same story." This translates the Asian story into a shared kind of folklore, but the specificity is uncanny, as the southwestern Indian equals the Asian "other" in numerous stories.[50] This, as we have seen, involves a process underway since the 1800s, if not earlier, as travelers believed the Indians were representatives of Asian or Middle Eastern tribes, as reflected in their physiognomy and culture (notably folklore, ceremonies, and the like).

Travelers seeking Oriental symbolism in the modern Southwest should visit artist Roy Purcell's Chloride Murals, which are tucked away in a small canyon near the former mining town of Chloride, Arizona. Purcell's murals are among the most fascinating Orientalist works in the modern American West. Jim Eidel of Carson City notes that Purcell "found a desert dream and followed it," creating the Chloride Murals in 1966 "on house-sized granite boulders and immense cliff faces with enamels and bits of desert" (fig. 8-10a). The murals, which were restored in 2006, are startling, a reminder of how much the desert itself is like a canvas, and how readily the artistic imagination can add to the desert's drama, but Purcell abstracted their imagery into a painting that explicitly lays out the Oriental symbols. Called *The Goddess Rising*, it places in context a wealth of symbols from both Easts—Near East and Far East (fig. 8-10b). The centerpiece is a stylized sun held up by a buxom female goddess whose outstretched arms are entwined by two serpents with their mouths open to encircle her breasts. The goddess holds an all-seeing eye as she stands in the maw of a huge serpent. Her ample breasts suggest the fertility rites of ancient Hindu India, while her vagina is a yin and yang symbol from East Asia. Overhead, two ibises, sacred to the Egyptians, fly on either side of the sun symbol. One bears a branch in its beak, while the other spreads its wings majestically. From sky to ground, a river adorned with stylized fish—presumably the Nile—crosses diagonally like a lightning bolt. From ground level, palm trees and vines rise skyward above a tent. A camel and rider appear, as does that other enduring symbol for the ancient Near East, a pyramid. Adding to the mystery, a winged creature (griffin) stands at the lower right.

Serpents are a central motif in the Chloride Murals, and on the original murals, they twist their way about the rocks like huge roots. Eidel notes that Purcell was fascinated by the religious traditions of the Old World and is currently engaged in Native American studies, as well as "visual exploration of the goddesses from ancient historical traditions and civilizations." Interestingly, the way in which Purcell presented these scenes suggests a Native American influence in that the assemblage and its very location bring to mind an elaborate rock art pictograph. As Eidel concludes: "Chloride has certainly never been the same, nor have countless visitors who, over the years, have wound their way into the little canyon to study the Murals and be profoundly changed in some quiet way."[51] For his part, Purcell was deeply aware of the rich iconography associated with the Oriental world, and he easily merged that identity into a western landscape. To Purcell, the mural represents "The Journey," which, he told me, turned out to be a prediction of how his own life would develop, though he had no idea at the time. Purcell, it should be noted, was a devout Mormon until images like these came to him and called in question that faith. Purcell, when he created the Chloride Murals, built on a time-honored tradition of exploring the connections between the landscape and memory, but modern-day tourists seek the place out for enlightenment.

Some historians, including the late Hal Rothman, critique the imitative and exploitative aspects of tourism. Rothman called it a "Devil's Bargain that has compromised the American West." In clever pop culture–tinged phrasing right out of Steely Dan's song "Deacon Blues," Rothman observed that "tourism created a culture, languid and bittersweet that has as its object participation in consumption." Like the human viper in that song who crawls through suburban streets making love to "women languid and bittersweet," tourism represented the seductive side of capitalism and materialism to Rothman. As a historian interested in deeper meanings of the ordinary, Rothman further

Fig. 8-10a. Roy Purcell's stunning Chloride Murals near Chloride, Arizona, offer a remarkable vision of Oriental symbolism in the American West.

suggested that "as the American West became the psychic location of the national creation myth, Americans understood their experience and identity as a people as being formed and refashioned." [52]

Rothman persuasively argued that the West itself was powerful enough to shape this identity, but it should again be noted that this could not have happened without that of other more distant places being employed first. As I have shown, these were places that, like the fabled East(s), had the strongest presence in the imagination and the greatest similarity, visually speaking, to their western counterparts. This process required that the landscape here be branded, in part, with an Oriental identity *before* it could become wholly American.

However, because our own Southwest was once part of Mexico and still shares a border with that country, it remains foreign to us in many ways despite the fact that it is indisputably part of the United States. What borderlands historian James Brooks describes as "strands of desire and repulsion that stretched across the cultural frontiers" [53] can still be glimpsed in folklore and popular culture. This is explicit in the 2006 film *Bordertown*—a gritty exposé of the murders of approximately four hundred young women in the vicinity of the Juárez (Chihuahua) *maquiladoras*. When an enthusiastic journalist (Jennifer Lopez) arrives in El Paso/ Ciudad Juárez, she finds another world south of

Painting courtesy Roy Purcell

Fig. 8-10b. Artist Roy Purcell's painting of *The Goddess Rising* features serpents, yin/yang, and other Oriental symbols.

the border. To decipher the mysteries here, she connects with a local newspaper editor (Antonio Banderas) who operates at considerable peril to himself, as the government intends to suppress news about the murders. As configured by director Gregory Nava and cinematographer Rey Villalobos, Juárez has a decidedly infernal and Oriental quality. The city is teeming with an erotic quality of sexual abandonment associated with Sodom and Gomorrah. Lopez seeks a young Mexican woman who miraculously managed to escape the clutches of a serial killer who raped her and buried her alive. The Mexican woman rises from her would-be grave and returns to Ciudad Juárez only to find herself in a kind of hell dominated by mysterious strangers who have no regard for human life. The movie's musical score has a decidedly Arabic quality, and numerous scenes in Juárez, including a huge sign for a bar that is a brightly colored replica of King Tut, add to the film's sinister Oriental quality. So too do several Middle Eastern men who are part of the nefarious dealings in Juárez.

Bordertown is a reminder that the Southwest has long been vulnerable territory in the eyes of Americans. It was first threatening country as it entered the United States after the US-Mexican War, perceived as a thorn-ridden land full of Apaches, Comancheros, bandits, and other miscreants. Anglo-American enthocentrism played a role, as the popular press portrayed the region as so lawless and ethnically alien that it took nearly fifty years of intense lobbying for Arizona and New Mexico to become states. However, even after the region gained statehood in 1912, the Mexican Revolution (circa 1910–1920) reminded Americans of the region's vulnerability when Pancho Villa invaded Columbus, New Mexico, in 1916, killing about a dozen Americans.[54] More recently, with illegal immigration a growing concern, the Southwest seemed once again threatened, and Arizona passed controversial legislation in response. In addition to undocumented workers, though, two bigger concerns loom. The first, heavily armed and particularly savage drug lords who operate with impunity, have left thousands dead (some beheaded) across the border in Mexico. The second concern is the fear that al-Qaeda-inspired Islamist terrorists may slip into the United States across the border. That present-day fear of savagery and terror has resulted in what geographer Daniel Arreola calls the "hardening" of the border,[55] and is a dark reminder not only of the region's own sometimes troubled past but also of current events playing out in destabilized Middle Eastern countries such as Iraq, Afghanistan, and Pakistan.

9

Another Place, Another Time
The Modern West as the Far East

"Welcome to the home of our Pan-Asian American communities. It's the only neighborhood in America where Chinese, Filipino, Japanese, Vietnamese and Southeast Asians live and work together, side by side."

Discover Seattle's Chinatown/International District website

In the Far West from California into the Pacific Northwest, the Far East has remained a major theme throughout the twentieth century. China and Japan, in particular, are the major areas of Asia represented, but other Asians are increasingly becoming part of the region's identity. California was a leader in perpetuating an Asian character for the West, and it developed in two major centers there. As Asian American art historian Gordon Chang recently noted, "San Francisco may be unique for the degree to which it has embraced an Asian cultural identity."[1] In that city, Asian art and culture flourished despite considerable racial animosity. Building on the momentum of the Panama Pacific International Exposition in 1915, San Francisco's Chinatown became one of the city's most recognizable and heavily visited neighborhoods. In the era that saw private automobile ownership soar, Chinatown was now filled with traffic and presented a bustling appearance to tourists. It was among the most popular of subjects for San Francisco postcards in the 1930s, keeping its place along with another icon, the new Golden Gate Bridge whose stunning orange-colored superstructure formed a portal through which ships passed on the way to exotic ports. Within the sight of the bridge, equally exotic Chinatown experienced a facelift aimed at making it more accessible and visible. Using new printing techniques, postcards of Chinatown further emphasized the bright colors of the buildings and signs (fig. 9-1). Color is the operative word here, for Chinatown represented the colorful side of ethnicity.

Fig. 9-1. A brightly colored postcard, ca. 1940, depicts San Francisco's Chinatown as an enduring tourist attraction.

Pretty much missing were threatening images such as highbinders, which were now replaced by polychrome dragons and other symbols of Chinese culture. Chinatown had now become a largely commercial district, with fewer Chinese living in this part of the city.

If San Francisco helped establish a Chinese identity in the entire West, however, Los Angeles helped further that connection in twentieth-century popular culture. This began well before Grauman's Chinese Theatre (fig. 9-2) opened its doors in 1927, but that spectacular theater symbolizes the city's modern fascination with Asian culture. The brainchild of showman Sid Grauman, it was built near Grauman's earlier Egyptian Theatre. Constructed to look like a real Chinese pagoda, Grauman's Chinese Theatre features several iconic touches, including a huge dragon writhing across the facade, two stone lions that perpetually stand guard at the front entrance, and a copper roof decorated with the silhouettes of dragons. When completed, Grauman's Chinese Theatre epitomized Hollywood's insatiable interest in the exotic as represented by stylized icons. Such faux architecture is both a tribute to authentic Chinese buildings and a whimsical addition to an eclectic streetscape along Hollywood Boulevard. As a mecca to film aficionados in Southern California, Grauman's Chinese Theatre has become an icon in its own right, appearing in movies that make inside references to Hollywood filmmaking. And yet beneath the veneer of cinematic tributes is the theater's ultimate bow to fantasies about the Far

Fig. 9-2. As seen in this 1940s-era postcard, Grauman's Chinese Theatre became a Hollywood icon after its grand opening in 1927.

East itself, which has been the subject and locale of hundreds of Hollywood movies. These included the popular Charlie Chan series of detective films, which, of course, employed highly made-up Anglo-Americans in the lead Asian roles—a racializing of characters now disparagingly called "yellowface."

Grauman's vision of building an Asian-style wonder in Hollywood may have been inspired, at least in part, by two wealthy businessmen, brothers Charles and Adolph Bernheimer. As New Yorkers who had made their fortunes in the cotton and dry goods trade, the Bernheimers were attracted by California's climate and well aware of its proximity to the Far East. Avid Orientalists who traveled frequently to the Far East—Adolph is said to have made seventeen trips there—the brothers knew the Orient well. In 1914, the brothers amazed Hollywood by constructing an impressive Japanese style home and gardens on a hilltop overlooking the city. The Bernheimer mansion was both unique and magisterial. It was, in fact, a replica of a palace at Yamashiro, near the Japanese city of Kyoto. To ensure accuracy, the brothers imported Japanese craftsman and laborers. The impressive, Japanese style home not only made an Asian statement in the California landscape; it also housed the brothers' fabulous collection of Asian art and artifacts. Inside and out, the home possessed the feel of an imperial palace. One might say that it not only conveyed or revealed the brothers' appreciation of the Orient; it also positioned them as Oriental-style nabobs in a community that appreciated the exotic and admired fame and fortune. That the Bernheimers were able to pull off their Oriental dream so effectively was due, in part, to the similarity between the original setting in Japan and the setting of their replica in California—rugged hills overlooking cities on coastal plains bordering the Pacific Ocean. More to the point, the Bernheimer's palatial Japanese style home was visited by many of the budding film industry's elite. Following Charles's death in 1922, Adolph built the even more impressive Asian style Oriental Japanese Gardens on a bluff overlooking the ocean in Pacific Palisades. Given the public's interest in things Asian, it is no surprise that both of the Bernheimer sites were heavily visited and admired in the 1920s and 1930s. Regrettably, the Pacific Palisades site was vandalized during the Second World War, in part a result of anti-Japanese sentiment. However, the Bernheimer's fabulous Hollywood home still enchants as an artifact of the Orient, for it is now the upscale Yamashiro Restaurant.[2]

The Second World War marked a turning point for Asians in California. During that conflict, Japanese Americans paid a high price, as those living in cities on the West Coast were deported for security reasons. These temporary relocation camps were located far inland, as officials worried that Japanese Americans sympathetic to the emperor would sabotage shipbuilding plants or harbors. Unpleasant popular stereotypes of Asians, regardless of country of origin, persisted into the 1950s, as evident in a black-and-white photographic postcard titled "Chinese Laundry in Ghost Town" (fig. 9-3). It features a lone male figure, but the text here is both explicit and degrading. That familiar phrase mocking Chinese-American speech—"No Tickee No Shirtee"—was a staple "in-joke" (which, like all such stereotypical sentiments, had some basis in reality because laundries were very often owned and operated by Chinese). Here, however, it not only takes on a comical or mocking quality but also has an element of the theatrical because the entire scene itself is fabricated in Knott's Berry Farm (erroneously called "Knotts Berry Place" on the postcard). Archconservative Walter Knott created the theme park in 1951, four years before Disneyland opened, and it featured vignettes from the "real" past of the American West. The building's interior itself looks credible enough, and Walter Knott likely pulled it out of a real mining camp such as Calico in the Mojave Desert. Hoping to keep the western past alive, Knott not only partly reconstructed Calico in Buena Park, but also obtained buildings and artifacts from many other western locales. The Chinese laundry was such a common business in western towns that we see it here as a cliché, for both a man and his occupation are reduced to a marketable stereotype. In this image, the Chinese man appears to be a caricature of a "Chinaman," his features accentuated

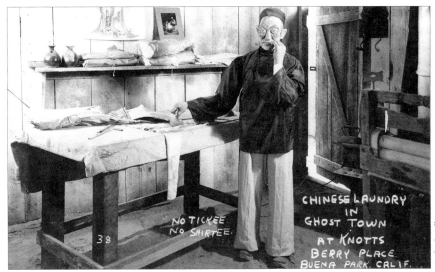

Fig. 9-3. Building on venerable stereotypes, a photographic postcard of the Chinese laundry in Ghost Town, Knott's Berry Farm (ca. 1953) portrays a stereotyped Chinese man.

either by makeup or photographic retouching. People viewing this card might wonder, is he real, or a wax figure?

Despite these attempts to perpetuate anti-Asian sentiment, or at least mock Asians, the media and Hollywood began to defend them. With the bitterness of the Second World War subsiding by the late 1950s, for example, Japan began to be portrayed favorably, its geographical similarities to California and the richness of its traditions noted in television and film. In a 1959 episode of the popular television show *Perry Mason* titled "The Case of the Blushing Pearls," a Japanese artist named Mitsu Kamuri (played by actress Nobu Atsumi McCarthy) rents a home overlooking the rugged Pacific coastline near Los Angeles so that she can paint pictures of the beautiful scene, which, she tells her attorney Mason, reminds her of her home in Japan. As in many films now portraying Asians sympathetically during this period, Mitsu's talents and dignity are respected rather than ridiculed.

This positive portrayal of Asians in California is also evident in popular cartoons in the 1950s. Again, San Francisco took the lead in celebrating rather than denigrating Chinese people. Cartoonist Albert Tolf included several vignettes of them in his popular cartoon-filled book, *This Was San Francisco*. Tolf's book, produced from his cartoons that ran from 1956 through 1958, depicts "A Walk Through Old Chinatown" as a positive experience wherein a boy's fortune is told ("You grow up to be a great man") and Chinese people converse with each other, sometimes about their beliefs and superstitions ("Fifth day of month lucky for me"). The Chinese people depicted are industrious ("A few steps away might be a shoe repairman") and their architecture elaborate and exotic. In his cartoon titled "A Corner of San Francisco in 1900," Tolf depicts "the Chinese Shrimp Camp"—which, he noted, was "a thriving village and a marketplace for seafood which was built and inhabited by Orientals and located in the southeast part of the city." Shrimp Camp became a magnet and "kids would hike [to] it from afar to bring home cornucopias of fresh shrimp"[3] (fig. 9-4). It is worth noting that Tolf went out of his way to include only the positive attitudes of Chinese culture. Gone are the aspersions cast at such "Orientals." Now, the Chinese are instead woven into a sanguine, multiculturally inclusive urban world.

Chinatown became the most enduring stereotype of Asian-American life on the West Coast. Of the many Chinatowns here, however, none has earned more cinematic acclaim than Chinatown in Los Angeles. In a sense, Los Angeles was the perfect place for such an exotic ghetto, as it were, existing as an island in a sea of Anglo-American fantasies about the region's cultural identity. One factor that helps explain Los Angeles's propensity to experiment with identity is its relative recency compared to, say, New York. The city's Anglo-American population began to grow rapidly during the real estate boom of the 1880s, transforming the former Mexican pueblo. As Mike Davis put it, Los Angeles "had no compelling image in American letters," and that anonymity made it a tabula rasa. Then, too, Hollywood had already given the city a cinematic quality in the early twentieth century. By the 1920s, "L.A. was all (stage) set, which is to say, it was utopia: literally, no-place (or thus any place)." The movie set had become the "architectural zeitgeist" of Southern California. An eclectic built environment blossomed with the likes of "Spanish Colonial" houses, "Egyptian revival" apartments, and Masonic temples.[4] In the twentieth century, film studios repeatedly used Los Angeles's Chinatown to convey a myriad of plots and themes, many of them sinister. Of all those films, none has portrayed the mystery of Chinatown better than Roman Polanski's *Chinatown* (1974). Although filmed several decades after the film noir period of the 1940s and early 1950s, *Chinatown* is often considered to be of that genre, or better yet neo-noir, because it reveals anew the seamier underside of life in otherwise prosperous and happy mid-twentieth-century California.

The action in *Chinatown* initially focuses on the rural landscape at Los Angeles's periphery, where land grabbing and water dealing are exposed. Significantly, it is a Chinese gardener who helps private detective J. J. "Jake" Gittes (Jack Nicholson) ultimately solve the case. The film's name, however,

Fig. 9-4. In Albert Tolf's book *This Was San Francisco* (1958), the Chinese section called "Shrimp Camp" is portrayed nostalgically.

concerns the more sinister parts of the plot. The most poignant scene—the climactic shooting death of the mysterious woman (Evelyn Cross Mulwray, played by Faye Dunaway) with whom Jake falls in love—takes place in Chinatown. When trying to console Jake about Evelyn's senseless death in that seemingly foreign part of Los Angeles, an associate tells him to "forget it" because he will never have an answer. As his friend concludes with simple resignation, "It's Chinatown." That parting line reminds us that the Orient is associated with mystery and inscrutability. Moreover, Chinatown as both disquieting film and indifferent place personifies the arbitrariness of fate. The premise that something greater than the individual is in control and predestines events is one of Orientalism bedrock themes.

Noir, particularly Los Angeles noir, has been associated with a grim pre-destination since the 1948 release of *Criss Cross*, a film whose plot Mike Davis brilliantly summarizes as "industrial strength sexual obsession unraveling through complex duplicities to the final betrayal of the otherwise-decent protagonist by the *femme fatale*." Some critics and moral guardians objected to the film's theme of predestination—as when protagonist Steve (Burt Lancaster) tells femme fatale Anna (Yvonne De Carlo), "It's all in the cards." That, however, is precisely the point of noir. It challenges the largely Protestant model of a controllable fate, replacing it with a darker, largely Orientalist theme that fate is predetermined. More to the point, Los Angeles's gritty, decadent, multiethnic Bunker Hill neighborhood steals the show as the place where nightmares come true.[5] Ethnic neighborhoods—Chinatown was the supreme example but others like Tokyotown and Koreatown can also serve as stand-ins—bring the Anglo-American face-to-face with the "other"; in this case, the "other" is not only other peoples, but their timeless philosophies.

The film *Chinatown* is worth additional comment, for it is an excellent example of just how compelling film is at moving a story to an inevitable, place-bound conclusion. As cultural geographers Gary Hausladen and Paul Starrs recently observed, film has a unique ability to depict peoples and places in a viselike grip. Like the Orient itself, film presents a scenario that seems predetermined, inevitable. Hausladen and Starrs put it succinctly: "Settings transform character, and rarely is choice involved; film is a deterministic medium, which gives a movie maker rare and exotic power."[6] Even more to the point is their observation that if we "start with landscape and lead character—noir, especially on screen, works toward the strengths of film, the conveyance of an evolving society that foists unwanted change on the world around, alterations transforming the land and tormenting the victim."[7] In *Chinatown*, Los Angeles and Southern California are in flux, driven by nefarious forces that finally express themselves in a timeless setting—the mysterious and unchanging Oriental core of the ironically named City of Angels. *Chinatown*, then, is beautifully situated in the dark and complicated world of Los Angeles noir.

Los Angeles was a natural for the setting. Fueled in part by booster literature and word of mouth, the city's experienced phenomenal population growth in the early 1880s slowed only occasionally, with strong rebounds continuing to bring in those searching for sunnier climes and the good life. As Norman M. Klein described in *The History of Forgetting*, Los Angeles boosters had an evangelical spirit: "They were selling," as Klein put it, "the City on the Hill . . . the new Jerusalem, first come, first served, at the semi-arid, most westerly—and newly civilized—corner of the great frontier." Like a manuscript taking shape, the cityscape of Los Angeles contained some elements which remained from the outset, while others were obliterated through the eraser or delete key. Klein uses the term "social imaginary" to describe an ethos about the "built environment, particularly sites that were destroyed or severely altered"—to "make the fictions of erasure easier to describe."[8]

The creation of the new Los Angeles through additions and erasures was achieved largely by the development of several myths. One of these is the "myth of Chinatown, 1887–1973," which involved "a nest of catacombs where inscrutable sins were committed," and "'hatchetmen high binders' dressed in purple silks . . . killed to win 'slave' women, like the famous Helen of Chinatown." These fantasies were resurrected in the film *Chinatown*, which was based on a screenplay by Robert Towne. Using information obtained by a vice cop—"that police were better off in Chinatown doing nothing, because you could never tell what went on there" anyway—Towne's Chinatown helped "the legend of the underground downtown" resurface. Klein confesses, or rather laments: "As much as I love noir, and find it compelling, it is nevertheless often utterly false in its visions of the poor, of the non-white in particular." The problem, as Klein sees it, is that *Chinatown* itself is a fabrication, that is, part of Anglo-American mythmaking and erasure. As Klein concluded: "Chinatown may be the Ur-text for L.A. political history, but it obscures as much as it clarifies."[9] Similar questions about the validity of a work of art often arise when one considers their political implications in light of modern sensitivities. The point to be remembered here, however, is that noir is valuable precisely *because* it so essentializes, even stereotypes, culture—in this case, Asian culture.

Before leaving Los Angeles's fabled Chinatown, it should be noted that some films about it draw from both the Near East and the Far East for inspiration. In the classic 1982 science-fiction film *Blade Runner*, for example, the entire Orient lingers in postapocalyptic Los Angeles. The year is 2019, and the functioning center of a perpetually dark and rainy Los Angeles is Tyrell Corporation's headquarters, which resembles a truncated pyramid. Harrison Ford is the Blade Runner, a man who searches out and destroys Replicants—robots who have rebelled and attempted to take over what is left of the world. In seeking them out, Ford enters Chinatown, where he hopes to learn the identity of a piece of evidence he has found. It seems to be a fish scale, but the Chinese informants tell him it is a snake scale. This clue leads him to an Arab merchant, Amin Assad, who in turn leads Ford to a woman who carries a snake, which wraps itself around her sequined, nude body like a mink stole. This woman is mysterious and erotic—and dangerous. In an instant, she subdues Ford and escapes. The Oriental part of Los Angeles, in Ridley Scott's vision of the future, is still a place of mystery, intrigue, and danger. But it is also a place where answers to enigmas can be found.

In addition to popular depictions of places like Chinatown, the West's Orientalization occurred in one highly unlikely form, namely, the classic American Western. From its origins as the dime novel of the 1870s and 1880s, the Western evolved into a quintessentially American genre. By the 1950s, during the early Cold War, the Western was not only one of the most popular forms of entertainment but also a metaphor for America's engagement in a broader, polarized world of good and evil. Although seemingly indigenous in that it took place on American soil, the Western frequently calls upon ancient stories from the Orient as it explores subjects like good vs. bad, individual will vs. fate, and the like.

Building on a long tradition, American writer Louis L'Amour (1908–1988) crafted stories about the American West by essentially retelling Asian stories in a new setting. L'Amour became a household name after he was discovered as a Western writer in 1958, but he never forgot his literary debt to the Orient. He was, in a sense, a child of the bleak Great Plains, where the imagination could be stimulated to see more than what the eye beheld. Growing up in North Dakota, L'Amour became fascinated by the unusual sights that Marco Polo had encountered on his epic journey to China. Like Polo's tales, L'Amour's stories are steeped in the romance of travel to exotic and dangerous places. After all, this is the same L'Amour who, in his autobiography *Education of a Wandering Man*, revealed his fascination with Rudyard Kipling and recounted his own travels to Singapore and Arabia. These readings and travels helped fill his nearly insatiable appetite for the far-off continent of Asia. As a young man, L'Amour was especially influenced by an Arab boy he had met in Indonesia—a boy who related stories of Asia to the spellbound writer who would publish some of the most popular fiction about the American West.

We must also credit L'Amour's much earlier fascination with Orientalist literature. As L'Amour put it, "It would be impossible for me to explain my early fascination with Asia, although it could well have sprung from reading a child's version of *The Arabian Nights*." That legendary story apparently got him started, but L'Amour confessed that "years later, when I acquired the full set in the Sir Richard Burton translation [of the *Arabian Nights*], I was content that I had the best." Particularly impressive to L'Amour was "Burton's knowledge of the Arabic language, of the customs and mores of Near Eastern and African peoples." What fascinated L'Amour about the *Arabian Nights*, though, was his perceptive realization that "the stories largely originated in India or farther east."[10] They were, in his opinion, Pan-Asian. Although L'Amour devoured all kinds of literature, he was especially captivated by Asian stories, including *Shah-nama*, Iran's *Book of Kings*, which, as he romantically put it, "are still told along the caravan trails with some minor variations here and there, as are stories of that other hero of Central Asia and Tibet, Kesar of Ling."

L'Amour especially admired "one of the greatest works any man ever attempted" to write—*Science and Civilization in China*, a monumental twenty-seven-volume work orchestrated by Joseph Needham, a British China scholar and biochemist. L'Amour also noted his appreciation of two Chinese classics—*The Scholars* (a novel about the Qing Dynasty written by Wu Junzu in 1750), and *The Romance of Three Kingdoms* (an 800,000-word epic historical novel written by Luop Guanzhong in the fourteenth century). At a time of seeming American supremacy in the world, L'Amour humbly concluded, "We must take heed of India and China, Pakistan and Southeast Asia." This, from the same man who simultaneously admired Joseph McCoy's *Historic Sketches of the Cattle Trade of the West and Southwest*, and J. Frank Dobie's *The Longhorns*. Like William Roberts, who wrote the screenplay of *The Magnificent Seven* using *The Seven Samurai* as inspiration, L'Amour noted, "Long before the appearance of Samurai films in this country I knew their stories." That rich Asian source material, including exposure to "the history of Japanese martial arts, and the Legends of the Samurai and the *bushido* code,"[11] give L'Amour's stories both an ageless quality and an Asian feel. Leaving little doubt about his debt to Asian literature as an influence, L'Amour candidly noted: "As I was researching the American West, I was also delving into the histories of India, China, and Southeast Asia." According to L'Amour, "That Arab boy, long ago in Indonesia had no idea what he started, but I owe him a debt." L'Amour concluded: "He opened a door for me that has never closed."[12]

That may help explain the Oriental quality of L'Amour's descriptions that blur distinctions between Asian and Native American spirits and people. For example, in the Western novel *The Lonesome Gods* (1983), an Anglo-American named Peg-Leg describes Tahquitz, who "is supposed to be an evil spirit." Hinting at origins far from the American West, L'Amour noted that "some say he's a monster of some kind, even a dragon. Once in a while, the mountains rumble and they say Tahquitz is trying to escape."[13] In *The Lonesome Gods*, L'Amour makes a revealing comment about the antiquity of the American West: "The 'Old World'" one character says, "is no older than this, if as old." Even though in the Old World, men "knew of the Egyptians and Babylon," this American desert had mysteries of equal importance. L'Amour's character asks the question that brings both identity and time into focus: "Who knows when men first came here? Who knows how many people were here before you whom we call Indians? So much decays. So much disappears in the passage of years."[14]

In keeping with L'Amour's fascination with the Orient, *The Lonesome Gods* makes frequent reference to Japan, China, and Korea—no doubt an autobiographical comment based on L'Amour's own extensive travels in Asia. L'Amour constantly compared the trappings of this West to the Orient: "An attractive Indian woman opened the door for me, and I was shown into the shadowed quiet of a rectangular room carpeted with Oriental rugs."[15] L'Amour also describes a mysterious Asian man who is "not a Chinese, although he comes from what is part of China. From Khotan," which we learn is "in Turkestan, against the Kunlun Mountains." A character in *The Lonesome Gods* put it, as only L'Amour could: "I believe Marco Polo was there on the old Silk Road that led from China to the Mediterranean." Here in L'Amour's West, this man "has found a place he loves, and he lives there."[16] Like this Asian dweller in the West, L'Amour himself recognized that the Western was the vehicle by which East and West could be united, or rather reunited.

It should be underscored that L'Amour the Orientalist was decidedly *not* an exploiter of the East. Rather, he used the literature and oral traditions of the East respectfully. In a sentiment that Edward Said himself might have appreciated, L'Amour noted that "unfortunately, in most of our [American] schools the history of Europe and North America is taught as if it were the history of the world." L'Amour added, "We do not at the present educate people to think but, rather, to have opinions, and that is something altogether different."[17] Valuing both the oral and literary tradition, L'Amour confessed: "That book or that person who can give me an idea or a new slant on an old idea is my friend."[18] The sentiment here is that Orientalism can inform and enrich—and reveal debts to the East that few Western critics acknowledge. We Orientalize the West in part because we inherently value the Orient and its peoples.

Hollywood played a major role in putting these Easternized Westerns on the screen in the 1960s and 1970s. In the enigmatic 1964 film *The Seven Faces of Dr. Lao*, a mysterious Asian man named Dr. Lao (played by an Asianized Tony Randall) arrives in the West to lead a circuslike entourage. Although based on the 1935 fantasy novel *The Circus of Dr. Lao* by Charles Finney, the film version provides an almost surreal critique of 1950s-era American conformity and morality. In the film, Dr. Lao beguiles the circus goers into questioning their beliefs and values. In this regard he is both Asian and Bohemian. As the movie poster declared, "Bolt the Doors! Lock the Windows! Dr. Lao's coming to town!"[19] Metaphorically speaking, those doors and windows would not hold, and Dr. Lao's circus would soon appear in, appropriately enough, San Francisco's Haight-Ashbury district, as an age-old Oriental combination of drugs, sex, and spirituality (namely, Zen-inspired pacifism) swept the nation from the West Coast to the East Coast.

The tumultuous sixties witnessed the toppling of the Western as the most popular form of nightly television show, in part because the Vietnam War now cast doubt on both simplistic good vs. evil plots and the veracity of authority in general. As an outcome of that disenchantment, the television Western became darker and more sophisticated despite its waning popularity. The Western television series *Kung Fu*, featuring a stoic David Carradine as a man of part-Chinese heritage who roams the American West barefoot dispensing wisdom and justice, revealed how flexibly western identities could be cast. There was a certain revisionist irony to *Kung Fu*, for as we have seen, real Asians in the Old American West had so often been marginalized, and sometimes brutally harassed. This again underscores the flexibility of a western America that serves as a stage upon which dramas of all kinds can be acted, and then reenacted.

The *Kung Fu* series lasted only three seasons (1973–75) but deserves additional scrutiny here because it made such a deep impression on popular culture. As a website dedicated to the show observes, *Kung Fu* is an "Eastern Western."[20] As such, it builds on the rich traditions of giving the American West an Eastern character—literally and metaphorically. *Kung Fu*'s main character is Kwai Chang Caine, the orphaned son of a Chinese woman and an American man. From the outset, Caine's biracial status raises interesting questions and creates interesting dilemmas regarding his identity. Caine was raised in a Shaolin monastery in the province of Honon, and he became a Shaolin master there. However, because Caine killed the emperor's nefarious nephew, he left China to avoid being imprisoned or executed. Caine's name suggests the biblical Cain, who slew his brother and was forced to flee. At any rate, like many nineteenth-century wanderers, "Caine ended up in the American Old West." While wandering there, Caine discovers that he has a half brother named Danny.

As an Orientalized icon, Caine was the right man in the right place at the right time. He epitomized the romanticized Asian: given his instilled sense of social responsibility and his training as a priest, he is highly ethical and spiritual. A seeming loner with a burning passion for social justice, he soon puts everything to the test in the West. Given Caine's martial arts skill and his concern about civil rights, he becomes the quintessential 1970s hero/antihero. The American West of the 1870s was the perfect place and time for Caine, whose "desire for anonymity and a sense of social responsibility is conveyed through the frequent use of flashbacks." To add to the drama and create even more cross-cultural identity tension, Caine is pursued by both American bounty hunters and Chinese assassins. One of the most notable and haunting things about Caine is his uncanny ability to seem detached and highly engaged simultaneously. He is catlike—one might say tigerlike—in his demeanor and movements. His combination of lethality and compassion are characteristically Oriental in that they create one character with two opposite identities. By this, I mean much more than Asian and American, but also pacifist and violent— the perfect yin and yang character for a time of tremendous social change. Tellingly, perhaps, *Kung Fu* aired during the Vietnam War and concluded a year after the United States pulled out of that quagmire. The Old West also proved the perfect locale for Caine's persona to operate—a land of permeable borders, moral ambiguity, and stunning, almost otherworldly scenery.

Caine was played by David Carradine, whose unusual facial features, willowy body, and graceful moves were perfect for the role despite the fact that Asian actor Bruce Lee had tried for the part. Ironically, Lee's audition had proved him to be too intense and frenetic to play Caine's serene, Asian persona. The series featured many actors who have become Hollywood legends in their own right, including Harrison Ford, Jodie Foster, and William Shatner, but Carradine became the icon for the series. The show also spawned martial arts epic films such as *The Circle of Iron* (1978) and a later television series— *Kung Fu: The Legend Continues*—which also starred David Carradine. As a testimony to the endurance of the West-as-East theme, the latter ran for five years (1993–1997).[21] *Kung Fu* also spawned two books that interpret the series.[22]

Few characters ever ventured forth into the American West more purposefully, but impassively, than *Kung Fu*'s Caine. Film studies scholar Yvonne Tasker observed that *Kung Fu* possesses "that peculiar mix of violence and stoicism so characteristic of the Western in its various fictional incarnations." And yet the show emphasized philosophy over violence, making *Kung Fu* "in some ways contradictory . . . a 'pacifist' action series." This helps *Kung Fu*, to use Tasker's deliberate play on words, "re-Orient" the television Western. Caine serves two roles or purposes in the series—as a "witness to human frailty and diversity . . . and dispenser of justice." A promotional illustration for the series reveals the contrast between the bald-headed, cloth-costumed Caine and the hard-edged, leather-clad westerner. However, it is the stoic-looking Caine alone who appears on the packaging for the three-part DVD series, which includes every episode of the show's three-season run (fig. 9-5). Despite the show's—and Carradine's—insistence that nonviolence was the message, *Kung*

Fig. 9-5. The cover image used on Warner Bros.
Entertainment's complete three-season DVD set of *Kung Fu*
features a bald-headed David Carradine as the Shaolin priest
Kwai Chang Caine.

Fu is credited with starting the martial arts craze that continues to the present in the United States. Tasker perceptively observes that the flashbacks to
Caine's Chinese past, as well as his simplicity and his simple questions (in one
episode, he asks "What is a railroad?"), render him as a "child-man." Tasker
also notes that Caine's reluctance to be violent and his gentle demeanor essentially feminize him.[23]

Throughout the series, Caine's identity confounds many who encounter
him as he wanders the western frontier. Although most people simply call him
a "Chinaman," others mistake him for a Native American. For example, in
the episode titled "Chains," which aired on March 15, 1973, a fellow prison
escapee tells Caine, "You sure act like an Indian," because Caine knows where
to find and how to use medicinal herbs. In the episode "Alethea," which aired

two weeks later, a stage stop owner tells Caine, "You got a sorta Injun look." Hearing this, Caine does not answer. Instead, a far-off look comes over his face, adding to the enigma of his identity while also perpetuating the long-held popular belief that Indians and Asians are somehow related. Other people that Caine encounters recognize him as mystical or almost superhuman. For example, in the episode titled "The Brujo," which aired on October 10, 1973, a Mexican priest informs Caine: "You are not like any other man in this part of the world; you are strange." In "The Spirit Helper," which aired two weeks later, a young Indian man on a vision quest prays for a spirit to advise him just as Caine serendipitously appears to fulfill that request. Although Caine is both Asian mystic and transcendent wise man, he does indeed take on more of an American Indian countenance as the series develops: he begins the series with his head shaven, but by the second season his straight, dark brown hair has grown to shoulder length and he wears a headband much like an Apache Indian (or, as some critics observed, a hippie). Then, too, Caine plays a flute as he travels, its haunting tone as reminiscent of Native American flute playing as it is Chinese. In *Kung Fu*, the landscape itself helps conflate the American West and Asia. Flashbacks to Caine's youth in China feature the same rugged, scrub-covered landscape, as both were shot in Southern California. A reed-choked streambed or mountainous scene in one episode might be a setting in China, while in another it is the frontier American West. In one particularly humorous but revealing episode in the second season titled "The Cenotaph II," a trapper asks Caine what he seeks and Caine answers the "Tao." Unaware that *Tao* refers to an ancient Chinese philosophy, the trapper informs Caine that he means "Taos" (New Mexico), which, he states authoritatively, lies a few miles to the north. This, of course, is a play on words, for that *Tao* literally means "the way" or "the path."

As Herbie J. Pilato observes in *The Kung Fu Book of Caine: The Complete Guide to TV's First Mystical Eastern Western*, the show "was a story about love overcoming hate, good triumphing over evil," and in each episode, Caine "struggled with the oldest of human questions"—namely, how should a good man behave in a violent world? In answering this question weekly, Caine "becomes almost the inadvertent symbol, the unsought-for . . . champion of the underdog, with whom we can empathize only too well." He doesn't seek out action; rather, it comes to him. Pilato notes that because Caine is "a man who cannot endure injustice, he must act on it."[24] Although Kung Fu is widely regarded as socially progressive, scholars and the Asian-American community are ambivalent about it. As Jane Naomi Iwamura observes in *Virtual Orientalism*, the show represents "a hegemonic statement of a post

1960s liberal audience" that was not as socially and politically progressive as is often claimed.[25]

This series helped Carradine become one of America's most popular actors. However, ironically—or perhaps prophetically—Carradine's death in 2009 had an aura of Oriental intrigue. After the actor's naked body was found hanging in a closet in his hotel room in Bangkok, Thailand, authorities listed his cause of death as accidental autoerotic asphyxiation. In life, Carradine savored roles that were enigmatic, philosophical, and mysterious; now, in death, he became associated with forbidden, exotic, and dangerous behavior. Ironically, all of these are common themes in portraying the Orient.

In a sense, *Kung Fu* was parodied in the popular film *Shanghai Noon* (2000), whose plot involves a Chinese martial arts–savvy imperial guard (Jackie Chan) searching for a kidnapped Chinese princess (Lucy Liu) in nineteenth-century Nevada. More comedy and action film than drama, *Shanghai Noon* is a tongue-in-cheek homage to Westerns—for example, the film's title mocks *High Noon*, and Jackie Chan's character is named Cho Wang (pronounced "John Wayne").[26] And yet this film team presents Chinese and American characters as more or less equals rather than hero and sidekick. For that matter, it actually cast real Chinese and Chinese American actors in lead roles. *Shanghai Noon* above all symbolized the growing acceptance of China as a player in both the heroic Western and Hollywood itself.

Hollywood's fascination with the Orient continues to play out closer to home as it imagineers the built environment into exotic locales.[27] California had, from the 1890s onward, reproduced portions of the Far East—for example, the Japanese Tea Garden in Golden Gate Park in 1894, which was the first Japanese garden in America—a trend that culminated in the Golden Gate International Exposition on Treasure Island in San Francisco Bay in 1939. Faux Oriental locales not only were popular places to visit but could become film shooting locales in their own right. Those closest to Hollywood had an advantage, as film crews could shoot there conveniently. Small wonder that the 2005 movie *Memoirs of a Geisha* was filmed in part at the famed Japanese Garden at the Huntington Gardens in San Marino. Offering enough stereotypically Asian settings, including a Japanese house, Zen court, moon bridge, rock garden, and the like, it proved the perfect locale to simulate the Orient.

In capturing the visual character of Japan, or at least the popular view of Japan, the Huntington built on its long history of interest in the culture of Asia. In 2006, it began a new venture aimed at reproducing "one of the world's largest classical Chinese gardens outside of Asia." When completed in several phases over perhaps a decade or more, the new Chinese Garden will feature

中國園 The Huntington
Chinese Garden

Fig. 9-6. Conceptual drawing of the Huntington Chinese Garden, slated for development in San Marino, California, from 2009 to 2019, shows the proposed arrangement of pavilions, waterways, and forested areas.

a lake, bridges, pavilions, and "poetic views"—all set among native Chinese plants (fig. 9-6). In design, the fourteen-acre Huntington Chinese Garden is configured something like a mandala, for the seasons will be represented by the four compass directions (summer in the south, spring in the east, autumn in the west, and winter in the north). Ultimately, more than thirty major structures, all Chinese-style, will grace the site. One of the Huntington Chinese Garden's main objectives is to "feature plants rich in literary and symbolic associations."[28] After an elaborate process, the Huntington Chinese Garden was given a name, Liu Fang Yuan, which means "Garden of Flowering Fragrance." The selection of this name was considered to be crucial because "according to Confucius . . . 'If a name is not correct, speech will not flow smoothly [and] it will even imperil the harmony of all under heaven.'" This is in stark contrast to the Western tradition immortalized by Shakespeare, who opined: "That which we call a rose by any other name would smell as sweet." Liu Fang Yuan, then, involves not only the importation of physical elements from China, such as rocks and plants, but also the philosophical spirit of the Chinese garden.

Given the Huntington's interest in art, it is not surprising that the garden's connection to painting is stressed. Interestingly, Liu Fang was also the name of a famous Chinese painter during the Ming Dynasty. The Huntington notes that "gardens were always seen as three-dimensional paintings." Moreover, "painters designed many celebrated gardens of the 16th and 17th centuries, the golden age of gardens in China."[29] In part educational and in part thera-peutic, the Huntington Chinese Garden promises to be much more than a contemplative setting: it will also be a tribute to New Age sensitivities that embrace the rich Oriental (in this case Chinese) heritage of California.

In any event, the fact that the Chinese Garden will be developed well into the second decade of the twenty-first century confirms that California's fasci-nation with the Far East endures. Nearby, throughout the San Gabriel Valley, a thriving Asian American community has shaped Southern California's sub-urban landscape into a remarkable amalgam of Buddhist temples, apartments, shops, and other businesses. These comprise the authentic modern American "Chinatown" of the twenty-first century—functional, oriented to the auto-mobile and public transportation, unselfconscious—continuously altering and reshaping Anglo-American suburbs into vibrant ethnic communities. Then, too, an Asian consciousness can infiltrate even modern Los Angeles, as is evident in the recent book *The Bodhi Tree Grows in L.A.*, where the serene Theravada Buddhist Temple sits just a few blocks from the perpetually con-gested Santa Monica freeway.[30]

California is the undisputed hearth of popular culture embracing the Far East, but farther up the Pacific Coast, the Pacific Northwest is also enmeshed in its aura. Although this region is in a sense a step or two behind, and in the shadow of, California when it comes to creating an Oriental identity, it too has flowered. Given the Pacific Northwest's long-held dream of connecting with Asia, it should come as no surprise that it enthusiastically embraced a modernized connection with Asia in the latter half of the twentieth century.

This time, though, it was the airline industry rather than the railroads that led the way. Aptly named Northwest Orient Airlines was a major player in this process. Beginning in the Midwest as Northwest Airlines in 1926, this airline expanded after the Second World War, making the first flight from the United States to Japan in 1947. In 1949, it was rebranded as Northwest Oriental Airlines, but ultimately dropped the *al* and became simply Northwest Orient. Interestingly, however, the legal name of the company remained a more American-sounding Northwest Airlines.

At its zenith, Northwest Orient Airlines produced a wealth of Oriental images aimed at getting American travelers to Japan, and vice versa. The airline's colorful postcards from the early 1960s feature scenes of "majestic" Mount Fuji, and Japan as "the land of picturesque gardens." A common theme is a traditionally clad Japanese woman, parasol in hand, standing on stumplike stones in a serene pond. More often than not the woman's dress is pink (reminiscent, perhaps, of cherry blossoms) and the vegetation is an intense green. This, in fact, is imagery that Portland Oregon would soon adopt as the popularity of Asian gardens increased. One card reminds prospective travelers that "Japan [is] the land of Oriental classicism and Western modern-ism" where "you'll see trees and temples . . . ponds and pagodas . . . shrubs and shrines . . . in delightful picturesque harmony." This wording builds on many of the sophisticated themes in Victorian-era travel literature that were so well represented by Raphael Pumpelly nearly a century earlier. However, it now had a more candid and more modern connection to a globalizing America that had made Japan part of its own hinterland.

More to the point, though, by the time that postcards touted the airline's "Orient Express"—which operated on "Northwest's Great Circle shortcut across the Pacific to the Orient"—the Pacific Northwest was poised to more fully embrace Asia as a partner in image building. This happened for a good reason: Japan was now, as a postcard put it, "just a day away."[31] That country was also one of the United States' most important trading partners and becoming an economic giant in its own right. In the 1960s and early 1970s, Northwest Orient advertised on radio and television, its name sung as a jingle:

Author photograph, 2010

Fig, 9-7 The Poetry Stone in the Japanese Garden (Portland, Oregon) features a *haiku* (traditional Japanese poem) reading "Here, miles from Japan, I stand as if warmed by the spring sunshine of home."

"Northwest Orient . . . [followed by the single clash of a gong] . . . Airlines." That gong reminded one of the huge metal disks struck at strategic places in orchestrated Asian symphonies and in popular movies set in Asia. It not only signalled that something important was about to happen, such as the arrival of an emperor. It also conveyed a sense of the difference between Western music and its more mysterious counterpart from the Orient.

In the late 1950s, when Portland became a sister city to Sapporo, Japan, leaders in the community sought a way to offer a glimpse of the Orient closer to home. The result was Portland's stunning Japanese Garden. Designed by Professor Takuma Tono in 1963, it consists of five separate gardens that were opened to the public in 1967. As the Japanese Garden's website reminds visitors, because they were "influenced by Shinto, Buddhist, and Taoist philosophers, there is always 'something more' in these compositions of stone, water and plants than meets the eye"[32] (fig. 9-7). As another website observes, the gardens take full advantage of Portland's setting at the base of the towering Cascades, which yields an "unsurpassed view of Mt. Hood,"[33] a subliminal reference, perhaps, to its similarity to Mount Fuji. In their elaborate design, the gardens juxtapose small and large objects as a way of fostering contemplation and appreciation.

In addition to Japan, the sprawling country of China also offers important models of landscape appreciation and contemplation in the Pacific Northwest. In Portland, the Classical Chinese Garden recognizes the city of Suzhou in China, in that it uses an "authentic" Suzhou-style garden as its prototype. Opened in 1990 and occupying a full city block at the north edge of downtown, the garden was designed by Chinese architects and artisans. Situated behind a wall, the Classical Chinese Garden features "serpentine walkways, a bridged lake, and open colonnades" that "set off a meticulously arranged landscape of plants, water, stone, poetry, and buildings." According to a promotional brochure, the Classical Chinese Garden's design "embodies the duality of nature, yin and yang." Like all such gardens, this one involves miniaturization and abstraction of the real world—and is carefully designed to appeal to the senses during all seasons, "each one as lovely as the last." That miniaturization of topography here is achieved by Taihu rocks that are meant to symbolize high mountain peaks framed by a waterfall. Not far from Portland, the surrounding landscape also features high peaks and waterfalls aplenty. And yet the fact that this garden is within the city—and is a miniaturization of a larger, similar landscape—makes it all the more intriguing. The brochure concludes that "the yin and yang of the Garden take you to another place and time." In addition to the basic environmental designs, the architecture here features a pavilion and teahouse, which offers "Chinese teas to calm and refresh you."[34]

The Classical Chinese Garden's promise to "take you to another place and time" touches on the essence of American Orientalism. The place is ostensibly the Orient, specifically China, at some time during the classical period before modernization and industrialization sullied so much of the real world. In other promotional information, the Classical Chinese Garden quotes Wen Zhengming (1470–1559): "Most cherished in this mundane world is a place without traffic; truly in the midst of the city, there can be mountains and forest."

With its two Asian gardens, Portland now had an embarrassment of riches. Upon its tenth anniversary in January of 2010, Portland's Classical Chinese Garden changed its name to the Lan Su Chinese Garden—in part to avoid confusion with the Japanese Garden. As the *Oregonian* reported, the new name builds on the Chinese name for Portland (*Lan*), and the name of Portland's Chinese sister city, Suzhou (*Su*).[35] Still, the city's pride in both gardens is evident. Graciously, the brochure for the Chinese Garden also takes a bow to the city's other Asian sister garden, as it were, noting it has been "proclaimed one of the most authentic Japanese gardens outside [of] Japan." As "a haven of tranquil beauty," as the brochure puts it, the Japanese Gardens' five components "combine to capture the mood of ancient Japan."[36] Although

Asian gardens can be found in other cities nationwide, the fact that Portland has two—and two Asian sister cities—serves as a reminder that the Pacific Northwest is oriented to the Orient. Seattle has an equally strong Asian identity, but it is not confined to just the Northwestern United States. Across the Canadian border, Vancouver, British Columbia, emphasizes that heritage, too. The late actor-photographer Dennis Hopper recently named Vancouver "one of the most exquisite, aesthetically pleasing cities in the world" because, as he put it, "you can really see the Chinese influence in the new skyscrapers towering above the sea."[37]

It is in the arts, letters, and film, however, that the Pacific Northwest has made original contributions to Orientalizing the American West. Seattle was a major center in this process. As Asian American art historian Kazko Nakane recently observed, "In this quiet city, Asian American artists have long asserted a prominence equal to that of other local artists developing their own artistic identity, rooted in their Asian heritage but adapted to the new life in America."[38] They and their work also influenced European American artists living in the city. Paintings hanging in Pacific Northwest art galleries and museums confirm the connection between this region and Asia. Since the 1950s, several famous regional artists have used Asian themes to link life and landscape across the Pacific. Of the three great Northwestern artists who came to prominence in the mid-twentieth century, for example, one looked to the eastern United States, but two "look[ed] west across the Pacific to the orient as a source of inspiration."[39] These two artists—Mark Tobey and Morris Graves—used different styles, but their work clearly owes a debt to Japan and China.

Tobey was born in Centerville, Wisconsin, in 1890 and died in his adopted homeland of the Pacific Northwest in 1976. Between these two dates and places, he did a lot of traveling. After converting to the Baha'i world faith in 1918, Tobey moved to Seattle, where he became one of the Northwest's most recognized modern artists. Tobey's Oriental influences include extensive travel to China and the Middle East, where he became interested in Arabic and Persian scripts. However, Chinese calligraphy, which he learned from the masters, was his forte.[40] By the 1950s, Tobey's work helped the Pacific Northwest segue into an Asian-influenced cultural hearth that not only honored the logging and fishing of the Northwest but also introduced an element of Oriental mysticism.

It was Morris Graves (1910–2001), however, whose work more clearly reflected Asian influences. As biographer Delores Tarzan Ament observed, Graves found inspiration in Japan, where he learned to see the world and the Pacific Northwest anew. Ament noted that Graves's "time in Japan was brief, but for the rest of his life, his art reflected a spare Japanese aesthetic." Ament also noted that "it is unlikely that any artist will ever again capture the popular imagination and the public heart of Northwesterners in quite the same way Graves did."[41] Several of Graves's paintings of various subjects, for example a still life and a forest, epitomize Asian art in its American northwestern context. His interpretation of a pine forest in particular (fig. 9-8) is simultaneously Asian and northwestern. In this young forest, the new green stems resemble fragile asparagus shoots, and the scene is seemingly enveloped in mist. On Graves's canvas, we experience the Northwest not only through an Asian lens but in the electric incandescence of modern American painting.

In 1975, a remarkable documentary film called *Northwest Visionaries* explored the factors that inspired northwestern artists to create such energetic yet strangely serene works of art. After describing Seattle in the early 1930s, the filmmakers let those people who were actually involved with the arts there tell the story from their own perspective. These included art dealers and the artists themselves. One interviewee recalled that there were two main groups of artists—the serious artists who were influenced by Paris (and New York), and the commercial artists who "painted pretty pictures that sold well." In this regard, Seattle was much like other places. However, a third and much smaller group emerged in the 1930s that would have the most lasting influence. Called "the Northwest School," it consisted of three artists: Kenneth Callahan, Mark Tobey, and Morris Graves. As noted above, two of these artists—Tobey and Graves—exerted a tremendous influence, but others, including Margaret Thompkins, George Tsutakawa, Paul Horiuchi, Helmi Juvenen, and Guy Anderson were also significant players.

Throughout *Northwest Visionaries*, several themes emerge. The first is the significance of the natural environment, which is often "wet, dark, gloomy and gray," but richly textured. Its primary themes are forests, mountains, and water. The coastal margin of the region, as well as the Cascades, which form the veritable backbone of the Northwest, is topographically varied, spectacularly verdant, and awash in streams and waterfalls. As hinted by J. Russell Smith, a second and equally important factor is the region's proximity to Asia. As one informant candidly put it, the Pacific Northwest is "close to the water—the Japan current—that brings Zen influences." This current, which Japanese fishermen call *Kuroshio*, brings relatively warm water from the eastern Pacific far northward, circulating it to the Pacific Northwest. Here, although considerably cooler at this point, the Kuroshio Current helps explain the mild, damp quality of winter, and sometimes summer, in the Pacific Northwest. Driven by

Fig. 9-8. Morris Graves's painting *Young Pine Forest in Bloom* (1947) uses Asian techniques to depict a Pacific Northwest landscape.

the prevailing westerly winds at this latitude, the cool, moist air moves across the coastal ranges, where it rises and further cools, depositing as much as 120 inches (300 centimeters) of rain a year in some locations. These coastal ranges are the wettest places in North America, veritable rain forests shrouded in clouds for a substantial portion of the year.

The supposed connection between Asia and the Pacific Northwest by ocean currents may sound whimsical, but some of the topography here was literally part of Asia in the ancient geological past. Geologists believe that a Jurassic crocodile fossil recently found in the Blue Mountains of eastern Oregon originated in "an area from Japan to East Timor, somewhere in the western Pacific in a tropical estuarine environment." What used to be called continental drift and is now plate tectonics was evidently operative here: the terrane (huge block of strata) in which the fossil was found moved here by "floating" on the more pliable surface below. As veteran Oregon geologist William Orr put it: "Fossils similar to the Oregon crocodile appear today in [rocks in] many areas around South China." These moving blocks are called exotic terranes, "exotic" referring to their origin elsewhere. Some of these terranes are larger than mountain ranges, yet they moved pretty much intact for hundreds, and sometimes thousands, of miles. Earth history is replete with many such examples. These exotic terranes remind us that what we think of as "American" or "Asian" topography may have been connected in the distant geological past—in the case of the Jurassic crocodile, about 150 to 180 million years ago.[42]

The more recent, but still prehistoric, past also links the Pacific Northwest and Asia in the popular mind. If, as one artist claimed, even Native American art in the Pacific Northwest is based on "early Chinese" culture from which the natives were descended,[43] then this made the region a natural to be Orientalized. According to some in the artistic community here, the Native Americans themselves have had a role in the complicated process through which this part of North America has become Oriental in nature. The Indians, of course, may have been unwitting actors in this complex dramatic process of Orientalization, but they are extremely important nonetheless. By the late 1960s and early 1970s, it became increasingly clear that Asian and native were being compared, and sometimes conflated. Interestingly, in his soul-searching book *Haunted by Waters*, Japanese American writer Robert Hayashi observed that growing up in the interior Pacific Northwest involved, as Gary Okihiro observed earlier, being "neither 'black nor white' but red." Both the Japanese Americans and Native Americans not only faced discrimination but were mythically united by language. Upon arriving at Idaho's Minidoka internment camp during the Second World War, for example, the Japanese Americans did not know what that name meant in Indian, but it sounded much like the Japanese expression *mina do ka*, or "how is everyone?" That name resonated as an ironic joke, given that those interned here had been displaced from their homes in the green, forested western portion of the region.[44] For the most part, it is that moist, lush part of the Pacific Northwest that resonates as Asia's surrogate.

In literature, too, the misty and wet western margin of the Pacific Northwest has embraced the Far East. In the 1950s and 1960s, Oregon celebrated a rising star in a regional literary field that was becoming crowded with moody poets and brilliant novelists. That star, Gary Snyder, was claimed to be a native son, and quickly became a regional poet laureate to both mainstream and underground. Snyder's poems seemed delightfully exotic and yet familiar. At this time, Snyder was breaking new ground by creating his own Northwest based on Asian prototypes. This was, after all, the poet who could describe the winter landscape of the Cascade Range as a "Chinese scene of winter hills and trees."[45]

This eloquent poet who could so easily conflate West and East was actually born in California in 1930, but became a northwesterner at an early age. When he was two years old, Snyder's family moved to the state of Washington. At twelve, he was living in Portland, Oregon. In his midteens, Snyder attended a camp at Spirit Lake, in the shadow of Washington's spectacular Mount Saint Helens, and in his late teens he worked a series of jobs in radio and journalism, including copy boy for the *Oregonian* in Portland. Despite claims as a northwestern native, Snyder had, as do many northwesterners, a close if ambivalent connection to California. After attending Reed College in Portland, Snyder enrolled at the University of California at Berkeley, where he majored in Oriental languages. In the mid-1950s, Snyder began associating with San Francisco beats, including Allen Ginsberg and Jack Kerouac. By 1956, the pull of the Orient proved irresistible, and Snyder left for Japan. A decade later, he was famous as the author of *Riprap and Cold Mountain Poems* and *Mountains and Rivers Without End*. The 1960s witnessed Snyder's coronation as the king of northwestern poets.

With one foot in the Pacific Northwest and the other in Asia, Snyder straddled two continents. Traveling back and forth across the Pacific Ocean, Snyder personified the intense relationship between two very distant but somehow connected locales. In a sense, Snyder represented Orientalism's role in creating the cultural "Pacific Rim," only his role was more literary than economic. Snyder's writing reveals his Zen Buddhist philosophy and the influences of Japanese haiku poetry, Chinese poetry, and Oriental (Asian) art. In other words, Snyder's American genius and talent plumbed an eclectic set of elements before it blossomed into a characteristically regional form of expression. One of these elements was his fascination with the evocative Pacific Northwest landscape for both the physical attributes (forests, mountains, coasts, rivers) and cultural traditions (a deeply rooted Japanese presence). Blending these with the Orient, Snyder created something radically new. And yet the haunting subliminal presence of the real Orient—which is to say the

Orientalist impulse that has run so deeply through American history and has played out so richly in the American West—is part of the equation in Snyder's brilliant work.

Snyder's work combines East and West in remarkable ways. It builds on the delicacy of the "Northwest Coast Indian myths and folktales" and Japanese Zen. However, it fuses this Oriental softness with what Snyder's biographer Bob Steuding calls the virility of "the rough-and-tumble world of the Far West."[46] In a very real sense, Snyder's strong advocacy of ecology represented an Asian sensitivity to the landscape coupled with an active sense of American individualism. One can, in fact, identify two sources of Snyder's inspiration— the early New England Orientalism of Ralph Waldo Emerson (1803–1882) (and Walt Whitman), and the mid to late twentieth century revival of Oriental sensitivities in West Coast artists and writers—to understand the Orientalist foundations of the American environmental movement itself. Consider these connections: early (nineteenth century) and later (twentieth century) conservation narratives reveal the subtle influences of Native American mythology on the European American mind. The fact that these Indians were both indigenous and exotic (that is, often Orientalized) helped suggest the timeless "wisdom" of their beliefs about the sacredness of the land.

Snyder was able to draw from varied cultural and artistic traditions in a way that epitomized the mind-set of the Pacific Northwest, or at least the elite in that region. As Steuding astutely notes, "The elements of a typical Snyder poem are: (1) a wilderness, or Oriental setting; (2) an avoidance of abstraction and an emphasis on the concrete; (3) a simple, organic form, with generally imagistic lines; (4) the use of colloquial language, with the exploitation of oral aspects; (5) esoteric allusion; (6) occasional erotic overtones." In demonstrating that in Snyder's work, "images are concrete; they are held to objects that are visual and generally sensuous," Steuding observes that several factors, including Oriental poetry, influenced Snyder.[47] To these, we should add the very landscape and cultural traditions of a Pacific Northwest (and Northern California) that had been Orientalized for nearly a century before Snyder began publishing. In phrases like: "Creating empty caves and tools in shops / And holy domes, and nothing you can name; / The long old chorus blowing under foot / Makes high wild notes of mountains in the sea," Snyder's poems reveal "his explorations in the mythology of other cultures—in this case, essentially that of India." Moreover, Snyder's work was influenced by Ezra Pound, who "was thoroughly familiar with the technical aspects of the Imagistic Chinese and Japanese poems." Snyder himself also "acknowledged his debt" to the original Chinese and Japanese poets.[48]

There is an ethereal, almost surreal, quality to Snyder's poems, for example "Riprap," which is essentially Asian in construction. Steuding observed that this poem is more Asian than American in its "evocation of solitary objectivity and a melancholy that is both sad and somehow strangely pleasant." Snyder himself admitted that "Riprap" was in part "influenced by the five and seven character line Chinese poems I'd been reading, which work like sharp blows to the mind." These are sharp blows, indeed, for they hammer home an American's exposure to an Oriental way of expressing the relationship between individual and environment.

As Nicholas O'Connell observes in *On Sacred Ground: The Spirit of Place in Pacific Northwest Literature* (2003), "After immersing himself in Chinese and Japanese poetry, he [Snyder] began to produce some of his best work." More specifically, "as a result of his intensive training in Buddhist meditation, Snyder is able to see things from the inside out, and embody them with great concreteness in his poetry." The result of this, O'Connell concludes, is that Snyder's "practice of Zen Buddhism and familiarity with Asian poetry in the original laid the groundwork for an art that achieves the interpenetration of people and place." Snyder reanimates the landscape of North America, particularly the Northwest, using ecological, anthropological, and Oriental writing strategies, all of which "are designed to convey a sense of the landscape as a living entity, entitled to respect and reverence."[49] The American literati became cognizant of the Northwest's connection to Asia through an article that northwestern poet Carolyn Kizer wrote in 1956: "In this same rainy, misty area, on which the sun never (or almost never) rises, with a climate tempered by the Japanese current and protecting mountains . . ." Kizer declared, "a new Pacific School of poets is emerging."[50]

Oregon poet Clemens Starck frequently uses Asian imagery. His poem "Practising Archery," for example, juxtaposes Oregon's beautiful landscape, with its "Mist in the firs, Moss on the oaks . . . Snow on the mountains— no, those are clouds!" with "Two little Chinamen kneeling, / one is in brick-colored pajamas, the other / in charcoal colored pajamas, each / drawing a bow." Starck asks if one of the Chinese figures might be "the young Buddha practising archery?" and he uses the illustration of them on the cover of his book of poems. A central theme in this poem is that in many things, including vegetation, climate, and the search for deeper meaning, "Oregon is not so far from China."[51]

When did the Pacific Northwest's literature begin to take on an Asian quality? In his essay "Inventing the Pacific Northwest: Novelists and the Region's History," historian Richard Etulain notes that this region's literature evolved through several stages. Between the 1920s and early 1930s, "a new wave of regionalism flooded over the section, baptizing numerous writers and editors alike." Slowly, "a new way of viewing the region, one that continued to gain strength in the next generation," took hold.[52] Etulain suggests that the region's literary identity was linked to other areas in the United Sates, including Montana, but that a distinctively northwestern style began to develop in the 1960s. To Etulain's influences should be added a strong Asian undercurrent that was part of that new regional style.

Consider lastly how popular film incorporates Asia in Pacific Northwestern identity. A major theme is Asian identity in what remains a largely European-American region. The 1999 movie *Snow Falling on Cedars*,[53] which is set in the fictional Puget Sound community of San Piedro, plumbs a sore subject—the harsh treatment of Japanese Americans. Although this story is set in 1951, it features the enduring theme of European American pioneer identity confronting people of Japanese descent. The struggle is ultimately between white, nativist, blue-collar workers and the enigmatic and proud Japanese, and the outcome is predictably tragic. Although nominally historical, *Snow Falling on Cedars* is a reminder that Asian-northwestern identity is still taking shape, as novelists address one of the growing literary and academic themes of the early twenty-first century, namely, the mistreatment of minorities regarded with suspicion in times of national crises. When the Japanese American population living along the Pacific Coast was sent to internment camps in the interior American West during the Second World War for "security reasons," the foreignness of even long-term residents was underscored.

Another side of the same coin—the European-American fascination with, and appreciation of, the Pacific Northwest's Oriental identity—is evident in the film *Little Buddha* (1994). The perspective here is more sanguine. This transcultural film begins as two Buddhist monks travel from Bhutan to Seattle in search of their master, who has been reincarnated as a boy there. Upon arriving in Seattle, they visit a family living in a house that one of the monks has "seen in a dream." They announce to the stunned family that their son Jesse is the reincarnated lama. In this surreal film by Bernardo Bertolucci, images of Bhutan are interspersed with scenes in Seattle, thereby giving that American locale a connection with the Orient. The boy's Anglo-American mother is surprisingly receptive to the monks, as she herself is not only open-minded but also in search of alternative explanations to the ultimate meaning of existence. Bertolucci has an ulterior motive—to introduce the audience to Buddhist philosophy. Given Seattle's proximity as the place in the continental United States closest to Asia, and its receptivity to alternative spirituality, it is a perfect place for revelation. Possessing vaguely ethnic features, Keanu Reeves is cast as Siddhartha—the man who will become Buddha. After traveling to Kathmandu, Nepal, the American boy experiences the story of Siddhartha's transcendence as he too is validated as a lama. The revelation comes full circle as the boy returns to Seattle with the ashes of the monk who first found him. In the film's finale, the monk's ashes are placed in a bowl and set afloat in the Seattle harbor; in this symbolic act, the Orient and America are (re)united in the most natural locale—the Pacific Northwest.

In the 2008 romantic comedy *Management*, a young man named Mike (Steve Zahn) pursues Sue (Jennifer Aniston) from Arizona to Maryland and then to Washington State. Here in the Pacific Northwest, Mike meets an Asian American man named Al (James Hiroyuki Liao) who offers him a job at his folks' Asian restaurant. In one scene, Al shares his insights about Asia with Mike: "China is not only going to kick America's economic butt, but it's going to invade your whole country. I'm talking about you guys getting like a whole new flag and whatnot." In a play on words, Al adds, "You need to re-orient the way you think about the Asians, Mike, because we will blow your minds with our uniqueness and [our] inner beauty." Mike evidently heeds Al's advice and attempts to become a Buddhist monk. His spiritual mentor, an older monk from Vietnam, teaches Mike something about accepting life when he reveals that even though American troops killed his parents during the Vietnam War, he moved to the United States to fulfill his destiny. Filmed in portions of Oregon, including Portland's Japanese Gardens, this film reinforces the proximity of Asia not only to the Pacific Northwest but also to the nation as a whole.

10

Full Circle
Imagining the Orient as the American West

> *"California's economy is increasingly tied to Asia. And China is a huge part of this trend."*
>
> Governor Arnold Schwarzenegger, "Selling California,"
> radio address, November 19, 2005

As historian David Wrobel recently noted, what we know as the West today was not really the West at all throughout much of the nineteenth century. Instead, it was widely perceived "as a global West, as one developing frontier, one colonial enterprise, among many around the globe."[1] In this conclusion I would like to portray the Orientalized American West as a fragment of the larger United States. Like portions of the earth's crust that are part of the American mainland but were once fragments of Europe, Africa, and Asia, this region has a complicated past that can be understood only by tracing material back to its original source areas. As human artifacts, those tectonically shifted cultural fragments are in some ways even more difficult to decipher than pieces of the earth's crust. They are both idiosyncratic—the result of individual perception—and collective in that they coalesce in a popularly constructed set of shared images. Moreover, to complicate things, these images change as soon as they become recognizable. The truth is, they are in a constant state of flux.

Even today, when the West seems so exceptionally American, why does Orientalism constitute such a strong undercurrent in the region's art, film, literature, and tourism? My search through hundreds of examples found in primary sources confirms Wrobel's findings that people originally viewed the American West as something other than the West we know today because that West hadn't yet been imagined into existence. Moreover, Orientalism is still a component in how the region is viewed today because we have not finished shaping that region through the creation of surrogate identities.

In this conclusion, however, I would like to explore something that is in itself both characteristically American and yet somewhat subversive—namely, that the Orientalization of the American West was not only one stage in the process by which a broader American identity was formed but also a stepping stone to our exporting that American West to far corners of the globe. By Orientalizing the West, we made it familiar to ourselves by making it the exotic, by giving it a recognizable though strange identity, and we could in turn now use this Orientalized West to spread our typically expansive American culture to similar parts of the world, namely the Near East and Far East, and make the exotic familiar. At first glance, this may seem paradoxical because the Orientalized West seems to take a backseat to twentieth-century visions of a West filled with cowboys and Indians, miners and pioneers, and the like. But upon closer examination, a subtly (and not so subtly) Orientalized West is a component in spreading a western American mystique worldwide. How this is occurring represents one of the most exciting subjects for scholar and citizen alike, that is, anyone interested in the American West and its worldwide influence.

First, though, consider Governor Schwarzenegger's quote above in historical context, that is, part of the United States' long tradition of engaging the Orient as an extension of American expansion. At first we looked directly east—that is, across the Atlantic Ocean—to accomplish this. In the 1780s and 1790s, the Barbary Wars along Africa's north coast in the late eighteenth century represented America's first encounter and conflict with Islam. These conflicts occurred when American sailors were taken for ransom, and they represented the United States' first foreign policy challenge. However, we also always looked westward toward the east. The earliest American national movement westward, which began at about the same time, involved the agenda of reaching Asia. In the June 1853 issue of *Knickerbocker Magazine*, an anonymous writer asked a geopolitical question that resonates today. "What part have we of America in the Orient?" Although the United States was not yet considered a serious player on the world stage at that time, the writer was sure that destiny would involve his country in the East. As that writer put it, "No power but the ALMIGHTY can prevent the Democratic element of America from making its impress upon the Orient."[2] That same year, American warships under the command of Admiral Perry steamed into Edo (now Tokyo) and—under the banner of "friendship" and "commerce"—demanded an audience with the Tokugawa Shogunate. This bold act effectively opened American commerce with the Orient, but the subtle threat of those modern, steam-powered vessels should not be overlooked. Truth be told, winning the

US-Mexican War in 1848 had emboldened the United States and made the world its oyster. The pearl, as it soon made clear, was the Orient itself. During the nation's centennial in 1876, John Greenleaf Whittier wrote a hymn to the process of a peaceful and profitable engagement, which includes the lines

> Thou, who has here in concord furled
> The war flags of a gathered world,
> Beneath our Western skies fulfill
> The Orient's mission of good will,
> And, freighted with love's Golden Fleece,
> Send back the Argonauts of peace.[3]

What historian William Goetzmann called "the irresistible western drive to the Far East" became, as he so eloquently put it, "part of the whole romantic urge to reach out to the remote corners of the globe; the belief that somewhere, over the horizon, beyond the ken of ordinary rational man, lay some sublime truth, and the possible meaning of human existence." These possibilities, as Goetzmann concluded, "became the vogue among romantics both in Europe and in America." In addition to numerous factors that contributed to a fascination with the East—including "tradition, history, fable, philosophy, Christianity, mystery and science," Goetzmann added yet another—"the economic motive." This made the attraction to the East, to introduce a relevant dichotomy, both "rational and irrational." It also ensured that the Orient would be a vital element in American westward expansion.[4] In a sense, effective American expansion into Asia depended in part on its well-established tradition of Orientalizing American soil itself. The Orient, after all, was subliminally part of the nation's own fabric now. In other words, the Orientalization of the western American frontier created and constituted a bridge, so to speak, that facilitated the nation's expansion into the Orient.

Orientalism is far more than solely aesthetic or cultural, then, but also had considerable potency as a subliminal force in geopolitics. This could work both culturally and politically and be manifested internally as well as internationally. As Islamic art historian Holly Edwards observes, in the mid-nineteenth century, American Orientalism was "a therapeutic response to changing circumstances rather than a static intellectual stance on a monolithic phenomenon."[5] The word "therapeutic" suggests that Orientalism was a fix or solution to conditions or maladies—rapid urbanization, social instability, increasing commercialism, and the like—and that certainly had some validity. It was Orientalism, after all, that could offer escape from the complications and uncertainties, as well as from the boredom and malaise, of everyday life.

However, Orientalism could do much more. As Edwards further observed, Orientalism also provided "images of universality when regional or sectional differences were divisive and painful," adding that "the Orient may have served to focus public attention on larger horizons and more inclusive 'truths.'"[6] Whether or not regional tensions were a factor in American Orientalism's increasing popularity at this time may be debated, but an important spatial and temporal aspect is quite significant: this vigorous Orientalism flowered at exactly the time that the western American frontier was being explored and colonized—that is spread, and not only in the American West but also to Asia.

It is widely recognized that Orientalism played a strong role in European expansion into both the Near East and Far East, but the degree to which the tropes of the *American* frontier were involved in this process is virtually unknown. Consider, though, the case of early nineteenth century Russian career foreign service officer Aleksandr Griboedov, who assisted Russian colonial expansion into Persia in the 1820s. According to Russian literature scholar Angela Brintlinger, the ambitious Griboedov was both a Russian Orientalist and would-be literary hero who called upon America's growing frontier literature to assist that expansion. Brintlinger notes that James Fenimore Cooper's evocative works about civilization moving into wild, open frontiers served as a yardstick for Griboedov's literary imagination and geographical ambition. Griboedov, however, was not only an incurable romantic, but egomaniacal in his belief that his life of adventure eclipsed all others, even the characters that Cooper employed to push the American frontier westward. As Griboedov immodestly put it in 1828, when he helped Russia expand its frontier southeastward in steppe and desert, "forget your Trapper and Cooper's *Prairie*, my living novel is right before your eyes and a hundred times more interesting." Griboedov's living novel, as he called it, was both intoxicating and exhilarating. Unlike a regular novel, it would not be published but rather lived. In this living novel, Griboedov fantasized that "something new happens to me which I never considered, never guessed might occur." This sentiment was not only romantic but also prophetic. After Russia defeated Persia, and its diplomatic delegation arrived in Teheran, resentment mounted as something Griboedov never guessed would occur was about to: on January 30, 1829, with little or no warning, an angry mob whipped into a frenzy by a firebrand mullah tore the entire unarmed Russian delegation, including Griboedov, to pieces in the street.[7]

The United States offered Josiah Harlan (1799–1871) as a counterpart to the Russian diplomat who would have been feted for his part in expanding the frontier into Southwestern Asia, had a cruel Persian fate not intervened.

Harlan traveled to the Orient in 1820 after being exposed to adventure stories as a youth in Pennsylvania. As a young man who did, indeed, go East, ex-pat Harlan hired on as a surgeon in the British East India Company, and found himself face to face with the real Orient. Like his American homeland, Harlan was imaginative and ambitious—an adventurer in the nineteenth century tradition. By the 1830s, the restless Harlan found himself involved in political intrigue in the desert-mountain empire of Afghanistan. Impressed by the potential to create something of an empire for himself, Harlan took up arms in raging battles for control there. In 1838, Harlan became the Prince of Ghor, a landlocked mountain province in central Afghanistan. His combination of romanticism and intelligence was infectious, and his exploits intrigued Americans back home. In fact, it was Harlan who reportedly lobbied Jefferson Davis to import Afghan camels to the American Southwest as a way of helping the U.S. take control over that similarly arid portion of the West. Above all, it was Harlan's political exploits that riveted Americans' attention, providing a glimpse of his nation's future role in Oriental exploits. Although Harlan escaped the gruesome fate that awaited Griboedov, he was ultimately unable to maintain his grasp on central Afghanistan. Disillusioned, Harlan returned to the United States. In 1871, he died in what soon became the undisputed center of American Orientalism—San Francisco. Harlan himself was all but forgotten, though his role was immortalized in Rudyard Kipling's 1888 short story *The Man Who Would be King*—a tale of colonial ambition gone awry that was made into a feature-length film of the same name by John Huston in 1975. It was not until the search for Osama bin Laden in the post 9/11 War on Terror that Harlan's story was rediscovered and told anew by journalist-writer Ben Macintyre in his 2004 book, *The Man Who Would Be King: The First American in Afghanistan.*

In turning east rather than west, Harlan proved that the adventurous, entrepreneurial westering spirit of Jacksonian America could be applied to the Orient as well as the American West. As Griboedov further demonstrated, American depictions of the frontier could serve as inspiration for those hoping to colonize other frontiers, namely the Orient. That was true in the nineteenth century, but does Orientalism today play any role in international affairs? More specifically, what lessons can an Orientalized American West offer about the way American culture diffuses to the real Orient? A closer look at popular culture here suggests that by Orientalizing its own frontier, the United States found Americanizing Oriental frontiers easier. This, of course, is the flip side of a well-worn coin. I am not the first to suggest that the American western experience would ultimately be part of the United States' expansion as a world power. In fact, that premise was central to Frederick Jackson Turner's 1893 paper "The Significance of the Frontier in American History" presented in Chicago at, as historian John White has astutely pointed out, the exact same time as Chicago's Columbian Exposition. In building on such visionary, if controversial, ideas, I shall now show that an Orientalized West is part of the complex process by which American values find a more or less natural stage abroad, namely in the Middle East and Asia. I hasten to add that although Americans may find this natural, peoples of the Orient may have differing views on the subject.

Although it is now widely agreed that the United States' rise as a world power and the rise of the American Western as an art form were not coincidental—after all, both happened at about the same time and ostensibly involved good triumphing over long-entrenched evils such as despotism—I here seek to explore how the American Western is used in American encounters with the Orient and its peoples. I am referring to something different here than the more or less natural tendency for an American in the Middle East in the nineteenth century to compare people there to the Santa Fe traders or Indians he knew in the West. I have in mind something far more significant, some might say troubling, and that is the more recent tendency to transform the real Orient itself into the American West in popular culture.

Even though the vision of the Far East as an extension of western frontier expansionism dates back at least two centuries, it could only become a real possibility given developments in the Second World War. The vision is beautifully portrayed in a 1945 advertisement for Shell Oil Company (fig. 10-1). Using the metaphor of Pony Express relays, the *U.S. News and World Report* advertisement's map features a horse and rider galloping toward the Chinese mainland, hell-bent-for-leather. This metaphor is both symbolic and pragmatic in that Shell here touted the importance of its motor oils to the aircraft flying supply routes during the Second World War; these supplies would help keep China free of the menace posed by Japan. This ingenious advertisement rests on that familiar western icon of horse and rider, contrasted with the exotic and traditional people of the Orient. In this advertisement, though, China is part of the Western frontier of democracy. The message here is unity with the Chinese in the effort to stop another Asian power, the sinister Japanese.[8]

This advertisement was no mere eccentric vision but rather reflected an increasingly attractive prospect after the War. In 1946, for example, Northwest Airlines ran a provocative ad in *Time* magazine promoting its soon-to-be-initiated air service to Tokyo, Shanghai, and Manila. These venerable cities were recently brought back into the travelers' reach following the War, and

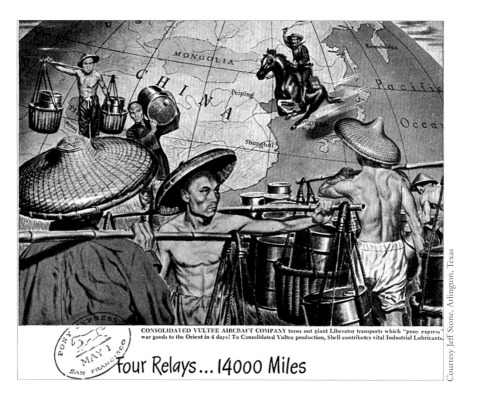

Fig. 10-1. A 1945 Shell Oil Company advertisement in *U. S. News & World Report* uses the frontier metaphor of the Pony Express relay to "westernize" the Orient.

they had tremendous economic and cultural appeal. While touting its modern "4-engine, 44-passenger luxury service," the airline also reminded prospective travelers that this amounted to "fulfilling America's historic dream of a short-cut to the Orient . . . [the] *Northwest Passage*!"[9] In emphasizing the historic dream, the airline juxtaposed two earlier methods of travel—an old sailing vessel of the type that would have been used by European powers searching for the fabled passage in the 1700s, and a covered wagon from America's west-ward-moving frontier. These contrasted with the then-modern four-engine, propeller-driven Stratocruiser airliner, but the message was explicit. Northwest Airlines was helping a westward-looking America fulfill an early dream, to reach—and ultimately have an impact on—the Orient. Another 1946 adver-tisement by Northwest Airlines uses only the prairie schooner juxtaposed with the modern four-engine aircraft to confirm the validity of a long-held dream: "You were right, Pioneers . . ." the ad claims, the route connection from the United States to Asia via the "NORTHWEST PASSAGE" is indeed a "short cut to opportunity!" (fig. 10-2).

Fig. 10-2. In 1946, Northwest Airlines used this advertisement in *Time* magazine to resurrect the fabled "Northwest Passage" as a way of linking West and East in modern times.

The railroads also participated in this westernization of the Orient, although their power would rapidly diminish as rail passenger ridership dropped off and trucks siphoned off considerable freight traffic in the 1950s. In 1946, though, the Great Northern Railway was still optimistic. It ran a revealing advertisement in *Newsweek* magazine touting its connections to the Far East (fig. 10-3). This ad featured a map of the Northwest with the Great Northern's bright red lines extending off that map toward Asia, where a drawing of a Chinese man dressed in a western suit was positioned to signify China. Noting that the Great Northern Railway was now "an 'old hand' in Pacific trade," the advertisement bore the familiar "Rocky" mountain goat

Fig. 10-3. In a 1946 advertisement that appeared in *Newsweek* magazine, the Great Northern Railway used a map of its system as the "Open Door to Modern China."

followed by the words "the 'open door' to MODERN CHINA." Significantly, the latter was written in the "Chinese style" letters so commonly seen on everything Chinese American, from fireworks packages to menus. The purpose of the advertisement was to announce that "something big and important is happening in China . . . the awakening of new ideas of China's 450 million people." That idealism lasted only long enough to be shattered by the rise of Chinese Communism in the late 1940s, but it revealed more than a century of interest in stimulating China's millions into "real"—which is to say Western—development.

In 1959, Hawaii and Alaska became states, in effect finishing the United States' geopolitical growth westward toward the Orient. Alaska had its own Oriental mystique, for it shared a border with (and was once a part of) Orientalism-inspired Russia. Hawaii—recognized as an East-West crossroads since the nineteenth century—was home to native peoples of East Asian and South Pacific origin and thus was literally the Orient in the popular mind. Although the annexation of these two territories can be seen as a fulfillment of an American Orientalist impulse, the geopolitics of the Cold War was also a factor. As the 1960s would prove, America did indeed have an "impress" to make on Asia. It would come in the form of covert and overt military action, and also through the kinder and gentler vehicle of cultural exchange, including the arts, literature, and popular culture.

In a sense, the Western novel and Western films provided an irresistible vehicle for the transmission of American popular culture to the Orient, all the more so because they embodied some inherently Asian elements in their storylines. However, although some of these stories were themselves Asian in origin, they represented the American West and the American spirit to audiences worldwide. *The Magnificent Seven*'s origins in Akira Kurosawa's Japanese film *The Seven Samurai* (1954) were palpable when the American film appropriated the Japanese one in 1960. Shortly thereafter, Kurosawa's epic standoff drama *Yoshimbo* (1961) was appropriated by Sergio Leone as a *Fistful of Dollars*, which was released in Italy in 1964 and the United States in 1967. This may seem to suggest that the West was the sole appropriator, but it should be understood that Kurosawa himself grew up watching, and fell under the spell of, American Westerns such as those featuring William Hart.[10] In other words, a genre as powerful and well-articulated as the American Western could not be limited to American soil. The first step in the diffusion of the Western to the Orient witnessed its arrival in Asia as more or less a curiosity in the 1920s and 1930s, but in the hands of Asians themselves it would ultimately become a new breed of Westerns set on Asian soil.

The recent popular Chinese film *Crouching Tiger, Hidden Dragon* (2000) is nominally a *wuxia* story featuring a hero who operates using a code of chivalry and fighting oppression as he protects powerless people. That alone subliminally links *Crouching Tiger* to the American Western, but the film also uses cinematic techniques such as camera movement, plot devices, and character development from the American Western movie genre to make this a Western-style fantasy film. With its desert bandits and heroic action, *Crouching Tiger* pays homage to the American Western. There is something universal about a lone hero meeting challenges in distant locales, his strict moral codes evident despite the fact that he operates in areas where laws are not (yet) established. *Crouching Tiger*, which represents the fusion of not only styles but also production, as it was a partnership between Chinese and American producers, became a surprise international success.[11] Interestingly, as a reminder of the genre's versatility, its director, Wang Lee, later produced the revisionist Western *Brokeback Mountain* (2005).

Taking yet another cue from the American Western, Chinese filmmakers are now casting that country's own desert interior as a parallel to the American West. The most noteworthy of the recent Chinese Westerns is the stunning *Warriors of Heaven and Earth* (2003). The plot is nominally Asian enough—a warrior is sent to the Gobi Desert by the emperor to apprehend a lawbreaker and along the way has many encounters with local tribes and bandits. However, the picaresque story is developed and filmed much like an American Western. The warrior Lai Xi is an outsider (Japanese) of few words and impressive stature. Like Palladin in the edgy 1960s-era television Western *Have Gun, Will Travel*, he wears black and possesses a stoic honor and integrity in any assignment. Lai Xi's journey westward takes him to Frontier Pass, beyond which military outposts (forts) become scarce and the law virtually nonexistent. On his journey, Lai Xi experiences mystical events and encounters a tribe of troublesome Turks, the latter reminiscent of recalcitrant Indians and a reminder that all cultures have their "others." Significantly, the rebellious folk on the frontier are Muslims, and they have a modern counterpart that fights to retain its own lifestyle amid globalizing trends that have made modern China an economic superpower. China's recent confrontation with the Uighurs represents that nation's bid for complete control on what may be seen as its own western frontier, albeit in modern times. In any event, *Warriors of Heaven and Earth* resonates as an American Western in that Lai Xi makes short work of several would-be assassins at the gates of a livestock enclosure, his swift swordsmanship bringing to mind film versions of the gunfight at the OK Corral in Tombstone, Arizona.

Scenery is a contributing factor in *Warriors of Heaven and Earth*. The superb cinematography by Zhao Fei captures the stark beauty of the Gobi Desert, just as John Ford's classic *Stagecoach* (1939) helped put Monument Valley on the map. But Fei's brilliant use of color cinematography recalls the best of more recent American Westerns (for example, *The Professionals* and *Dances with Wolves*). In Fei's desert landscape, indigenous people and outsiders interact and spar in scenes of incredible natural beauty—mesas, sand dunes, bluffs, and mountain ranges—all the staples of "western" scenery that the Chinese now film with aplomb in places like the once remote Tulufan region in Xinjiang Province. In the English-dubbed version of *Warriors and Heaven and Earth*, one canyon is called "Red Rock Gorge." At the end of *Warriors of Heaven and Earth*, when Chinese warrior Li asks Lai Xi where he is from, he simply replies, "Japan." When Li asks, "Where is that?" Lai Xi replies, "To the East"—a reminder that there are many Easts.

Speaking of Japan, it too has recently experimented with the American Western, as is evident in the 2008 Japanese film *Sukiaki Western Django*. Even the title of this film suggests fusion, for *Sukiaki* refers to a Japanese dish, while *Django* derives from Sergio Carbucci's spaghetti Western of the same name. The *Western* in the title, of course, leaves no doubt as to the ultimate source of inspiration. *Sukiaki Western Django* is set in the period of Japanese history when brutal clans dominated the countryside and the samurai rose to take control. Although a Japanese production with an almost entirely Japanese cast, *Sukiaki Western Django* takes place in a fictional locale that is simultaneously Western and Oriental—that is, American and Asian. The two rival clans have a showdown in the nominally western town of Yuta, Nevada, where mayhem breaks loose as old scores are settled. Symbolically, these clans are called the "reds" and the "whites"—a use of color that has roots in Japanese culture but also resonates in the American Western as a battle between European Americans and Indians. The main figure in *Sukiaki Western Django* is a nameless gunfighter who arrives in time to assist a prostitute in getting justice—a familiar formula in American Westerns, including Clint Eastwood's *Unforgiven* (1990), which breathed new life into the American Western and impressed filmmakers worldwide. *Sukiaki Western Django*'s only American character is Quentin Tarantino, who plays Ringo; his presence here is appropriate given Tarantino's reputation as the purveyor of hip, cool violence in American film. Otherwise, the Japanese characters act out not only an epic period in their own country's history but also a drama that is unmistakably western American in form and style. A particularly noteworthy scene in this film features a painted backdrop landscape complete with a yellow, disklike setting sun and a towering, black, volcanic mountain. This backdrop abstracts both Western and Eastern landscape elements to underscore the similarities between the two imagined places. Similarly, the wildly mixed architectural sets combining ancient Japanese structures and western false front buildings are mind-boggling. *Sukiyaki Western Django* is both a tribute to the American Western and a metaphor for how seamlessly it can travel back to one of its sources of inspiration, namely, the Far East during its lawless "frontier" period. Looked at in a broader context though, this film reminds one how dominant the West (both the United States and its art form, the Western) is in modern-day Japan.

To a lesser extent, other Asian countries, for example Thailand, are also producing Westerns, even though they may be set in modern times and locales far removed from the American West. In *The Protector* (2006), a Thai police chief is called upon to travel to Australia to free two very different kinds of victims—endangered animals captured by smugglers, and a beautiful Thai girl who has been "forced into modern-day slavery"—which is to say prostitution.[12] In his brashness and certitude, though, the police chief as protector is a characteristically western hero in that he embodies attitudes about good vs. evil, retribution and justice, and the like. Significantly, he operates by his own rules rather than relying on established legal conventions. The 2008 Korean film *The Good, The Bad, The Weird*, is even more explicitly western. Although the time period is the 1940s and the locale is Manchuria, the entire film, from premise to plot, pays homage to Sergio Leone's classic spaghetti Western *The Good, The Bad, and The Ugly*. Like its predecessor, this film directed by Ji-woon Kim centers on three outlaws searching for a lost treasure, in this case what they believe to be an ancient Chinese treasure. Shot in the deserts of China, which double for the barren American West, *The Good, The Bad, The Weird* features plenty of masterful gunplay, spectacular hell-bent-for-leather horsemanship, and gritty, conflicted characters, one of whom dresses like a cowboy right out of the American Wild West. In stunning action sequences that modern moviegoers demand, the film's main characters are pursued across the sweeping deserts by the Japanese army, Korean freedom fighters, and a Manchurian crime syndicate. Although making such a patently Western-style film involved a risk—it was, after all, ground that others had traversed in both serious and comical films—*The Good, The Bad, The Weird* became an overnight sensation in Asia, riding high in the number one position at the Korean box office for several months. In 2010, it was imported to the United States, appearing in theaters before being released on DVD. The latter contains an interview with Kim, who calls his film an "Oriental Western"—a reminder of the enduring international appeal of this characteristically American genre.

The theme of the East as West also plays out in another part of the Orient in modern times, namely the Middle East, but its purveyors are American, not Middle Eastern. For example, the 2004 film *Hidalgo*, based very loosely on the real story of Frank Hopkins, an American westerner who is part Native American and an excellent horseman, brings the American West into the heart of Arabia. In this Western played out in the early twentieth-century Middle East, Frank, played by Viggo Mortensen, plans to enter his stallion, Hidalgo, in the premier horse race that traverses the Arabian Peninsula. As an American, Frank finds himself up against not only the physical obstacles posed by the Arabian environment—including sweltering heat and a ferocious sandstorm—but also cultural obstacles, including dishonest and sinister Arabs who attempt to scuttle his plans for victory. Frank, though, prevails—and why not? He is a genuine westerner who can ultimately show the Arabs a thing or two about not only good horsemanship but also heroism and fair play. In the process, he also gets the girl. The film *Hidalgo* presents some Arabs as duplicitous, which is part of Hollywood's long tradition of creating what Jack Sheehan sarcastically called "Reel Bad Arabs."[13]

Some critics of the war in Iraq saw *Hidalgo* as the parable of a "Cowboy President" (George W. Bush) attempting to reform the Arab world through seemingly chivalrous deeds much like a hero in a Western movie. After all, shortly after September 11, 2001, Bush stated that Osama bin Laden was "wanted dead or alive," and even made a reference to the "old wanted posters," as he announced the United States' search for this mastermind of the attacks. Six years later, with al-Qaeda inflicting its particularly savage brand of warfare on civilians in portions of Afghanistan, Pakistan, and Iraq, a weary (and perhaps wiser) President Bush still used the analogy, only he now qualified it. "This is wild country," Bush observed of the Middle East, but he now added the sobering and humbling confession, "This is wilder than the Wild West."[14] Actually, it has been this wild for quite some time, as Eric Margolis aptly observed before the United States went after the Taliban. As Margolis put it, the area along the Afghanistan-Pakistan border "was a combination of Dodge City and the Arabian Nights."[15] Bush sought to emulate President Ronald Reagan, who also owned a ranch, dressed like a cowboy from time to time, and did not hesitate to use military action when it seemed the right thing to do. Reagan had famously used the term "Evil Empire" to refer to the Soviet Union, which stretched across a large portion of the East. Taking a cue, perhaps, Bush later used the term "Axis of Evil" to refer to Libya, Iran, and North Korea, which likewise are troublesome spots scattered across much of the Arab world and Asia. Critics of President Bush saw him as unable to conceptualize the post-9/11 world in terms other than simple, Orientalist-inspired distinctions like Christian vs. Muslim or good vs. evil. Nevertheless, those who viewed the peoples of Afghanistan or Iraq as unable to become Western enough to support democracy also used an enduring Orientalist prejudice built on the stereotype of unchanging and unchangeable Easterners.

Disenchantment with such aggressive policies motivated reviewers of Oliver Stone's film *Alexander* to see parallels between the monomaniacal Alexander the Great and President Bush.[16] Both envisioned expanding Western civilization into an East that proved reluctant to accept it. It is very tempting—but likely too easy (and perhaps even still too early)—to claim that Bush-era policy in the Arab/Muslim world was simply a reenactment of Western/European expansion, whether by Alexander or the Crusaders. It might just as easily be regarded as a result of an American exceptionalism based in large part on the nation's perceptions of ever-expanding frontiers (the West, outer space, the hearts and minds of mankind).[17] Certainly, there are enough tempting similarities to make Orientalists of all political persuasions speculate about the global consequences of such a western/frontier American *mentalité*.

Popular film can, and has, influenced American foreign policy in Asia and may also have done so in the Middle East.[18] The antiwar movie *Three Kings* (1999) is a case in point. It follows the exploits of three American soldiers who go rogue and plunder treasure in Iraq during the Persian Gulf War in 1991. Influenced by Orientalist fantasy stories such as *The Man Who Would be King* and spaghetti Westerns such as *The Good, the Bad, and the Ugly*, its would-be kings run roughshod over a desert frontier. *The Three Kings* castigates the United States for its failure to support anti-Saddam forces who were crushed by Saddam Hussein's Baathist regime, as the insurgency was initially encouraged and then betrayed by the first Bush administration. This betrayal was still palpable when neocons in the Bush administration formulated Middle Eastern policy as the War on Terrorism heated up in 2001–2002. The logical conclusion? To set things right, the United States should again intervene or face eternal condemnation. Ironically, by intervening, the United States would soon face that same fate, as much of the world opposed the US invasion of Iraq.

Although 2008 marked a change in power in Washington with the election of antiwar President Barack Obama, things did not change as quickly as some predicted or hoped. In accepting the Nobel Peace Prize in December of 2009, Obama stood tall at the podium and delivered a sobering message to the committee and to the world, namely, that violence can be justified when reason fails and the cause is just. While downplaying military excess and abuse, Obama nevertheless called on American exceptionalism based in part on American expansionism. He noted that it is America's responsibility to not only defeat al-Qaeda, but also to foster prosperity and democracy worldwide, a point upon which his western-inspired Republican predecessor(s) likely agreed. Obama observed that Americans protect noncombatants rather than slaughtering them as do terrorists and, one might add, as did bad guys bent on terrorizing the frontier American West in popular film.

Obama finally brought frontier justice to bin Laden in 2011. The U.S. military's code word for this top-secret operation in Pakistan—and for bin Laden himself—was "Geronimo." Although some Native Americans quickly deplored that comparison between an Apache chief and an Arab terrorist, it was certainly understandable given bin Laden's Geronimo-like ability to elude the US military for so long in an arid part of the Muslim world that had long been equated with the frontier American West. That such a comparison could be made by the normally politically savvy Obama administration serves as a reminder that American Orientalism is remarkably persistent and easily exported overseas to the real Orient.

How the Old West plays out in films about the Arab/Muslim world speaks volumes about America's (and Americans') desire to set things straight using Western-style characters and impulsive action. In the movie *Sahara* (2005), underwater archaeologist (and Texan) Clive Cussler tells a fanciful story of a team scouring Muslim West Africa for the wreckage of a Confederate ironclad steamship, the *Texas*. This ship was reportedly lost on a clandestine voyage at the end of the American Civil War, and the intrepid archaeologists search the now bone-dry desert interior of Mali for it. These archaeologists are, in effect, modern-day versions of hardworking cowboys and good gunslingers—honest, impulsive, and brave men of action. Under the direction of swashbuckling archaeologist Matthew McConaughey, the Americans begin searching for the vessel—that is, reclaiming a piece of American history. By coincidence, they meet up with a fetching European woman, a doctor who works for the World Health Organization and is investigating an outbreak afflicting the locals in the southern Sahara. The movie features a mysterious, sinister Tuareg and a few other stereotypical characters but otherwise treats Arabs (and Africans) with respect. The real villains in *Sahara*, in fact, are US government bureaucrats who turn a blind eye to the problem. As free agents with a conscience, though, the Texan-led team comes to the rescue by not only solving a pollution problem but also finding the *Texas*, and considerable treasure, under the desert sands. Again, this plot suggests that Americans can right wrongs in the Arab world and in the process unearth those treasures that inevitably await the enterprising and ingenious people brave enough to pull it off. In popular culture, the American archaeologist is often a crusader-cowboy who encounters corruption and sets things right, usually single-handedly, and often woos (and wins) an attractive woman in the process.[19] In a sense, then, *Sahara* leads us to rethink the notion of an "American Sahara," one that now exports the American frontier into that legendary Old World desert rather than the other way around.

But the Muslim world of the Middle East and North Africa has proven especially tough to influence positively about western American values—much tougher than Asia. This may reflect a simmering resentment that the United States has helped rob the Arab world of its own history as manifested in the growing Pan-Arab/Muslim fundamentalism that would ban all "infidels," especially Christians, from business ventures in Arabia and its environs. Bitter memories of the Crusades are often cited, but this mistrust is in effect a more recent phenomenon exacerbated by American support for Israel during and after the humiliating Arab-Israeli War of 1967. It should be remembered that Cecil B. DeMille's film *King Richard and the Crusaders* received a warm reception in Egypt in the mid-1950s.[20] The point worth noting here is that films produced in the Middle East in recent times are so universally pro-Arab and often anti-American that the likelihood of a western American theme being embraced is remote. Instead, Americans must content themselves with historically themed films such as *Hidalgo* and *Sahara*, and modern-era action films such as *Body of Lies* (2008), in which a cowboylike CIA agent risks all to stop al-Qaeda, bring peace and prosperity to the region, and woo a beautiful local Muslim woman in the process.

Visions of an American West continue to influence what Americans experience as they travel in the Middle East and Asia. In writing about Mongolia's Gun-Galuut Nature Reserve, for example, environmentalist Heidi Landecker noted that "the landscape, wild and treeless, is very like the American West; the theme music from *Bonanza* keeps playing unbidden in my head." *Bonanza*, which ran for fourteen years as a television series and lives eternally as reruns into the twenty-first century, epitomized the serialized television Western. Further drawing the comparison between West and East, Landecker observed that "Mongolia, twice the size of Texas, has [only] 2.8 million people, more than two thirds of them nomads."[21] This topic—the westernizing (by which I mean the western Americanization) of the real East itself—remains one of the most fertile frontiers of scholarship on American Orientalism. One of the more vivid references to finding the American West in arid interior Asia is found in Nicole Mones's 1998 bestseller *Lost in Translation*, when peripatetic protagonist Alice Mannegan encounters Erem Obo, a Mongolian "desert town frozen in time" and imagines it to be "another Tonopah, Nevada." For Alice, "just the sight now of these low sand-colored buildings, this contained little grid backed right up to a tributary range of brown desert mountains and the blazing blue sky, brought back memories" of the similarly situated former mining town in Nevada that made such an impression on her during her youthful travels through the West.[22]

This vision of Asia as somehow akin to the American West is worth further exploration. It persists as an element of Asia's modern development, which, although it may not mention the Western by name, certainly alludes to the western spirit of economic, colonial-inspired expansion. In describing his first trip to China, American architect Michael Sorkin first quoted Benjamin Disraeli ("The East is a Career"), then became even more candid about the opportunities there. "China" as Sorkin put it, "has become American architecture's wet dream." Sorkin went on to say that China "evoked in me a colonial fantasy that was surely of a piece with the acquisitive incursions of centuries." Realizing that China had succumbed to westernization, or rather Americanization, Sorkin concluded: "China is building U.S.-style McCities that put L.A. or Phoenix to shame."[23] In other words, not only has the East seduced Americans with the possibility of becoming rich there (a common theme of Orientalism), but we have now seduced the East itself, or at least

Author's collection, courtesy *The Economist*

Fig. 10-4. As a metaphor for the changing balance of power between the United States and China, a February 2010 cartoon in *The Economist* shows President Obama as a cowboy sheriff about to meet the wrath of a kickboxing Chinese warrior.

parts of the East, into becoming more like America. Sorkin's mentioning Phoenix and Los Angeles is on target, for these are quintessential western cities whose identities embody considerable Orientalization. Then, too, Sorkin's use of the term "wet dream" is especially apt here, as such dreams are likely to be associated with *adolescence or youth* and involve *subconscious fantasizing* (most often by young men) about *sexual or sensual pleasure*—three ingredients associated with Orientalism itself. That the Chinese government may not always see eye to eye with such enthusiastic American ambition was made abundantly clear in the February 6–12, 2010, issue of *The Economist*, which featured a cartoon depicting President Obama dressed as a cowboy sheriff about to be assaulted by a traditionally clad Chinese martial artist (fig. 10-4). In this symbol-rich cartoon, Obama wears a Stetson hat decorated with an American flag, while the Chinese warrior wears a red headband bearing the Chinese Communist government's signature star. Mesas and saguaro cacti form the backdrop for Obama, and the Great Wall lies behind the Chinese warrior—icons of West and East, respectively. Tellingly, Obama is leaning backward, away from the warrior, who is flying toward the president in an aggressive kickboxing move that is likely to upset the balance of power. As *The Economist* article makes clear, the traditional relationship between China and the United States has now changed, and Americans are no longer able to call all the shots, so to speak.

In his commentaries about the United States and China, Sorkin astutely notes how closely landscape symbolizes culture. Throughout this book I have referred to features in the landscape, such as topography and vegetation, which become symbols that facilitate comparisons between America and the Orient. As noted earlier, plants such as sagebrush, date palms, and alfalfa readily serve as metaphors for people(s) because they are easily anthropomorphized. Like people, they prefer certain habitats, have identifiable visual characteristics, and suggest places of origin. If one plant in particular has become a symbol for the restlessness of the western American frontier, it is tumbleweed (*Salsola kali*). At first glance, what could be more western American than this plant, which becomes a dust-colored, ball-shaped bush that blows along in the wind as its seeds begin to ripen? However, its less familiar name—Russian thistle—reveals its real source of origin. Native to the steppes of southwestern Asia, the tumbleweed is one of the characteristic invaders that accidentally found its way here in the nineteenth century. Significantly, this foreigner adjusted so well that it appears native. In other words, the tumbleweed is really as western American as Genghis Khan.

The tenacious, ever-mobile tumbleweed took center stage in a recent opinion article expressing disenchantment with Bush-era US foreign policy. Its author, a university student originally from the desert lands of eastern Oregon, urged Americans to "rethink" their popular affection for this "weed of the West." Upon returning home from a trip abroad, she now found the tumbleweed to be an "indescribably ugly" plant that could serve as a "double-sided" metaphor for American expansion and insensitivity worldwide. As she critically observed, "I often wonder if we [Americans] move as freely through the world as the tumbleweed does across an open landscape, spreading the seeds of our culture and government in our path." Because the United States is often considered to spread its own values "with little regard for the culture, the people, or the way of life that was there before us," she then asked: "Is it going too far to say that much of the world, in this present era, thinks of us as a noxious weed?"[24]

That, of course, is a far different sentiment than that expressed in the romantic ballad "Tumbling Tumbleweeds" from the 1936 Gene Autry movie of the same name. In that movie and song, the tumbleweed symbolized something noble, a wanderer who moves through the land in search of something. The tumbleweed personified the American cowboy, who has an overall attachment to the concept of the land, but never any one particular place. That sentiment used to be laudable but is now increasingly suspect in an age that questions mobility in favor of localism and sees globalization as unsustainable.

Still, though, American Orientalism is not a one-way street in that it can play a valuable role in cultural exchange and cooperation. Again, the landscape offers symbols upon which to build. In 2010, for example, the National Park Service launched a new initiative—*The Mount Rainier-Mount Fuji Sister Mountain Curriculum*. This project, which "builds on the long history of connections between Mount Rainier and Mount Fuji," not only created a curriculum but also involved a partnership between American and Japanese teachers and their students. As the Park Service website put it, this project uses "Mount Fuji and Mount Rainier as a lens to learn about the history, culture, geography and environmental uses of each others' countries."[25] That creative use of surrogate landscapes for yet another purpose, namely cultural understanding, is a reminder of western American Orientalism's versatility. It also leads one to conclude that a phenomenon this versatile, deep seated, and potent is likely to play a role in future relationships between the United States and the real Orient.

Notes

Introduction

1. Karlinsky, *California Dreaming.*
2. Barrett, "Servants of the Map," 1–43.
3. Doughty, *At Home in Texas*, 4.
4. Grammer, "'April in Andalusia,'" 222–33.
5. Twain, *The Innocents Abroad.*
6. Walker, *Irreverent Pilgrims*, 174–75, 180.
7. Pomeroy, *In Search of the Golden West*, 30–34.
8. Harris, *The Artist in American Society*, 158–60.
9. Borges, *Seven Nights*, 48, 51.
10. Weiss, *Translating Orients*, 22.
11. For a more complete discussion of this, see Francaviglia, "Crusaders and Saracens."
12. Note that the first definition seems objective despite the fact that identifying these traits (etc.) and the people who exhibit them involves considerable subjectivity. The second definition also seems objective, but the decision to use something from another culture again involves subjectivity, as choices have to be made as to what is studied and how it is used. The third definition—imitation or assimilation of that which is Oriental—is clearly subjective.
13. MacKenzie, *Orientalism: History, Theory, and the Arts.*
14. Liebersohn, *Aristocratic Encounters*, 8–9.
15. Wrobel, "Global West, American Frontier," and "Exceptionalism and Globalism."
16. Said, *Orientalism.*
17. Adopting Said's use of limited sources while opposing his conclusions, some Orientalist scholars restrict the definition of Orientalism to the serious academic scholarship about the East (and Easterners) and thereby disregard any popular interest in the Orient. This is regrettable. Using this type of restricted definition led British Orientalist Robert Irwin to entirely dismiss American Orientalism: as he put it categorically, "There is little to say about American Orientalism in the nineteenth or early twentieth centuries." Irwin believed this because, in his opinion, America offered little substantive study of the Orient at this time. Irwin urged that "the American Oriental Society, founded in 1842," be disregarded because it "was at first an association for interested amateurs." Irwin, *The Lust of Knowing*, 213–14. Only in the later twentieth century could Irwin grudgingly admit an American scholar into the ranks of the Orientalists. Irwin misses the point. Simply because scholars have not studied something does not mean it is not significant. My point here is that there is indeed much to say about how Orientalism has functioned in the United States from the late eighteenth century into the early twenty-first century. Moreover, I shall show that amateurs as well as professionals were involved in making Orientalism an important factor in American life for at least two centuries. My point here is not to establish boundaries but rather to suggest that we have much to gain by considering how those American "amateurs" reacted to the East. By being more inclusive than Edward Said or Robert Irwin, my definition of Orientalism includes voices that are less often, and less seriously, considered.
18. MacKenzie, *Orientalism.*

19. Orientalism thus reflects the dualism embedded in our own "western" culture. The binary thought system—light vs. dark, good vs. evil, saved vs. damned—that underlies much Western thinking, has roots in the Judeo-Christian tradition that originated in the Orient. Christianity (and, for that matter, Judaism and Islam) are inheritors of this tradition. Orientalism, it can be argued, reveals the Orient to be the ultimate source of the Western world's most basic cultural values and beliefs.

20. See Leal, *Wilderness in the Bible.*

21. Lears, *No Place of Grace,* 142–43, 168, and 225–41.22. Henry Nash Smith, *Virgin Land.*

23. Henry Nash Smith, *Virgin Land*, 15–22.

24. Hernán Cortés (as quoted in Watkins, *Gold and Silver in the West.*)

25. Grabar, "Roots and Others," 3–9.

26. See Francaviglia, *Believing in Place.*

27. The late Edward Said might have considered the Orientalization of the American West's landscapes by writers, artists, and others as one more appropriative and racist act. However, as *The Cambridge Companion to Travel Writing* makes clear, "over recent years students of British travel writing have contested the Saidian paradigm and modified it considerably." These scholars include Ali Behdad, Charles Issawi, Billie Melman, and Lisa Lowe—all of whom "have pointed out that travelers' representations were not homogenous but were inflected by gender, class, and nationality." A growing number of scholars also believe not only that Orientalism changes (that is, has changed) over time but that simple binary interpretations (for example, good vs. bad) of the East do not hold up under closer scrutiny. Melman, "The Middle East/Arabia," 105–21.

28. Orientalism in the United States certainly deserves greater study by historians and historical geographers. The Orient's grip on the West, including the United States, is very powerful and quite enduring. In fact, no understanding of American culture is complete without factoring in the Orientalist impulse.

29. Adair, *The History of the American Indians*, 366–67.

30. A Lieutenant of the Left Wing, *Sketch of the Seminole War*, 121.

31. Rafn, *America Discovered in the Tenth Century*, 18.

32. Sigourney, *Scenes in My Native Land*, 51.

33. Sanders, *A History of the Indian Wars*, 228.

34. Gilleland, *The Ohio and Mississippi Pilot*, 162.

35. Yu, *The Great Circle*, 26.

36. Stowe, *Uncle Tom's Cabin*, 232–33. I thank former University of Texas at Arlington student Zachary Wingerd for bringing this quote to my attention.

37. Stowe, "Uncle Lot," 31.

38. Russell, *Pictures of Southern Life, Social, Political and Military*, 17.

39. Russell, *My Diary North and South*, 157.

40. Martineau, *Society in America*, 127–29.

41. Trafton, *Egypt Land*, 16

42. Schoolcraft, *Information Respecting the Indian Tribes*, 38, 343.

Chapter 1

1. Brackenridge, *Journal of a Voyage up the River Missouri.*

2. Tudor, *Narrative of a Tour in North America*, 41–43.

3. Ibid., 260.

4. Irwin, *The Lust of Knowing*, 2.

5.   Irving, *Astoria Or, Anecdotes Beyond the Rocky Mountains*, 179.

6.   Willis, *American Scenery*, 120.

7.   St. John, *The Trapper's Bride*, 39–40

8.   Hall, *The New Purchase*, 281–82.

9.   Henry Nash Smith, *Virgin Land*, 1–3.

10. Mason, *Infelicities*, 126–27.

11. LeMenager, *Manifest and Other Destinies*, 79, 110.

12. Ludlow, *The Heart of the Continent*, 268.

13. Irving, *The Adventures of Captain Bonneville*, 206.

14. Pattie, *The Hunters of Kentucky*, 67.

15. Nuttall, *Journal of Travels into the Arkansas*, 54.

16. Ludlow, *The Heart of the Continent*, 287–88.

17. Ibid., 294.

18. Sarmiento, *Life in the Argentine Republic*, 33–35.

19. Ibid., 39.

20. The Sam Houston Museum at Sam Houston State University, Huntsville, Texas, provides many examples of Houston's eccentricities.

21. Matthews, "The Family," 17.

22. Sarmiento, *Life in the Argentine Republic*, 29–30.

23. Irving, A Tour on the Prairies, 65.

24. McLeod to Mirabeau Lamar, Red River Country, Below Clarksville 60 Miles, January 9, 1839, Papers of Mirabeau Lamar, vol. 2, 406.

25. Thorpe, *The Mysteries of the Backwoods*, 13–15.

26. Lanman, *A Summer in the Wilderness*, 58.

27. Galveston Bay and Texas Land Company, *Emigrants' Guide to Texas*, 30.

28. Brackenridge, *Journal of a Voyage up the River Missouri*, 133.

29. Dodge, *The Plains of the Great West and Their Inhabitants*, 378–79.

30. Dunraven, *The Great Divide*, 22, 169.

31. Leavitt, "California Again!"

32. Morgan, ed., *Overland in 1846*, 559–60.

33. Ibid., 485–87.

34. Journal of Horace K. Whitney, May 12, 1847; see also Bennett, *We'll Find the Place*, 148–49.

35. Harmon, *Appleton Milo Harmon Goes West*, 22.

36. Spec, *Line Etchings*, 63.

37. Irving, *Astori, Or Anecdotes of the Rocky Mountains*, 232.

38. Langworthy, *Scenery of the Plains, Mountains and Mines*, 42.

39. Actually, as many as nine Egyptian obelisks existed in Egypt, and three were later placed in major cities (Paris, London, and New York). Cleopatra's Needle(s) symbolized the accomplishments of the ancient Egyptians, but ironically, these obelisks are actually associated with Tuthmosis III, rather than Queen Cleopatra herself. This was not the first time that powerful outsiders repositioned the venerable obelisks. Originally erected in Heliopolis, the obelisks were later moved by the Romans to Alexandria. They also found their way into Europe. As early as 1819, plans were made to move one obelisk to London as the pasha of Egypt had given it to England.

40. Historian Gregg Cantrell uses the term "divided mind" to characterize the American psyche in the early to mid-nineteenth century. By this he means the discrepancy between the present (a buoyant belief in the ascendancy of their Republic) and the past (all such Republics have crumbled, leaving only venerated ancient ruins). Cantrell suggests that Manifest Destiny worked to resolve this tension, and to dispel fears by

sustaining enthusiasm and offering "self assurance." So, too, did an Orientalizing of the American landscape, which offered a reassuring sense of antiquity in an otherwise new land. See Gregg Cantrell, "Manifest Destiny," presented at *The West and the Shaping of America*, Institute for Texas Teachers, Texas Christian University, June 3, 2007.

41. Harris, *The Artist in American Society*, 192–99.

42. Despite initial concerns about obelisks, then, they soon became a cherished symbol for a new nation proudly rescuing ancient forms from the graveyards of history. With ease, the new nation now ingeniously employed them as American symbols for strength, power, and durability. With their acceptance came an ease in equating the richness of the ancient past with the vibrancy and enthusiasm of a new America.

43. Langworthy, *Scenery of the Plains, Mountains and Mines*, 108.

44. It is no coincidence that at exactly this time, American gravestones also emulated the obelisk, becoming a standard feature in cemeteries from coast to coast. See Francaviglia, "The Cemetery as an Evolving Cultural Landscape," 501–9.

45. The social gospel movement, which urges action based on socially responsible Christian traditions, was yet another aspect of this impetuous American expansion. In the twentieth century, it required a renunciation of the isolationism that has characterized the United States from time to time.

46. White and Hopkins, *The Social Gospel*, 40–41.

47. Burton, *The City of the Saints*, 19–21.

48. Ibid., 25.

49. Ibid., 30–31.

50. Ibid., 45, 47.

51. Ibid., 57.

52. Ibid., 62.

53. Ibid., 62.

54. Given the tendency to Orientalize the western American landscape, it is not surprising that the native peoples here seemed to have a decidedly Oriental quality—at least in the eyes, and imaginations, of Europeans and European Americans. But some travelers sought to explore beyond mere visual connections; they searched for deeper, genetic connections. This, after all, represented the dawn of ethnography and anthropology. As an inveterate explorer in a world searching for connections, Burton was fascinated by the Native Americans—particularly their beliefs, which he sought to connect with Old World origins. "The religion of the North American Indians" he began, "has long been a subject of debate." Burton was particularly interested in the sources of Native American religions. "Some see in it traces of Judaism, others of Sabaeanism; M. Schoolcraft detects a degradation of Guebrism." In this statement, we can sense a common belief that native religions—and native peoples themselves—originated elsewhere. Yet, there was also an assumption of primitivism, for, as Burton clearly put it, "they have not yet risen to monotheism." The Indians were "superstitious," as if most Christians had totally shed this trait. Burton noted that "some tribes, as the Cheyennes, will not go to war without a medicine man, others without sacred war-gourds containing the tooth of the drum-head fish." As a Christian, Burton believed that two things that elevated Native American religions—"namely, the Great Spirit or Creator, and the Happy Hunting Grounds in a future world—were the results of Christian missionary teaching." See Burton, *The City of the Saints*, 84–86. By contrast, as Burton put it, the Indians' fetishism "leads to Pantheism and Polytheism" and no belief in the human soul. Burton, though, was impressed by the depth of Indians' belief in "Manitou . . . which gave the spark from the flint, lived in every blade of grass, flowed in the streams, shone in the stars, and thundered in the waterfall," and yet he pointed out that this belief in the

Deity was "particular and concrete" rather than the Judeo-Christian belief in a single God.

55. Lockwood, *Locust*.

56. The South Western Immigration Company, *Texas: Her Resources and Capabilities*, 14, 54.

57. John Runnels, untitled speech, *Report of the Fourth Tri-State Reunion*, 56–59, cited in Wrobel, *Promised Lands*, 143.

58. Howett, "Grounding Memory and Identity," 25, 19–38.

59. See Kolodny, *The Land Before Her*, 8–10.

60. Worster, "Cowboy Ecology," 3.

61. Leonard Collection, I:1:13, typed extract credited to *Boston Traveler*, Aug. 8, 1868, UPRR Archives, Council Bluffs, Iowa.

62. "Bryan," *National Republican*, March 11, 1869.

63. Webb, *Buffalo Land*, 118.

64. US Congress, *Railroad Reports*, vol. 2, 62; see also Hyde, *An American Vision*, 56.

65. Lubetkin, *Jay Cooke's Gamble*, 104.

66. Winchell, *Sketches of Creation*, 205–9.

67. Ibid., 148.

68. In the introduction to his 1982 book *Scenes in America Deserta*, Peter Reyner Banham candidly confessed that "I have given this book a title that deliberately echoes Charles Doughty's classic *Travels in Arabia Deserta*." Banham admitted that he owed a debt to British travel writers who wrote such stirring accounts of the Middle Eastern deserts. See Peter Reyner Banham, *Scenes in America Deserta*, 1. More to the point here, however, is that the American deserts were, and still are, perceived in terms of their Old World counterparts. In the nineteenth century, both were similar enough—sparsely populated, but possessing intriguing villages of either sedentary or seminomadic peoples, and landscapes that are ultimately stony, sandy, arid, exotic, hazardous—that they could serve as literary landscape surrogates. Even today, in the popular imagination, American deserts convey the mystique of the Sahara and Arabian Deserts. The key operative idea here is romanticism, which has long been an element in the American ethos.

69. Although the term "siesta" suggests a Spanish or Mexican location, the painting's premise—a lounging odalisque—is far more Middle Eastern than Spanish or Native American.

70. Dilworth, *Imagining Indians in the Southwest*, 5–6.

71. This critique would seem to indict capitalism per se, but then again, imperial nostalgia may be part of a larger and fairly recent trend, what Jean Baudrillard saw as a "species-wide sense of remorse . . . inducing humanity to resurrect the whole of its past just when it is losing the thread of its memory." Regardless, the quest still results in the same enigma: by trying to return fossilized cultural relics to life, "we shall turn them from something buried and living into something visible and dead." See Baudrillard, "The Dance of the Fossils," 72–77.

72. J. W. Dawson, *Modern Science in Bible Lands*, 349–53.

73. Morris, "When Corporations Rule the Llano Estacado," 44–93.

Chapter 2

1. Varga, "Pyramids of the World, True or False," A63.

2. Herodotus, *History*, 131.

3.   Nisbet, *The Mapmaker's Eye*, 110.

4.   Frémont, *Memoirs of My Life*.

5.   Dawson, *Modern Science in Bible Lands*, 336.

6.   Stephens, *Incidents of Travel in Egypt*, 32–33.

7.   Stephens, *Incidents of Travel in Egypt*, xi.

8.   Frémont, *Exploring Expedition to the Rocky Mountains*, 217–18.

9.   Calculated from longitude 112° to 120° west at 38° latitude.

10. Like the nineteenth-century British explorers, Frémont was engaged in expanding empire—in this case the American empire to the Pacific Coast. When Frémont experienced (and named) Pyramid Lake, he was, in fact, in Mexico, more properly the Mexican province of Upper or Alta California. Frémont was more than an impartial observer here. He was on a mission to obtain strategic geographic information for the US government. In this regard, Frémont was part of a broader mission to expand the territory of the United States from the Atlantic to the Pacific. Manifest Destiny is commonly referred to as the motive for such expansive American exploration, and it was both metaphorical and military. The passions it excited would ignite within two short years as the US-Mexican War broke out in 1846.

11. Ridgway, *Geological Exploration of the Fortieth parallel*, 343.

12. Said, *Orientalism*.

13. Stephens, *Incidents of Travel in Egypt*, 259–61.

14. Deveney, *Paschal Beverly Randolph*, 152. That spelling, "Zahara," was common among mid-nineteenth century Anglo-American explorers, who coined the term "American Zahara" for the driest parts of the American West.

15. Burton, *The Look of the West*, 273.

16. Ibid., 307–9.

17. *Sacramento Daily Union*, December 9, 1867, as cited in Hyde, *An American Vision*, 139.

18. The Sahara-as-quintessential-desert metaphor still works today in parts of the American West. In a 2007 opinion piece on how "the annual rite known as the family trip allows you to rediscover your heart, laugh deeply and skid closer than you'd like to the gates of hell," columnist William McKenzie described various vacation trips to the West. Of a trip to Colorado, he recalled that "one Sunday evening, a cellist played for a handful of us in an amphitheater at the Great Sand Dunes National Park and Preserve." The music was probably fine, but what impressed McKenzie most about the experience was the sand dunes themselves: "The sun was settling down, casting a red glow against the chalk-like dunes that rise out of southern Colorado like towers in the Sahara." It was, as he put it, an "overpowering moment." By the early twenty-first century, it is impossible to separate the numerous factors that enabled McKenzie to so easily fall under the romantic spell of the dunes. Given cinema's impact on us, the music probably helped, as did the fresh late afternoon rain that helped cool the air. Then, too, the spectacular lighting—almost painterly—may have helped. "But . . ." as McKenzie put it, "the combination of family, color, sound and sense was so strong" that they contributed to the experience. Interestingly, McKenzie seems to be describing something akin to the family watching a film (or television), but his point was that the experience was real—or so it seemed.

19. Davis, *Dead Cities and Other Tales*, 40–41.

20. This plays out in interesting ways. In the days after 9/11, watching video footage of Osama bin Laden pontificating from some unidentified scrub-pine highland location in, most likely, northeastern Afghanistan, made it easy to imagine this fugitive holding court on a New Mexico mountainside somewhere northwest of Santa Fe—until, that is, one looked very closely at the species of pine trees in the background.

21. For more information, see Neil A. West, *Ecosystems of the World*, 279–421.
22. Monoghan, "The Dunes that Roar," A64.
23. Curzon, *Tales of Travel*, 313–98.
24. Williams, *Refuge*, 109.
25. Chandler and Goldthwaite, eds., "Sound Ground to Stand On," 81–94.
26. Robinson, *Sinners and Saints*, 280.
27. Ibid., 208.
28. Robinson continues the cultural comparison much of the way across Nevada. But the ever-critical Robinson did mention one redeeming aspect of the Silver State. Nevada's desert wasteland, as he put it, "thus keeps apart the two American problems of the day—pigtails and polygamy." Interestingly, both of those "problems"—the Chinese presence in California, and the Mormons' practice of polygamy in Utah—were fodder for Robinson's Orientalist impulses.
29. Twain, *The Innocents Abroad*, 441.
30. Fowler, *Camels to California*, 1–8.
31. Ibid., 18.
32. Ibid., 19.
33. Ibid., 30.
34. Ibid., 41–42.
35. Ibid., 54, 59.
36. See Jackson and Jackson, *Dr. J. R. N. Owen*, 2.
37. In Reel 59, Incoming Brigham Young Correspondence, Archives, Church of Jesus Christ of Latter-day Saints, Salt Lake City.
38. Corinne *Daily Utah Reporter*, July 7, 1869.
39. Woodward, *Camels and Surveyors in Death Valley*, 8–11.
40. Ibid., 16–17.
41. Ibid., 21.
42. Lingenfelter, *Death Valley & the Amargosa*, 89.

Chapter 3

1. Bushman, *Joseph Smith: Rough Stone Rolling*.
2. Barlow, "Toward a Mormon Sense of Time," 24; see also LeSueur, "The Community of Christ," 9.
3. See John Davis, *The Landscape of Belief*, 13–16.
4. Grabar, "Roots and Others," 4.
5. See Wood, *The New England Village*.
6. John C. Bennett, *The History of the Saints*, 306.
7. Marr, *The Cultural Roots of American Islamicism*, 7–8.
8. Then, too, the Mormons were increasingly marginalized from an organization to which many of their leaders had belonged—Freemasonry. Non-Mormon Masons complained that the Mormons were making membership in their church a prerequisite for joining Masonic lodges in Nauvoo. After Joseph Smith's death, the two organizations grew increasingly estranged.
9. See Richard Jackson, "The Mormon Experience," 68.
10. Francaviglia, *The Mormon Landscape*.
11. Burton, *The City of the Saints*, 240.
12. See Tuveson, *Redeemer Nation*, 184–85.
13. The closest comparison in the twentieth century was the creation of Israel in 1947, which also associated a migration with "Zion."

14. John Davis, *The Landscape of Belief*, 21.
15. O'dea, *The Mormons*, 1.
16. Doctrine and Covenants 133:25, 29.
17. Hyde, *Journal of Discourses*, vol. 2, April 6, 1853, 11.
18. Smith, *Journal of Discourses*, vol. 11, October 7, 1865, 157–58.
19. Pratt, *Journal of Discourses*, vol. 12, August 11, 1867, 93.
20. Pratt, *Journal of Discourses*, vol. 15, December 18, 1870, 58–59.
21. Jackson also noted that the Saints generally regarded the Great Plains as a rather attractive area for raising stock, though some did mention that the landscape became increasingly dry, dusty, and barren the farther west they traveled. Looking back on their journey across the plains in hindsight, though, many were tempted to claim it was a harsh desert that they traversed to get to Utah. Similarly, they rejoiced at the sight that greeted them upon their arrival to the Great Salt Lake valley rather than characterizing it as inhospitable desert. Wilford Woodruff described his joy in seeing "the most fertile valley spread out before us . . . clothed with a heavy garment of vegetation in the midst of which glistened the waters of the Great Salt Lake, with mountains all around towering to the skies, and steams, rivulets, and creeks of pure water running through the beautiful valley." This, as Jackson put it, was typical of "the overwhelmingly favorable view of the Great Salt Lake Valley by the initial pioneer party and subsequent immigrants." Within a few years, though, the Saints' characterization of a fair land changed to a harsh place. Challenges and privations abounded, or so claimed the people writing in the 1850s. Had the environment really changed? The evidence that Pratt provided above suggests that a fluctuation in climate may have been significant enough to support the Mormons' claims. But Jackson does make a good point when he suggests that people in the post–frontier period tended to look back to the early years and see them as a wilderness challenge.
22. Richard Jackson, "The Mormon Experience," 41–58.
23. Epistle dated December 23, 1847, *Millennial Star*, vol 10, 82–83.
24. Historical records of Parowan, Utah, 1856–1859 (August 23, 1857) 25, Salt Lake City, Church Historian's Office.
25. Micah 4:15.
26. The Mormons strongly supported the creation of Israel in the mid-twentieth century; their pro-Israel sentiment remains very strong in the early twenty-first century.
27. John Davis, *The Landscape of Belief*, 22.
28. Davies, "Israel," 85.
29. Ibid. 86.
30. The belief that the American Indians were descended from the "lost" tribes of Israel actually predates the Mormons. In a seminal book on this subject—*View of the Hebrews: or the Tribes of Israel in America*—the Reverend Ethan Smith (no relation to the Mormon prophet) claimed in 1825 that the American Indians' ancestry could be traced directly to the lost tribes of Israel. In yet another testimony to the importance of New England in such matters, Ethan Smith's book was published in Vermont, the same state in which Joseph Smith was born in 1805. *View of the Hebrews* was published five years before Joseph Smith publicly claimed that the same belief was divinely revealed to him; this, as might be anticipated, led to claims of plagiarism, which Joseph Smith effectively refuted. Located in a frontier area, the young Mormon prophet was not likely to know about Ethan Smith's book. More likely, both Smiths tapped into a growing belief that Native Americans were not really indigenous, but connected to an epic biblical history.

31. Although not normally considered in this light, the belief rectifies something that had long troubled religious people since Columbus reached the New World; if the Bible is God's perfect word, how could it fail to mention the peoples of a hemisphere that he also created? The discovery of the Americas, which we take for granted, was truly disconcerting for theologians and common folk alike, who placed absolute faith in the Bible.

32. Peter Martyr, *De Orbe Novo, the Eight Decades of Peter Martyr d'Anghera*, translated by Francis August MacNutt, as referenced in Benjamin Mark Allen's "Naked and Alone in a Strange New World: Early Modern Captivity and Its Mythos in Ibero-American Consciousness" (unpublished PhD diss., University of Texas at Arlington, 2008), 211.

33. Berkhofer, *The White Man's Indian*, 34–35.

34. Stephens, *Incidents of Travels in Egypt*, 104, 223.

35. Twain, *The Innocents Abroad*, 348. I am indebted to University of Texas at Arlington student Greg Kosc for bringing this passage to my attention.

36. Noted by Farmer in *On Zion's Mount*, 34; see also Walker, "Wakara Meets the Mormons," 215–37.

37. Hamer, "Timeless Histories," 281; see also Ahmed, *Women and Gender in Islam*, 152.

38. Burton, *The City of the Saints*, 5.

39. Grabar, "Roots and Others," 3.

40. Robinson, *Sinners and Saints*, 262–63.

41. Ibid., 170–71.

42. Ibid., 219.

43. Landon, ed., *The Journals of George Q. Cannon*, 43.

44. "The Joshua Palm abounds throughout certain sections of the Great American Desert." (Los Angeles: Western Publishing & Novelty Co., C.T. Art-Colortone, n.d.).

45. Christensen, *Nevada*, 108.

46. Whipple, *This is the Place: Utah*, 84.

47. By one account, she was associated with the theater—some said she was a prominent actress of the day (Corinne LaVaunt)—but more likely she was a character of that name in a French novel. Another account holds that Corinne's namesake was the "beautiful and accomplished daughter" of J. A. Williamson—the town's founder.

48. The would-be "Chicago of the West" boomed for a while, but never became a large city. Being the "Only Gentile City in Utah," as some ambitiously branded it, Corinne became a haven for anti-Mormons, including Irish-born Patrick Connor, "the arch-enemy of Brigham Young and the Mormons."

49. Huchel, *A History of Box Elder County*, 123–45.

50. See Richard Bennett, *We'll Find the Place*, 254; also, "General Epistle from the Council of the Twelve Apostles," December 23, 1847 (LDS Church Archives).

51. Robinson, *Sinners and Saints*, 68–71. In Genesis 46:31–47, Goshen is described as a land where the Israelites could remain four hundred years until Moses led them to the Promised Land. In this passage, Robinson appears to be positioning the Mormons as Israelites, though one wonders just how "beautiful" Goshen really was.

52. Streit, *Die Vereinigten Staaten von Nord-Amerika* (Map) (Leipzig, 1851), Virginia Garrett Cartography Collection, University of Texas at Arlington Special Collections #00157 @132/4.

53. Stansbury, *Exploration of the Valley of the Great Salt Lake*, 129.

54. Sir Walter Scott, *The Talisman*.

55. Stephens, *Incidents of Travel in Egypt*, 74.

56. Burton, *The City of the Saints*, 210–15.

57. Stout, *On the Mormon Frontier*, 456.

58. Twain, *The Innocents Abroad*, 91.

59. Unbeknownst to Farandoul, however, trouble is brewing in paradise. The difficulties begin when Brigham Young becomes envious and orders Farandoul to be abducted by Apache Indians. During Farandoul's absence, the disingenuous Young claims that Farandoul has neglected the women. To make matters even worse, Young declares that "after your incomprehensible flight, which showed that you were not a sincere Mormon, your spouses, blushing for shame at having ever, for one instant, been united to a man so bereft of convictions, are petitioning for divorce." Young's telegram continues to inform Farandoul that "an honorable Mormon, Matheus Bikelow, appointed Bishop in your stead, has afforded the shelter of his home to them." Young concludes by stating that Bikelow "has married them and will not abandon them" and warns Farandoul that because he has "been unworthy . . . I would suggest that you never show yourself again in the city of the Saints." The hijinks continue as Farandoul prepares to challenge Bikelow to a duel, reconsiders and renounces all claim to the Mormon women, and continues his journeys through the West with his sailors. Ultimately traveling to South America, Farandoul meets up with characters from Jules Verne's *Around the World in Eighty Days*. Robida's book *Voyages très extraordinaires de Saturnin de Farndoul dans les 5 ou 6 parties du mondo et daris tous les pays connus et meme inconnus de M. Jules Verne*, is discussed in Homer, ed., *On the Way to Somewhere Else*, 217–26.

60. Allen, "The Garments of Instruction From the Wardrobe of Pleasure."

61. Ibid., 74.

62. Langworthy, *Scenery of the Plains, Mountains and Mines*, 75.

63. Stanfield, *Diary of Howard Stillwell Stanfield, 1864–1865*, 82.

64. Domenech, *Voyage Pittoresque dans les grands déserts du Nouveau monde*.

65. Domenech, *Seven Years' Residence*, 269.

66. Ibid., 269.

67. Ibid., 269–70.

68. "Eugene Buissonet Diary," 198–200.

69. *Nelson's Pictorial Guide-Books, the Central Pacific Railroad: A Trip Across the North American Continent from Ogden to San Francisco* was also published with a paper cover, entitled *The Scenery of the Central Pacific Railroad* (New York: T. Nelson and Sons, 1871).

70. *Nelson's Pictorial Guide Books, The Central Pacific Railroad*, 8–10.

71. Langworthy, *Scenery of the Plains, Mountains and Mines*, 101.

72. Ibid., 89.

73. McCormick and McCormick, "Saltair," 168.

74. Ibid., 170–71.

75. Great Salt Lake lantern slides, PH 4579, Archives, Church of Jesus Christ of Latter-day Saints, Salt Lake City, Utah.

76. See Baudrillard, *The System of Objects*, 73–84.

77. Stegner, "Xanadu by the Salt Flats: Memories of a Pleasure Dome."

78. *Deseret Evening News*, Monday, January 1, 1917.

79. See Waite, "The Cedar City Branch and the Utah Parks Company," 17–34.

80. For more about how natural features in Utah were given cultural identities, see Farmer, *On Zion's Mount*.

Chapter 4

1. Flint and Flint, Documents of the Coronado Expedition, 1539–1542, 596–97.

2. Interestingly, the Spaniards regarded turquoise with considerable contempt, as it was

relatively soft and altogether opaque—unlike the clear, hard gems such as diamonds, emeralds, or rubies that they highly prized. The Spaniards' haughty attitude was an affront to the native peoples who considered turquoise sacred, but at least the Spaniards were disinterested enough to leave the natives' turquoise unmined rather than haul it back to Spain, as they did South American emeralds. Turquoise provides yet another example of the transfer of a material object's association with a part of the world and its people to a new context, so much so that even today it is known by the Spanish term rather than the Indian.

3. Irwin, *The Lust of Knowing*, 62; see also Matar, Turks, *Moors and Englishmen in the Age of Discovery*, 100–27.
4. Marryat, *Narrative of the Travels and Adventures of Monsieur Violet*, 21.
5. Howe, *Historical Collections of the Great West*, 375–76.
6. Justin Harvey Smith, *The War with Mexico*, 268.
7. Ibid. 35, 268.
8. Emory, *Report on the United States and Mexican Boundary Survey*.
9. Cozzens, *The Marvellous Country*, 19.
10. Ibid., 163.
11. DeJong, "'Good Samaritans of the Desert,'" 457–96.
12. In the 1940 Wesley Ruggles film *Arizona*, a guide described the sedentary Pima as "good" Indians who "hate the Apache more than we do."
13. James Martineau Diary, 38–39 and 42.
14. Ibid.
15. Shohat, "Gender and Culture of Empire," 54. An example of this type of Oriental-ized sexuality can also be found in popular as well as adult (pornographic) films in the twenty-first century. The former feature mysterious women whose "charms" can intro-duce Westerners to a myriad of secrets guaranteed to enchant. The latter simply make explicit that which is covert in popular culture. Of these, *The Lost Treasure of Ali Baba* is a XXX-rated version of an old story. The plot (what there is of it) is familiar enough and may actually be closer to *Aladdin and the Magic Lamp*. In this film, an American globetrotter who returns home from world travels experiences some tough times and finds an old book revealing a legend about a lost cave laden with treasure. After securing an old map of Syria, he travels there to search the area and ultimately finds the treasure. The cave is strewn with coins and jewels, but the real treasure is Jessica, a veiled, scantily clad, and totally uninhibited woman whose sole dialogue consists of "your wish is my command." After their explicit activities, he awakens in the United States. The encoun-ter was but a dream—or was it? With a smile, he realizes that the coins he pulls from his pocket are from that treasure; hence, his encounter with Jessica was real though magical. Unwittingly, perhaps the producers of this video built on one of the most enduring aspects of Eastern identity—that it is both real and imaginary simultaneously. *The Lost Treasure of Ali Baba, Nineteen*, *Video Magazine*, Volume 45, Chatsworth, CA: DANE Productions, 2002. A couple of lines from Robin Cook's 1979 novel *Sphinx*, which is set in Egypt, remind us how enduring these concepts are in literature. When Egyptologist Erica Barton of Harvard University is surprised by a man with "pure Bedouin features" in Cairo, she is powerless: he is like a terrifying sculpture in deep bronze. Although back home Erica had fantasized how violently she would react if she were ever threatened with rape, now she did nothing. *Sphinx* features many of the standard tropes about the Middle East—treasures and riches, murderous Arab thieves and wise Arab elders, intercultural romance, and sexual awakening. These, of course, reveal more about the Western imagination than they do about the real Middle East, but they confirm the power of combined stereotypical elements in conveying images of,

and attitudes about, that region and its peoples. In *Sphinx*, the landscape is exotic and enigmatic, with treasure and danger lurking just below the surface, while the human encounters are either sexually charged, fraught with danger, or both. Cook, *Sphinx*, 65.

16. Poston, "Building a State in Apache Land," 87–98.
17. Billington, *Land of Savagery, Land of Promise*, 126.
18. Norris, Milligan, and Faulk, *William H. Emory, Soldier-Scientist*, 55–56.
19. Pumpelly, *Across America and Asia*, 13, 17.
20. May, *Oriental Odyssey II*, 36.
21. Dunraven, *The Great Divide*, 117. This, as one might expect, led some Europeans to secretly sympathize with the plight of American Indians. Another British observer traveling through the West grudgingly admitted that "I can feel a sympathy for the red man" despite the fact that "it may be true that neither gunpowder nor the Gospel can reform him." Why? In a moment of unusual candor, he admitted that "a people cannot be altogether worthless that in the deepest depths of their degradation still maintain a lofty wild-beast scorn of white man, and think them something lower than themselves." This statement must be understood in its historical context. It is based on the premise that western European culture was the most advanced, and that all other cultures were below it in the natural order. Despite, or perhaps because of, this "fact," the writer felt it chivalrous that "the red man holds sacred everything that his tribe is guarding." Because he felt that American Indians were destined to disappear soon under American colonialism, which he felt was more brutal than the colonialism that other governments had initiated elsewhere, the writer asked a penetrating question that still resonates today: "Why should not this chivalry, common to every savage race on earth, and largely utilized by other governments in Asia as in Africa, be turned to account in America too, and Indians be entrusted with the peace of Indian frontiers?" (Robinson, *Sinners and Saints*, 271–72.) This, of course, is a question that has been asked many times since, most recently in Afghanistan and Iraq.
22. Breeden, ed., *A Long Ride in Texas*, 52–53.
23. Cozzens, *The Marvellous Country*, 80.
24. Meline, *Two Thousand Miles on Horseback*, 151–52.
25. Twitchell, "An Old-World City in the New: the Place that gave Santa Fe its Name," 2; see also Dye, *All Aboard for Santa Fe*, 25–31.
26. Dilworth, *Imagining Indians in the Southwest*, 5.
27. Ibid., 6.
28. Harmsen, *Harmsen's Western Americana*, 56.
29. Brooks, *Captives & Cousins*, 18–22.
30. There is yet another similarity to military action in both places: in the American Southwest, the multiyear searches for Cochise, Geronimo, and other Indian leaders who seemingly vanished into thin air despite the fact that thousands of forces were bent on capturing them proved good (and sobering) training for American troops in pursuit of terrorist leaders in present-day Afghanistan, Pakistan, and Iraq. Given the tasks facing our military leaders, it is surprising that these early Indian feats of escape have not been studied carefully; they could provide valuable lessons in the difficulties of suppressing indigenous insurgencies among mobile populations in rugged areas.
31. Cozzens, *The Marvellous Country*, 15.
32. Ibid., 20–21.
33. Ibid., 22.
34. Ibid., 22.
35. Hyde, *An American Vision*, 198–202.
36. Ferguson and Coldwell-Chanthaphonh, *History is in the Land*, 31.

37. Alas, however, the original Orient railroad never even made it all the way to the Pacific. Nevertheless, its route into the United States was well planned enough to be incorporated into the lines of the Santa Fe Railroad, which purchased the Orient in the 1920s. But while it lasted, the KCM&O recognized that the "Orient" in its title was exotic enough to distinguish it from all the other railroads. For much of its life, the KCM&O painted the name orient in huge white letters on its cars and locomotive tenders. Even today, more than eighty years since the Orient was purchased by the Santa Fe, railroaders still refer to operating sections of the old KCM&O line as "The Orient"—a testimony to how evocative and enduring a name can be. Moreover, an independent short-line that took over a section of the line in Texas in the 1990s still proudly calls itself "The Orient" in the twenty-first century.

38. Although the origins of Phoenix are usually associated with only Anglo-Americans, the city also has a long and rich Hispanic past. See Oberle and Arreola, "Resurgent Mexican Phoenix," 171–196.

39. "The Swastika cross of benediction and good will . . . copied from the red sandstone of Arizona, appears in the hieroglyptric inscriptions and decorative designs of the Egyptians, Chaldeans, Scandinavians, Chinese and North American Indians." *Overland Monthly and Out West Magazine*, vol. 42, San Francisco, 1868–1935, 110.

40. Baudrillard, "The Order of the Simulacra," 50–86.

41. West and Augelli, *Middle America: Its Lands and Peoples*.

42. Auerbach, *Explorers in Eden*, 20.

43. Ibid., 28–29.

44. Ibid., 57.

45. See Don D. Fowler, *A Laboratory for Anthropology*, 112–13.

46. Ibid., 213–19.

47. Auerbach, *Explorers in Eden*, 77.

48. Aleš Hrdlička, 1912, as quoted in Matthew Bokovoy, *The San Diego World's Fairs*, 77–78.

49. Incidentally, Taylor dedicated his book about the Saracens (i.e., Muslims) to Washington Irving, who "more than any other American author, have [sic] revived the traditions, restored the history, and illustrated the character of that brilliant and heroic people" (Taylor, *The Lands of the Saracens*, 32). For their part, Saracens were people of Islamic faith who occupied the Middle East; some Christians despised them, but others lauded their long list of accomplishments. For his part, Washington Irving was now an important element in American Orientalism. He traveled widely through portions of the American West and portions of the East, in addition to serving as ambassador to Spain and thus imbibing huge doses of Moorish heritage.

Chapter 5

1. Wierzbicki, *California as it is, and As it May Be*, 24–25.

2. Fleming, *California*, 82.

3. Francaviglia, "The Treasures of Aladdin."

4. See *Dreams of the West*, 17–18.

5. Conti, "Seeing the Elephant."

6. "Seeing the Elephant," Nebraska State Historical Society, http://www.nebraskahistory.org/publish/publicat/timeline/seeing_the_elephant.htm.

7. "First in the West," 5.

8. See Evans, *A la California*, chap. 12.

9.   GMD to A. Burlingame, Washington, June 15, 1866. (W) GMD papers, box 337, GMD & China. Union Pacific Archives, Council Bluffs, Iowa.

10. Parson, *An American Engineer in China*, 198.

11. Murphy, "Like Standing on the Edge," 4–11.

12. *Great Trans-Continental Tourists' Guide*, n.p.

13. H. T. Williams, ed., *The Pacific Tourist*, 166.

14. MacGregor, *The Birth of California Narrow Gauge*, 556.

15. Daniel, "'The Various Celestials Among Our Town," 93–104.

16. Maffly-Kipp, "Engaging Habits and Besotted Idolatry," 60–88.

17. Lemon, *The Harmony Borax Works of Death Valley, California*, 13.

18. For example, Francaviglia, "Landscape and Cultural Coninuity," *The Changing Faces of the West*.

19. Speer, *The Oldest and the Newest Empire*, 21–22.

20. Meriwether, *Harper's Weekly*, Oct. 13, 1888.

21. Ames, *Death in the Dining Room*, 1.

22. Conn, *Museums and American Intellectual Life*, 1876–1926, 14, 18.

23. Giedion, *Mechanization Takes Control*.

24. Ames, *Death in the Dining Room*, 123, 236.

25. MacKenzie, *Orientalism: History, Theory, and the Arts*, 133.

26. "Gems of Art Contributed by Local Painters," *San Francisco Call*, January 21, 1900.

27. Goss, *Gold and Cinnabar*, 233.

28. Pine, *Beyond the West*, 433.

29. J. Russell Smith, *North America*, 587.

30. Zesch, "Chinese Los Angeles in 1870–71," 109–58.

31. Yip, "A Time for Bitter Strength," 4.

32. Leung, "One Day, One Dollar—Delta Heritage," 41–43.

33. Hoover, Hoover, and Rensch, *Historic Spots in California*, 453

Chapter 6

1.   See "Exploring Colonial Mexico," Espadaña Press website, http://www.colonial-mexico.com.

2.   Lawrence W. Levine, *The Unpredictable Past*, 144.

3.   Morgan, ed., *Overland in 1846*, 721–22.

4.   See Kalmar and Penslar, *Orientalism and the Jews*.

5.   See Manly, *Death Valley in '49*, 98–99.

6.   Sidney Smith, *The Settler's New Home*, 129.

7.   Special one-sheet flyer [unattributed to any newspaper], "What the Religious Press of New York says of the Pacific Railroad" in MSC 159, Box 32, Levi Leonard Railroad Collection, University of Iowa Special Collections.

8.   Browne, *Crusoe's Island*, 172–77.

9.   Ibid., 238–48.

10. Pumpelly, *Across America and Asia*, 65.

11. In 1885, geologist Israel Cook Russell noted that the Great Basin was markedly different from other regions of the United States. Russell observed that "the traveler in this region . . . must compare it rather to the parched and desert areas of Arabia and the shores of the Dead Sea and the Caspian." See Padget, *Indian Country*.

12. Stevenson, "The Silverado Squatters," 31.

13. Taylor, *The Lands of the Saracens*, 99–100.

14. Worster, *Under Western Skies*, 56.
15. Ibid.
16. Ibid., 55.
17. Wrobel, *Promised Lands*, 38.
18. Taylor, *The Lands of the Saracens*, 425–26.
19. DeLyser, *Ramona Memories*.
20. Helen Hunt Jackson, *Ramona*, 43–45.
21. Helen Hunt Jackson, "Outdoor Industries in Southern California," 257; see also Padget, *Indian Country*, 83–101.
22. Austin, *The Land of Little Rain*, 99–100.
23. Ibid., 109.
24. *The Huntington Library: Thesaurus from Ten Centuries*, 137.
25. McClelland and Last, *California Orange Box Labels*, 5, 20.
26. Walker Tompkins, "Santa Barbara, CA Samarkand History."
27. Reid, "Original Sketch: The Entry of the American Army into Puebla," 1.
28. We tend to associate such Spanish/Moorish architecture with California or the Southwest, but it could be built anywhere. Consider, for example, the spectacular Broadwater Natatorium in Helena, Montana, described by a Great Northern Railway writer in superlatives, including the "finest specimen of Moorish architecture in the world." Chacón, "Creating a Mythic Past: Spanish-Style Architecture in Montana," 46. The natatorium and hotel was the brainchild of Montana entrepreneur Charles A. Broadwater, who poured money into the place in an effort to make Helena one of the best, that is, most idyllic, places during the Gilded Age. What better way to achieve this than using exotic Oriental motifs? Locals believed that Broadwater's spectacular hotel and natatorium, with their stained glass windows and dome, illuminated a "scene of Oriental magnificence such as we dreamed of when reading Arabian Nights." The natatorium, with its "Moorish architecture," was evocative and exotic. A postcard featuring a photograph of the natatorium as well as an ode to that building by Thomas Murray Spencer of Butte, Montana, noted: "Full well the sturdy master builder in wilderness Egyptian-like of old," a place where those seeking "health, wealth and merriment achieve" could find a state of bliss. The ode was apparently to Broadwater the man (or master) and Broadwater the place. Rejuvenation was the theme. As Spencer put it, in a world where "Time—Death's great derider, was spreading his dusty pall," the Broadwater rose to experience "its palmiest day." This amounted to "a day of resurrection surely," for "its pristine glory is not past." To people who sensed that time was fleeting, this building offered "a second time for playing." Spencer, *Helena, Montana*, 58, 59, 117.
29. See Padget, *Indian Country*.
30. This play on regional identity needs just a bit of clarification, because "West" or "East" could refer to either the western or eastern United States (as in that line from the musical Oklahoma [1948], "East is East, and West is West") as well as Western culture and Eastern (i.e., Oriental) culture.
31. Bokovoy, *The San Diego World's Fairs*, 64.
32. MacCannell, "Ideological Castles," 33.
33. Buel, *The Magic City*.
34. Findlay, *Magic Lands*.
35. Sackman, *Orange Empire*, 24.
36. Ibid., 92.
37. Ibid., 120, 133.
38. Ironically, this Eastern philosophy has as much to do with the training of rather wealthy, elite easterners in Western/American schools having strong anticapitalist,

left-wing philosophies—which may explain the tendency of the left to support radical Occidentalists' interests. See Buruma and Margalit, *Occidentalism*.

39. Worster, "Landscape with Hero," 29.
40. Smythe, "The Blooming of a Sahara," 1261.
41. Sauder, *The Yuma Reclamation Project*, 22-23.
42. It should be noted that the Salton Sink has held water in earlier times, especially during the Pleistocene epoch when wetter, cooler conditions prevailed.
43. Gudde, *California Place Names*, 210.
44. Signor, *Beaumont Hill*, 42, 73, 126.
45. "Date Palms."

Chaper 7

1. See McClain, *In Search of Equality*.
2. Nokes, *Massacred for Gold*.
3. Cover, *West Shore*, 42.
4. Cover, *West Shore*.
5. McArthur, *Oregon Geographic Names*, 175.
6. American Baptist Home Missionary Society, *Baptist Home Missions in North America*, 113.
7. Speer, *The Oldest and the Newest Empire*, 27–28.
8. *Oregonian*, June 21, 1909; June 22, 1909; June 30, 1909.
9. Harvey Whitefield Scott, ed., *History of Portland, Oregon*. See also *Dreams of the West*, 66–67.
10. O'Connell, *On Sacred Ground*, 41.
11. Pumpelly, *Across America and Asia*, 66–67.
12. Ibid., 93.
13. Ibid., 95–96.
14. Ibid., 133.
15. Anis, "Pacific NW Skiing at its Best at Mt. Hood Meadows."
16. That not all imagery is as Orientalist-inspired as it might at first seem is evidenced in Rainier Fruit Company's labels for Fuji apples (a variety introduced into the Pacific Northwest from Japan in the 1980s). The labels depict the company's trademark, showing a snow-capped mountain (evidently Mount Rainier) in this case crowned by the name "fuji." Although at first glance, the mountain appears to be the venerable Mount Fuji, one must realize this simply represents a way of identifying both the company and a variety of apples marketed by the company—and not the Orientalization of Mount Rainier. On the other hand, that juxtaposition of the Fujilike mountain profile and the name Fuji over the mountain works subliminally to reaffirm a connection between the Pacific Northwest and Japan.
17. Kessler, "Spacious Dreams: A Japanese American Family Comes to the Pacific Northwest," 163–65.
18. Pumpelly, *Across America and Asia*, 131–32.
19. J. Russell Smith, *North America*, 605.
20. "Seattle" in *Choir's History, Business Directory, and Immigrant's Guide Book* (1878), 10.
21. See Boswell's account of this event in August 1896 in the *Seattle Times*, January 28, 1996, as recounted in "Partners Across the Pacific."
22. Lee, "The Contradictions of Cosmopolitanism," 278–79, 302.

23. Panero, "Outside the Frame: How Asia Changed the Course of American Art," 18.
24. Doyle, "The Oriental Limited."
25. Shaffer, See *America First*, 74.

Chapter 8

1. Wister, *The Virginian: A Horseman of the Plains*, 10.
2. Baum, *The Wizard of Oz*, 3.
3. Ibid., 115–16.
4. Harmetz, *The Making of The Wizard of Oz*.
5. See "David Russell: Concept Illustrator/Storyboard Artist," David Russell website, http://www.dynamicimagesdr.com/index1.php.
6. Fleishman, "It's Love, Saudi Style," *Dallas Morning News*, January 15, 2008, 10A.
7. Ironically, the United States was attempting to rid the Middle East of faux (or at least dictatorial) potentates and poppy fields in the early twenty-first century, as events in the War on Terrorism unfolded.
8. J. B. Jackson, "The Necessity for Ruins," 101–2.
9. Malamud, "Pyramids in Las Vegas and Outer Space," 31, 35.
10. Dodds, "Myst," 180.
11. Papanikolas, *American Silence*, 78.
12. "Luxor Las Vegas," http://www.luxor.com.
13. Shohat, "Gender and Culture of Empire," 48.
14. See http://www.lyricsmode.com/lyrics/b/brand_new_heavies/midnight_at_the_oasis.html. Consulted January 15, 2011.
15. This type of self-confidence and intense sexuality is, of course, very Western. Many Muslim men would find this woman to be disarmingly aggressive, even predatory, certainly more of a "whore" than a concubine or odalisque.
16. *Year One*, Columbia Pictures, 2009.
17. Miller, "Inside the Glitter: Lives of Casino Workers," 237.
18. In the mid-twentieth century, Pyramid Lake's setting doubled for the landscape of the desert Levant in a popular movie. In 1965, when international tensions kept film crews out of the Holy Land during the filming of *The Greatest Story Ever Told,* they sought a double for the Sea of Galilee, selecting Pyramid Lake as a credible substitute. Even though perceptive people who had actually been to the Sea of Galilee might have noted some discrepancies, the geographic feature in Nevada worked well enough. Filmgoers were none the wiser, and that intense blue sheet of water and its desert surroundings seemed credible enough to earn the film's cinematography accolades.
19. Field, *From Egypt to Japan*, 82.
20. Moreno, *Roadside History of Nevada*, 169.
21. Said, "Orientalism Reconsidered," 90, 103.
22. Lant, "The Curse of the Pharaoh, or How Cinema Contracted Egyptomania," 91.
23. David S. Boyer, "Geographical Twins A World Apart," 848–59.
24. Ibid., 71.
25. In the interior West, Peery's Egyptian Theater (Ogden, Utah) was one such copy, representing Egyptian revival at its finest. Opened in 1923 and recently restored as part of Ogden's downtown revitalization, Peery's Egyptian Theater possesses all the characteristic elements of the genre: viewed from the outside, its polychromatic, highly detailed Egyptian-style columns stand in contrast to the more mundane buildings in the streetscape. Just behind the freestanding ticket booth, a striking Egyptian vulture adorns

the doorway into the theater. Once inside, the patron experiences an ornately decorated lobby, but the auditorium portion of the interior is the tour de force. The decoration here gives the patron the feeling that he or she is outside again, only this time under an Egyptian night sky, as the azure-colored ceiling is filled with lights simulating the stars. Then, too, the stage curtain is richly evocative of stylized Egypt, featuring seated statues of Ra, and the pyramids studding a sandy plain that is punctuated by date palm trees. The Egyptian revival architecture of such theaters (forty-two of which were built in the United States) is itself highly eclectic. As critic Gary Parks has observed, "So it is with Egyptian movie palaces, which often borrow shamelessly from [all Egyptian] Dynasties I - XXX in a single building, yet somehow . . . work." Parks noted that both the interior and exterior of Peery's Egyptian in Ogden is "Ptolemaic in feeling although painted scenes in the auditorium appear to be New Kingdom in flavor, with the Viceroy of Kush seeking audience with Tutankhamen." Some of the Egyptian icons in this theater are authentic in appearance. However, as Parks also noted, the Peery Egyptian is decorated with Egyptian icons that never would have been placed together in ancient Egypt; these he calls "bits of humor that an Egyptophile who also loves old theatres can enjoy." Some of the seemingly Egyptian icons in this theater's decoration are more clearly whimsical, apparently depicting events surrounding the construction of the theater in the ancient Egyptian style. See Parks, "Pharaoh Comes to Main Street."

26.   The appeal of a building like Peery's Egyptian Theater in Ogden, Utah, depends on its ability to convince (some might say deceive) those who enter it that it is just like the original. With its many Egyptian-style elements, the theatre convinced some theare goers that it was a copy of an actual Egyptian structure. Further conflating ancient Egypt with the American West was the film shown at the theater's opening—Zane Grey's *Wanderer of the Wasteland*—a dramatic Western film portraying love, greed, and spiritual challenges in the Mojave Desert.

27.   "Rosicrucian Egyptian Museum," Rosicrucian Order, http://www.egyptianmuseum.org.

28.   One aspect of New Age religion and spirituality that deserves greater study is its close relationship to Orientalism in addition to its fascination with Native American spirituality.

29.   Staton, "Wait Watchers," 104.

30.   Interestingly, Cher—like the Pyramids—endures: she is reportedly the only singer to have a top-selling original song in every decade since the 1960s.

31.   "Sands of Oblivion," Sci-Fi Channel premiere, October 13, 2007.

32.   Bob Dylan, "The Groom's Still Waiting at the Altar," words and music Bob Dylan, released on *Biograph* (1985) and on the CD edition of *Shot of Love* (1981).

33.   Auerbach, *Explorers in Eden*.

34.   See Wilson, *The Myth of Santa Fe*.

35.   Sorkin, *Some Assembly Required*, 55.

36.   Austin, *The Land of Journeys' Ending*, 228.

37.   Alter, "Revising a Pulp Prodigy"; see also Finn, *Blood & Thunder*.

38.   Howard, *Conan the Barbarian*, 10.

39.   Slotkin, *Gunfighter Nation*, 412.

40.   "Rock Camel" postcard.

41.   Sorkin, *Some Assembly Required*, 82.

42.   Pronk, "Camels at Home on the Range," 31.

43.   Garrigues, *West of Babylon: A Novel*, 3–6.

44.   Ibid., 91.

45.   A sexual encounter in Garrigues's *West of Babylon* is as Oriental as anything out of the Kama Sutra.

46. Garrigues, *West of Babylon*, 15.
47. Estival, *Stars Over the Desert*, author's profile on back cover
48. Auerbach, *Explorers in Eden*, 150–51.
49. At this point, however, Auerbach himself makes something of a problematic assumption about Orientalism: If not all visitors and explorers to the Southwest were exploiters, and not all southwestern natives were exploited, then how could the mind-set that the former possessed really be "Orientalism" in the Saidian sense? In order to be considered Orientalists, Auerbach suggests, these image builders would have had to process the negative views of racist appropriators. Auerbach here does not take the next step, namely, to challenge Said's core assumptions and claims about Orientalism. In this book I claim that travelers who were entranced by and succumbed to the Southwest as "a land in which foreign people, with foreign speech and foreign ways" lived amid "spectacles which can be equaled in few Oriental lands" should be considered Orientalists in a broader sense of the term.
50. How direct is the connection observers have made between Asia and the Indian Southwest? Some nineteenth-century scholars believed that the Apache Indians' ceremonies and language identified them as a mysterious group that had been driven from China in the twelfth century AD, thus making them very recent arrivals indeed. Of course, the fact that Native Americans do have Asian ancestry is not only apparent from the anthropological record but is also evident from the facial characteristics of Native Americans like the Hopis and Navajos. In early photographs of Native Americans in a southwestern village, it may be challenging to identify the location. Is it American, or is it Asian? That question is difficult to answer, as the scene, or rather the people, look so Asian. These similarities intrigued scholars and the public in the nineteenth century, when people were obsessed with origins and ancestry.
51. Eidel, Foreword to *Portraits of Nature*, by Roy Purcell; personal communication, author with Roy Purcell, June 9, 2010, Green Valley, Arizona.
52. Rothman, *Devil's Bargains*, 19, 44.
53. Brooks, *Captives & Cousins*, 21.
54. Like the filmmakers who made *Bordertown*, filmmakers have long given the Mexican and Native American peoples here an Asian quality. When director Elia Kazan wanted to make Marlon Brando more Indian in appearance in *Viva Zapata!* (1952), he used makeup that gave Brando's eyes "an Oriental look" and also imparted "a darker skin tone, especially early in the film" to help contrast the Anglo-American actor with his Anglo-American female love interest (Jean Peters). See Slotkin, *Gunfighter Nation*, 423.
55. Arreola, "The Mexico-US Borderland," 348-350.

Chapter 9

1. Chang, ed., *Asian American Art: A History, 1850–1970*, 1.
2. "Bernheimer Residence and Oriental Japanese Gardens."
3. Tolf, *This Was San Francisco*, 4, 32.
4. Mike Davis, "Bunker Hill: Hollywood's Dark Shadow," 35.
5. Ibid., 38–40.
6. Hausladen and Starrs, "L.A. Noir," 46.
7. Ibid., 47–48.
8. Klein, *The History of Forgetting*, 9, 27.
9. Ibid., 61–62, 79, 247.
10. L'Amour, *Education of a Wandering Man*, 66.

11. Ibid., 128–32.
12. Ibid., 147.
13. L'Amour, *The Lonesome Gods*, 45.
14. Ibid., 241.
15. Ibid., 264.
16. Ibid., 269–70.
17. L'Amour, *Education of a Wandering Man*, 72–74.
18. Ibid., 3.
19. "The Seven Faces of Dr. Lao," poster used as the cover for the VHS package, dates from 1964.
20. *Kung Fu*, popular culture study guide, BookRags, http://www.bookrags.com.
21. "*Kung Fu* (TV Series)," Wikipedia, http://en.wikipedia.org/wiki/Kung_fu_tv_series.
22. See Anderson, *The Kung Fu Book*; and Pilato, *The Kung Fu Book of Caine*.
23. Tasker, "Kung Fu: Re-orienting the Television Western," 115–116.
24. Pilato, *The Kung Fu Book of Caine*, 7, 28.
25. Iwamura, *Virtual Orientalism*, 111-157.
26. "Shanghai Noon," Internet Movie Database, http://www.imdb.com/title/tt0184894; and "Shanghai Noon," Wikipedia, http://en.wikipedia.org/wiki/Shanghai_Noon.
27. Adopted Californian Walt Disney knew this when he selected Orange County for the location of Disneyland in 1951. In 2005, Disneyland's fiftieth anniversary, it still worked as Fantasyland, and the section called "It's a Small World" offered a glimpse of the exotic.
28. The Huntington Chinese Garden, a two-sided card produced by the Huntington Chinese Garden Project, San Marino, California, n.d., ca. 2006.
29. Li, "Breathing Life into the Chinese Garden," 13–17.
30. See Piyananda, *The Bodhi Tree Grows in L.A.*
31. "Japan, the land of picturesque gardens" postcard.
32. "The Five Gardens," Portland Japanese Garden website.
33. "What People are Saying about the Japanese Garden," Portland Citysearch website.
34. Portland Classical Chinese Garden, brochure.
35. Beaven, "Portland Classical Chinese Garden celebrates."
36. "Things to See & Do [in] Oregon" brochure.
37. "My Favorite Place: Dennis Hopper, The Modern Renaissance Man tells Dan Shapiro about Vancouver, and its Mix of High Design and Natural Wonders," Travelandleisure.com, October 2009, 202.
38. Nakane, "Facing the Pacific," 55.
39. Johnson, *Kenneth Callahan*, 10.
40. "Mark Tobey,"Guggenheim Museum website.
41. Ament, "Morris Graves: The Bad-Boy Recluse of Northwest Art,"ArtGuide website.
42. "Jurassic Crocodile is Unearthed from Blue Mountains in Eastern Oregon." Science Daily website.
43. Kenneth Mark Levine, *Northwest Visionaries*.
44. Hayashi, *Haunted by Waters*, 7, 80.
45. Snyder, *Mountains and Rivers Without End*, 25.
46. Steuding, *Gary Snyder*, 18.
47. Ibid., 22.
48. Ibid., 32–33, 44.
49. O'Connell, *On Sacred Ground*, 146, 148.
50. Kizer, "Poetry: School of the Pacific Northwest," as cited in O'Connell, *On Sacred Ground*, 98.

51. Starck, *Journeyman's Wages*, 45.
52. Etulain, "Inventing the Pacific Northwest," 25.
53. The film, based on the novel by David Guterson (New York: Vintage Books, 1994), was released in 1999

Chapter 10

1. Wrobel, "Global West, American Frontier," 1.
2. *Knickerbocker Magazine*, June 1853; see also Edwards, "A Million and One Nights," 19.
3. "The 1876 Centennial Exhibition," Beinecke Rare Book & Manuscript Library, Yale University, http://www.library.yale.edu/beinecke/orient/centen.htm.
4. See Goetzmann, *When the Eagle Screamed*, 92–103.
5. Edwards, *Noble Dreams, Wicked Pleasures*, viii.
6. Ibid., 27.
7. Brintlinger, "The Persian Frontier," 228.
8. "Four Relays . . . 14000 Miles."
9. "Dream-Come-True!"
10. Rickman, "Japanese Cinema to 1960," website.
11. "Crouching Tiger, Hidden Dragon," Wikipedia, http://en.wikipedia.org/wiki/Crouching_Tiger,_Hidden_Dragon.
12. These commercials were seen on *The Closer* (TNT Time Warner Network), August 21, 2006, and, in slightly modified form, continued into 2011.
13. See Shaheen, *Reel Bad Arabs*.
14. Kruh, "Al-Qaeda Threat."
15. Margolis, *War at the Top of the World*, 30.
16. See, for example, the review of Alexander in *The American Conservative*, December 20, 2004.
17. Etulain, *Does the Frontier Experience Make America Exceptional?*
18. See Toplin, *History by Hollywood*.
19. In more recent times, of course, the archaeologist may be a woman—a condition that sets up considerable sexual tension, as the locals she encounters are often Muslim men.
20. DeMille, *The Autobiography of Cecil B. DeMille*, 544.
21. Landecker, "From Steppe to Campus, Maybe," A56.
22. Mones, *Lost in Translation*, 239.
23. Sorkin, *Some Assembly Required*, 38.
24. McQuerry, "Tumbleweed Invasive, Tumbleweed Tough," 19.
25. "Mount Rainier," National Park Service, http://www.nps.gov/mora/index.htm.

Bibliography

Adair, James. *The History of the American Indians, Particularly Those of the Nations adjoining to the Mississippi, East and West Florida, Georgia, South and North Carolina, and Virginia.* London: Edward and Charles Dilly, 1775.

Ahmad, Diana L. *The Opium Debate and Chinese Exclusion Laws in the Nineteenth-Century American West.* Reno and Las Vegas: University of Nevada Press, 2009.

Ahmed, Leila. *Women and Gender in Islam: Historical Roots of a Modern Debate.* New Haven: Yale University Press, 1992.

Allen, Brian T. "The Garments of Instruction From the Wardrobe of Pleasure: American Orientalist Painting in the 1870s and 1880s." In *Noble Dreams, Wicked Pleasures,* edited by Holly Edwards. Princeton, NJ: Princeton University Press, 2000.

Alter, July. "Revising a Pulp Prodigy." [Texas Letters] *Dallas Morning News,* January 20, 2008.

Ament, Delores Tarzan. "Morris Graves: The Bad-Boy Recluse of Northwest Art." *Art Guide Northwest.* http://www.artguidenw.com/Graves.htm. Accessed July 27, 2006.

American Baptist Home Missionary Society. *Baptist Home Missions in North America.* New York: Baptist Home Mission Society, 1883.

Ames, Kenneth. *Death in the Dining Room and Other Tales of Victorian Culture.* Philadelphia: Temple University Press, 1991.

Anderson, Robert. *The Kung Fu Book: The Exclusive, Unauthorized, Uncensored Story of America's Favorite Martial Arts Show.* Orem, UT: Pioneer Books, 1994.

Anis, Nickl. "Pacific Northwest Skiing at its Best at Mt. Hood Meadows." http://www.travel-watch.com/mt.hood.htm. Accessed January 12, 2011.

Arreola, Daniel D. "The Mexico-US Borderlands through Two Decades." *Journal of Cultural Geography* 27, no. 3 (2010): 331–51.

Auerbach, Jerold S. *Explorers in Eden: Pueblo Indians and the Promised Land.* Albuquerque: University of New Mexico Press, 2006.

Austin, Mary. *The Land of Journeys' Ending.* Tucson: University of Arizona Press, 1983.

———. *The Land of Little Rain.* New York: American Museum of Natural History, 1962.

Babcock, Barbara. "A New Mexican Rebecca: Imaging Pueblo Women." *Journal of the Southwest* 32, no. 4 (1990): 400–37.

Banham, Peter Reyner. *Scenes in America Deserta.* Salt Lake City: Peregrine Smith Books / Gibbs M. Smith, 1982.

Barlow, Philip L. "Toward a Mormon Sense of Time." *Journal of Mormon History* 33, no. 1 (2007): 24.

Barrett, Andrea. "Servants of the Map." In *The Best American Short Stories,* edited by Barbara Kingsolver. New York: Houghton Mifflin, 2001.

Baudrillard, Jean. "The Dance of the Fossils." In *The Illusion of the End.* Stanford, CA: Stanford University Press, 1994.

———. "The Order of the Simulacra." In *Symbolic Exchange and Death.* London: Sage Publications, 1993.

———. The *System of Objects.* London: Verso, 1996.

Baum, L. Frank. *The Wizard of Oz.* Chicago: M. A. Donahue, 1903.

Beaven, Steve. "Portland Classical Chinese Garden celebrates 10th anniversary with a new name – Lan Su Chinese Garden." Oregon Live. http://www.oregonlive.com/news/index.ssf/2010/01/portland_classical_chinese_gar.html. Accessed January 10, 2010.

Bennett, John C. T*he History of the Saints, or an Exposé of Joe Smith and Mormonism*. Boston: Leland & Whiting, 1842.

Bennett, Richard E. *We'll Find the Place: The Mormon Exodus, 1846–1848*. Salt Lake City: Deseret Book, 1997.

Berkhofer, Robert F., Jr. *The White Man's Indian: Images of the American Indian from Columbus to the Present*. New York: Alfred A. Knopf, 1978.

"Bernheimer Residence and Oriental Gardens." Image-Archeology.com/Bernheimer_residence_CAhtm. Consulted 7 February, 2011.

Bernstein, Matthew, and Gaylyn Studlar. *Visions of the East: Orientalism in Film*. New Brunswick, NJ: Rutgers University Press, 1997.

Billington, Ray Allen. *Land of Savagery, Land of Promise: The European Image of the American Frontier in the Nineteenth Century*. New York: W. W. Norton, 1981.

Bokovoy, Matthew F. *The San Diego World's Fair*s and Southwestern Memory, 1880–1940. Albuquerque: University of New Mexico Press, 2005.

Borges, Jorge Luis. *Seven Nights*. New York: New Directions, 1984.

Boswell, Sharon. "Partners Across the Pacific." *Seattle Times,* January 28, 1996. http://seattletimes.nwsource.com/special/centennial/january/partners.html. Accessed January 15, 2010.

Boyer, David S. "Geographical Twins a World Apart." *National Geographic*, December 1958, 848–59.

Brackenridge, Henry Marie. *Journal of a Voyage up the River Missouri*: Performed in Eighteen Hundred and Eleven. Baltimore: Coale and Maxwell, 1816.

Breeden, James O., ed. *A Long Ride in Texas: The Explorations of John Leonard Riddell*. College Station: Texas A&M University Press, 1994.

Brintlinger, Angela. "The Persian Frontier: Griboedov as Orientalist and Literary Hero." *Canadian Slavonic Papers,* 4, no. 3-4 (2003): 371-393.

Brooks, James F. *Captives & Cousins*: Slavery, Kinship, and Community in the Southwest Borderlands. Chapel Hill: University of North Carolina Press, 2002.

Brown, Rollo W. *I Travel by Train*. New York: D. Appleton-Century, 1939.

Browne, J. Ross. *Crusoe's Island*: A Ramble in the Footsteps of Alexander Selkirk: with Sketches of Adventure in California and Washoe. New York: Harper & Bros., 1864.

Buel, James W. *The Magic City*. St. Louis: Historical Publishing, 1894.

Burton, Richard F. *The City of the Saints and Across the Rocky Mountains to California*. New York: Alfred A. Knopf, 1963.

———. *The City of the Saints: Among the Mormons and Across the Rocky Mountains to California*. Santa Barbara, CA: Narrative Press, 2003.

———. T*he Look of the Wes*t. Lincoln: University of Nebraska Press, 1963.

Buruma, Ian, and Avishai Margalit. *Occidentalism: The West in the Eyes of its Enemies*. New York: Penguin Press, 2004.

Bushman, Richard L. *Joseph Smith: Rough Stone Rolling*. New York: Alfred A. Knopf, 2005.

Cannadine, David. *Ornamentalism: How the British Saw their Empire*. Oxford: Oxford University Press, 2001.

Chacón, Hipólito Rafael. "Creating a Mythic Past: Spanish-Style Architecture in Montana." *Montana, the Magazine of Western History* 51, no. 3 (Autumn 2001): 46.

Chandler, Katherine, and Melissa Goldthwaite, eds. "Sound Ground to Stand On: Soundscapes in Williams' Work." In *Surveying the Literary Landscapes of Terry Tempest Williams: New Critical Essays*. Salt Lake City: University of Utah Press, 2003.

Chang, Gordon H., ed. *Asian American Art: A History, 1850–1970*. Stanford, CA: Stanford University Press, 2008.

Choir, Melody. *Choir's Pioneer Directory of the City of Seattle and King County, History, Business Directory, and Immigrant's Guide to and throughout Washington Territory and Vicinity*. Pottsville, PA: Miners' Journal Book and Job Rooms, 1878.

Christensen, Jan. Nevada. Portland, OR: Graphic Arts Center, 2001.

The Closer. Television show on TNT Time Warner Network, August 21, 2006.

Conn, Steven. *Museums and American Intellectual Life, 1876–1926.* Chicago: University of Chicago Press, 1998.

Conti, Gerald. "Seeing the Elephant." *Civil War Times,* June 1984. http://wesclark.com/jw/elephant.html. Accessed October 16, 2008.

Cook, Robin. *Sphinx.* New York: G. P. Putnam's Sons, 1979.

Cozzens, S. W. *The Marvellous Country; or Three Years in Arizona and New Mexico. London*: S. Low, Marston, Low, and Searle, 1875.

"Crouching Tiger, Hidden Dragon." *Wikipedia.* http://en.wikipedia.org/wiki/Crouching_Tiger,_Hidden_Dragon. Accessed February 24, 2006.

Curzon, Nathaniel. *Tales of Travel.* New York: George H. Doran, 1923.

"Date Palms." Natural Color Card, Kodachrome K39A. Published and distributed by Bob Petley, Phoenix, AZ.

Davies, W. D. "Israel, the Mormons and the Land." In *Reflections on Mormonism: Judaeo-Christian Parallels,* edited by Larry E. Dahl and Charles D. Tate Jr. Provo, UT: Religious Studies Center, Brigham Young University, 1978.

Davis, John. *The Landscape of Belief: Encountering the Holy Land in Nineteenth-Century American Art and Culture.* Princeton, NJ: Princeton University Press, 1996.

Davis, Mike. "Bunker Hill: Hollywood's Dark Shadow" in Mark Shiel and Tony Fitzmaurice, eds. *Dead Cities and Other Tales*: Film and Urban Societies in Global Context. New York: New York Press, 2002. 33-45.

Dawson, J. W. *Modern Science in Bible Lands.* New York: Harper & Brothers, 1889.

DeJong, David H. "'Good Samaritans of the Desert': The Pima-Maricopa Villages as Described in California Emigrant Journals, 1846–1852." *Journal of the Southwest* 47, no. 3 (2005): 462–69.

DeLyser, Dydia. *Ramona Memories*: Tourism and Shaping of Southern California. Minneapolis: University of Minnesota Press, 2005.

DeMille, Cecil B. *The Autobiography of Cecil B. DeMille.* Englewood Cliffs, NJ: Prentice-Hall, 1959.

Deveney, John P. *Paschal Beverly Randolph: A Nineteenth-century Black American Spiritualist, Rosicrucian, and Sex Magician.* Albany: State University of New York Press, 1997.

Dilworth, Leah. *Imagining Indians in the Southwest: Persistent Visions of a Primitive Past.* Washington, DC: Smithsonian Institution Press, 1996.

Dodds, Jerrilynn D. "Myst." In *Analyzing Ambasz,* edited by Michael Sorkin. New York: Monacelli Press, 2004.

Dodge, Richard Irving. *The Plains of the Great West and Their Inhabitants, Being a Description of the Plains, Game, Indians & C. of the Great North American Deser*t. New York: Archer House, 1959.

Domenech, Emmanuel. *Seven Years' Residence in the Great Deserts of North America.* London: Longman, Green, Longman, and Roberts, 1860.

———. *Voyage Pittoresque dans les grands déserts du Nouveau monde.* Paris: Morizot, 1862.

Doughty, Robin. *At Home in Texas: Early Views of the Land.* College Station: Texas A&M University Press, 1987.

Doyle, Theodore F. "The Oriental Limited." Great Northern Historical Society, Reference Sheet No. 217, June, 1994.

"Dream-Come-True!" Northwest Oriental Airlines advertisement in Time, November 4, 1946, 51.

Dreams of the West: A History of the Chinese in Oregon, 1850–1950. Portland, OR: Ooligan Press and the Chinese Consolidated Benevolent Association, 2007.

Dunraven, Windham Thomas. *The Great Divide: Travels in the Upper Yellowstone.* Lincoln: University of Nebraska Press, 1967.

Dye, Victoria E. *All Aboard for Santa Fe: Railway Promotion of the Southwest, 1890s to 1930s*. Albuquerque: University of New Mexico Press, 2005.

Dylan, Bob. "The Groom's Still Waiting at the Altar." Words and music Bob Dylan. Released on *Biograph* (1985) and on the CD edition of Shot of Love (1981).

Edwards, Holly. *Noble Dreams, Wicked Pleasures: Orientalism in America, 1870–1930*. Princeton, NJ: Princeton University Press, 2000.

Eidel, Jim. Foreword to *Portraits of Nature*, by Roy Purcell, xi–xiii. Las Vegas, NV: K.C. Publication, 2001.

Eliason, Eric. "Pioneers and Recapitulation in Mormon Popular Historical Expression." In *Usable Pasts*, edited by Tad Tuleja. Logan, UT: Utah State University Press, 1997.

Emory, William H. *Report on the United States and Mexican Boundary Survey*. Washington, DC: C. Wendell, 1857–1859.

Etulain, Richard. *Does the Frontier Experience Make America Exceptional?* Gordonsville, VA: Bedford / St. Martin's, 1999.

———. "Inventing the Pacific Northwest: Novelists and the Region's History." In *Terra Pacifica: People and Place in the Northwest States and Western Canada*, edited by Paul W. Hirt. Pullman: Washington State University Press, 1998.

"Eugene Buissonet Diary [1868-1869]." Unpublished manuscript, Utah State Historical Society Archives, 1869.

Evans, Albert S. *A la California: Sketch of Life in the Golden State*. San Francisco: A. L. Bancroft, 1873.

Farmer, Jared. *On Zion's Mount: Mormons, Indians, and the American Landscape*. Cambridge, MA: Harvard University Press, 2008.

Ferguson, T. J., and Chip Coldwell-Chanthaphonh. *History Is in the Land*. Tuscon: University of Arizona Press, 2006.

Field, H. M. *From Egypt to Japan*. New York: Charles Scribner's Sons, 1897.

Findlay, John M. *Magic Lands: Western Cityscapes and American Culture After 1940*. Berkeley: University of California Press, 1992.

Finn, Mark. *Blood & Thunder: The Life & Art of Robert E. Howard*. Austin, TX: MonkeyBrain Books, 2006.

"First in the West: Sacramento Valley Railroad of One Hundred Years Ago, is Oldest Link in SP's Western Lines." *The Western Railroader* 18, no. 10 (1955): 5.

"The Five Gardens." Portland Japanese Garden. http://www.japanesegarden.com. Accessed January 17, 2010.

Fleishman, Jeffrey. "It's Love, Saudi Style." *Dallas Morning News*, January 15, 2008.

Fleming, G. A. *California: Its Past History, its Present Position, its Future Prospects*. London: McGowan, 1850.

Flint, Richard, and Shirley Flint. *Documents of the Coronado Expedition, 1539–1542*. Dallas, TX: Southern Methodist University Press, 2005.

"Four Relays . . . 14000 Miles." Shell Oil Co. advertisement in *U.S. News and World Report*, May 4, 1945, 69.

Fowler, Don D. *A Laboratory for Anthropology: Science and Romanticism in the American Southwest, 1846–1930*. Albuquerque: University of New Mexico Press, 2000.

Fowler, Harlan D. *Camels to California: A Chapter in Western Transportation*. Stanford, CA: Stanford University Press, 1950.

Francaviglia, Richard. *Believing in Place: A Spiritual Geography of the Great Basin*. Reno: University of Nevada Press, 2003.

———."The Cemetery as an Evolving Cultural Landscape." *Annals, Association of American Geographers 61*, no. 3 (1971): 501–9.

———. "Crusaders and Saracens: The Persistence of Orientalism in Historically-Themed Films About the Middle East." In *Lights, Camera, History: Portraying the Past in Film,* edited by Richard Francaviglia and Jerry Rodnitzky. College Station: Texas A&M University Press, 2007.

———. "Landscape and Cultural Continuity: The Case of the Southwest." *Journal of the West* 37, no. 3 (1998): 9–21.

———. *The Mormon Landscape: Existence, Creation and Perception of a Unique Image in the American West*. New York: AMS Press, 1979.

———. "The Treasures of Aladdin: Orientalizing the Mining Frontier." Paper presented at the Mining History Association meeting in Silver City, New Mexico, June 11, 2010.

Frémont, John Charles. *A Report of the Exploring Expedition to the Rocky Mountains and to Oregon and North California in the Years 1843–'44*. Washington DC: Blair and Rives, 1845.

———. *Memoirs of My Life*. Chicago: Belford, Clark and Co., 1887.

Galveston Bay and Texas Land Company. *Emigrants' Guide to Texas: Containing Important Statements and Documents Concerning that Interesting Country*. New York: H. Mason, 1834.

Garrigues, Eduardo. *West of Babylon: A Novel*. Albuquerque: University of New Mexico Press, 2002.

"Gems of Art Contributed by Local Painters." *San Francisco Call [The Sunday Call],* January 21, 1900.

"General Epistle from the Council of the Twelve Apostles to The Church of Jesus Christ of Latter Day Saints Abroad Dispersed Throughout the Earth." LDS Church Archives. December 23, 1847.

Giedion, Siegfried. *Mechanization Takes Control*. New York: Norton, 1969.

Gilleland, J. C. *The Ohio and Mississippi Pilot . . .* Pittsburgh: R. Patterson & Lambdin, 1820.

GMD to A. Burlingame, June 15, 1866. (W) GMD papers, box 337, GMD & China. Union Pacific Archives, Council Bluffs, Iowa.

Goetzmann, William. *When the Eagle Screamed*: *The Romantic Horizon in American Diplomacy, 1800–1860*. New York: John Wiley & Sons, 1966.

Goss, Helen Rocca. *Gold and Cinnabar: The Life of Andrew Rocca,* California Pioneer. Montgomery, AL: H. R. Goss, 1990.

Grabar, Oleg. "Roots and Others." In *Noble Dreams, Wicked Pleasures: Orientalism in America*, *1870–1930*, edited by Holly Edwards. Princeton: Princeton University Press, 2000.

Grammer, Timothy. "'April in Andalusia': Geographic Parallelisms in the Diario of Columbus' First Voyage." *Journal of Caribbean History* 35, no. 2 (2001): 222–33.

Great Salt Lake lantern slides, PH 4579. Archives, Church of Jesus Christ of Latter-day Saints, Salt Lake City, Utah.

Great Trans-Continental Tourists' Guide . . . from the Atlantic to the Pacific. New York: G. A. Crofutt, 1870.

Gum San: Land of the Golden Mountain; An Exhibit on Chinese Life and Labor in the West. Bend, OR: High Desert Museum, 1991.

Gunn, Giles. *Readings on the Religious Meaning of the American Experience*. New York: Oxford University Press, 1981.

Hall, Baynard Rush. *The New Purchase, or, Early Years in the Far West*. New Albany, IN: Jno. R. Nunemacher, 1855.

Hamer, Mary. "Timeless Histories: A British Dream of Cleopatra." In *Visions of the East: Orientalism in Film*, edited by Matthew Bernstein and Gaylyn Studlar. New Brunswick, NJ: Rutgers University Press, 1997.

Harmetz, Aljean. *The Making of the Wizard of Oz*. New York: Knopf, 1977.

Harmon, Appleton Milo. *Appleton Milo Harmon Goes West*. Berkeley, CA: Gillick Press, 1946.

Harmsen, Dorothy. *Harmsen's Western Americana: A collection of One Hundred Western Paintings*. Denver, CO: Harmsen Publishing, 1978.

Harris, Neil. *The Artist in American Society: The Formative Years, 1790–1860*. New York: George Braziller, 1966.

Hausladen, Gary, and Paul Starrs. "L.A. Noir." *Journal of Cultural Geography* 23, no. 1 (2005): 46.

Hayashi, Robert T. *Haunted by Waters: A Journey through Race and Place in the American West*. Iowa City: University of Iowa Press, 2007.

Herodotus. *History*. Hentfordshire, UK: Wordsworth Editions Ltd., 1996.

Historical Records of Parowan, Utah, 1856–1859. Salt Lake City, Church Historian's Office (August 23, 1857): 25.

Homer, Michael, ed. *On the Way to Somewhere Else: European Sojourners in the Mormon West, 1834–1930*. Spokane, WA: Arthur H. Clark, 2006.

Hoover, Mildred Brooke, Hero Eugene Hoover, and Ethel Grace Rensch. *Historic Spots in California*. Palo Alto, CA: Stanford University Press, 1966.

Howard, Robert E. *Conan the Barbarian*. New York: Gnome Press, 1954.

Howe, Henry. *Historical Collections of the Great West . . .* vol. 1. Cincinnati, OH: Henry Howe, 1853.

Howett, Catherine. "Grounding Memory and Identity: Pioneering Garden Club Projects Documenting Historic Landscape Traditions of the American South." In *Design with Culture: Claiming America's Landscape Heritage*, edited by Charles A. Birnbaum and Mary V. Hughes. Charlottesville: University of Virginia Press, 2005.

Hrdlička, Aleš. 1912. Quoted in Matthew Bokovoy, *The San Diego World's Fairs and Southwestern Memory, 1880–1940*. Albuquerque: University of New Mexico Press 2005.

Huchel, Frederick M. *A History of Box Elder County*. Utah State Historical Society and Box Elder County Commission, 1999.

Hurlbut, Jesse Lyman. *Bible Atlas: A Manual of Biblical Geography and History*. Chicago: Rand, McNally, & Company, 1884.

Hyde, Anne Farrar. *An American Vision: Far Western Landscape and National Culture, 1820–1920*. New York: New York University Press, 1990.

Irving, Washington. *The Adventures of Captain Bonneville, or, Scenes Beyond the Rocky Mountains*. London: R. Bentley, 1837.

———. *Astoria Or, Anecdotes of an Enterprise Beyond the Rocky Mountains*. Philadelphia: Carey, Lee & Blanchard, 1836.

———. *A Tour on the Prairies*. Philadelphia: Carey, Lee & Blanchard, 1835.

Irwin, Robert. *The Lust of Knowing: The Orientalists and Their Enemies*. London: Allen Lane, 2006.

Iwamura, Jane Naomi. *Virtual Orientalism: Asian Religions and American Popular Culture*. Oxford: Oxford University Press, 2011.

Jackson, Helen Hunt. *Outdoor Industries in Southern California*. Century Magazine, October 1883. Reprinted in her edited book *Glimpses of California and the Missions*. Boston: Little, Brown, 1902.

———. *Ramona*. New York: Little, Brown, 1884.

Jackson, J. B. "The Necessity for Ruins." In *The Necessity for Ruins, and Other Topics*, edited by J. B. Jackson. Amherst: University of Massachusetts Press, 1980.

Jackson, Jean, and LeRoy Jackson. *Dr. J. R. N. Owen, Frontier Doctor and Leader of Death Valley's Camel Caravan*. Death Valley, CA: Death Valley '49ers, 1996.

Jackson, Richard. "The Mormon Experience: The Plains as Sinai, the Great Salt Lake as the Dead Sea, and the Great Basin as Desert-cum-Promised Land." *Journal of Historical Geography* 18, no. 1 (1992).

———. "Mormon Perception and Settlement." *Annals, Association of American Geographers* 68 (1978).

James Martineau Diary. Huntington Library, San Marinp, California, FAC 1499, Box 2, Folder 2 (February 13, 1986): 38–39, 42.

"Japan, the land of picturesque gardens." Northwest Orient Airlines postcard, TRAD 335. Printed in USA, 1961.

Johnson, Michael B. *Kenneth Callahan*: *Universal Voyage*. Seattle, WA: Henry Art Gallery, 1973.

"Jurassic Crocodile is Unearthed from Blue Mountains in Eastern Oregon." *Science Daily,* March 19, 2007. http:www.sciencedaily.com/releases/2007/03/070319112538.htm. Accessed June 11, 2007.

Kalmar, Ivan Davidson, and Derek Jonathan Penslar. *Orientalism and the Jew*s. Waltham, MA: Brandeis University Press; Hanover, MA: University Press of New England, 2005.

Karlinsky, Nahum. *California Dreaming: Ideology, Society, and Technology in the Citrus Industry of Palestine.* New York: State University of New York Press, 2005.

Kessler, Lauren. "Spacious Dreams: A Japanese American Family Comes to the Pacific Northwest." *Oregon Historical Quarterly* 94, no. 2-3 (1993): 163–65.

Kizer, Carolyn. "Poetry: School of the Pacific Northwest." *The New Republic*, July 16, 1956. Cited in Nicholas O'Connell, *On Sacred Ground*: *The Spirit of Place in Pacific Northwest Literature.* Seattle: University of Washington Press, 2003.

Klein, Norman M. *The History of Forgetting*: *Los Angeles and the Erasure of Memory*. New York: Verso, 1997.

Kolodny, Annette. *The Land Before Her: Fantasy and Experience of the American Frontiers, 1630–1860.* Chapel Hill: University of North Carolina Press, 1984.

Kruh, Nancy. "Al-Qaeda Threat." *Dallas Morning News*, Friday, July 20, 2007.

L'Amour, Louis. *Education of a Wandering Man*. New York: Bantam Books, 1989.

———. *The Lonesome God*s. New York: Bantam Books, 1983.

Landecker, Heidi. "From Steppe to Campus, Maybe." *The Chronicle of Higher Education*, May 11, 2007, A56.

Landon, Michael N., ed. *The Journals of George Q. Cannon: Vol. 1 To California in '49.* Salt Lake City: Deseret Book, 1999.

Langworthy, Franklin. *Scenery of the Plains, Mountains and Mines: or A Diary Kept Upon the Overland Route to California.* Ogdensburgh, NY: J. C. Sprague, 1855.

Lanman, Charles. *A Summer in the Wilderness: Embracing a Canoe Voyage up the Mississippi and around Lake Superior.* New York: D. Appleton, 1847.

Lant, Antonia. "The Curse of the Pharaoh, or How Cinema Contracted Egyptomania." In *Visions of the East: Orientalism in Film*, edited by Matthew Bernstein and Gaylyn Studlar. New Brunswick, NJ: Rutgers University Press, 1997.

Leal, Robert Barry. *Wilderness in the Bible: Toward a Theology of Wildernes*s. New York: Peter Lang, 2004.

Lears, T. J. Jackson. *No Place of Grace: Antimodernism and the Transformation of American Culture, 1880–1920.* New York: Pantheon Books, 1981.

Leavitt, D. G. W., "California Again!" In *Arkansas Gazette*, October 27, 1845. Reed Papers, Sutter's Fort Historical Monument Collection, 1845.

Lee, Lawrence. "William E. Smythe and San Diego, 1901-1908." *The Journal of San Diego History* 19, no. 1 (1973):10-24; see also http://www.sandiegohistory.org/journal/73winter/smythe.htm.

Lee, Shelly S. "The Contradictions of Cosmopolitanism: Consuming the Orient at the Alaska-Yukon-Pacific Exposition and the International Potlatch Festival, 1909–1934." *Western Historical Quarterly* 38, no. 3 (2007): 278–79, 302.

LeMenager, Stephanie. *Manifest and Other Destinies: Territorial Fictions of the Nineteenth-Century United States*. Lincoln: University of Nebraska Press, 2004.

Lemon, Dean. *The Harmony Borax Works of Death Valley, California.* Bishop, CA: Community Printing and Publishing, 2000.

LeSueur, Steven C. "The Community of Christ and the Search for a Usable Past." *John Whitmer Historical Association Journal* 22 (2002):1-24.

Leung, Peter C. Y. "One Day, One Dollar—Delta Heritage." In *150 Years of the Chinese Presence in California: Honor the Past, Engage the Present, Build the Future.* Sacramento Chinese Culture Foundation and Asian-American Studies, University of California, Davis, 2001.

Levine, Kenneth Mark. *Northwest Visionaries.* Video recording. Seattle, WA: Iris Films, 1979.

Levine, Lawrence W. *The Unpredictable Past: Explorations in American Cultural History.* New York: Oxford University Press, 1993.

Li, T. June. "Breathing Life into the Chinese Garden." *Huntington Frontiers* 3, no. 1 (2007): 13–17.

Liebersohn, Harry. *Aristocratic Encounters: European Travelers and North American Indians.* Cambridge, MA: Cambridge University Press, 1998.

Liestman, Daniel. "'The Various Celestials Among Our Town': Euro-American Response to Port Townsend's Chinese Colony." *Pacific Northwest Quarterly* 85, no.3 (1994): 93–104.

A Lieutenant of the Left Wing. *Sketch of the Seminole War: and Sketches During the Campaign.* Charleston, SC: Dan J. Dowling, 1836.

Lingenfelter, Richard E. *Death Valley & the Amargosa: A Land of Illusion.* Berkeley: University of California Press, 1986.

Lockwood, Jeffrey. *Locust: The Devastating Rise and Mysterious Disappearance of the Insect That Shaped the American Frontier.* New York: Basic Books, 2004.

Long, Burke O. *Imagining the Holy Land: Maps, Models, and Fantasy Travels.* Bloomington: Indiana University Press, 2003.

Lubetkin, M. John. *Jay Cooke's Gamble: The Northern Pacific Railroad, the Sioux, and the Panic of 1873.* Norman: University of Oklahoma Press, 2006.

Ludlow, Fitz Hugh. *The Heart of the Continent: A Record of Travel Across the Plains and in Oregon.* New York: Hurd and Houghton, 1870.

MacCannell, Dean. "Ideological Castles." In *Analyzing Ambasz*, edited by Michael Sorkin. New York: Manacelli Press, 2004.

Macfie, A. L. *Orientalism.* New York: Longman, 2002.

MacGregor, Bruce. *The Birth of California Narrow Gauge: A Regional Study of the Technology of Thomas and Martin Carter.* Stanford, CA: Stanford University Press, 2003.

Macintyre, Ben. *The Man Who Would be King: the First American in Afghanistan.* New York: Farrar, Straus, Giroux, 2004.

MacKenzie, John. *Orientalism: History, Theory, and the Arts.* Manchester, NY: Manchester University Press, 1995.

Maffly-Kipp, Lauri. "Engaging Habits and Besotted Idolatry: Viewing Chinese Religions in the American West." In *Race, Religion, Region: Landscapes of Encounter in the American West*, edited by Fay Botham and Sara M. Patterson. Tucson: University of Arizona Press, 2006.

Malamud, Margaret. "Pyramids in Las Vegas and Outer Space: Ancient Egypt in Twentieth-Century American Architecture and Film." *Journal of Popular Culture* 34, no. 1 (2000): 31, 35.

Manly, William Lewis. *Death Valley in '49: Important Chapter of California Pioneer History.* San Jose, CA: Pacific Tree and Vine, 1894. Reprinted by Ann Arbor. University Micro-films, 1966.

Margolis, Eric S. *War at the Top of the World: The Struggle for Afghanistan, Kashmir, and Tibet.* New York: Routledge, 2002.

"Mark Tobey." Guggenheim Museum. http://www.guggenheimcollection.org/site/artist_bio_1538.html. Accessed July 27, 2006.

Markwyn, Abigail. "Economic Partner and Exotic Other: China and Japan at San Francisco's Panama-Pacific International Exposition." *Western Historical Quarterly,* 34 no. 4 (2007): 439–466.

Marr, Timothy. *The Cultural Roots of American Islamicism.* Chapel Hill: University of North Carolina Press, 2006.

Marryat, Frederick. *Narrative of the Travels and Adventures of Monsieur Violet in California, Sonora, and Western Texas.* New York: Harper Brothers, 1843.

Martineau, Harriet. *Society in America*, vol. 2. New York: Saunders and Otley, 1837.

Mason, Peter. *Infelicities: Representations of the Exotic.* Baltimore, MD: Johns Hopkins University, 1998.

Matar, Nabil. *Turks, Moors and Englishmen in the Age of Discovery.* New York: Columbia University Press, 1999.

Matthews, Sallie Reynolds. "The Family." In *Interwoven, A Pioneer Chronicle,* 17. College Station: Texas A&M University Press, 1982.

May, Karl. *Oriental Odyssey II: In the Shadow of the Padishah. The Devil Worshippers.* Originally published in *Deutscher Hausschatz* in serial format, 1881–1888. Psi Computer Consultants, 1999, 2002.

McArthur, Lewis A. *Oregon Geographic Names.* Portland: Oregon Historical Society Press, 1992.

McClain, Charles J. *In Search of Equality: The Chinese Struggle Against Discrimination in Nineteenth Century America.* Berkeley: University of California Press, 1994.

McClelland, Gordon T., and Jay T. Last. *California Orange Box Labels: An Illustrated History.* Beverly Hills, CA: Hillcrest Press, 1985.

McCormick, Nancy D., and John S. McCormick. "Saltair." In *Great Salt Lake: An Anthology,* edited by Gary Topping. Logan: Utah State University Press, 2002.

McQuerry, Claire. "Tumbleweed Invasive, Tumbleweed Tough." *Oregon Quarterly* 87, no. 1 (2007): 19.

Meline, James F. *Two Thousand Miles on Horseback: Santa Fé and Back, A Summer Tour Through Kansas, Nebraska, Colorado, and New Mexico, in the Year 1866.* New York: Hurd and Houghton, 1867.

Melman, Billie. "The Middle East/Arabia: 'The Cradle of Islam.'" In *The Cambridge Companion to Travel Writing,* edited by Peter Hulme and Tim Youngs. Cambridge, MA: Cambridge University Press, 2002.

Miller, Kit. "Inside the Glitter: Lives of Casino Workers." In *The Grit Beneath the Glitter: Tales from the Real Las Vegas,* edited by Hal Rothman and Mike Davis. Berkeley: University of California Press, 2002.

Momaday. Scott N., "The American West and the Burden of Belief." In *The Man Made of Words: Essays, Stories, Passages.* New York: St. Martin's Press, 1997: 89-110.

Mones, Nicole. *Lost in Translation: A Novel.* New York: Dell, 1998.

Monoghan, Peter. "The Dunes that Roar." *The Chronicle of Higher Education,* Nov. 2005, A64.

Moreno, Richard. *Roadside History of Nevada.* Missoula, MT: Mountain Press, 2000.

Morgan, Dale, ed. *Overland in 1846: Diaries and Letters of the California-Oregon Trail,* vol. 2. Georgetown, CA: Talisman Press, 1963.

Morris, John Miller. "When Corporations Rule the Llano Estacado." In *The Future of the Southern Plains,* edited by Sherry Smith. Norman: University of Oklahoma Press, 2008.

Murphy, Deirdre. "Like Standing on the Edge of the World and Looking Away Into Heaven." *Common-Place* 7, no. 3 (2007): 4.

Nakane, Kazuko. "Facing the Pacific: Asian American Artists in Seattle, 1900–1970." In *Asian American Art: A History, 1850–1970,* edited by Gordon H. Chang. Stanford, CA: Stanford University Press, 2008.

Nelson's Pictorial Guide-Books, the Central Pacific Railroad: A Trip Across the North American Continent from Ogden to San Francisco. Also published with a paper cover, entitled *The Scenery of the Central Pacific Railroad.* New York: T. Nelson and Sons, 1871.

Nisbet, Jack. *The Mapmaker's Eye: David Thompson on the Columbia Plateau.* Pullman: Washington State University Press, 2005.

Nokes, R. Gregory. *Massacred for Gold: The Chinese in Hells Canyon.* Corvallis: Oregon State University Press, 2009.

Norris, L. David, James C. Milligan, and Odie B. Faulk. *William H. Emory, Soldier-Scientist*. Tucson: University of Arizona Press, 1998.

Nuttall, Thomas. *Journal of Travels into the Arkansa* [sic] *Territory, During the Year 1819: With Occasional Observations on the Manners of the Aborigines*. Philadelphia: Thomas H. Palmer, 1821.

Oberle, Alex P., and Daniel D. Arreola. "Resurgent Mexican Phoenix." *Geographical Review* 98, no. 2 (2008): 171–96.

O'Connell, Nicholas. *On Sacred Ground*: T*he Spirit of Place in Pacific Northwest Literature*. Seattle: University of Washington Press, 2003.

O'dea, Thomas F. *The Mormons.* Chicago: University of Chicago Press, 1957.

Padget, Martin. *Indian Country*: *Travels in the American Southwest, 1840–1935*. Albuquerque: University of New Mexico Press, 2004.

Panero, James. "Outside the Frame: How Asia Changed the Course of American Art." *Humanities: The Magazine of the National Endowment for the Humanities* 30, no. 2 (2009): 18.

Papanikolas, Zeese. *American Silence*. Lincoln: University of Nebraska, 2007.

Parks, Gary. "Pharaoh Comes to Main Street: American Movie Palaces in the Egyptian Style." American Research Center in Egypt / Northern California. http://home.comcast.net/~hebsed/parks.htm. Accessed on January 15, 2011.

Parson, William Barclay. *An American Engineer in China.* New York: McClure, Phillips, 1900.

Pattie, James Ohio. T*he Hunters of Kentucky, or, the Trials and Toils of Trappers and Traders, During an Expedition to the Rocky Mountains, New Mexico, and California*. New York: W. H. Graham, 1847.

Pike, Zebulon Montgomery. *Expedition of Zebulon Montgomery Pike to Headwaters of the Mississippi River, through Louisiana Territory, and in New Spain, during the Years 1805–6–7.* New York: Francis P. Harper, 1895.

Pilato, Herbie J. *The Kung Fu Book of Caine*: *The Complete Guide to TV's First Mystical Eastern Western.* Boston: Charles A. Tuttle, 1993.

Pine, George W. *Beyond the West: Containing an account of two years' travels in the other half of our Great Continent far beyond the Old West* . . . Utica, NY: T. J. Griffiths, 1870.

Piyananda, Bhante Walpola. *The Bodhi Tree Grows in L.A.*: *Tales of a Buddhist Monk in America*. Boston: Shambhala, 2008.

Pomeroy, Earl. *In Search of the Golden West: The Tourist in Western North America.* New York: Alfred A. Knopf, 1957.

Portland.Citysearch. http://portland.citysearch.com/profile/8452942portland_or/the_japanes_garden.html. Accessed on January 15, 2011.

Portland Classical Chinese Garden. Brochure for the Portland Classical Chinese Garden, 2002.

Poston, Charles D. "Building a State in Apache Land." *Overland Monthly, and Out West Magazine* 24 (July 1894): 89–90.

Prevost, Louis. *California Silk Grower's Manual.* San Francisco: H. H. Bancroft and Company, 1867.

Pronk, John. "Camels at Home on the Range." *Dallas Morning New*s, January 8, 2006.

Pumpelly, Raphael. *Across America and Asia*: *Notes on a Year's Journey Around the World.* New York: Leypoldt & Holt, 1870.

Purcell, Roy. *Portraits of Nature*. Las Vegas: KC Publications, 2001.

Rafn, Carl Christian. *America Discovered in the Tenth Century*. New York: W. Jackson, 1838.

Reid, Mayne. "Original Sketch: The Entry of the American Army into Puebla." *The Saturday Evening Post,* February 25, 1849, 1.

Rickman, Gregg. "Japanese Cinema to 1960." Green Cine, http://www.greencine.com/static/primers/japan-60-1-jsp. Accessed January 29, 2010.

Ridgway, Robert. *United States Geological Exploration of the Fortieth parallel, Part III, Ornithology.* Washington: US Government Printing Office, 1870.

Robinson, Phil. *Sinners and Saints: A Tour Across the States and Round Them; with Three Months Among the Mormons*. Boston: Roberts Brothers, 1883.

"Rock Camel." Postcard of Petley Color Cards, Bob Petley, Phoenix, Arizona, K-226, n.d., ca. 1960.

Rothman, Hal. *Devil's Bargains: Tourism in the Twentieth-Century American West*. Lawrence: University Press of Kansas, 1998.

Runnels, John. Untitled speech. Report of the Fourth Tri-State Reunion, 56–59, 1884–1887. Cited in David Wrobel, *Promised Lands: Promotion, Memory, and the Creation of the American West*. Lawrence: University of Kansas Press, 2002.

Russell, William Howard. *My Diary North and South*. Boston: T. O. H. P. Burnham, 1863.

———. *Pictures of Southern Life, Social, Political and Military*. New York: J. G. Gregory, 1861.

Sackman, Douglas Cazaux. *Orange Empire: California and the Fruits of Eden*. Berkeley: University of California Press, 2005.

Sacramento Daily Union, December 9, 1867. Cited in Anne Farrar Hyde, *An American Vision: Far Western Landscape and National Culture, 1820–1920*. New York: New York University Press, 1990.

Said, Edward W. *Orientalism*. New York: Vintage, 1979.

———. "Orientalism Reconsidered." *Cultural Critique,* Fall 1985, 90, 103.

Sanders, Daniel Clark. *A History of the Indian Wars with the First Settlers of the United States, Particularly in New-England*. Montpelier, VT: Wright and Sibley, 1812.

"Sands of Oblivion." Sci-Fi Channel premiere, Saturday, October 13, 2007.

Sarmiento, D. F. *Life in the Argentine Republic in the Days of the Tyrants*. New York: Collier Books, 1961.

Sauder, Robert A. *The Yuma Reclamation Project: Irrigation, Indian Allotment, and Settlement Along the Lower Colorado River*. Reno: University of Nevada Press, 2009.

Schoenbauer, Susan, ed. *Nineteenth Century Travels, Explorations, and Empires: Writings from the Era of Imperial Consolidation, 1835–1910; Vol. 2, North America*. London, UK: Pickering Chatto Publishers, 2003.

Schoolcraft, Henry Rowe. *Information Respecting the History, Condition and Prospects of the Indian Tribes of the United States.* Philadelphia: Lippincott, Grambo, 1851–57.

Scott, Harvey Whitefield, ed. *History of Portland, Oregon: With Illustrations and Biographical Sketches of Prominent Citizens and Pioneers*. Syracuse, NY: D. Mason, 1890.

Scott, Sir Walter. *The Talisman*. New York: Dodd, Mead, 1943.

Shaffer, Marguerite. *See America First: Tourism and National Identity, 1880–1940*. Washington, DC: Smithsonian Institution Press, 2001.

Shaheen, Jack. *Reel Bad Arabs: How Hollywood Villifies a People.* New York: Olive Branch Press, 2001.

"Shanghai Noon." *Wikipedia*. http://en.wikipedia.org/wiki/Shanghai_Noon. Accessed January 27, 2010.

Shohat, Ella. "Gender and Culture of Empire: Toward a Feminist Ethnography of the Cinema." In *Visions of the East: Orientalism in Film*, edited by Matthew Bernstein and Gaylyn Studlar. New Brunswick, NJ: Rutgers University Press, 1997.

Signor, John R. *Beaumont Hill: Southern Pacific's Southern California Gateway.* San Marino, CA: Golden West Books, 1990.

Sigourney, Lydia Howard. *Scenes in My Native Land*. Boston: James Munroe, 1845.

Slotkin, Richard. *Gunfighter Nation: The Myth of the Frontier in Twentieth Century America.* Norman: University of Oklahoma Press, 1992.

Smith, Ethan. *View of the Hebrews: or the Tribes of Israel in America*. Poultney, VT: Smith & Shute, 1825.

Smith, Henry Nash. *Virgin Land: The American West as Symbol and Myth.* New York: Vintage Books, 1957.

Smith, J. Russell. *North America: Its People and Resources, Development, and Prospects of the Continent as an Agricultural, Industrial, and Commercial Area.* New York: Harcourt, Brace, 1925.

Smith, Justin Harvey. *The War with Mexico.* New York: Macmillan, 1919.

Smith, Sidney. *The Settler's New Home, or, Whether to go, and Whither?* London: J. Kendrick, 1850.

Smythe, William E. *The Conquest of Arid America.* New York: Harper and Brothers, 1900.

———. "The Blooming of a Sahara." *World's Work, II* (October 1901): 1261–70.

———. "San Diego Owns the Future." *Out West* 23 (August 1905): 193–196.

Snyder, Gary. *Mountains and Rivers Without End.* Washington, DC: Counterpoint, 1996.

Sorkin, Michael. *Some Assembly Required.* Minneapolis: University of Minnesota Press, 2001.

South Western Immigration Company. *Texas: Her Resources and Capabilities: Description of the State of Texas and the Inducements She Offers to those Seeking Homes in a New Country.* New York: E. D. Slater, 1881.

Spec [pseud.]. *Line Etchings: A Trip from the Missouri River to the Rocky Mountains, via the Kansas Pacific Railway.* St. Louis: Woodward, Tiernan & Hale, 1875.

Speer, William. *The Oldest and the Newest Empire*: *China and the United States.* Cincinnati, OH: National Publishing, 1870.

Spencer, Patricia. *Helena, Montana: The Queen City of the Rockies and the Broadwater Hotel.* Chicago: Arcadia Publishing, 2002.

Stanfield, Howard Stillwell. *Diary of Howard Stillwell Stanfield, 1864–1865.* Bloomington: Indiana University Press, 1969.

Stansbury, Howard. *Exploration of the Valley of the Great Salt Lake.* Washington, DC: Smithsonian Institution Press, 1988.

Starck, Clemens. *Journeyman's Wages.* Brownsville, OR: Story Line Press, 1995.

Staton, Tracy. "Wait Watchers: True Road Warriors Know that a Long Layover at the Airport Doesn't Have to be a One-Way Ticket to Boredom." *American Way,* 2005 Road Warrior Issue, 104.

Stegner, Wallace. "Xanadu by the Salt Flats: Memories of a Pleasure Dome." *American Heritage* 32, no 4 (1981):81-87. http://americanheritage.com/articles/magazine/ah/1981_4_81print.shtml.

Stephens, John Lloyd. *Incidents of Travel in Egypt, Arabia Petraea and the Holy Land.* New York: Harper, 1837.

Steuding, Bob. *Gary Snyder.* Boston: Twayne Publishers, 1976.

Stevenson, Robert Louis. "The Silverado Squatters: Sketches from a Californian Mountain." *The Century Magazine* 27, no. 1 (1883): 31.

St. John, Percy B. *The Trapper's Bride; a Tale of the Rocky Mountain*s. London: Hayward and Adam, 1845.

Stout, Hosea. *On the Mormon Frontier: The Diary of Hosea Stout, 1844–1861,* edited by Juanita Brooks. Salt Lake City: University of Utah Press, 1964.

Stowe, Harriet Beecher. "Uncle Lot." In *The Mayflower and Miscellaneous Writings.* Boston: Phillips, Sampson, 1855.

———. *Uncle Tom's Cabin.* New York: Modern Library, 2001.

Streit, F. W. *Die Vereinigten Staaten von Nordamerika. (*Map) Leipzig, 1851. Virginia Garrett Cartography Collection, University of Texas at Arlington Special Collections #00157 @132/4.

Tasker, Yvonne. "Kung Fu: Re-orienting the Television Western." In *Action TV: Tough Guys, Smooth Operators and Foxy Chicks*, edited by Bill Osgerby and Anna Gough-Yates. New York: Routledge, 2001.

Taylor, Bayard. *The Lands of the Saracens; or Pictures of Palestine, Asia Minor, Sicily and Spain.* New York: G. P. Putnam's Sons, 1904.

"Things to See & Do [in] Oregon." 18" x 21 ½" two-sided, 12-fold color brochure for MEDIAmerica, Inc., in partnership with the Portland Oregon Visitors Association and Travel Oregon, n.d.

Thompson, David. *Travels*, iii. Cited in Jack Nisbet, *The Mapmaker's Eye: David Thompson on the Columbia Platea*u. Pullman: Washington State University Press, 2005.

Thorpe, Thomas Bangs. *The Mysteries of the Backwoods, or, Sketches of the Southwest: Including Character, Scenery, and Rural Sports*. Philadelphia: Carey and Hart, 1846.

Tolf, Albert. *This Was San Francisco*. San Francisco: Albert B. Tolf, 1959.

Tompkins, Walker A. "Santa Barbara, CA Samarkand History." http://www.thezia group.com/SamarkandHistory.php.

Toplin, Robert. *History by Hollywood: The Use and Abuse of the American Past*. Champaign: University of Illinois Press, 1996.

Trafton, Scott. *Egypt Land: Race and Nineteenth-Century American Egyptomania*. Durham, NC: Duke University Press, 2004.

Tudor, Henry. *Narrative of a Tour in North America: Comprising Mexico, the Mines of Real del Monte, the United States, and the British Colonies*. London: J. Duncan, 1834.

Tuveson, Ernest Lee. *Redeemer Nation: The Idea of America's Millennial Role*. Chicago: University of Chicago Press, 1968.

Twain, Mark. *The Innocents Abroad, or The New Pilgrims' Progress* . . . Hartford, CT: American Publishing, 1869.

———. *The Innocents Abroad*. New York: Viking Press, 1984.

———. *The Innocents Abroad*. New York: The Modern Library, 2003.

Twitchell, Ralph E. "An Old-World City in the New: The Place that Gave Santa Fe its Name." *Old-New Santa Fe and Roundabout*. Atchison, Topeka and Santa Fe Railway, 1912.

Varga, Robert. "Pyramids of the World, True or False." Letters. *The Chronicle of Higher Education*, April 27, 2007.

Waite, Thornton. "The Cedar City Branch and the Utah Parks Company." *The Streamliner—the Official Publication of the Union Pacific Historical Society* 12, no. 3 (1998): 17–34.

Walker, Franklin. *Irreverent Pilgrims: Melville, Browne, and Mark Twain in the Holy Land*. Seattle: University of Washington Press, 1974.

Watkins, T. H. *Gold and Silver in the West: An Illustrated History of an American Dream*. Palo Alto, CA: American West Publishing, 1971.

Webb, W. E. *Buffalo Land: An Authentic Narrative of the Adventures of a Late Scientific and Sporting Party Upon the Great Plains of the West*. Cincinnati, OH: E. Hannaford, 1872.

Weber, David J. *Bárbaros: Spaniards and their Savages in the Age of Enlightenment*. New Haven: Yale University Press, 2005.

Weigle, Marta, and Barbara A. Babcock, eds. *The Great Southwest of the Fred Harvey Company and the Santa Fe Railway*. Phoenix: Heard Museum, 1996.

Weiss, Timothy. *Translating Orients: Between Ideology and Utopia*. Buffalo, NY: University of Toronto Press, 2004.

West, Neil A. *Ecosystems of the World,* Vol. 5, *Temperate Deserts and Semi-Deserts*. New York: Elsevier Scientific Publishing, 1983.

West, Robert C. and John P. Augelli. *Middle America: Its Lands and Peoples*. Englewood Cliffs, NJ: Prentice-Hall, 1966.

"What the Religious Press of New York says of the Pacific Railroad." MSC 159, Box 32, Levi Leonard Railroad Collection, University of Iowa Special Collections.

Whipple, Maureen. *This is the Place: Utah*. New York: Alfred A. Knopf, 1945.

White, Ronald, Jr., and C. Howard Hopkins. *The Social Gospel: Religion and Reform in Changing America*. Philadelphia: Temple University Press, 1976.

Wierzbicki, Felix Paul. *California As It Is, and As It May Be, or A Guide to the Gold Region*. San Francisco: Printed by W. Bartlett, 1849.

Williams, H. T., ed. *The Pacific Tourist: An Illustrated Guide to the Pacific R.R. [and] California, Pleasure Resorts Across the Continent.* New York: Adams & Bishop, 1879.

Williams, Terry Tempest. *Refuge: An Unnatural History of Family and Place.* New York: Pantheon Books, 1991.

Willis, Nathaniel Parker. *American Scenery, or Land, Lake, and River Illustrations of Transatlantic Nature.* London: George Virtue, 1840.

Wilson, Chris. *The Myth of Santa Fe: Creating a Modern Regional Tradition.* Albuquerque: University of New Mexico Press, 1997.

Winchell, Alexander. *Sketches of Creation: A Popular View of the Grand Conclusions of the Sciences in Reference to the History of Matter and of Life.* New York: Harper & Brothers, 1871.

Wister, Owen. *The Virginian: A Horseman of the Plains.* New York: Macmillan, 1904.

Wood, Joseph. *The New England Village.* Baltimore, MD: Johns Hopkins University Press, 1997.

Woodward, Arthur. *Camels and Surveyors in Death Valley.* Palm Desert, CA: Desert Printers, 1961.

Worster, Donald. "Cowboy Ecology: A New Look of an Old West." In *The Charles L. Wood Agricultural History Lecture Series.* Lubbock, TX: International Center for Arid and Semi-Arid Land Studies, Texas Tech University, 1991.

———. "Landscape with Hero: John Wesley Powell and the Colorado Plateau." *Southern California Quarterly* 79, no. 1 (1997): 29.

———. *Under Western Skies: Nature and History in the American West.* New York: Oxford University Press, 1992.

Wrobel, David. "Exceptionalism and Globalism: Travel Writers and the Nineteenth Century American West." *The Historian* 68, no. 3 (August 2006): 431–460.

———. "Global West, American Frontier." *Pacific Historical Review* 78, no. 1 (2009): 1.

———. *Promised Lands: Promotion, Memory, and the Creation of the American West.* Lawrence: University of Kansas Press, 2002.

Yip, Christopher L. "A Time for Bitter Strength: The Chinese in Locke, California." *Landscape* 22, no. 2 (1978): 4.

Yu, Beongcheon. *The Great Circle: American Writers and the Orient.* Detroit, MI: Wayne State University Press, 1983.

Zesch, Scott. "Chinese Los Angeles in 1870–71: The Makings of a Massacre." *Southern California Quarterly* 90, no. 1 (2008): 109–58.

Index

A

Acoma Pueblo, 128, 132
Across America and Asia (1870), 136–37, 181–82, 209–12, *212*
Adam-ondi-Ahman, 88
advertising, 187, *188*, 189, 217–18, *219, 249*, 293–96, *294, 295, 296*
Afghanistan, 256, 291–92
African Americans, 19, 75
airlines, 240, 276, 293–94, *295*
Aladdin and the Magic Lamp story, 141, 143, 156, 179, 187, *188*, 227
Alaska, 296
Albuquerque, New Mexico, 244
al-Qaeda, 256, 301–2
American Arabs, 53–54, 104–5, 265
Apache Indians, 128, 133, 134, 135–37, 139, 140, 145, 149, 256, 272
Arabian Desert, 28, 32–33, 58
Arabian Nights, 27–29, 38, 39, 120, 140–41, 145, 155–56, 179–80, 187, 188, 189, 192, 193–94, 224, 225, 301, 322n28
Arabs, 47, 56, 104–5, 179, 256, 265, 300–303
archaeologists, 241, 303
architecture (Oriental style), 120, *121*, 122, 138, 141–42, 143–44, *144, 153, 167*, 172, *173, 174–75*, 184–85, 190–91, *192*, 193–94
Argentine Pampas, 34, 36–37
Arizona, 2–3, 131–32, 134, *135*, 136–37, 145–46, 147–48, 209
art and artists, 59–61, *60, 61*, 66–67, *67*, 114–15, *115*, 130–31, 143, *144*, 211, *212*, *213*, 215, 217–19, *219*, 252–55, *254, 255*, 279–82, *281*
Artemisia (genus), 77, 100, 306
Asia Minor, 63, 152
Asian people and culture, 171–73, 207, 211, 257
Austin, Mary, 186–87
Axis of Evil, 301

B

Baghdad, 157, 226
Bamberger, Simon, 122–23
Bangkok, Thailand, 273

Barbary Coast, 26, 158
Barbary Wars, 289
Bath House, Redondo Beach, California, *192*
Baum, Lyman Frank, 224–27
Beale, Lieutenant Edward Fitzgerald, 83
Bedouins, 34, 38, 47, 98, 150
Bennett, John C., 90
Berbers, 184
Berkhofer, Robert F., Jr., 98
Bernheimer, brothers Charles and Adolph, 259–60
Bertolucci, Bernardo, 286–87
Bigelow, William Sturgis, 11
bin Laden, Osama, 292, 300–302
Blade Runner (1982 film), 265
Body of Lies (2008 film), 304
Bonaparte, Napoleon, 68
Bonneville, Captain Eulalie de Benjamin Louis, 32
Bordertown (2006 film), 254–56
Boston, 11
Brackenridge, Henry Marie, 25–26
Bridgeman, Frederick Arthur, 59–60, *60*
British Isles, 215–16
Browne, J. Ross, 180–81
Bryce Canyon National Park, 123, *124*, 125
Buckingham, James S., 19
Buddhism, 11, 269, 277, 283, 285–87
Buel, J. W., 194
Buissonet, Eugene, 112–13
Burlingame Treaty, 202–3
Burton, Sir Richard F., 47–48, 75–77, 92, 99, 105–6, *107*, 266–67
Bush, George W., 301–2

C

Cabeza de Vaca, Álvar Núñez, 126–27, 190
Caine, Kwai Chang. See *Kung Fu*
California, 117, 155–75, 176–201, 203, 206, 207, 209–10
camels, 16, 81–85, *83*, 146, 231, 246–49, *247, 248, 249*
Camelback Mountain, Arizona, 247–48, *248*
Camel Rock, New Mexico, 246, 247
Canaan, 184

Canada, 62–63, 279
Cannon, George Q., 101
captivity narratives, 133–34, 139, 318n15
Carbucci, Sergio, 298
Carradine, David, 270–73, *271*
Cascade Range, 208–9, 212–14, 277, 282
Casino and Natatorium, Santa Cruz,
   California, 192
Catholicism, 185, 190
Catlin, George, 30
Cedar Breaks National Monument, Utah, 123,
   125
Central Pacific Railroad, 159–60, *161*, 162,
   179–80
Chamberlain, Sam, 130
Chan, Charlie, 259
Chan, Jackie, 273
Chemehuevi Indians, 85
Cher, 240–41
Child, Thomas, 236–37, *237*
Chimney Rock, Nebraska, 41, 48
China, 12, 155, 159–60, 288, 293–96, *294,
   295, 296,* 304–6, *305*
China Hat, 205, *206*
Chinatown, 164–65, 166–69, *167, 168,* 206–
   7, 257–58, *258,* 261–62, 263, 264–266,
   275
Chinatown (1974 film), 262–64
Chinese Exclusion Act of 1882, 171
Chinese Massacre of 1871, 172
Chinese people and culture, 155–59, *159,
   161,* 161–71, *161, 167, 168, 170,* 173–75, *174,
   175,* 202–4, *204,* 205–7, *208,* 257–260,
   261–266, *261, 263*
Chloride Murals, Arizona, 252–53, *254, 255*
Christian attitudes, 43, 53, 57–58, 149–50,
   162–63, 179, 205–7, 235
Church, Frederick, 109
Church of Jesus Christ of Latter-day Saints.
   See Mormons
City of Rocks, Idaho, 44–45, *45*
Ciudad Juárez, Mexico, 254–56
Classical Chinese Garden, Portland, Oregon,
   278–79
Cleopatra's Needle, 42–45
Coachella Valley, California, 1, 197, 199
Cochise, 149
Colorado, 4, 41–42
Colorado Desert, California, 81, 181, 197
Colorado River, 198, 245
Columbian Exposition of 1893, Chicago,
   Illinois, 230, 293
Columbus, Christopher, 3, 316n31
Columbus, New Mexico, 256

Comanche Indians, 36, 37, 133, 139
Conan the Barbarian (1933 short stories, 1954
   book, and 1982 film), 245–46
Coolie (Chinese Worker), 159–60, *161*
Coolie Hats, *159, 161, 204,* 205, *206, 294*
Cooper, James Fenimore, 291
Corinne City, Utah, 103
Coronado, Francisco Vázquez de, 127
Corps of Discovery, Lewis and Clark, 15, 203
Cortés, Hernán, 12
cowboys, ix, 52–53, *54–55,* 302–3
Cozzens, S. W., 131–32, 137–38, 140–42
Cree Indians, 62–63, *63*
Criss Cross (1948 film), 264
Crocker, Charles, 159, 160
Crouching Tiger, Hidden Dragon (2000 film),
   297
Cushing, Frank Hamilton, 147–48

D

Dakota Territory, 47, 62
Damascus, Syria, 2
date palms, 1, 188, 199, *200,* 201, 305
Davis, Jefferson, 81–82, 292
Dawson, J. W., 62–63
Dead Sea, Palestine, 1, 2, 93, 104, 110–12,
   113, 198
Death Valley Scotty, 85, *86,* 190
Death Valley, California, 83, 163, 164, 178,
   190
De Anghiera, Pedro Mártir, 97
DeMille, Cecil B. 237, 241, 303
De Peralta, Juan Suárez, 97
Deseret, 91
deserts, 17, 64–86
Diamond of the Desert, Salt Lake City as the,
   104–5
Diné. *See* Navajo Indians
Disney, Walt, 194
Dobie, J. Frank, 267
Dodge, Grenville, 159–60
Dodge, Richard Irving, 39
Domenech, Emmanuel Henri, 11013
Domínguez, Francisco Atanasio, 64
Domínguez-Escalante Expedition of 1776,
   64–65
Donner Party, 177–78
Doré, Gustave, 114, *115*
Driving Cattle into a Corral in the Far West
   (1875 illustration), 51–53, *54–55*
Dromedary Peak, Arizona, 248
Dumont Dunes, Mojave Desert, California,
   79
Dutton, Major Clarence E., 143

E

Earl of Dunraven, 39
Egypt, 65–75, 103, 223, 236–42
Egyptomania, 19, 66–71, 227–34, 236–41
Eidel, Jim, 252–53
El Paso, Texas, 143, 144
Emerson, Ralph Waldo, 18, 284
Emory, William, 135–36
Enoshima Island, Japan, 211, *212*
Escalante, Francisco Silvestre, 64
Estevanico the Moor, 126–27
Estival, Francesc, 251
Ethnogrophers, 147–48, 149, 151
Evil Empire, 301
exceptionalism, 288
Exodus, Jewish, 91
Expulsion from the Garden, The (1728 painting), 176

F

Field, Henry M., 233
Film (Cinema), 223, 224, 226, 231, 234–35, 237, 241, 246, 254–56, 258–59, 262–66, 273, 286–87, 292, 297–303
Film Noir. *See* Noir
Fook, Yee, 174
Freemasons, 241
Frémont, John Charles, 66–69, 71–73, 85, 87, 91, 135, 227
Friedman, Kinky, *249*
Fuller, Margaret, 51

G

Garden of Eden, 50–51, 88–89, 94–95, 176–77, 195–97, 234
gardens, Asian-style, 172–73, *173*, 214–15, 260, 273–76, *274*, 277–79, *277*
Garrigues, Eduardo, 249–251
Genghis Khan, 242, 306
geologists, 57–59, 62–63, 104–5, 136–37, 143, 181–82, 197, 209–12, 214–16, 321n11
Geronimo, 149, 302
Gilgal Garden, Salt Lake City, Utah, 236–37, *237*
Gilgamesh epic, 249–250
Gilleland, J. C., 17
Glacier National Park, Montana, 220
Glacier Park Hotel, 220
globalization, 288–307
Gold Mountain (Gum Shan)(California), 156
Gold Rush, California, 155–59, 178, 180
Golden Gate Park, San Francisco, California, 172–73, *173*, 239, 273

Gomorrah. *See* Sodom and Gomorrah
Good Samaritans, 132-33
Good, the Bad, and the Weird, The (2008 film), 299–300
Goss, Helen Rocca, 169
Grand Canyon, 142–43
Grauman's Egyptian Theatre, Hollywood, California, 237–38
Grauman's Chinese Theatre, Hollywood, California, 258, *259*
Graves, Morris, 279–80, *281*
Great American Desert, 31, 32, 95
Great Basin, 66–69, 71–73, 77, 91, 113
Great Northern Railway, 218, 220, 295–96, *296*
Great Plains, 28–34, 38–41, 91, 133–34, 266
Great Salt Lake, Utah, 79, 93, 110–11, *112*, 114–16, *117, 118*
Great Wall of China, 42
Greeley, Horace, 40, 231
Griboedov, Aleksander, 291, 292
Guangdong Province, China, 156
Guangzhou, Canton, China, 156
Gun-Galuut Nature Reserve, Mongolia, 303–4
Gypsies. *See* Roma

H

Hadji Ali. *See* Hi Jolly
Hall, Baynard Rush, 29
harem, 59, 106, 109, 231
Harlan, Josiah, 291–92
Harroun, Philip E., 150
Harum Scarum (1965 film), 231
Hawaii, 296
Hells Canyon, Idaho, Chinese Massacre, 203–4
Hewett, Edgar, 191
Hidalgo (2004 film), 300–301, 303
Highbinders, 169, *170*
Hi Jolly (Hadji Ali), 81, 248–49
Hi Jolly Monument, *24,* 248-49
Hill, James J., 218
Hillerman, Tony, 252
Himalayan Blackberry, *Rubus armeniacus,* 215–16
Hinduism, 59
Hohokam, 135
Holley, Mary Austin, 51
Hollywood, 258–60
Holy Land, 2, 35, 46, 88–89, 92, 96, 101, 117–18, 235–36
Hood River, Oregon, 214
Hopi Indians, 134, 150
Hopi Snake Dance, 150
Hopper, Dennis, 279
horses, 37, 38–39, 51–52

Houston, Sam, 35–36
Howard, Robert E., 245–46
Howe, Henry, 129
Howett, Catherine, 51
Hrdlička, Aleš, 151
Huntington Chinese Garden, 273–75, *274*
Hurlbut, Reverend Jesse Lyman, 152, *152*
Hussein, Saddam, 301–2
hydraulic civilizations, 183

I

Idaho, 32, 44–45, 209, 282
imperial nostalgia, 62, 137
Imperial Valley, California, 1, 197–201
Incidents of Travel in Egypt, Arabia, Petraea, and the Holy Land, 69–71, 74
India, 59, 101, 193, 266–67
Indies, 3
Innocents Abroad, The (1869), 3–4, 13, 98, 106
Intermountain West, 64–86, 87–125, 227–37
Iraq, 242, 256, 300-302
irrigation, 93–95, 183–84, 197–98, 235
Irving, Washington, 37, 185
Isaiah, Book of, 92–95, 178
Islam, 90
Israel, 1, 91, 132
Israelites, 96

J

Jackson, Helen Hunt, 185–86, 191
James, George Wharton, 150
Japan, 12, 209–11, *212, 213,* 214–15, 259–60, 261, 276
Japanese, 170–71, 172–73, *173,* 214–17, 261, 282
Japanese Garden, Portland, Oregon, 277–79, *277*
Japanese Relocation Camps, 282, 286
Japanese Tea Garden, San Francisco, California, 172–73, *173,* 273
Jefferson, Thomas, 203
Jerusalem, 92, 97, 103, 104, 106, 177, 243–44, 264
Jews, Orientalism and, 178
Jordan River, 2, 95–96, 119, 235–36
Joshua trees, 101–2, *102*
Joss Houses (Chinese Temples), 174–75, *175*
Joss House State Historical Park, California, 174–75, *175*
Juárez. *See* Ciudad Juárez

K

Kashmir, 101
Kathmandu, Nepal, 287

Keeoma, 1896 painting, 59–60, 61, 62, *62*
Kim, Ji-woon, 299–300
Knott, Walter, 260–61
Koran, the, 76, 98
Koreatown, 264
Kung Fu (television series), 269–73, *271*
Kuroshio Current, 280–81, 285
Kurosawa, Akira, 297

L

La Grande Station, Los Angeles, California, 192
Laguna Pueblo, New Mexico, 142, 152, *153*
Lake Texcoco, Mexico, 176
Lamanites. *See* Lost Tribes of Israel
L'Amour, Louis, 266–68
landscape, 1–3, 13–14, 93, 110, 130, 152–54, 211–15, 305–6
Langworthy, Franklin, 42–43, 44–45, 116
Lan Su Chinese Garden, Portland, Oregon, 278
Las Vegas, Nevada, 227–28, 229–33
Leavitt, D. G. W., 177
Le Baron, Alan, 234
Lee, Wang, 297
Leone, Sergio, 297
Little Buddha (1994 film), 286–87
Locke, California, 173–75, *175*
locusts, 49
Lodge, George Cabot, 11
Lonesome Gods, The (1983 novel), 267–68
Los Angeles, California, 85, 172, 183, 192, 258–66
Lost in Translation (1998 novel), 304
Lost Tribes of Israel, 15, 97–99, 315n30
Lowell, Percival, 11
Ludlow, Fitz Hugh, 33–34
Lummis, Charles, 184, 185, 189–90
Luxor Hotel, Las Vegas, Nevada, 227–28, *228,* 229–31, 233

M

Magnificent Seven, The (1960 film), 267, 297
Management (2008 film), 287
Manifest Destiny, 93, 180
Man Who Would be King, The (1888 short story and 1975 film), 292, 302
Marlboro Man, 249
Marryat, Frederick, 128–29
Martineau, Susan Ellen Johnson, 133–34
Marvellous Country, The (1875 book), 131–32, 137–38, *140, 141, 142*
Mathewson, A. J., 113, *114*
Mauvaises Terres or Bad Lands of Dacotah (1871 illustration), 57, *58*
May, Karl, 137

McLeod, Hugh, 37
Mecca, ix, 13, 82, 104, 106
Memoirs of a Geisha (2005 film), 273
Métis, 62–63
Mexicans, 129–30, 138, 189–90, 254–56
Mexico, 27, 129–30, 143, 147, 176–77, 191, 245, 254–56
Middle East, 6, 39, 109, 139–40, 300–303
Miller, Joaquin, 208–9
minarets, 57, 122, 141, *225*
Minidoka Internment Camp, Idaho, 282
mirages, 180
mission style achitecture, 191–92, 193
Moab, Utah, 93
modernity, 34
Mohammed, 37, 82, 90
Mojave Desert, California, *33,* 79, 81, 101
monad, 217–18, *219*
Mongolia, Mongolians, 52, 81, 151, 162, 303–4
Moorish architecture, 120, *121,* 138, 190–91, *192,* 322n28
Moors, 126, 128, 184, 185, 189
Mormons, ix, 14–15, 87–125, 235–37
Morocco, 7, 63
mosques, 43, 57, 180
Mount Fuji[ama], Japan, 211, *212, 213,* 214, 215, 306–7
Mount Hood, Oregon, 209, 212, 277
Mount Rainier, Washington, 212, 214, *214,* 306–7
Mount Rainier-Mount Fuji Sister Mountain Curriculum, 2010 National Park project, 306–7
Mount Saint Helens, Washington, 212*, 213*
Muldaur, Maria, 231
museums, 165, 238–40
Muslims, 90, 99, 109, 128, 151

N

Native Americans, 14, 17, 36, 39, 47, 59–63, *63,* 97–99, 128–29, 132–33, 134–37, 143–44, *143,* 150–51, 153, *154,* 267, 271–72, 282, 299, 302, 311n54
Navajo Indians. 14, 149, 252
Nebraska, 41, 47–48, 197
Nevada, 66–81, *83,* 84–85, 105, 227–34, 273, 304
New England, 18, 20–21, 89–90
New Mexico, 138, 141–42, *142,* 152, *153,* 154, 197
Nile River and Valley, Egypt, 44, *46,* 49, 65, *67,* 191, 198
noir, film and literature, 262–64

Nomads, 26, 53–54, 80–81, 304
North Coast Limited, 218–19, *219*
North Dakota, 266
Northern Pacific Railroad, 217–18, *219*
Northwest Orient Airlines, 276–77
Northwest Passage, 203, 294, *295*
Northwest School, Regional Art Style, 280–82, *281*
Nuttall, Thomas, 33

O

oasis (oases), 231–32, 235
Obama, Barack, 302, 304–5, *305*
obelisks, 42–45, *46*
Occidentalism, 196
Ocean Park, California, 192
odalisques, 59, *60*
Olympia, Washington, 214, *214*
Oraibi, 148–49, *148*
Oregon, 92, 203–9, 212–14, 215–16, 276, 282–86, 287, 306
Organ Mountains, New Mexico, 141, 142, *142*
Orient Railway, 145, 320n37
Oriental Limited, 218, 220
Orientalism, 8–9, 10–13, 53, 109, 217, 220, 251–52, 290–91
Orientalism, American, 11–12, 59–62, 109, 220
Orientalization, 15–16, 17, 21, 32–33, 100–101, 209–17, 223–27, 289
Owens Valley, California, 183
Oz, land of, 224–27

P

Pacific Northwest, 202–20, 257, 276–87
Pacific Railroad, 159–62, 179–80
Paiute Indians, 183
Pakistan, 256, 301
Palmer, W. J., 51–53, *54–55*
palm trees, native, (*Washintonia filifera*), 199
Pasadena Grand Opera House, California, 192
Pattie, James Ohio, 32
Pawnee Indians, 47
Pecos and Northwestern Railroad, 146
Peery's Egyptian Theater, Ogden, Utah, 236, 324n25
Perry Mason (television series), 261
Perry, Admiral, 289
Persia, 291
Phoenix, Arizona, 2, 145–46
Pike, Zebulon, 25
Pima-Maricopa Indians, 132
place names, ix, 12–13, 26–27, 142–43, 205
poetry, 284–85

Point of the Mountain, Utah, 113, *114*
Polo, Marco, 78
polygamy, 105–7, 109, 236
Pony Express, 293, *294*
pornography, 232, 318n15
Porter, Dixon, 81–83
Portland, Oregon, *204–6*, 212, 277–79, *277*
Poston, Charles D., 135
Powell, John Wesley, 196–97
Pratt, Orson, 94–95
Presley, Elvis, 231
Preuss, Charles, 72
Promised Land, the, 92, 96, 117, *118*, 179
Pueblo architecture, 147, *153*, 244
Pueblo Indians, 153
Pumpelly, Raphael, 136–37, 181–82, 197, 209–12, *212*, 214–16
Purcell, Roy, 252, 253, *254, 255*
Pyramid Lake, Nevada, *22*, 66–68, 71–73, *73*, 227, *233*, 324n18
pyramids, 42, 48, 49, 57, 58, 64–67, *67*, 68–73, *73*, 75, 81, 227–28, *228*, 229–31, 234

R

railroads, 55–56, 116–17, 123, 144–46, 210, 295–96
Ramona (1884 novel), 185–86, 191
ranching, 51–53, *53–55*
Randolph, Paschal Beverly, 75
Reagan, Ronald, 301
Redondo Beach, California, 192, *192*
Red Pheasant (Cree Indian Chief), 62, *63*
Reeves, Keanu, 286–87
Remington, Frederick, 143, *144*
Riddell, John Leonard, 137
Ridgway, Robert, 72
Rio Grande, 245,
Rio Grande Western Railroad, 116–17, 118–19
River Jordan. *See* Jordan River
Riverside, California, 184
Roberts, David, 66, *67*
Robida, Albert, 106–9
Robinson, Phil, 80, 100–101
Rocky Mountains, 5, 91
Rogue River, Oregon, 203
Roma (Gypsies), 240–41
romanticism, 25–26, 34–35, 37–38, 290, 291
Rosetta Stone, 236–37, *237*
Rosicrucian, 75
Rosicrucian Egyptian Museum, San Jose, California, 238–39, *239*, 240
ruins, *46*, 57, *58*, 59, 228–29
Runnels, the Honorable John, 50–51

Russell, Charles M., 59–62
Russell, William Howard, 18–19
Russia, 291, 296

S

Sacramento Valley Railroad, 157
sagebrush. See *Artemisia*
Sahara (2005 film), 302–3
Sahara Desert, 31–32, *33*, 59, 63, 181–82, 248, 302–3, 313n18
Said, Edward, 8–9, 217, 251–52, 268
Salsola Kali (tumbleweed), 78, 305–6
Saltair Pavilion and Beach, Utah, 119–20, *121*, 122
Salt Cedar (Tamarisk), 78
Salt Lake City and Valley, Utah, 91, 103–6, 116–17, *118*
Salton Sea, California, ix, 1
Samarkand, Persian Hotel, Santa Barbara, California, 189
San Antonio, Texas, 137
San Bernardino, California, 193
sand dunes, 78–80, 181
San Diego, California, 191, 197
Sands of Oblivion (2007 film), 241
San Francisco, California, 165, 166–71, 209, 239, 257–58, 261–63, 273, 292
San Gabriel Valley, California, 275
San Joaquin Valley, California, 240
San Pedro, Los Angeles and Salt Lake Railroad, 123
Santa Barbara, California, 181, 189
Santa Cruz and Felton Railway, 162
Santa Fe, New Mexico, 138, 151, 243–44
Santa Fe Railway, 144–45, 149
San Xavier del Bac, Arizona, 138
Sarkisian, Cherilyn, *See* Cher
Sarmiento, Domingo, 34, 36–37
Schoolcraft, Henry Rowe, 20–21
Schwarzenegger, Arnold, 246, 288, 289
Scotch Broom (*Cytisus scoparius*), 215
Scott, Harvey Whitefield, 207
Scott, Sir Walter, 105
Scotty's Castle, 190
Sea of Galilee, 2, 95
Seattle, Washington, 212, 216–17, 257, 286–87
Seeing the Elephant, 157–58
Seven Faces of Dr. Lao, The (1964 film), 268–69
Seven Samurai, The (1954 film), 267
sexual abuse, abduction and, 133–34, 318n15
sexuality, 59–62, 127, 128–30, 180–81, 187, 230–35, 265–66, 318n15
Shanghai, 293

Shanghai Noon (2000 film), 273
Shell Oil Company, 293–94, *294*
Shoshone Indians, 128–29
Sierra Nevada, 160–61, *161,* 164
Siesta, The (1878 painting), 59–60
Siddhartha, 286–87
Silverado Squatters (1883 story), 182
Sinners and Saints (1883 novel), 100–101
sister cities, 278, 279
Smillie, James David, 130, *131*
Smith, George Albert, 94, 96
Smith, Joseph, 87–88, 90–91
Smith, J. Russell, 215–16
Smythe, William E. 176, 197
Snake River Plain, Idaho, 32
Snow Falling on Cedars (1999 film), 286
Snyder, Gary, 283–85
Sodom and Gomorrah, 53, 103, 116, 232–33, 255
Sonoran Desert, Arizona, *33*
Soule, John B. L., 40, 231
Southern Pacific Railroad, 145, 198
Southwestern United States, 126–54, 245–56
Spaniards, 3, 12, 34, 36–37, 64–65, 126–28, 137, 138, 249–51
Spanish identity, 185, 189–91
Speer, William, 164
Sphinx, the, 33, 57, 85–86, *86,* 188, 223, *228, 233*
Spirit Lake, Washington, *213,* 283
St. John, Percy B., 29
Stansbury, Howard, 104–5
Starck, Clemens, 285
Stegner, Wallace, 122
Stephens, John Lloyd, 69–71, 74, 105
Stevenson, Matilda Cox, 148–49, *148*
Stevenson, Robert Louis, 182
Stowe, Harriet Beecher, 18
Streit, Dr. F. W., 104, *104*
Sukiaki Western Django, (2008 film), 298–99
swastika, 146–47
Swastika Coal Company, 146
symbols, 217–18, *219,* 252–53, *254, 255,* 304–5
Syria, 176, 235

T

Tadmor, 137
Taoism, 272, 277
Taos, New Mexico, 272
Tarantino, Quentin, 299
Taylor, Bayard, 184–85
Temple of Osiris, *124,* 125
Tepemazalco, Mexico, 176–77

Terranes, 281–82
terrorism, 256, 302
Texas, 37, 126, 137, 143, 144, *152,* 245, 304
This Was San Francisco (1956–58 cartoon book), 261–62, *263*
Thompson, David, 65–67
Thoreau, Henry David, 18
Three Kings (1999 film), 301–2
time, 57–58
Tobey, Mark, 279, 280
Tokugawa Shogunate, 289
Tokyo, Japan, 289, 293
Tokyotown, 264
Tolf, Albert, 261–62, *263*
Tombstone, Arizona, 298
Tong War of 1854, 175
Tonopah, Nevada, 304
tourism, 189, 253–54
Tower of Babel, 113–14, *115*
Transcontinental Railroad, 159–62
Treaty of Tien-tsin, 202
Treaty Regulating Immigration from China, 171
tumbleweed, 305–6. See also *Salsola*
Turco, El, 127
Turks, 81–82, 127, 128
Turner, Frederick Jackson, 292–93
Tutankhamen, King, 228, 237, 255–56
Twain, Mark, 3–4, 13, 80–81, 106
Twitchell, Ralph E., 138

U

Uighurs, 298
Ukraine, 37
Union Pacific Railroad, 123, 159–60
US-Mexican War, 129, 130, 180
Utah, ix, 64, 77, 79, 89–125, 235–36, 237
Utah Lake, Utah, 95, *118*

V

Vancouver, British Columbia, 279
Victorian Culture, 59, 70, 149, 165, 166, 180, 182
Vietnam War, 252, 270, 287
Villa, Poncho, 256
Virginia City, Nevada, 84, 165
Virginian, The (1902 novel), 223–24
Voyages Trés Extraordinaires (1885 illustration), 106–7, *108,* 109

W

Wakara (Walkara, Walker), 99
Walls of Jericho, *125*
War on Terrorism, 300–302

Warriors of Heaven and Earth (2003 film), 297–98
Wasatch Range, Utah, 96
Washington, 212–14, 215–17, 257, 279–80, 283, 286–87
Washington Monument, Washington D. C., 43
Watsonville, California, 174–75, *175*
Wayne, John, 242, 273
Wayne, Major Henry Constantine, 81–84
Weaverville, California, 174–75, *175*
westerns (genre), 223–24, 242, 266–73, 297–300, 304–5
West of Babylon (2002 novel), 249–51
Whipple, Maureen, 101–2
Whistler, Joseph Nelson Garland, 57
Whitman, Walt, 142
Whitney, Horace K., 41
Whittier, John Greenleaf, 290
Wierzbicki, Felix Paul, 155–56
Willis, Nathaniel Parker, 28–29
Winchell, Alexander, 57–58, *58, 59*

Wister, Owen, 223–24
Wizard of Oz (1899 novel and 1939 film), 224, *225*, 226–27
women, 17, 36, 50–51, 52, 59–60, *60*, 61, 62, 106–8, 127, 128–30, 133–34, 135–36, 139, 143, *144, 150*, 180–81, 231–33, 235, 245–46, 252–53, 265–66, 299
Wyoming, 224

Y

Yamashiro Restaurant, 260
yellowface, 259
Yokohama, Japan, 216
Yosemite Valley, California, 233
Young, Brigham, 90–91, 99, 123, 142
Yukon-Pacific Exposition, 217

Z

Zion, 97
Zion National Park, Utah, 123–24